Fifth Edition

The Canadian Writer's Workplace

Gary Lipschutz Centennial College

John Roberts Mohawk College

John Scarry Recently with the Office of Academic Affairs, City University of New York

Sandra Scarry Hostos Community College, City University of New York

Australia Canada Mexico Singapore Spain United Kingdom United States

The Canadian Writer's Workplace
Fifth Edition

by Gary Lipschutz, John Roberts, John Scarry, and Sandra Scarry

Editorial Director and Publisher:
Evelyn Veitch

Executive Editor:
Anne Williams

Marketing Manager:
Lisa Rahn

Senior Developmental Editor:
Mike Thompson

Permissions Coordinator:
Patricia Buckley

Production Editor:
Julie van Veen

Copy Editor:
Lisa Berland

Proofreaders:
Lisa Berland
Wayne Herrington

Indexer:
Belle Wong

Production Coordinator:
Ferial Suleman

Creative Director:
Angela Cluer

Interior Design:
Kevin Connoly, revised by
Liz Harasymczuk

Cover Design:
Anne Bradley

Cover Image:
© Rafael Goldchain 1986.
All rights reserved.

Compositor:
Nelson Gonzalez

Illustrations (pages 347, 349, and 383):
Jock MacRae

Printer:
Webcom

Printed and bound in Canada
3 4 07 06 05

For more information contact Nelson, 1120 Birchmount Road, Toronto, Ontario, M1K 5G4. Or you can visit our Internet site at http://www.nelson.com

National Library of Canada Cataloguing in Publication

The Canadian writer's workplace / Gary Lipschutz ... [et al.]. — 5th ed.

Includes index.
Fourth ed. written by: John Roberts, John Scarry and Sandra Scarry.
ISBN 0-17-641579-3

1. English language—Rhetoric—Textbooks. 2. English language—Rhetoric—Problems, exercises, etc. 3. English language—Grammar—Problems, exercises, etc. I. Lipschutz, Gary, 1964– II. Roberts, John A., 1944– . Canadian writer's workplace.

PE1413.C355 2004 808'.042
C2003-906804-8

Brief Contents

Contents

Preface

The Canadian Writer's Workplace, Fifth Edition, is a complete program of grammar and writing activities for students who need to build their writing skills in order to produce college-level work. This book gives the student the ability to write with control, a crucial skill that is needed not only in English courses but also in virtually every other course taken in college and/or university. *The Canadian Writer's Workplace* can help students get the most out of any college/university course that calls for the ability to write clearly and effectively.

Many of the features that proved successful for students and faculty who worked with the first four editions of the book have been retained in this fifth edition.

Completeness

The book begins with a detailed study of sentences, then helps students practise solid paragraph development, and finally shows them how to develop the complete essay. At each step along the way, numerous practice exercises and writing assignments reinforce what is being learned. The reading section in this edition has been revised and expanded to include more serious essays with particular appeal to postsecondary students.

The approach taken in *The Canadian Writer's Workplace* is convenient in that grammar and writing skills are taught in detail between the covers of a single book. When you use *The Canadian Writer's Workplace*, there is no need to look for a supplemental book containing grammar work or a book to teach writing skills; everything you need for teaching grammar skills and writing development is contained in the book you are now holding. You will be pleased to find that the grammar work of the book has been especially selected with one major goal in mind: to meet the needs of the student writer who must understand how sentence parts work together. The grammar presented in this book is intended to help the student writer feel comfortable using a variety of sentence structures when composing paragraphs and essays.

Flexibility

The format of *The Canadian Writer's Workplace* enables an instructor to work on different exercises with an entire class, gives individual students opportunity to work by themselves or with a tutor in a lab, and encourages students to work in groups. The book is flexible, also, in that certain sections can be skipped if the material is not needed for a particular class—or a class might begin with a later section, with the earlier chapters being used as a review. Students or faculty can use the Quick Quiz at the beginning of each chapter in Unit I to determine whether students' skills are strong enough in a particular area to move on to the next chapter right away or not.

Stimulating Content

The assignments in the book feature material that deals with current events or subjects that are of contemporary interest. Many of the exercises are based on material from such fields as history or science. And the readings throughout the text are extremely varied: they include model paragraphs and essays in Unit III and major readings in Unit IV. Some of the works in Unit III are by student writers; others are taken from a wide range of novels, essays, short stories, and books of nonfiction by world-famous authors. Unit IV is made up of three genres: mostly nonfiction and some fiction and poetry. The writers of the readings in Unit IV are exclusively Canadian, and they are all seasoned writers and/or academics. The strong Canadian flavour of the text offers the postsecondary student in Canada an insight into various aspects of Canadian culture.

Features of the Fifth Edition

Many features of the first four editions of the book have been retained. As mentioned above, they include the in-depth treatment of grammar skills and the step-by-step approach to the writing process. This fifth edition, however, offers some exciting and innovative changes:

- Most readings in the major reading section toward the back (Unit IV) are new, and the number of readings has been increased. New readings in the fifth edition include works by Mordecai Richler, Rachel Manley, Tomson Highway, and Rosemary Sullivan.
- The pedagogy for each reading in Unit IV has been enhanced. Now, four sections of questions and writing ideas follow every major reading in Unit IV: Comprehension Questions, Questions about Form, Questions for Discussion, and Writing Ideas.
- A new annotated listing of readings is included in the Table of Contents, offering a glimpse into what each reading in Unit IV is about. A short biographical sketch of the author accompanies each reading in Unit IV. As well, a short glossary (of approximately four to six terms from the reading) accompanies each reading in Unit IV to help students with their reading comprehension.
- Unit I (Grammar) now contains more chapters on specific points of grammar, making the text easier for students and instructors to use.

- Major reorganization of Units II and III eliminates former repetition in the discussion of rhetorical modes (writing strategies). For example, no longer is there one chapter in Unit II on the narrative paragraph and another chapter in Unit III on the narrative essay. Rather, Chapter 21 in Unit III (Writing Strategies) deals with both the narrative paragraph and the narrative essay. Unit II is now devoted to the writing process. This process includes steps taken to achieve effective writing results for both the paragraph and the essay. Such steps include prewriting techniques, outlining, writing the rough draft, and revising.
- A new introductory chapter on the four stages of writing, Chapter 14, has been added in Unit II. This chapter includes prewriting techniques such as diagramming and keeping a journal. Chapters on the paragraph and the essay now contain illustrations of their structural models. Exercises have been added throughout the text to enhance the learning opportunities offered in previous editions.
- Much of the material in the book is followed by two types of assignments: one is called "Practice;" the other is called "Exercise." These assignments have been reorganized so that answers to all "Practices" appear in Appendix D at the end of the book, enabling instructors to use "Practices" for in-class activity. Answers to "Exercises," on the other hand, are not provided at the back of the text so that instructors can either assign these exercises for homework or use them for testing.

An **Instructor's Manual** and **Test Bank** are available for use with this book. The manual contains answers to the Exercises; hints for teaching students writing skills, including techniques for using groups in the classroom; and specific suggestions for activities that can be used with the material in the book.

The Canadian Writer's Workplace is a flexible tool, one that works for the instructor and with the student. It strengthens grammar skills and places special emphasis on strong paragraph writing, which is the basic building block of the complete essay. It also enables the student to understand and construct a complete essay, often the goal of the English instructor at this level. The student who carefully uses this book and works consistently with his or her instructor throughout the semester should be able to look forward with confidence to success in college or university writing.

Features Retained from the Fourth Edition

- Each chapter in Unit I begins with a Quick Quiz, designed to assess students' skills in the material in that chapter. Based on the results of this quiz, the instructor can choose either to skip over the material in the chapter, or to spend extra time on the material in question if the students' skills in this area are shown to be weak.

- A valuable feature, Working Together, can be found at the end of every chapter in the book. Working Together gives the student an additional opportunity to confirm the work that has just been finished. Each Working Together section enables the class to break into groups, an approach that provides opportunities for the peer editing and peer review that many instructors use to enhance their classes today. Working Together is a versatile resource for the instructor who uses *The Canadian Writer's Workplace*, extending the work of the book into different classroom activities. Each activity is related to the work that the class has just completed.

Acknowledgments

This fifth edition of *The Canadian Writer's Workplace* has been dedicated to Norman Lipschutz (1921–2002). You were my first editor, Dad, and you continue to inspire me.

For their advice and/or personal support, thank you to Denvil Buchanan, Diane Fagel, Nancy Sukornyk, Geri Dasgupta, Rose Lipschutz, Nina Keren, Ilana Indaig, Ben Labovitch, Dan Holbrook, John Artibello, Alexis Pereria, Paul Tamblyn, Leah Robinson, and George Thomas.

Kudos and thanks go to the winning team at Nelson—Anne Williams, Mike Thompson, and Julie van Veen—as well as to our copy editor and proofreader, Lisa Berland. Their hard work and dedication have helped make this edition what it is.

The comments and advice from the following reviewers of the fourth edition and the first draft of the fifth edition were indeed invaluable:

Marlet Ashley, Kwantlen University College
John Carroll, University College of the Fraser Valley
Robert Einarsson, Grant MacEwan College
Robert Fleming, Kwantlen University College
Kathy Hamilton, Okanagan University College
Rhonda Hustler, Centennial College
Peter Lovrick, George Brown College
Helen Mildon, Nova Scotia Community College
Deanna Roozendaal, Camosun College
Rhonda Sandberg, George Brown College
Doreen Williams, Northern Alberta Institute of Technology/University of Alberta

To the student essayists who have generously given permission to publish their work in this edition of *The Canadian Writer's Workplace*, the author and editors wish to thank them most sincerely. They are Jenny Yuen, Alexandra Savage-Ferr, Akis Stylianou, Leanne C. Southall, Margo Fine, Zack Goodman, and Donald Pianissimo.

UNIT ONE

I

Grammar

CHAPTER ONE

1

Parts of Speech: Overview

The Canadian Writer's Workplace begins with an overview of grammar to ensure that you have an understanding of basic terms. Such an understanding will help you succeed with the rest of this text. Words can be divided into nine categories called **parts of speech**. Understanding these categories will help you work with language, especially when it comes to revising your own writing.

QUICK QUIZ

Test your knowledge of the various parts of speech. Fill in the blank with the correct part of speech for the underlined words in the following sentences. The answers to the questions are beside the quiz.

1. By installing the service, you agree to the following conditions.
2. Follow the instructions on the screen to uninstall the older version of the program.
3. Running the program is easily handled if you pay attention to the next part of the video.
4. Everything you need to do is explained in ten easy steps.
5. If you have any questions, call our toll-free number.

Answers:

1. noun, verb, article
2. verb, preposition, adjective, preposition, noun
3. gerund (*-ing* word acting as a noun), adverb, pronoun, adjective
4. pronoun, infinitive (*to* + a verb), preposition, adjective
5. conjunction, noun, verb, adjective

1. What Are Nouns?

DEFINITION ➤ A **noun** is a word that refers to a person, place, or thing.

TYPES OF NOUNS

There are two types of nouns: common nouns and proper nouns.

Types of Nouns

Common Nouns	**Proper Nouns**
officer	Michael Johnson
station	Union Station
magazine	*Canadian Geographic**
university	Centennial College

* When a title is that of a major publication such as a book or a magazine (see *Canadian Geographic* above), the title should be italicized or underlined (the equivalent of italicizing when handwriting).

Common nouns are nouns that are not names or titles. For this reason, common nouns do not begin with a capital letter (unless, of course, the word begins a sentence):

I plan to attend university next fall.

The word *university* is a common noun in this sentence because it is not part of a specific name or title. The *u* must not be capitalized.

Proper nouns are names or titles. Every significant word of these titles starts with a letter that must be capitalized.

Carleton University is in Ottawa, our nation's capital. The University College of Cape Breton, on the other hand, is in Sydney, Nova Scotia.

In the above two sentences, the *U* in University (the word immediately following *Carleton* and the second word in the second sentence) must be capitalized because the word *University* in both cases is now a proper noun; it is part of the title of a specific university. (See Chapter 12: "Capitalization.") The University College of Cape Breton includes the word *of*, whose first letter is not capitalized because *of* is a *preposition* (see below), and a preposition is not considered a significant word of a title.

Concrete vs. Abstract Nouns

Nouns are said to be **concrete** if they represent things you can see or touch.

window	river
paper	finger

Nouns are said to be **abstract** if they represent things you cannot see or touch. These words can be concepts, ideas, or qualities.

meditation	carelessness
honesty	fearlessness

To test for a noun, it may help to ask these questions:

- Can I put the article *the* in front of the word?
- Is the word used as the subject or object of the sentence?

A noun may be the subject of a sentence, but it may not be. All subjects are nouns. But not all nouns are subjects. For example, a noun might be an object, instead.

Marissa gave me the book.

Marissa is the first noun in the sentence. *Marissa* is also the subject of the sentence. *Me* is the second noun (more specifically, a pronoun); it is an indirect object (the indirect receiver of the action). Finally, *book* is the third noun of the sentence. It is a direct object. It is the direct receiver of the action.

2. What Are Pronouns?

DEFINITION ➤ A **pronoun** is a word that takes the place of a noun. Just like a noun, it is used as the subject or object of a sentence. Pronouns can be divided into several classes (*see below*).

Pronoun Cases

A personal pronoun will be in one of three cases depending on how it is used in a sentence: subjective, objective, or possessive.

	Subjective	Objective	Possessive
Singular			
1st person	I	me	my (mine)
2nd person	you	you	your (yours)
3rd person	he	him	his (his)
	she	her	her (hers)
	it	it	its (its)
Plural			
1st person	we	us	our (ours)
2nd person	you	you	your (yours)
3rd person	they	them	their (theirs)

Relative Pronouns	Demonstrative Pronouns	Indefinite Pronouns
who, whom, whose	this	all, both, each, one
which	that	nothing, nobody, no one
that	these	anything, anybody; anyone
what	those	something, somebody, someone
whoever, whichever		everything, everybody, everyone

3. What Are Adjectives?

DEFINITION ➤ An **adjective** is a word that modifies a noun or pronoun.

Adjectives usually come before the nouns they modify, but they can also come after the verb.

The *unusual* letter was delivered to my house.
It felt *heavy*.

4. What Are Verbs?

DEFINITION ➤ A **verb** is a word that is used to indicate an action, state, or occurrence as well as the time at which the action, etc., takes place.

Verbs can be divided into three classes: action verbs, linking verbs, and helping verbs.

Action Verbs

An action verb tells us what the subject is doing. Most verbs are action verbs.

The athlete *cycles* 20 km every morning.
(The action takes place in the present.)
The crowd *applauded* the sax player.
(The action takes place in the past.)

Linking Verbs

A linking verb joins the subject of a sentence to one or more words that describe or identify the subject.

He *is* a jazz musician in his twenties.
She *seemed* excited about getting married.

Common Linking Verbs		
be (am, is, are, was, were, have been)	become	look
act	feel	seem
appear	grow	taste

Helping Verbs (also called Auxiliary Verbs)

A helping verb, or an "auxiliary," is any verb used before the main verb.
It could show the tense of the verb:

It *will* rain tomorrow.
(Shows future tense.)

It could show the passive voice (see pp. 38–39 for more on active and passive voice):

The new concert hall *has been* finished.

It could give a special meaning to the verb:

Avril Lavigne *may be* singing at that concert.

Common Helping Verbs

can, could
may, might, must
shall, should
will, would
forms of the irregular verbs *be*, *have*, and *do*

See Appendix C at the back of the text for more on Irregular Verbs.

5. What Are Adverbs?

DEFINITION ➤ An **adverb** is a word that modifies a verb, an adjective, or another adverb. It often ends in *-ly*, but a better test is to ask yourself if the word answers the question how, when, or where.

She is sure to succeed *eventually*.

- The adverb *eventually* answers the question "When?"
- It ends in *-ly*, and it modifies the verb *succeed*.

It will be *very* cold tomorrow.

- The adverb *very* answers the question "How?"
- It modifies the adjective *cold*.

Winter has come *too* early.

- The adverb *too* answers the question "How?"
- It modifies the adverb *early*.

Here are some adverbs to look out for:

Adverbs

Adverbs of Frequency	Adverbs of Degree	
always	even	quite
ever	extremely	surely
never	just	too
often	more	very
seldom	much	
sometimes	only	

6. What Are Prepositions?

DEFINITION ➤ A **preposition** is a word used to relate a noun or pronoun to some other word in the sentence. The preposition with its noun or pronoun (object of the preposition) is called a prepositional phrase.

Example: The gift is *from* my mother.
The card is addressed *to* my aunt.

Common Prepositions			
about	below	in	since
above	beneath	inside	through
across	beside	into	to
after	between	like	toward
against	beyond	near	under
along	by	of	until
among	down	off	up
around	during	on	upon
at	except	outside	with
before	for	over	within
behind	from	past	without

7. What Are Conjunctions?

DEFINITION ➤ A **conjunction** is a word that joins or connects other words, phrases, or clauses.

Connecting two words

Sooner *or* later, you will have to pay.

Connecting two phrases

The story was on the radio *and* in the newspaper.

Connecting two clauses

Dinner was late *because* I had to work overtime at the office.

Since one word can function differently or have different forms or meanings, you must often study the context in which the word is found to be sure of its part of speech.

The parent makes sacrifices *for* the good of the children.

In this sentence, *for* is a preposition.

The parent made sacrifices, *for* the child needed a good education.

In this sentence, *for* is a conjunction meaning "because."

Conjunctions

Coordinating Conjunctions	**Subordinating Conjunctions**	
and	after	provided that
but	although	since (meaning "because")
nor	as, as if, as though	unless
or	because	until
for (meaning "because")	before	when, whenever
yet	how	where, wherever
so	if, even if	while

Correlative Conjunctions	**Adverbial Conjunctions** (also known as "conjunctive adverbs")	
either...or	To add an idea:	furthermore
neither...nor		moreover
both...and		likewise
not only...but also	To contrast:	however
		nevertheless
	To show results:	consequently
		therefore
	To show an alternative:	otherwise

Where coordinating conjunctions are concerned, you can use the word *fanboys* (an acronym) as a way to remember them: *f* for *for*, *a* for *and*, *n* for *nor*, *b* for *but*, *o* for *or*, *y* for *yet* and *s* for *so*.

For
And
Nor
But
Or
Yet
So

8. What Are Interjections?

DEFINITION ➤ An **interjection** is a word that expresses a strong feeling and is not connected grammatically to any other part of the sentence.

Example: *Oh*, I lost my wallet.
Well, that means I'll have to borrow cash from a friend.

9. What Are Articles?

DEFINITION ➤ An **article** is a word that identifies a noun in a general sense.

Articles are considered to be adjectives. There are two types of articles: definite (*the*) and indefinite (*a, an*).

She read *the* magazine (a particular magazine).
She read *a* magazine (some magazine not identified).

Do not use *a* or *an* with non-countable nouns (things that can't be counted separately, such as *water*).

Water leaked under my roof during the rainstorm.

Use the indefinite article *a* or *an* before nouns that can be counted when you don't specify the thing counted.

An open window allowed the fresh air in (any one of a number of windows).

Use *a* before nouns beginning with a consonant or *u* pronounced as *y*. Use *an* before words beginning with a vowel or a silent *h*.

a vacation
a unit, *a* eulogy (*u* and *eu* are pronounced "*yu*")
an automobile
an hour

Working Together: *Puzzle Pieces and Sentence Parts*

Review the names for sentence parts by doing this crossword puzzle. Feel free to look back in the chapter for the answers.

Crossword Puzzle: Reviewing the Terms for Sentence Parts

Across

1. Verbs like *hop, sing,* and *play* are called _________ verbs.
4. A helping verb
6. Every sentence has a _________ and a verb.
8. A helping verb
9. Which of the following is a preposition?
   must, upon, they
12. A preposition
14. *Word, witch, wall,* and *willow* are examples of the part of speech called a _________.
15. Most nouns are _________ nouns. They are not capitalized.
18. In the following sentence, which word is an adjective?
   His pet theory was disproved.
21. A preposition
22. In the following sentence, which word is an abstract noun?
   The era was not economically successful.
23. A preposition
24. A word that can take the place of a noun

Down

1. *Joy, confidence, peace* are examples of this kind of noun; the opposite of a concrete noun.
2. Which word is the subject in the following sentence?
   Here is the tube of glue for Toby.
3. An indefinite pronoun
4. A plural pronoun
5. *Look, appear, feel,* and *seem* are examples of _________ verbs.
7. Which word is the object of the preposition?
   He made sure to call her before ten.
10. The opposite of a common noun
11. A pronoun
13. A preposition
16. A helping verb
17. Which of the following is a proper noun?
   king, Nero, hero, teen
19. Which of the following is an adjective?
   net, tan, Nan, man
20. Which word is the verb in the following sentence?
   Run down to the car for our bag.
21. A common linking verb

CHAPTER TWO

2

Recognizing Subjects and Verbs

QUICK QUIZ

Test yourself on your knowledge of subjects and verbs. In each of the following sentences, find the subject and verb. Write your answers in the spaces provided. The answers to the questions are beside the quiz.

Subject	Verb	
______________	______________	1. The definition of marriage has become a major issue in Canada.
______________	______________	2. Studies show that many people are getting married later than their parents did.
______________	______________	3. In Quebec, a large proportion of people have chosen to live in common-law relationships.
______________	______________	4. Researchers have given more attention to divorces than to successful marriages.
______________	______________	5. A positive attitude toward the partner appears to be the most important quality in a successful marriage.

Answers:
1. Subject: definition
   Verb: has become
2. Subject: studies
   Verb: show
3. Subject: proportion
   Verb: have chosen
4. Subject: researchers
   Verb: have given
5. Subject: attitude
   Verb: appears

Why Should We Use Complete Sentences When We Write?

If you walk up to a friend at noon and say "Lunch?", you are expressing an idea by using a short form of a complete thought: you are asking your friend to join you for lunch. Even though we do not always use complete sentences in daily conversation, we usually have complete thoughts in mind. We say and hear words and phrases such as "Lunch?" every day, and these words and phrases seem to be complete thoughts because both the speaker and the listener supply the missing words in their own minds. When your friend hears you say "Lunch?", he or she is able to quickly understand the meaning: "Would you like to join me for lunch?"

You are free to use language in this way when you speak, but you must use a different approach in more formal speaking and writing situations. In writing down your thoughts, you cannot assume that another person will finish your thoughts for you. Each of your written thoughts must be a complete expression of what is in your mind.

The purpose of writing is to communicate something of value to a reader. Once you understand how the parts of a complete sentence work, you will be able to focus as much attention on *what* you are saying as on *how* you are saying it. Once you understand how the parts of a complete sentence work, you can take control of the sentence. You will have the power to make words work for you.

What Is a Complete Sentence?

DEFINITION ➤ A **complete sentence** must contain a subject and a verb, as well as express a *complete thought.*

A *complete thought* is difficult to describe. It may be best understood by means of an example:

1. If you want an "A" in this course.
2. If you want an "A" in this course, you should do all your assignments and homework, attend all your classes, and communicate to your professor any difficulties you're having.
3. You want an "A" in this course.

The first thought is incomplete. The second thought is complete. The third thought is complete. Obviously, length does not determine completeness.

How Do You Find the Subject of a Sentence?

The subject of a sentence is the person or thing about which the rest of the sentence makes an assertion. Any sentence must be about someone or something; therefore, every sentence must have a subject. To find the subject of any sentence, ask yourself this question: Who or what is the sentence about? When you have answered this question, you have found the subject of the sentence. Try to zero in on one word that is the subject. Although it may not always be possible, it is possible most of the time. The subject in sentence #3 above is *you.* The words *"A"* and *course* are also nouns, but neither is the subject of the sentence.

EXERCISE

Recognizing Subjects

Examine each of the following sentences and ask yourself who or what each sentence is about. Draw a line under the subject in each sentence. (Underline only one word where possible.) The answers and explanations immediately follow the sentences.

1. The student graduated in the spring.

2. The unemployed Rick Daniels spent the summer looking for work.
3. He took a job as a security guard.
4. The building was near the waterfront.
5. The warehouse grew bitterly cold.
6. Cowardice was not the issue.
7. Tina and Margot listened to his complaints whenever they got together.

Since the subject of a sentence is made up of either one or more nouns (or a word, phrase, or clause that functions as a noun), learning some of the different terms used in traditional grammar to describe these different nouns is helpful.

1. The student graduated in the spring.

The sentence is about the *student*. In this case, the subject is a common noun.

DEFINITION ➤ **Nouns** refer to persons, places, and things. Most nouns are common nouns.

Common nouns are the general terms for all the persons, places, and objects around us. They are not specific names; therefore, they are not capitalized.

Examples: woman, city, cola

2. The unemployed Rick Daniels spent the summer looking for work.

The sentence is about *Rick Daniels*. In this case, the subject *Rick Daniels* is made up of two proper nouns.

DEFINITION ➤ **Proper nouns** name particular persons, places, or things. Proper nouns are always capitalized.

Examples: Juanita, Calgary, Pepsi

Notice that words like *unemployed* can be put in front of nouns to describe them further. These words are called **adjectives**. *The, a,* and *an* are called **articles**.

3. He took a job as a security guard.

The sentence is about *he*.

DEFINITION ➤ Words that can be used in place of nouns, such as *she, he, it, we, I, you,* and *they,* are called **pronouns**.

4. The building was near the waterfront.

The sentence is about the *building*, a common noun. Can you replace this noun first with a proper noun and then with a pronoun?

_______________ was near the waterfront.

_______________ was near the waterfront.

5. The warehouse grew bitterly cold.

The sentence is about the *warehouse*. Here the common noun is not about a person or place but a thing. What pronoun could take the place of *warehouse*?

_______________ grew bitterly cold.

6. Cowardice was not the issue.

The sentence is about *cowardice*.

7. Tina and Margot listened to his complaints whenever they got together.

The sentence is about *Tina* and *Margot*. The subject is made up of two proper nouns joined by *and*.

DEFINITION ➤ A **compound subject** is made up of two or more nouns joined together by *and*, *or*, *either/or*, or *neither/nor*.

Not *every* noun or pronoun functions as a subject. Nouns and pronouns can also function as **objects**. Can you find a noun in the following sentence that is not the subject of the sentence?

Marc bought a ticket.

Guide to Finding the Subject of a Sentence

Definition: The subject of a sentence is who or what the sentence is about.
How to find the subject: Ask yourself, "Who or what is this sentence about?"

- Subjects usually come early in the sentence.
- Subjects can be modified by adjectives.
- Subjects can be compound.

Look for these two kinds of words as your subjects:

1. **Nouns**: the names of persons, places, or things

Common	or	**Proper**	**Concrete**	or	**Abstract**
aunt		Aunt Giselle	face		loneliness
country		Ghana	people		patriotism
watch		Timex	jewellery		time

(continued)

Guide to Finding the Subject of a Sentence (continued)

2. **Pronouns:** take the place of nouns

Personal	**Indefinite**	**Relative**	**Demonstrative**
I	one	who	this
you	each	that	that
he, she, it	some, someone, somebody, something	what	these
we	any, anyone, anybody, anything	which	those
they	nobody, nothing		
	everyone, everybody, everything		
	all		
	many		
	several		

PRACTICE

Finding the Subject of a Sentence

Underline the subject in each of the following sentences. An example is done for you. Check your answers against those in the Answer Key on p. 433.

The seat belt <u>sign</u> switched on.

1. The plane landed.
2. Michelle Bates gathered her bags.
3. She was so excited.
4. Strange sounds filled her ears.
5. A mother and her three children shared a lunch.
6. The battered red taxi idled outside.
7. A light rain had fallen recently.

Finding the Subject in Sentences with Prepositional Phrases

The sentences you worked with in the Practice above were short and basic. If we wrote only such sentences, our writing would sound choppy. Complex ideas would be difficult to express. One way to expand the simple sentence is to add prepositional phrases.

Example: He put his suitcase on the seat.

On is a preposition. *Seat* is a noun used as the object of the preposition. *On the seat* is the prepositional phrase.

DEFINITION ➤ A **prepositional phrase** is a group of words containing a preposition and an object of the preposition with its modifiers. Prepositional phrases contain nouns, but these nouns are never the subject of the sentence.

In sentences with prepositional phrases, the subject may be difficult to spot. Consider the following sentence:

> In the young woman's apartment, paintings covered the walls.

In the sentence above, what is the prepositional phrase? Who or what is the sentence about?

To avoid making the mistake of thinking that a noun in the prepositional phrase could be the subject, it is a good practice to cross out the prepositional phrase.

> ~~In the young woman's apartment,~~ paintings covered the walls.

With the prepositional phrase crossed out, it now becomes clear that the subject of the sentence is the noun *paintings*.

When you are looking for the subject of a sentence, do not look for it within the prepositional phrase.

You can easily recognize a prepositional phrase because it always begins with a preposition. Study the following list so that you will be able to quickly recognize all of the common prepositions.

Common Prepositions

about	below	in	since
above	beneath	inside	through
across	beside	into	to
after	between	like	toward
against	beyond	near	under
along	by	of	until
among	down	off	up
around	during	on	upon
at	except	outside	with
before	for	over	within
behind	from	past	without

In addition to these common prepositions, English has a number of prepositional combinations that also function as prepositions.

Common Prepositional Combinations		
ahead of	in addition to	in reference to
at the time of	in between	in regard to
because of	in care of	in search of
by means of	in case of	in spite of
except for	in common with	instead of
for fear of	in contrast to	on account of
for the purpose of	in the course of	similar to
for the sake of	in exchange for	

Notice that when a prepositional phrase begins a sentence, a comma usually follows the phrase. (Sometimes, if the prepositional phrase is short, the comma is omitted.)

EXERCISE 1

Creating Sentences with Prepositional Phrases

Use each of the prepositions in the list below to write a prepositional phrase. Then write a sentence containing that prepositional phrase. Two examples are done for you.

Preposition	Prepositional Phrase	Sentence
before	before breakfast	My cousin called before breakfast.

Preposition	Prepositional Phrase	Sentence
between	between the two barns	Between the two barns, the old Buick lay rusting.

Preposition	Prepositional Phrase	Sentence
1. in	because of	he cried because of the punishment received.
2. with		
3. of	In case of a fire	emergency exits were ~~discussed~~ pointed out.
4. from		
5. during	the night	you could hear the owl.

6. by ____________ ____________

7. for ____________ ____________

EXERCISE 2

Finding Subjects in Sentences with Prepositional Phrases

Remember that you will never find the subject of a sentence within a prepositional phrase. In each of the following sentences, cross out any prepositional phrases. Then underline the subject of each sentence. An example is done for you.

> ~~On the circus grounds~~, Lisa wandered ~~among the elephants, horses, and camels~~.

1. Young people in the circus search for travel, adventure, danger, and romance.
2. However, after a few weeks of pulling cages and sleeping on hay, most of these people get tired of the circus and go back home.
3. The art of clowning, for instance, is very serious work.
4. Today, a circus clown must graduate from Clown College in Venice, Florida.
5. The staff of Clown College looks across the country for applicants.
6. Admission to the college is not easy.
7. Only 60 people out of 3000 applicants are admitted.

What Are the Other Problems in Finding Subjects?

Sentences That Are Questions

Some sentences begin with words that indicate that a question is being asked. Such words as *why, where, how,* and *when* give the reader the signal that a question will follow. Such opening words are not the subject. The subject will be found later on in the sentence. The following sentences begin with question words:

> Why is *he* going away?
> How did *he* find his sister in the city?

Notice that in each sentence the subject is not found in the opening part of the sentence. By answering questions or changing the question into a statement, you can make the subject easier to spot.

> *He* is going away ...
> *He* found his sister ...

Using *there*

The word *there* can never be the subject of a sentence.

There is a new teacher in the department.

Who or what is this sentence about? This sentence is about a teacher. *Teacher* is the subject of the sentence.

Commands

Sometimes a sentence contains a verb that gives an order:

Go to Halifax.
Help your sister.

In these sentences, the subject *you* is not written, but it is understood. This is the only case where the subject of a sentence may be left out when you write a sentence.

Sentences That Contain Appositive Phrases

DEFINITION ➤ An **appositive phrase** is a group of words in a sentence that gives us extra information about a noun in the sentence.

Example: Don Koyama, the retired chemist, sat at his desk.

In this sentence, the words *the retired chemist* make up the appositive phrase because they give you extra information about Don Koyama. Notice that commas separate the appositive phrase from the rest of the sentence. If you leave out the appositive phrase when you read the sentence, the thought will still be complete.

Don Koyama sat at his desk.

Now the subject is clear: *Don Koyama.*

When you are looking for the subject of a sentence, you will not find it within an appositive phrase.

PRACTICE

Finding Hidden Subjects

Each of the following sentences contains an example of a special problem in finding the subject of a sentence. First, cross out any prepositional phrases or appositive phrases. Then underline the subject of each sentence. An example is done for you. Check your answers against those in the Answer Key on p. 433.

What can <u>we</u> learn ~~from the study of an ancient civilization~~?

1. Look at a map of South America.
2. Where is the ancient city of Chan Chan?
3. Here on the coastal desert of northern Peru stand the remains of this city of the kings.
4. Chan Chan, once the fabulously wealthy centre of the Chimor, is situated in one of the driest, bleakest regions in the world.
5. It was the largest pre-Columbian city in South America.
6. In the ruins of this city, scientists have found fragments to piece together the mystery of the past.
7. How could this civilization have survived this hostile environment and become so advanced?

EXERCISE

Finding Hidden Subjects

Each of the following sentences contains an example of a special problem in finding the subject of a sentence. First, cross out any prepositional phrases or appositive phrases. Then underline the subject of each sentence. An example is done for you.

The <u>*Maid of the Mist*</u>, ~~an exciting boat ride~~, is a favourite stop ~~for many tourists to Niagara Falls~~.

1. How can you tell a stranger from a native?
2. There are sometimes unmistakable signs.
3. However, be careful not to assume too much.
4. A middle-aged man with three cameras around his neck and a family following behind him is nearly always a tourist.
5. On the other hand, a strange hairdo or an exotic outfit may just be the sign of a creative individual.
6. In Canada, even a foreign language is not always the sign of a stranger.
7. On your next trip, try to separate the strangers from the natives.

How Do You Find the Verb of a Sentence?

Every sentence must have a verb. Verbs can be divided into three classes:

1. Action: An **action verb** tells what the subject is doing.

   Simon Whitfield *ran* in the Olympics.

2. Linking: A **linking verb** indicates a state of being or condition.

   The crowd *seemed* exhausted during the triathlon.

3. Helping: A **helping verb** combines with a main verb to form a verb phrase and gives the main verb a special time or meaning.

   Canadians *can* expect strong performances from their Olympic athletes in the future.

Verbs tell time. Use this fact to test for a verb. If you can put the verb into different tenses in the sentence, that word is a verb.

> ***Present:*** (Today) he *runs.*
> ***Past:*** (Yesterday) he *ran.*
> ***Future:*** (Tomorrow) he *will run.*

Action Verbs

DEFINITION ➤ **Action verbs** tell us what the subject is doing and when the subject does the action.

The woman *studied* ballet.

What was the woman doing? studying
What is the time of the action? past (*-ed* is the past tense ending)

Action Verbs

Most verbs are action verbs. Here are a few examples:

arrive	learn	open	watch
leave	forget	write	fly
enjoy	help	speak	catch
despise	make	teach	wait

PRACTICE

Finding Action Verbs

Each of the following sentences contains an action verb. Find the action verb by first crossing out any prepositional or appositive phrases and underlining the subject of the sentence. Then circle the verb (the word that tells what the subject is doing). Note also the time of the action: past, present, or future. An example is done for you. Check your answers against those in the Answer Key on p. 433.

Many people (begin) hobbies ~~in childhood~~ (present) .

1. Some people collect very strange objects.
2. One man saved the fortunes from fortune cookies.
3. A group of people in Alberta often met to discuss their spark plug collections.
4. People in Brandon will gather many types of barbed wire.
5. Collectors take pride in the possession of unusual items.
6. A collection, like odd rocks or unique automobiles, will let a person express his or her individuality.
7. Collections keep us entertained from childhood to old age.

EXERCISE

Finding Action Verbs

Each of the following sentences contains an action verb. Find the action verb by first crossing out any prepositional or appositive phrases and underlining the subject of the sentence. Then circle the verb (the word that tells what the subject is doing). Note also the time of the action: past, present, or future. An example is done for you.

Attitudes ~~toward medical practices~~ (will change) (future).

1. Traditional Chinese medicine harnessed ancient healing techniques in the practice of "gigong."
2. Masters of this Chinese practice claimed the ability to cure many diseases.
3. The master will project a mysterious force into his students.
4. The hands of the Chinese gigong practitioner will pound at the air above a patient.
5. Many patients respond to this invisible force.
6. Some patients sway their bodies with the power of the force.
7. Some doctors conducted research in China in hopes of finding the secrets of this ancient art.

Linking Verbs

DEFINITION ➤ A **linking verb** is a verb that joins the subject of a sentence to one or more words that describe or identify the subject.

For example:

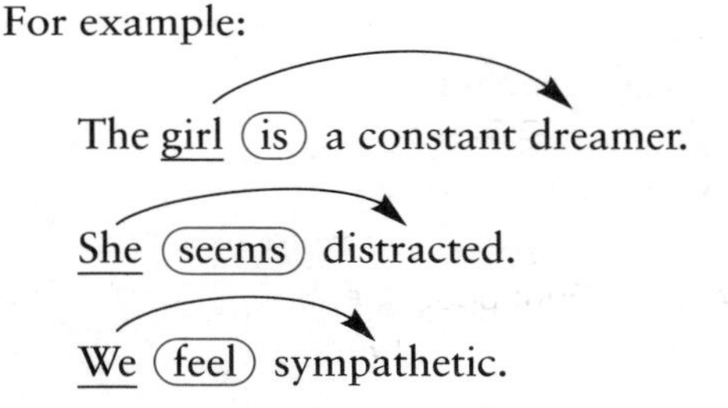

In each of these examples, the verb links the subject to a word that identifies or describes the subject. In the first example, the verb *is* links *girl* with *dreamer*. In the second example, the verb *seems* links the pronoun *she* with *distracted*. Finally, in the third example, the verb *feel* links the pronoun *we* with *sympathetic*.

Linking Verbs

Common linking verbs include:

act	feel
appear	grow
be (am, is, are, was, were, have been)	look
	seem
become	taste

EXERCISE 1

Finding Linking Verbs

Each of the following sentences contains a linking verb. Find the linking verb by first underlining the subject of the sentence. Then draw an arrow to the word or words that identify or describe the subject. Finally, circle the linking verb. An example is done for you.

Dreams (are) very important to the Aboriginal peoples of Canada.

1. My dream last night was wonderful.
2. I had become middle-aged.
3. In a sunlit kitchen with a book in my hand, I appeared relaxed and happy.
4. The house was empty and quiet.
5. In the morning light, the kitchen felt cozy.
6. I seemed to have grown calmer.
7. I felt satisfied with life.

EXERCISE 2

Finding Linking Verbs

Each of the following sentences contains a linking verb. Find the linking verb by first underlining the subject of the sentence. Then draw an arrow to the word or words that identify or describe the subject. Finally, circle the linking verb. An example is done for you.

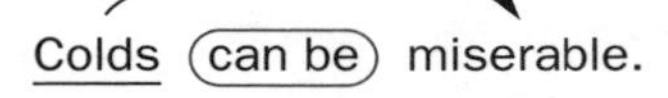

Colds (can be) miserable.

1. Monica was afraid of catching a cold.
2. She felt healthy.
3. Everyone in her family became sick.
4. Her brother looked horrible.
5. She seemed immune to the cold.
6. Soon Monica's head grew stuffy.
7. The chicken soup from the deli down the street tasted delicious.

Helping Verbs (also called Auxiliary Verbs)

Some verbs can be used to help the main verb express a special time or meaning.

Sentence Using Helping Verb	Time or Meaning Expressed
He *is* sleeping.	right now
He *might* sleep.	maybe now or in the future
He *should* sleep.	ought to, now or in the future
He *could have been* sleeping.	maybe in the past

Common Helping Verbs

can, could
may, might, must
shall, should
will, would
forms of the irregular verbs *be, do,* and *have*

REMEMBER that *be*, *do*, and *have* are also used as main verbs of sentences. In such cases, *be* is a linking verb while *do* and *have* are action verbs. All other helping verbs are usually used only as helping verbs.

WATCH OUT for adverbs that may come in between the helping verb and the main verb.

DEFINITION ➤ **Adverbs** are words that can modify verbs, adjectives, or other adverbs.

In the following sentence, the word *often* is an adverb coming between the verb phrase *can frighten*. For a list of adverbs, see p. 7.

Dreams (can) often (frighten) young children.

EXERCISE

Finding Helping Verbs

Each of the following sentences contains a helping verb in addition to the main verb. In each sentence, first underline the subject. Then circle the entire verb phrase. An example is done for you.

In some writing classes, students (must keep) a diary of their work.

1. There could be several advantages to keeping a diary.
2. In a journal, a person can safely express true feelings without fear of criticism by family or friends.
3. You will be able to capture your memories before they fade.
4. Important, too, would be the development of a writing style and the improvement of language skills.
5. A journal might awaken your imagination.
6. It may unexpectedly bring pleasure and satisfaction.
7. You should seriously consider the purchase of one of those lovely fabric-bound notebooks.

Chapter Review Exercises

PRACTICE

Finding Subjects and Verbs in Simple Sentences

In each of the following sentences, cross out any prepositional phrases or appositive phrases. Then underline the subject and circle the complete verb. An example is done for you. Check your answers against those in the Answer Key on p. 433.

The modern family (has been disrupted) ~~by many negative outside influences~~.

1. Mother and Dad always blame me for any trouble with my sister.
2. My sister, the most popular girl in her class, is two years older than I.
3. Yesterday, for instance, she was trying on her new graduation dress.
4. Helpfully, I took out her new shoes and purse for her.
5. Margaret instantly became furious with me.
6. I was only sharing Margaret's excitement about her new clothes.

EXERCISE 1

Finding Subjects and Verbs in Simple Sentences

In each of the sentences in the following paragraph, cross out any prepositional or appositive phrases. Then underline the subject and circle the complete verb.

Go West! Western Australia, one of the remaining great boom areas of the world, constitutes one-third of the Australian continent. Why did people by the tens of thousands go to western Australia in the late 1800s? In 1894, Leslie Robert Menzies jumped off his camel and landed in a pile of gold nuggets. In less than two hours, this man gathered over a million dollars in gold. He eventually took 5 t of gold to the bank by wheelbarrow! Kalgoorlie and Boulder, the two boom towns that grew up there, boast the richest golden mile in the world. With all the gold seekers, this surface gold did not last very long. Now the only bands of rich ore lie more than 1200 m down under the ground. There are many ghost towns with their empty iron houses and rundown chicken coops.

EXERCISE 2

Composing Complete Sentences

Below are two lists, one of subjects and one of verbs. Using any subject from one list and any verb from the other list, compose complete sentences. Use each subject and each verb only once. Try to vary the position of the subject in the sentence. An example is done for you. (Do not use it as one of your own sentences.)

The dentist looks very tired today.

1. dogs	is
2. nose	chased
3. she	are
4. dentist	was
5. Saskatchewan	singing
6. fishing	has
7. problems	screams
8. obeying	see
9. mailbox	approaches
10. storm	looks

1. ______________________________

2. ______________________________

3. ______________________________

4. ______________________________

5. ______________________________

6. ______________________________

7. ______________________________

8. ______________________________

9. ______________________________

10. ______________________________

Working Together: *Singling Out Subjects*

Student Profile: On a separate piece of paper, answer the following five questions about yourself. Write on every other line to make your writing more readable. Write freely for twenty minutes. Then exchange papers with another student. Using a pencil, circle the one-word (in most cases) subject in every sentence in your classmate's writing. Are you confusing subjects with objects? Be prepared to share examples with the class.

1. Tell about the first book you remember looking at or reading.
2. Who was your most memorable teacher in elementary school? What is it about this teacher that you remember?
3. Who was the person outside of school who taught you the most?
4. What are the magazines you subscribe to or would like to subscribe to and why?
5. When you have a day or half day to yourself, how do you spend that time?

CHAPTER THREE 3

More Work with Verbs

QUICK QUIZ

Test yourself on your knowledge of verb forms. In each of the following sentences, choose the correct verb tense for the verb in the dependent clause. Answers to the questions are beside the quiz.

1. The soccer game will continue only after the lightning and rain ____________ . (to stop)
2. Since he was poor and unappreciated by the music world when he died in 1791, Mozart did not realize the importance that his music ____________ (to have) in the twenty-first century.
3. My aunt told me yesterday that she ____________ (to buy) a new condo the day before that.
4. Hemingway wrote only about subjects that he ____________ . (to like)
5. I _______ (to see) the woman buy the purple hat yesterday.

Answers:
1. have stopped, stop
2. would have
3. had bought
4. liked
5. saw

Since every sentence contains at least one verb, and this verb can take one of many forms, it is worth a good deal of your time and effort to understand these many forms and their uses. In Chapter 2, you have learned to *recognize* verbs. In this chapter, you will study several other areas with respect to verbs that often cause difficulty for writers:

Irregular Verbs
Verb Tense Consistency
Sequence of Verb Tenses
Present Perfect and Past Perfect Tenses
Active and Passive Voice
The Subjunctive

What Are the Principal Parts of the Irregular Verbs?

The English language has more than 100 verbs that do not form the past tense or past participle with the usual *-ed* ending. Their forms are irregular. When you listen to young children, you often hear them utter expressions such as "Yesterday I *cutted* myself." Later on, they will learn that the verb *cut* is unusual, and they will change to the irregular form: "Yesterday I *cut* myself." The best way to learn these verbs is to listen to how they sound. Pronounce them out loud over and over until you have learned them. If you find that you don't know a particular verb's meaning, or you cannot pronounce a verb and its forms, ask your instructor for help. Most irregular verbs are very common words that you will be using often in your writing and speaking. You will want to know them well.

See more on "Irregular Verbs" in Appendix C in the back of the text.

Practising 50 Irregular Verbs

These are the three principal parts of irregular verbs:

Simple Form (also called **Infinitive Form**)	**Past Form**	**Past Participle** (used with perfect tenses after *has, have,* or *will have,* or with passive voice after the verb *to be*)

I. The following verbs do not change their forms:
(Notice they all end in *-t* or *-d*)

Simple Form	Past Form	Past Participle
bet	bet	bet
cost	cost	cost
cut	cut	cut
fit	fit	fit
hit	hit	hit
hurt	hurt	hurt
quit	quit	quit
spread	spread	spread

II. The following verbs have the same simple present form and past participle:

Simple Form	Past Form	Past Participle
come	came	come
become	became	become

EXERCISE 1

Knowing the Irregular Verb Forms

Fill in the correct form of the verb in the following sentences.

(cost) 1. Last year the tuition for my education ____________ 7 percent more than the year before.

(quit) 2. I <u>have</u> ____________ trying to guess my expenses for next year.

(spread) 3. The message <u>has</u> ____________ that college costs continue to spiral.

(hit) 4. Most parents <u>have been</u> ____________ with large tax increases.

(become) 5. Financing a child's higher education <u>has</u> ____________ a difficult task.

III. The following verbs have the same simple past form and past participle:

Simple Form	Past Form	Past Participle
bend	bent	bent
lend	lent	lent
send	sent	sent
spend	spent	spent
creep	crept	crept
keep	kept	kept
sleep	slept	slept
sweep	swept	swept
weep	wept	wept
teach	taught	taught
catch	caught	caught
bleed	bled	bled
feed	fed	fed
lead	led	led
speed	sped	sped
bring	brought	brought
buy	bought	bought
fight	fought	fought
think	thought	thought
seek	sought	sought

EXERCISE 2

Knowing the Irregular Verb Forms

Fill in the correct form of the verb in the following sentences.

(buy) 1. Last year the school district ___________ new chemistry texts.

(spend) 2. Some parents felt they had ___________ too much money on these new books.

(bleed) 3. They claimed the taxpayers were being ___________ dry.

(keep) 4. These parents argued that the school should have ___________ the old books.

(think) 5. The teachers ___________ the old books were worn out.

IV. The following verbs have all different forms:

Simple Form	Past Form	Past Participle
blow	blew	blown
fly	flew	flown
grow	grew	grown
know	knew	known
throw	threw	thrown
begin	began	begun
drink	drank	drunk
ring	rang	rung
shrink	shrank	shrunk
sink	sank	sunk
sing	sang	sung
spring	sprang	sprung
swim	swam	swum
bite	bit	bitten (or bit)
hide	hid	hidden (or hid)
drive	drove	driven
ride	rode	ridden
stride	strode	stridden
rise	rose	risen
write	wrote	written

EXERCISE 3

Knowing the Irregular Verb Forms

Fill in the correct form of the verb in the following sentences.

(grow) 1. Adventure holidays ___________ in popularity during the last decade.

(fly) 2. Years ago, travellers ___________ to Spain to see bullfights.

(throw) 3. Today, some clients dream of being ___________ by the bull.

(ride, swim) 4. As part of adventure trips, people have ___________ horseback, have ___________ across rivers, and have walked for days to get to their destinations.

(shrink) 5. Clients of a new trend called "reality tours" do not even ___________ from visiting jails.

EXERCISE 4

Knowing the Irregular Verb Forms

Supply the past form or the past participle for each verb in parentheses.

Ever since people __________ (begin) to write, they have __________ (write) about the great mysteries in nature. For instance, no one __________ (know) why the dinosaurs disappeared. Scientists now have __________ (bet) on one strong possibility. That possibility is that 65 million years ago, a 10-km-wide chunk of rock __________ (hit) the earth and __________ (throw) up a thick cloud of dust. The dust __________ (keep) the sunlight from the earth; therefore, certain life forms disappeared. Some scientists have __________ (think) that this could also have __________ (shrink) the earth's animal population by as much as 70 percent. Other scientists are not so sure that this is the answer. They believe time has __________ (hide) the real reason for the disappearance of the dinosaurs.

EXERCISE 5

Knowing the Irregular Verb Forms

Supply the past form or the past participle for each verb in parentheses.

Medical researchers have __________ (seek) a cure for the common cold, but so far they have __________ (fight) without success. The cold virus has __________ (spread) throughout the world, and the number of cold victims has __________ (rise) every year. Past experience has __________ (teach) us that people who drink plenty of liquids and take aspirin get over colds more quickly than those who do not, but this is not a good enough remedy. People have also believed that you __________ (feed) a fever and starved a cold, but recent research has __________ (lead) to a refutation of this belief. It has __________ (cost) a lot of time and effort to search for a vaccine, but so far the new knowledge has not __________ (bring) a cure.

Avoiding Unnecessary Shifts in Verb Tense

Do not shift verb tenses (move from past to present, for example) as you write unless you intend to change the time of the action.

Shifted tense: The customer *asked* (past tense) for the prescription, but the pharmacist *says* (present tense) that the ingredients *are being ordered* (present tense).

Revised: The customer *asked* (past tense) for the prescription, but the pharmacist *said* (past tense) that the ingredients *were being ordered* (past tense).

PRACTICE 1

Correcting Unnecessary Shifts in Verb Tense

Each of the following sentences has an unnecessary shift in verb tense. Revise each sentence so that the tense remains consistent. There may be more than one correct answer for each sentence. Check your answers against those in the Answer Key on p. 433.

1. After I complete that writing course, I took the required history course.

____

____

2. In the beginning of the movie, the action was slow; by the end, I am sitting on the edge of my seat.

____

____

3. The textbook gives the rules for writing a bibliography, but it didn't explain how to do footnotes.

____

____

4. I was walking in the park when all of a sudden I see her running toward me.

____

____

5. The encyclopedia gave several pages of information about astronomy, but it doesn't give anything about black holes.

____

____

6. The invitation requested that Juan be at the ceremony and that he will attend the banquet as well.

____

____

7. That Web site gives you excellent information, but it was too cluttered.

____

____

PRACTICE 2

Correcting Unnecessary Shifts in Verb Tense

The following paragraph contains unnecessary shifts in verb tense. Change each incorrect verb to past tense. Check your answers against those in the Answer Key on p. 434.

Doctor Norman Bethune grows up in Gravenhurst, Ontario. He was educated in Toronto and serves as a stretcher bearer in World War I. He contracted tuberculosis and thereafter devotes himself to helping other victims of the disease when he practises surgery in Montreal. He also invents or redesigned twelve medical and surgical instruments. Bethune travelled to Russia in 1935, joined the Communist party, and goes to Spain in 1936, where he organized the first mobile blood transfusion service during the Spanish Civil War. After returning to Canada, he shortly left for overseas again, this time to China, where he helped the Chinese Communists in their fight against Japan. "Spain and China," he writes, "are part of the same battle." While there, he contracted an infection and died. Mao's essay "In Memory of Norman Bethune," prescribed reading during China's Cultural Revolution, urges all Communists to follow Bethune's example of selfless dedication to others. Bethune is the best-known Canadian to the Chinese, and many Chinese visit his Canadian birthplace.

What Is the Sequence of Tenses?

DEFINITION ➤ The term **sequence of tenses** refers to the proper use of verb tenses in complex sentences (sentences that have an independent clause and a dependent clause).

DEFINITION ➤ The **independent clause (IC)** is a group of words that could be a simple sentence. *Independent* means that the words could stand alone as a sentence, and *clause* means there is a subject and a verb.

DEFINITION ➤ The **dependent clause (DC)** cannot stand alone as a simple sentence. Even though it has a subject and a verb, it depends on the rest of the sentence for completeness.

The verb tense in the independent clause determines the tense of the verb in the dependent clause. The guide that follows shows the relationship between the verb in the independent clause (IC) and the verb in the dependent clause (DC).

Sequence of Tenses

Independent Clause	Dependent Clause	Time of the DC in Relation to the IC
If the tense of the independent clause is in the **present** (he *knows*), here are the possibilities for the dependent clause:		
	that she *is* right.	same time
He knows	that she *was* right.	earlier
	that she *will be* right.	later
If the tense of the independent clause is in the past (he *knew*), here are the possibilities for the dependent clause:		
	that she *was* right.	same time
He knew	that she *had been* right.	earlier
	that she *would be* right.	later
IIf the independent clause is in the future (he *will tell*), here are the possibilities for the dependent clause:		
	if she *goes.*	same time
He will tell us	if she *has gone.*	earlier
	if she *will go.*	later

PRACTICE

Using the Correct Tense

In each of the following sentences, choose the correct tense for the verb in the dependent clause. Use the guide above if you need help. Check your answers against those in the Answer Key on p. 434.

1. The golf tournament will continue only after the thunder and lightning ________. (to stop)
2. Since he thought that he was buying a well-maintained car, Enzo did not realize the problems that this car ________ (to have) in the months to come.
3. I will know when I get my next paycheque whether or not I ________ (to buy) a stereo next week.
4. Albert Einstein failed the entrance exam at the Swiss Federal Institute of Technology because he ________ (to be) + never a very disciplined student.

5. Jacob ate only those foods that he __________.
   (to like)

6. Sasha believes that with a lot of hard work and a little luck, she __________ successful.
   (to be) + soon

7. I know that my best course of action __________ to tell the truth.
   (to be)

How Do You Use the Present Perfect and the Past Perfect Tenses?

Forming the Perfect Tenses

Present perfect tense: *has* or *have* + past participle of the main verb
has worked
have worked

Past perfect tense: *had* + past participle of the main verb
had worked

What Do These Tenses Mean?

DEFINITION ➤ The **present perfect tense** describes an action that started in the past and continues to the present time.

Elena *has worked* at the hospital for ten years.

This sentence indicates that Elena began to work at the hospital ten years ago and is still working there now.

Examine the following time line. What does it tell you about the present perfect tense?

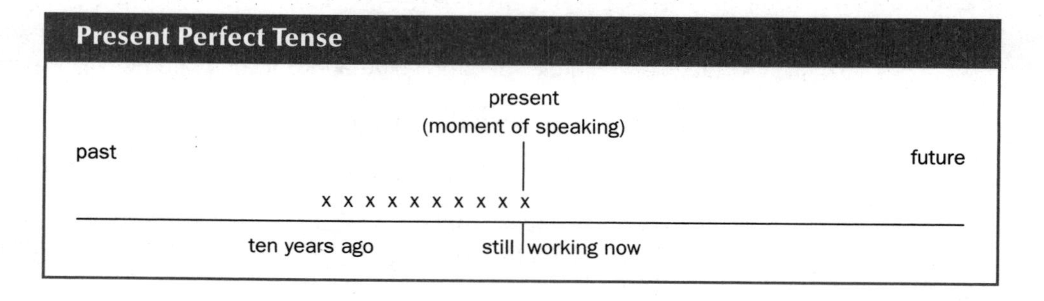

Other example sentences of the present perfect tense:

She *has studied* French since 1980.
I *have* always *despised* that television show.

DEFINITION ➤ The **present perfect tense** can also describe an action that has just taken place, or an action whose exact time in the past is indefinite.

Has Elena *found* a job yet?
Elena *has* (just) *found* a new job in Moncton.
Have you ever *been* to Kapuskasing?
Yes, I *have been* there three times.

If the time were definite, you would use the simple past:

Elena *found* a new job yesterday.
Yes, I *was* there last week.

DEFINITION ➤ The **past perfect tense** describes an action that occurred before another activity or before another point in the past.

Elena *had worked* at the hospital for ten years *before* she *moved* away.

In this sentence, there are two past actions: Elena *worked*, and Elena *moved*. The action that took place first is in the past perfect (*had worked*). The action that took place later, and was also completed in the past, is in the simple past (*moved*).

Past Perfect Tense

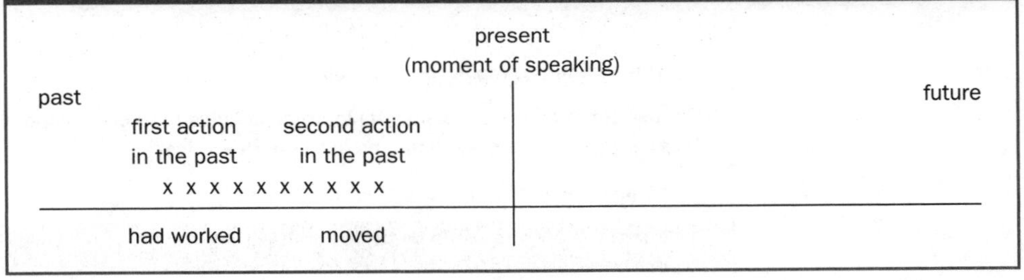

present
(moment of speaking)

past

future

first action in the past

second action in the past

x x x x x x x x x x

had worked

moved

Other examples using the **past perfect tense:**

I *had* just *arrived* when the alarm *rang*.

She *said* that Marty *had told* the class about the essay deadline.

He *had provided* the report *long before* last week's meeting.

EXERCISE

Using the Correct Verb Tense

Complete the following sentence by filling in each blank with either the present perfect tense or the past perfect tense of the verb given.

1. Yolanda told us that she ________________ (live) in Fort Smith before she moved to Mexico City.
2. Mexico City ________________ (fascinate) visitors for many years.
3. This city ____________ (become) the largest city in the world, and people ____________ (watch) it grow larger every year.
4. The suburbs of the city ________________ (overwhelm) old villages that ________________ (exist) peacefully since the days of the Aztecs.
5. Today, Mexico City ________________ (build) a computer-controlled subway system to deal with its huge transportation problem.

What Is the Difference between Active and Passive Voice?

Active and Passive Voice

In the **active voice**, the subject does the acting:

> **The committee made the decision.**

Choose the active voice generally in order to achieve direct, economical, and forceful writing. Most writing, therefore, should be in the active voice.

In the **passive voice**, the subject is acted upon:

> **The decision was made by the committee**
> or
> **The decision was made.**

Notice in these passive sentences, the actor is not only de-emphasized by being moved out of the subject place but may be omitted entirely from the sentence.

Choose the passive voice to de-emphasize the actor or to avoid naming the actor altogether.

Study the two sentences below. The first is in the active voice and the second is in the passive. In what situations would a writer want to use the active voice, and in what situations might the writer need to use the passive?

> Chris Hadfield orbited the earth in 2001.
> The earth was orbited by Chris Hadfield in 2001.

How might the passive voice be used in historical accounts? What are the disadvantages of the passive voice?

How Do You Form the Passive Voice?

The passive voice of a verb consists of a form of *be* (*am, is, are, was, were, being, be,* or *been*) plus the past participle of the main verb.

Cars and trucks *are built* in Oshawa.

1. Use the past participle, not the base form or past tense of a verb, to form the passive voice.
2. Identify the subject and make sure the form of the auxiliary verb *be* agrees with it.
3. Use only transitive verbs (verbs that take a direct object) in the passive voice.

Subject Acted Upon	+ Verb *to be*	+ Past Participle	+ *by* Phrase (Optional)
The race	was	won	(by the runner)
The fish	was	cooked	(by the chef)
The books	are	illustrated	(by the artists)

EXERCISE

Choosing the Right Voice

Fill in the following chart by making all sentences on the left active voice and all sentences on the right passive voice. Then discuss with your classmates and instructor why you might choose the active voice or the passive voice in each case.

Active Voice	Passive Voice
1. ______________________	1. The wrong number was dialled by the child by mistake.
2. ______________________	2. We went to the store where many shoes were available to be purchased.
3. The tornado struck Cherry Creek last spring.	3. ______________________
4. The wind blew the leaves across the yard.	4. ______________________
5. ______________________	5. In the 1970s, platform shoes were worn by many fashionable young men and women.

What Is the Subjunctive?

DEFINITION ➤ The **subjunctive** is a verb form used to express situations or actions that are desired or imagined but that are not true or are unlikely to be true.

Recognize these three situations that call for the subjunctive:

1. Unreal conditions using *if*, *wish*, *as if*, *as though*

   If he were my teacher, I would be pleased.
   He *wishes he were* in France.
   Try to act *as though you were* proud.

   Note that *as if* and *as though* don't always call for the subjunctive. It is correct to say: "It looks as if it is snowing." In this case, the speaker is simply describing what is very likely true. The difference is in the degree of doubt.

   The subjunctive verb form *were* shows that what is being wished for, or considered, is not (or not yet) a fact. Use *were* whether the subject is plural or singular. For example:

   If *I were* you ...(I can't be you.)
   I wish *I were* rich. (I'm not.)
   He acts as if *he were* the boss. (He's not.)

2. Clauses starting with *that* expressing demands, resolutions, or requests (after verbs such as *ask*, *command, demand, insist, move, order, recommend, suggest,* or *urge*)

   I *demand* that *she work* harder.
   Sullivan *insisted* that *Jones report* on Tuesday.

   Use the base form of the verb whether the subject is singular or plural.

3. Clauses starting with *that* after adjectives expressing urgency, as in *it is necessary*, *it is imperative*, *it is urgent*, *it is important*, and *it is essential*

   It is necessary that *she wear* a net covering her hair.
   It is essential that Robert *understand* the concept.

   Again, use the base form of the verb.

Other Problems with Verbs

Do not use more than one **modal auxiliary** (*can*, *may*, *might*, *must*, *should*, *ought*) with the main verb.

Incorrect: Ethan *shouldn't ought* to drop that course.

Correct: Ethan *ought not* to drop that course.
or
Ethan *shouldn't* drop that course.

Do not use *should of, would of,* or *could of* to mean *should have, would have,* or *could have.*

Incorrect: Alana *would of* helped you if she *could of.*
Correct: Alana *would have* helped you if she *could have.*

Chapter Review Exercises

PRACTICE

Solving Problems with Verbs

Revise each of the following sentences to avoid problems with verbs. Check your answers against those in the Answer Key on p. 434.

1. He hadn't ought to drive so fast.

   ___

2. It is essential that Lynn takes her dog to the vet.

   ___

3. I wish I was a chef.

   ___

4. She sung for a huge crowd Saturday night.

   ___

5. I was shook up by the accident.

   ___

6. The hill was climbed by the skiers.

   ___

7. My father ask me last night to help him build a deck.

   ___

EXERCISE

Solving Problems with Verbs

Some of the verbs in the following paragraph are incorrect. Find the errors and correct them.

I knowed I was in big trouble in chemistry when I took a look at the midterm exam. My semester should of been a lot better. The first day I had my new textbook, I put it on the back shelf of a taxi and forgot it when I got out. Then I catched a cold and miss the next two classes. When I finally start off for class, I missed the bus and walked into the classroom half an hour late. The teacher scowls at me and ask to speak to me after class. I use to always sit in the front row so I could see the board and hear the lectures, but now that I am late I have to take a seat in the last row. I wish I was able to start this class over again the right way. No one had ought to have such an unlucky start in any class.

Working Together: *Verbs, Not Verbiage*

Student Profile: On a separate piece of paper, answer the following five questions about yourself. Write on every other line to make your writing more readable. Write freely for twenty minutes. Then exchange papers with another student. Using a pencil, circle each verb in your classmate's writing. Are any of the verbs incorrect in their form or in their tense? Be prepared to share examples with the class.

1. Tell about the first car you remember owning or driving.
2. Who was the first person you were ever attracted to? What is one thing about this person that you remember?
3. Who was the person in school who taught you the most?
4. What is one television program you enjoy and why?
5. When you go away for the weekend, where is one place you like to go?

CHAPTER FOUR

4

Subject-Verb Agreement

QUICK QUIZ Test yourself on your knowledge of subject-verb agreement. On the line before each sentence below, write the correct form of the verb. Answers to the questions are beside the quiz.

_______________ 1. The history of humankind's attempts to fly (goes, go) back hundreds of years.

_______________ 2. An ancient myth that describes men trying to fly with wings made of feathers and wax (has, have) been passed on.

_______________ 3. The famous inventor Leonardo da Vinci made designs for a helicopter that (was, were) very detailed.

_______________ 4. Every aviator who set a new flying record in the early years of flight (was, were) treated as a hero.

_______________ 5. Not only helicopters but also the jet engine (was, were) among the advances that occurred during the Second World War.

Answers:
1. goes
2. has
3. were
4. was
5. was

For your sentences to be logical, all parts of each sentence must agree. Agreement is the correspondence between words in number, gender, or person. Subjects and verbs agree in number (singular or plural) and person (first, second, or third).

Since most students frequently have problems with agreement in their writing, you should work through this chapter carefully so that you will be able to look for these trouble spots in your own writing.

Subject-Verb Agreement within the Sentence

DEFINITION ➤ A verb must agree with its subject in **number**.

If the subject is singular, the verb must also be singular. Notice how singular and plural subjects are handled in the following chart:

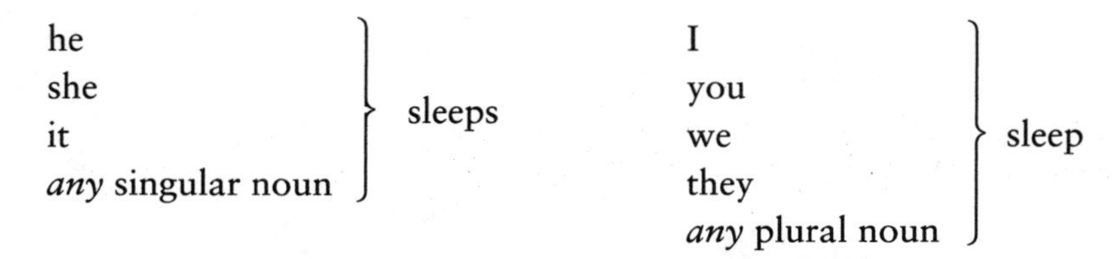

Example: The baby *sleeps*.

Example: The babies *sleep*.

Remember that a verb that goes with a singular noun or pronoun (except *I* or *you*) needs a final *s*.

PRACTICE

Making the Subject and Verb Agree

Underline the correct verb in the following sentences. Check your answers against those in the Answer Key on p. 434.

1. My uncle (cycle, cycles) 30 km a day.
2. He (amaze, amazes) the family.
3. His routes (varies, vary) with his mood.
4. Friends (cheers, cheer) him on.
5. I (hopes, hope) I'm that energetic at his age.

Special Problems in Making Verbs Agree with Their Subjects

RULE 1: **The subject is not always the noun closest to the verb. Remember, you will not find the subject of the sentence within a prepositional phrase.**

In the example that follows, the subject is underlined, the prepositional phrase is crossed out, and the verb is circled.

The hairline cracks ~~in the engine~~ (present) a serious threat to passengers' safety.

RULE 2: **Many indefinite pronouns take a singular verb.**

Indefinite Pronouns

Indefinite Pronouns Taking a Singular Verb:

-one	everyone	someone	anyone	no one
-body	everybody	somebody	anybody	nobody
-thing	everything	something	anything	nothing
	each	another	either	neither

Everyone *is* expecting a miracle.

Indefinite Pronouns Taking a Plural Verb:

	both	few	many	several

The talks between the two countries failed.
Both *were* to blame.

(continued)

(continued)

Indefinite Pronouns Taking a Singular or Plural Verb Depending on the Meaning in the Sentence:

any	all	more
none	some	most

The books are gone. **All were very popular.**
The sugar is gone. **All of it was spilled.**

The English language is constantly evolving. The word *none*, for example, is one of those words that is still in transition. The letters *one* inside the word *none* suggest that this indefinite pronoun should be singular. In formal usage, this is so. An example, therefore, of the correct formal usage of the word *none* would be the following:

None of my pens *is* working.

(*None,* being singular [in formal usage], would take a singular verb, in accordance with the subject-verb agreement rule.)

In general (less formal) usage, *none* (like the other indefinite pronouns listed with it above), is either singular or plural depending on the noun that the indefinite pronoun refers to (the noun that usually follows the preposition *of* which immediately follows the word *none*).

Example: None of the sugar is wasted.
None of the people are here yet.

This may be a case where you, the individual, have to make a decision. Do you go with formal or general usage? Your decision might depend on your audience and purpose (see Chapter 14: "The Four Stages of Writing").

RULE 3: **When a pair of conjunctions is used, the verb agrees with the subject closer to the verb.**

Neither the textbook nor my lecture notes (explain) the meaning of the term "tidal wave."

Textbook and *notes* together make up the compound subject. Since *notes* is closer to the verb, the verb agrees with *notes.*

Pairs of Conjunctions

neither ... nor	either ... or	not only ... but also

RULE 4: **In some sentences, the subject can come after the verb. In these cases, be sure that the verb agrees with the subject.**

Here (is) the surprise I promised you.

Who (were) the people with you last night?

RULE 5: **A group noun in Canadian English usually takes a singular verb if the group acts as a unit. (The test is to substitute the word *it* in place of the group noun.)**

The town council (is planning) a Canada Day celebration.

In this sentence, the council is acting as a unit. *It* is planning a celebration. Therefore, the verb is singular.

A group noun takes a plural verb if the members of the group act as individuals. (The test is to substitute the word *they* for the group noun and see if it sounds right.)

The town council (are preparing) their speeches for this event.

In this sentence, the council members are individually preparing speeches. *They* substitutes for the group noun in this sentence. Since the individuals are acting separately, the verb is plural.

Common Group Nouns				
audience	class	committee	council	crowd
family	group	jury	number	team

RULE 6: **The verbs *do* and *be* are often troublesome. Remember that standard English uses *s* for the third person singular.**

Verbs *do* and *be*

The Verb *to do*				The Verb *to be* (Past Tense)			
I do		we	do	I was		we	were
you do		you (plural)	do	you were		you	were
he	does	they	do	he	was	they	were
she	does			she	was		
it	does			it	was		

Example: She *does* the Christmas pageant every year.
They *do* everything they can to help others.
You *were* at the scene of the crime.
He *was* elected to the position.

Chapter Review Exercises

PRACTICE 1

Making the Subject and Verb Agree

Underline the verb that agrees with the subject. Check your answers against those in the Answer Key on p. 434.

1. He (doesn't, don't) study in the library anymore.
2. We (was, were) hoping to find him there.
3. The library (doesn't, don't) close until eleven o'clock.
4. (Was, Were) you late tonight?
5. Ann (doesn't, don't) care if you stay until closing time.

PRACTICE 2

Making the Subject and Verb Agree

In the blanks next to each sentence, write the subject of the sentence and the correct form of the verb. An example is done for you. Check your answers against those in the Answer Key on p. 434.

	Subject	Verb
The eleven proposals for the development of a new building at Laurier Circle (has, have) been submitted to the city.	proposals	have
1. The price of airline tickets to England (has, have) remained fairly reasonable.		
2. His decision (requires, require) a lot of thought.		
3. She (doesn't, don't) know the answer to any of the test questions.		
4. Either the guide or the security guard (see, sees) every visitor.		
5. The committee (agree, agrees) to the fundraising projects for this year.		
6. Potato chips and cola (is, are) most of her diet.		
7. One of the people in the audience (is, are) my brother.		

EXERCISE 1

Making the Subject and Verb Agree

In the blanks next to each sentence, write the subject of the sentence and the correct form of the verb.

	Subject	Verb
1. Included in the price of the trip (was, were) five nights in a lovely hotel and all meals.	________	________
2. None of the members (wants, want) to go.	________	________
3. Jerry and Aldo (works, work) well together.	________	________
4. The number of essay questions on the apprenticeship exam (seems, seem) to be increasing.	________	________
5. When (does, do) your parents return from their holiday?	________	________
6. In the whole town there (is, are) only two good restaurants.	________	________
7. Neither a piano nor Jim's guitar (was, were) available.	________	________

EXERCISE 2

Making the Subject and Verb Agree

Take your answers from the blanks in Exercise 1, and use them as the main subjects and verbs in your own sentences. For example, if the subject in the first column is *cars,* and the verb in the second is *perform,* your own sentence might look something like this:

Cars from Japan generally perform better than cars from the U.S.

The sentence *I prefer cars from Japan because they perform better than cars from the U.S.* does not work because in this sentence, the subject is not *cars* but *I.*

Working Together: *Employment Cover Letters*

Think of a job for which you might apply upon graduation from your school. Write a cover letter of approximately three to four paragraphs that might accompany your resume. When you're finished, deliberately change some of your verbs so they do not agree with the subjects they go with. Then exchange your letter with someone else in your class or group. Work on fixing the verbs in the letter you have. Then discuss some of the results with the class at the end.

CHAPTER FIVE

5

Coordination and Subordination

QUICK QUIZ 1

Test yourself on your knowledge of combining sentences using **coordination**. The following pair of sentences could be combined into a single sentence using coordination. Among the four choices given, place an *X* in front of the example that is correct. The answer to the question is beside the quiz.

Chocolate became a popular drink throughout Europe. It was thought to be good for your health.

_______________ 1. Chocolate became a popular drink throughout Europe, it was thought to be good for your health.

_______________ 2. Chocolate became a popular drink throughout Europe because it was thought to be good for your health.

_______________ 3. Chocolate became a popular drink throughout Europe, for it was thought to be good for your health.

_______________ 4. Chocolate became a popular drink throughout Europe and good for your health.

Answer:
Sentence 3 is correct. Sentence 1 is a run-on and sentence 4 is not parallel. Sentence 2 is grammatically correct, but it shows subordination rather than coordination.

QUICK QUIZ 2

Test yourself on your knowledge of combining sentences using **subordination**. Combine each of the following pairs of sentences using either a subordinating conjunction or a relative pronoun. More than one correct answer is possible. Sample answers are beside the quiz.

1. I live alone with two cats.
   They sleep on the braided rug in my bedroom.

   ____

2. The police stood by the door.
   They blocked our entrance.

   ____

3. She wore high heels.
   They made marks in the wooden floor.

   ____

Answers:
1. I live alone with two cats, who sleep on the braided rug in my bedroom.
2. The police stood by the door so that they blocked our entrance.
3. She wore high heels that made marks in the wooden floor.

4. My aunt is my favourite relative.
   Her name is Bharati.

   ____

5. He wore expensive designer clothes.
   He claimed to be struggling financially.

   ____

Answers:
4. My aunt, whose name is Bharati, is my favourite relative.
5. He wore expensive designer clothes although he claimed to be struggling financially.

Reading the above sentences, you will see that writing only simple sentences would result in a choppy style. Also, you would have trouble trying to express more complicated ideas.

You will therefore want to learn how to combine sentences. You can do this by using particular marks of punctuation and special connecting words called **conjunctions.** The two major ways of joining sentences together are called **coordination** and **subordination.**

What Is Coordination?

DEFINITION ➤ The pairing of similar elements—words, phrases, or clauses—to give equal weight to each pair is called **coordination**. Coordination can link two independent clauses to form a compound sentence.

I was sick, but I went to work anyway.

Combining Sentences Using Coordination

You can use coordination whenever you have two sentences that are related and that contain ideas of equal importance. There are three ways to combine such sentences. All three ways result in a new kind of sentence called a **compound sentence**. Before you study these three methods, however, it is important to understand the term *independent clause*. The **independent clause** is a group of words that could be a simple sentence. In a compound sentence we could say we are combining simple sentences, or we could say we are combining *independent clauses*. Don't let the term confuse you. *Independent* means that the words could stand alone as a sentence, and *clause* means that there are a subject and a verb. *IC* will mean *independent clause* in the work that follows.

Use a Comma Plus a Coordinating Conjunction

The first way to combine independent clauses is to use a comma plus a coordinating conjunction. A conjunction is a connecting or joining word.

IC	, and	IC
He spoke forcefully	, and	I felt compelled to listen.

Connectors: Coordinating Conjunctions

For easier remembering, spell *fanboys:*	Logical use:
for	to introduce a reason
and	to add an idea
nor (negative of "or")	to add an idea when the first clause is in the negative
but	to contrast two opposing ideas
or	to show a choice
yet	to contrast two opposing ideas (like *but*)
so	to introduce a result

Used in Pairs
either ... or
neither ... nor
not only ... but also

If any of the above "fanboys" conjunctions is used to separate two independent clauses, always place a comma before it.

PRACTICE

Recognizing the Comma and Coordinating Conjunction

In each of the following compound sentences, draw a single line under the subject and draw two lines under the verb for each independent clause. Then circle both the coordinating conjunction and the comma. An example is done for you. Check your answers against those in the Answer Key on p. 434.

The speaker rose to his feet (, and) the room became quiet.

1. The audience was packed into the room, for this was a man with an international reputation.
2. He could have told about all his successes, but instead he spoke about his disappointments.
3. His words were electric, so the crowd was attentive.
4. I should have brought a tape recorder, or at least I should have taken notes.

Did you find a subject and verb for both independent clauses in each sentence?

Now that you understand the structure of a compound sentence, you need to think about the meanings of the different coordinating conjunctions and how they can be used to show the relationship between two ideas, with each idea given equal importance.

EXERCISE

Combining Sentences Using Coordinating Conjunctions

Each of the following examples contains two simple sentences. In each case, join the sentences to form a new compound sentence. Use a comma and one of the seven coordinating conjunctions. There can be more than one correct answer for each example. Be sure the conjunction you choose makes sense in the sentence. An example is done for you.

Two simple sentences: Many farmers are desperate. They are going bankrupt.

Compound sentence: Many farmers are desperate, for they are going bankrupt.

1. The farmers in Canada want to work., so
   Some are experiencing severe financial difficulty.

2. Some people are losing their farms., and
   The banks are refusing to make further loans.

3. Many government programs have not been effective., nor can the public do anything.
   The public cannot do anything.
   (Use *nor*. You will have to change the word order in the second sentence.)

4. The farmers feel neglected., so
   They are protesting against the government.

5. There is an increased need for farm products., yet
   The government pays farmers not to grow food.

6. Everyone needs what the farmers produce., so
   We should be concerned about their problems.

7. In the future, fewer people will become farmers. The problem is likely to become increasingly serious.

____

____

Use a Semicolon, an Adverbial Conjunction, and a Comma

A second way to combine independent clauses is to form the compound sentence by using a semicolon, an adverbial conjunction, and a comma.

IC	; therefore,	IC
I had worked hard	; therefore,	I expected results.

Another set of conjunctions, which have meanings similar to the common coordinating conjunctions, are called **adverbial conjunctions** (or conjunctive adverbs). These connecting words will give the compound sentence you write more emphasis. They may also sound slightly more formal to you than the shorter conjunctions *and* and *but*. If an adverbial conjunction separates two independent clauses, place a semicolon before it. If it does not, use a comma before it instead.

Connectors: Frequently Used Adverbial Conjunctions

Addition (and)	Alternative (or)	Result (so)
in addition	instead	accordingly
also	otherwise	consequently
besides		hence
furthermore		therefore
likewise		thus
moreover		
Contrast (but)	**Emphasis**	**To Show Time**
however	indeed	meanwhile
nevertheless	in fact	
nonetheless		

PRACTICE 1

Recognizing the Semicolon, Adverbial Conjunction, and Comma

In each of the following compound sentences, draw a single line under the subject and draw two lines under the verb for both independent clauses. Then circle the semicolon, adverbial conjunction, and comma. An example is done for you. Check your answers against those in the Answer Key on p. 434.

The jet was the fastest way to get there ; moreover, it was the most comfortable.

1. The restaurant is always too crowded on Saturdays; nevertheless, it serves the best food in town.
2. The land was not for sale; however, the house could be rented.
3. The lawsuit cost the company several million dollars; consequently, the company went out of business a short time later.
4. The doctor told him to lose weight; furthermore, she insisted he also stop smoking.

PRACTICE 2

Combining Sentences Using Adverbial Conjunctions

Combine each pair of sentences below to make a compound sentence. Use a semicolon, an adverbial conjunction, and a comma. Be sure the conjunction you choose makes sense in the sentence. There can be more than one correct answer. An example is done for you. Check your answers against those in the Answer Key on p. 435.

Two simple sentences: Our family would like to purchase a computer. We must decide on which computer best serves our needs.

Compound sentence: Our family would like to purchase a computer; however, we must decide on which computer best serves our needs.

1. People once preferred to write with a pen or pencil.
   The computer has now become a favourite writing tool. (Show contrast.)

2. Computers provide a powerful way to create and store pieces of writing.
   They make the editing process fast and efficient. (Add an idea.)

3. Computers have revolutionized today's offices.
   No modern business is without them. (Show result.)

4. Computers have become relatively inexpensive.
   Most people own a computer. (Show result.)

5. Many children know more about computers than many adults.
   Many children are teaching adults how to operate computers. (Add an idea.)

nevertheless,

6. Professional writers have become enthusiastic about the use of computers; There are still some writers who will use only a ballpoint pen. (Show contrast.)

7. We have many technological aids for writing; however,
Let us not forget that the source of all our ideas is the human brain. (Show contrast.)

EXERCISE

Combining Sentences Using Adverbial Conjunctions

For each example, add the suggested adverbial conjunction and another independent clause that will make sense. There can be more than one correct answer for each example. Remember to punctuate correctly.

1. (however) I'll be at the library for a few hours; however, I might be late getting home tonight.
2. (therefore) James asked to borrow my notes; therefore, I told James I would.
3. (otherwise) I'm thinking about taking a part-time job; otherwise, I won't be able to pay bills.
4. (instead) Marcus is not going home for reading week; instead, he is going camping with friends.
5. (in fact) They haven't won a game this year; in fact, I don't think they will win a game.
6. (furthermore) Suzie has given up coffee and cigarettes; furthermore, she has decided to look after her health better.
7. (consequently) My computer keeps crashing; consequently, I will have to take it in for repairs.

Use a Semicolon

The third way to combine two independent clauses is to use a semicolon.

IC	;	IC
He arrived at ten	;	he left at midnight.

This third method of combining sentences is used less often. No connecting word is used. The semicolon takes the place of the conjunction.

Two independent clauses: I used to watch the Toronto Blue Jays play baseball at Exhibition Stadium. Tonight, I'm going to see them play at SkyDome.

Compound sentence: I used to watch the Toronto Blue Jays play baseball at Exhibition Stadium; tonight, I'm going to see them play at SkyDome.

The semicolon was used in this example to show that the content of the two clauses is closely related and, therefore, belongs together in one sentence.

When sentences are combined by using a semicolon, the grammatical structure of each sentence is often similar:

Gasoline prices increased; vacations became less frequent.

EXERCISE

Combining Sentences Using the Semicolon

For each of the independent clauses below, add your own independent clause that is a related idea with a similar grammatical structure. Join the two clauses with a semicolon. There can be more than one correct answer for each example. An example is done for you.

Independent clause: He wrote the speech.
Compound sentence: He wrote the speech; she gave it.

1. The apartment was light and airy.

____

____

2. Many students decorate their rooms wonderfully.

____

____

3. I plan to learn two foreign languages.

____

____

4. I tried to explain.

____

____

5. This rain will never stop.

___

___

What Is Subordination?

When you use coordination to combine sentences, the ideas in both of the resulting clauses are given equal weight. However, ideas are not always equally important. Subordination allows you to show which idea is the main idea.

DEFINITION ➤ **Subordination** is the method used to combine sentences whose ideas are not equally important.

I stayed home today because I was sick.

Combining Sentences Using Subordination

When you combine sentences using subordination, you make the most important idea an independent clause and the less important idea a dependent (subordinate) clause. The sentence that results is called a **complex sentence.** We identify the two or more ideas that are contained within this complex sentence by calling them **clauses**. The relationship between the main and secondary parts of a complex sentence is shown by the method of subordination you use. The various methods of subordination will be discussed below.

In a complex sentence, the main idea is called the **independent clause** because it could stand alone as a simple sentence. The less important idea is called the **dependent clause** because even though it has a subject and a verb, it is dependent on the rest of the sentence for its meaning. Consider the following clauses:

Independent clause: That girl leaves.
Dependent clause: If that girl leaves...

Notice that both clauses in the example above have a subject and a verb. (The subject is *girl*, and the verb is *leaves*.) The difference is that the dependent clause has an additional word. *If* is a special kind of connecting word that makes the clause "dependent" on an additional idea. A dependent clause does not make sense by itself; the thought is not complete. Below is the same dependent clause with an independent clause added to it.

If that girl leaves, I can finish my homework.

Now the thought is complete.

In your work with sentences, you will want to be comfortable writing sentences with dependent clauses. For this you will need to practise using two kinds of "connecting" words: subordinating conjunctions and relative pronouns. First, practise using subordinating conjunctions.

Use a Subordinating Conjunction to Create a Complex Sentence

Following is a list of subordinating conjunctions. These connecting words signal the beginning of a dependent clause. Be sure to learn them. It is a good idea to memorize them.

Connectors: Common Subordinating Conjunctions		
after	if, even if	unless
although	in order that	until
as, as if	provided that	when, whenever
as long as, as though	rather than	where, wherever
because	since	whether
before	so that	while
even though	though	

Function of Subordinating Conjunctions

To introduce a *condition*: if, even if, as long as, provided that, unless

I will go *as long as* you go with me.
I won't go *unless* you go with me.

To introduce a *contrast*: although, even though, though

I will go *even though* you won't go with me.

To introduce a *cause*: *because, since*

I will go *because* the meeting is very important.

To show *time*: after, before, when, whenever, while, until

I will go *whenever* you say.
I won't go *until* you say it is time.

To show *place*: where, wherever

I will go *wherever* you send me.

To show *purpose*: in order that, so that

I will go *so that* I can hear the candidate for myself.

You can choose between two ways of writing the complex sentence. You can begin with either the dependent clause or the independent clause.

First way:	DC	,	IC
Example:	If Barbara leaves	,	we can finish our homework.

Second way:	IC	DC
Example:	We can finish our homework	if Barbara leaves.

TIP **Use a comma when you begin a sentence with a dependent clause.**

From the above examples you can see that when a sentence begins with an independent clause, a comma may not always be needed. For example, the comma is omitted if the dependent clause is essential to the main idea of the speaker. This point of grammar is further discussed in Chapter 11, page 115, on punctuation.

PRACTICE 1

Recognizing Dependent and Independent Clauses

In the blank to the side of each group of words, write the letters *IC* if the group is an independent clause (a complete thought) or *DC* if the group is a dependent clause (not a complete thought even though it contains a subject and a verb). Check your answers against those in the Answer Key on p. 435.

DC 1. while the photographer was getting ready

DC 2. before the guests arrived

IC 3. I've been a bridesmaid for two of my friends

DC 4. even though we're all in our teens

IC 5. this one was more fun than most

DC 6. whenever I see you

DC 7. since I did not take the subway

PRACTICE 2

Combining Sentences Using Subordination

Combine each pair of sentences using subordination. Look back at the list of subordinating conjunctions if you need to. There may be more than one correct answer for each of these exercises. Check your answers against those in the Answer Key on p. 435.

1. He was eating breakfast, when
   The results of the election came over the radio.

   ____

   ____

2. Simon gave up his plan to launch a dot-com company.
   He felt it was too risky.

3. I will see my teacher tonight.
   She is speaking at the university this evening.

4. The designer hoped for a promotion.
   Not one person in the department was promoted last year.

5. The designer hoped for a promotion.
   She made sure all her work was done accurately and on time.

EXERCISE 1

Combining Sentences Using Subordination

Below are three pairs of sentences. Combine each pair by using a subordinating conjunction. Write the sentence two different ways. First, begin the sentence with the dependent clause and use a comma. Second, begin the sentence with the independent clause and use a comma only if necessary.

1. (Use *since*.) Wildlife habitats are being destroyed.
   Many species are in danger.
   a.
   b.

2. (Use *after*.) He won the wrestling match.
   He went out to celebrate.
   a.
   b.

3. (Use *when*.) Halyna returned from Europe this spring.
   The family was excited.

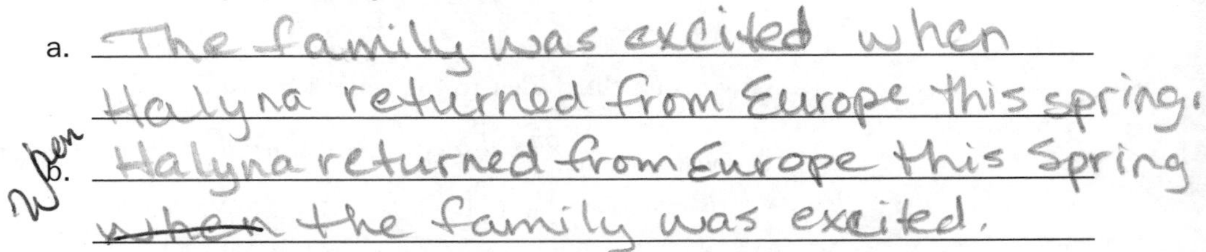

EXERCISE 2

Combining Sentences Using Subordination

Rewrite the following paragraph using subordination to combine some of the sentences wherever you feel it would be effective. Be prepared to discuss the reasons for your choices. You might also want to discuss places where coordination might be a good choice. More than one correct answer is possible.

> Many Canadian communities collect refuse from its source. Waste is delivered to a waste disposal site. Very little waste is recycled. Very little waste is burned. Many smaller towns and villages cannot afford a waste collection service or a proper waste disposal site. Smaller communities are prevalent in Canada. Improperly operated dumps outnumber the better-operated facilities used by larger communities. Over the next few years, many of our landfills will close. They are getting full. Some places in Ontario already truck their trash to the United States. The garbage continues to pile up. The newspapers print stories about it every week. Trash is not a very glamorous subject. People in every town talk about the problem.

Use a Relative Pronoun to Create a Complex Sentence

Often sentences can be combined with a relative pronoun.

Common Relative Pronouns		
who whose whom	refers to people	Note: "that" can also refer to people when a class or type is meant. Example: "The type of teacher I prefer is one that offers help outside of class."
which that	refers to things	

Two simple sentences: The researcher had a breakthrough.
He was studying diabetes.

These sentences are short and choppy. To avoid this choppiness, a writer could join these two related ideas with a relative pronoun.

Combining sentences with a relative pronoun: The researcher who was studying diabetes had a breakthrough.

Now join a third idea to the sentence (use *which*).

Third idea: He reported the breakthrough to the press.

Remember to put the relative pronoun directly after the word it relates to.

Incorrect: The researcher, which he reported to the press, had a breakthrough who was studying diabetes.

The relative pronoun *who* and its clause *who was studying diabetes* refers to *the researcher*, not to *a breakthrough*. The relative pronoun *which* and its clause *which he reported to the press* does refer to *breakthrough*. This clause will follow the noun *breakthrough*.

Correct: The researcher who was studying diabetes had a breakthrough, which he reported to the press.

PRACTICE

Combining Sentences Using a Relative Pronoun

Combine each of the three pairs of sentences below into one complex sentence by using a relative pronoun. Do not use commas. More than one correct answer is possible for each example. An example is done for you. Check your answers against those in the Answer Key on p. 435.

First sentence: That woman created the flower arrangement.
Second sentence: She visited us last weekend.
Combined sentence: That woman who visited us last weekend created the flower arrangement.

1. The chemistry lab is two hours long.
   I attend that chemistry lab.

   Combined: ______________________________

   ____

2. The student assistant is very knowledgeable.
   The student assistant is standing by the door.

   Combined: The student assistant that is standing by the door is very knowledgeable.

3. The equipment ~~was~~ purchased last year.
   ~~The equipment~~ will make possible some important new research.

   Combined: ______________________________

   ____

How Do You Punctuate a Clause with a Relative Pronoun?

Punctuating relative clauses can be tricky because there are two types of relative clauses.

1. One type of relative clause is basic to the meaning of the sentence:

   Never eat fruit *that hasn't been washed* first.

   The basic meaning of the sentence is not "never eat fruit." The relative clause is necessary to restrict the meaning. This clause is called a **restrictive clause** and does not use commas to set it off. *Note:* Clauses beginning with the pronoun *that* are usually in this category. Remember, the relative pronoun *that* always refers to things.

2. The other type of relative clause is **not** basic to the meaning of the sentence:

   Kim's famous salad, *which included spinach and almonds,* was delicious.

   In this sentence, the relative clause is not basic to the main idea. In fact, if the clause were omitted, the main idea would not be changed. This clause is called a **nonrestrictive clause.** Commas are required to indicate that the information is nonessential. *Note:* Clauses beginning with the pronoun *which* are usually in this category. Remember, the relative pronoun *which* always refers to things.

   Note: While *which* refers to things in a nonrestrictive clause and *that* refers to things in a restrictive clause, the relative pronouns that refer to people (*who, whom* and *whose*) are used either for nonrestrictive or restrictive clauses. Remember, restrictive clauses do not take commas to separate them from the rest of the sentence while nonrestrictive clauses do. (See Chapter 11: "Punctuation" for more on commas.)

PRACTICE

Recognizing Restrictive and Nonrestrictive Clauses

Choose whether or not to insert commas in the sentences below. Two examples have been done for you. Check your answers against those in the Answer Key on p. 435.

The man *who is wearing the Hawaiian shirt* is the bridegroom.

(The relative clause is essential. There are no commas.)

Al, *who was wearing a flannel shirt,* arrived late to the wedding.

(The relative clause is nonessential. Commas, therefore, are necessary.)

1. Canada's first census which was taken in 1667 showed 3215 non-Native inhabitants in 668 families.
2. Most of these families were French Canadians who lived near the St. Lawrence River.
3. By the time of Confederation, the population of the country had risen to 3 463 000 which was an increase of 1077 percent over 200 years.
4. If the population which is about 30 000 000 persons in Canada now increases by a similar percentage, we'll have a population of 280 200 000 by the year 2167.
5. Where do you think will we put everyone who will live in Canada then?

EXERCISE 1

Combining Sentences Using Relative Pronouns

Add a clause that begins with a relative pronoun to each of the sentences below. Use each of these possibilities at least once: who, whose, whom, which, that. Be sure to punctuate correctly. There may be more than one correct answer for each sentence. An example is done for you.

Simple sentence: The leader was barely 1.5 m tall.

Complex sentence: The leader, who was always self-conscious about her height, was barely 1.5 m tall.

1. The figure skaters ______________________________ began their program.
2. The music ______________________________ had a Latin beat.
3. Their first figure ______________________________ was a triple toe loop.
4. The crowd ______________________________ cheered wildly.
5. Even the judges ______________________________ seemed impressed.
6. Her triple axel ______________________________ was a little ragged.
7. Their coach ______________________________ was thrilled by the final score.

EXERCISE 2

Combining Sentences Using Relative Pronouns

Combine the following pairs of sentences using a relative pronoun. There may be more than one correct answer for each example.

1. Stress can do a great deal of harm.
   We experience stress every day.

   ____

   ____

2. People often use food to help them cope.
   Some people work long hours at demanding jobs.

   ____

   ____

3. The practice of eating to cope with stress is often automatic.
   The practice of eating to cope often goes back to childhood.

   ____

   ____

4. Foods can actually increase tension.
   People turn to foods in times of stress.

   ____

   ____

5. One of the biggest mistakes people make is to use alcohol as an aid to becoming calm.
   Alcohol is really a depressant.

   ____

   ____

6. People should eat three light meals a day and two small snacks.
   People want to feel a sense of calm.

   ____

   ____

7. Eat a good meal at regular intervals to help reduce stress.
   Binge eating puts on pounds, drains you of energy, and increases your stress level.

   ____

   ____

Chapter Review Exercises

PRACTICE

Combining Sentences Using Coordination and Subordination

Look over the following simple sentences, and rewrite the paragraph, combining sentences where you think it would improve the meaning and style. The Answer Key will give you one possible answer, but there are many ways of revising. Be creative, and don't be afraid to alter the wording to accommodate the changes you want to make. Check your answers against those in the Answer Key on p. 435.

The wind is strong. The waves are choppy. They are growing larger. I paddle my kayak harder. My arms are getting tired. The energy is draining from them. They grow limp and heavy. The other side of the harbour seems distant. The glow of the setting sun is behind me. It spreads orange and purple fingers across the sky. A wall of rocks lies offshore. It picks up the last light of the setting sun. It is a silver beacon. I focus on that wall and paddle harder. The sea smashes against my bow. It seems to push me away from shore. Flecks of spray hit my face. I taste the salt on my lips. With that taste of the sea, the beauty of the sea and shore strikes me. I am distracted from my labour and absorbed by the world around me. My kayak finally glides past the rocks to the sheltered beach beyond. I am exhilarated and exhausted.

EXERCISE 1 Combining Sentences Using Coordinating and Adverbial Conjunctions

Combine each pair of sentences below to make a compound sentence. Use a coordinating, subordinating, or adverbial conjunction, but be sure that the conjunction clearly shows the relationship between the ideas. There can be more than one correct answer for each example.

1. For many people, mathematics is a necessary evil., but
   To a few, mathematics provides a lifetime of challenge and fun.

   ____

   ____

2. Most Canadians have studied math only to Grade 12., therefore
   This limits their ability to understand new scientific developments.

   ____

   ____

3. Their knowledge extends to little more than basic arithmetic., yet
   People in the seventeenth century knew as much about math as most Canadians today.

   ____

   ____

4. Few Canadians study math at the university level., however
   Many promising mathematics graduates are offered employment in the United States.

   ____

   ____

5. Many schools form math teams to compete in area contests.
   Other schools encourage interest in math with math clubs.

6. Some schools suffer from a lack of science and math teachers.
   Mathematicians can find well-paid employment in industry.

7. It is important to increase the number of mathematics graduates.
   Canadian students may continue to trail behind those of many other countries in math and science ability.

EXERCISE 2

Combining Sentences with a Subordinating Conjunction or a Relative Pronoun

Combine each of the following pairs of sentences using either a subordinating conjunction or a relative pronoun. Be sure that the word you use makes sense in the sentence. There may be more than one correct answer for each example.

1. People have been fascinated for centuries by the problem of stuttering.
   Modern science is only beginning to understand some of the underlying causes of the problem.

2. For some people, stuttering disappears by itself.
   For others, stuttering continues into adulthood.

3. Stutterers usually keep their condition.
   They seek professional help.

4. It is true that there is some psychological basis for stuttering, even though.
   It is true that psychologists have not been able to solve the problem.

5. All kinds of scientists have looked at the problem from all different angles, yet
   There is no single answer to stuttering.

6. Stuttering runs in families, therefore
   Children of such families have greater chances of becoming stutterers.

7. You often hear someone say he or she knows the causes of stuttering, although.
   You know that person cannot be speaking scientifically.

Working Together: *Practising Coordination and Subordination*

A controversial issue today concerns the wide gap between the wages earned by people in some professions and the wages earned by people in other professions. For instance, some sports figures and entertainers earn millions every year. How are wages determined in our society? How do you think wages should be determined? Should there be a minimum wage in Canada? Should everybody earn the same salary? Divide into groups and discuss the subject for fifteen minutes.

Following the general discussion, practise combining sentences using coordination by writing ten sentences on the subject of wage differences. If you like, you may try to summarize the ideas of your group. The goal is to use each of the following coordinating conjunctions to combine two independent clauses:

and, but, or, nor, for, yet, so
either/or, neither/nor, not only/but also

Now, in each sentence you've written, combine two independent clauses with subordinating conjunctions instead. Consult the list of subordinating conjunctions on page 58.

After working on these sentences for fifteen minutes, exchange papers and answer the following questions about the sentences on the paper you have:

1. In each case, has the writer combined two independent clauses?
2. In each sentence, does the coordinating or subordinating conjunction carry the correct meaning for the sentence?
3. Is the punctuation correct?

CHAPTER SIX

6

Correcting Fragments

QUICK QUIZ Test yourself on your knowledge of fragments. Some of the examples below are complete sentences; some are fragments (only parts of sentences). Write *C* if the example is a complete sentence. Write *F* if the example is a fragment. The answers to the questions are beside the quiz.

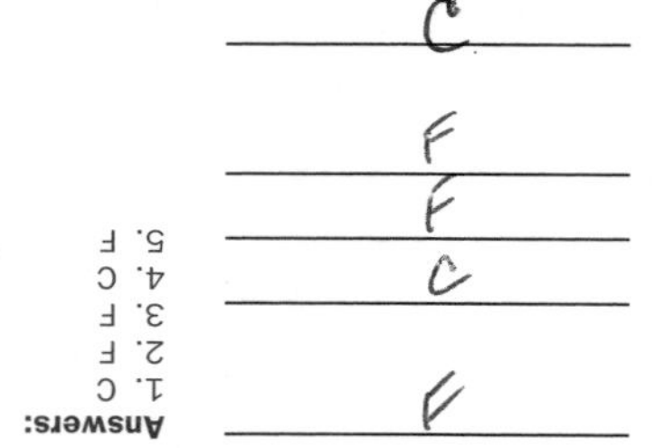

1. Whale watching is a popular tourist activity in British Columbia.
2. Although its effects are being studied.
3. Whales coping with heavy boat traffic.
4. The noise from engines can disturb the whales' communication.
5. Which may be changing their habitat.

Recognizing Sentence Fragments

Once you have learned that a sentence must have a subject and a verb, and that a sentence must also express a complete thought, you are on your way to correcting one of the most frequent errors in student writing—the fragment. A fragment is an incomplete sentence. Although many of our daily conversations are informal and sometimes contain fragments, standard writing is always more formal and requires complete sentences.

The fragment is a major problem for many student writers. In the writer's mind, a thought may be clear; however, on paper the idea may turn out to be incomplete, missing a subject or a verb. In this section, you will improve your ability to spot incomplete sentences or fragments, and you will learn how to correct them. This practice will prepare you to avoid such fragments in your own writing.

Practise Putting a Conversation into Complete Sentences

Remember the definition of a sentence:

DEFINITION ➤ A **complete sentence** has a subject and a verb and expresses a complete thought.

PRACTICE 1

Correcting Fragments

The following conversation is one that a couple of students might have at the start of their English class. Rewrite the conversation in complete thoughts or standard sentences. Check your answers against those in the Answer Key on p. 436.

JOHN: Early again.
LESIA: Want to get a front-row seat.
JOHN: Your homework done?
LESIA: Nearly.
JOHN: Think he'll give a quiz today?
LESIA: Hope not.
JOHN: Looks like rain today.
LESIA: Better not; haven't got a bag for these new books.
JOHN: Going to the game Saturday?
LESIA: Probably.

1. ______________________________
2. ______________________________
3. ______________________________
4. ______________________________
5. ______________________________
6. ______________________________
7. ______________________________
8. ______________________________
9. ______________________________
10. ______________________________

Remember, when you write in complete sentences, this writing may be somewhat different from the way you would express the same idea in everyday conversation with a friend.

Although you will occasionally spot incomplete sentences in professional writing, you may be sure the writer is using these fragments intentionally. In such cases, the fragment may capture the way a person thinks or speaks, or it may create a special effect. A student developing his or her writing skills should be sure to use only standard sentence form so that thoughts will be communicated effectively. Most of the writing you will do in your life—business correspondence, papers in school, or reports in your job—will demand standard sentence form. Fragments will be looked upon as a sign of poor writing skills rather than creative style!

What Is a Fragment?

DEFINITION ➤ A **fragment** is a piece of a sentence.

A fragment is not a sentence for one of the following reasons:

a. The subject is missing.

delivered the plans to my office

b. The verb is missing.

the architect to my office

c. Both the subject and verb are missing.

to my office

d. The subject and verb are present but the words do not express a complete thought.

when the architect delivered the plans

PRACTICE 2

Understanding Fragments

Each of the groups of words below is a fragment. In the blank to the right of each fragment, identify what sentence part could be added to make the fragment into a sentence. An example is done for you. Check your answers against those in the Answer Key on p. 436.

a. Add a subject.
b. Add a verb.
c. Add a subject and a verb.
d. The subject and verb are already present, but you need to add words to express a complete thought.

	Fragment	Add
	the red fox	b. verb
1.	returned to the river	a. subject
2.	a bird on the oak branch	b. verb
3.	between the island and the mainland	a. subject & verb
4.	the hawk in a soaring motion	~~b verb~~ d. verb
5.	the fishing boats on the lake	b. verb
6.	dropped like a stone into the water	a. subject
7.	the fisherman put	d. both present no thought

How Do You Correct a Fragment?

You can eliminate fragments in one of two ways:

1. Add the missing part or parts to develop the fragment into a complete sentence:

   Fragment: along the coastal road
   Add: subject and verb
   Sentence: He drove along the coastal road.

2. Join the fragment to another sentence. In order to do this, you will need to make use of the comma, the colon, or the dash, or you may not need to use punctuation. For example,
   a. Using the comma

   Fragment: including a stop at the shoe store
   Other sentence: He has to make a number of purchases.
   Fragment eliminated: He has to make a number of purchases, including a stop at the shoe store.

   b. Using the colon

   Fragment: action, science fiction, and comedy
   Other sentence: I like three types of movies.
   Fragment eliminated: I like three types of movies: action, science fiction, and comedy.

   c. Using the dash

   Fragment: more often than she should
   Other sentence: She goes to the casino every day.
   Fragment eliminated: She goes to the casino every day—more often than she should.

   d. Using no punctuation

   Fragment: on top of the mountain
   Other sentence: We planned to plant the flag.
   Fragment eliminated: We planned to plant the flag on top of the mountain.

PRACTICE 3

Turning Fragments into Sentences

Change the fragments of Practice 2 into complete sentences by adding the missing part or parts that you have already identified. There can be more than one correct answer. Check your answers against those in the Answer Key on p. 436.

1. returned to the river

   The beaver returned to the river.

2. a bird on the oak branch

   A bird was perched on the oak branch.

3. between the island and the mainland

   The best fishing was between the island & the mainland.

4. the hawk in a soaring motion

   The hawk flew by us in a soaring motion.

5. the fishing boats on the lake

   There were many fishing boats on the lake.

6. dropped like a stone into the water

   The loon dropped like a stone into the water.

7. the fisherman put

   The fisherman put all his tackle back into the fishing box.

EXERCISE

Turning Fragments into Sentences

Each of the following passages contains one or more fragments. First read each passage, then locate the fragments in it. Correct the fragments by joining them to other sentences, using either a comma, a colon, a dash, or no punctuation.

1. Fishing is one of the oldest sports in the world. And can be one of the most relaxing. Someone with a simple wooden pole and line can have as much fun as a professional angler. With expensive equipment. For busy executives, overworked teachers, and even presidents of nations. Fishing can be a good way to escape from the stress of demanding jobs.
2. The first electric car was built in 1887. Six years later, it was sold commercially. At the turn of the century, people had great faith in new technology. In fact, 300 electric taxicabs were operating in New York City by 1900. However, electric cars soon lost their popularity. The new gasoline engine became more widely used. With our concern about pollution. Perhaps electric cars will become desirable once again.
3. Most sports evolve over many years. But not basketball. A Canadian-born teacher invented basketball in December 1891. Working at a YMCA training school in Massachusetts. The coach needed an indoor game to keep his students fit over the winter. Dr. James Naismith created goals. By nailing two peach baskets to the gym balcony.

Don't Confuse Phrases with Sentences

Fragments are usually made up of phrases. These phrases are often mistaken for sentences because they are groups of words. However, they do not fit the definition of a sentence.

What Is a Phrase?

DEFINITION ➤ A **phrase** is a group of words that go together but that lack one or more of the elements necessary to be classified as a sentence.

How Many Kinds of Phrases Are There?

In English, there are a number of types of phrases that you should learn to recognize. Some of them you have already studied in the previous chapter. Remember, a phrase is not a complete sentence; it is a sentence fragment, and as such must be either joined to another sentence or made into a complete sentence.

1. **Noun phrase:** a group of words that functions as a noun.

   Noun phrase: large square bricks
   Complete sentence: The garage is built out of large square bricks.

2. **Prepositional phrase:** a group of words beginning with a preposition.

   Prepositional phrase: on the porch
   Complete sentence: Many of our neighbours are sitting on the porch.

3. **Verb phrase:** a group of words that functions as a verb.

   Verb phrase: is walking
   Complete sentence: My best friend is walking to my house.

4. **Infinitive phrase:** a group of words beginning with an infinitive.

   Infinitive phrase: to have a good job
   Complete sentence: I think it's important to have a good job.

PRACTICE 1

Identifying Phrases

Identify each of the underlined phrases in the following sentences. Check your answers against those in the Answer Key on p. 436.

1. To visit Montreal is a thrill for most Canadians.
2. Many people love to see the French culture.
3. Museums, restaurants, shopping, and the varied night life offer endless possibilities for the tourist.
4. On the subways, tourists experience one of the cleanest underground transit systems in North America.

5. My brother Don rode the subway under the St. Lawrence River.
6. A landowner from the country, he enjoyed the continental atmosphere of Quebec's largest city.
7. Montreal's continual fascination is its rich mix of cultures and lifestyles from all over the world.

PRACTICE 2

Identifying Phrases

Identify each of the underlined phrases in the following sentences. Check your answers against those in the Answer Key on p. 436.

1. In Canada,① crime seems to be increasing② at an alarming rate.③
2. Stories about many major crimes④ can be seen⑤ almost daily in the newspapers.⑥
3. To avoid⑦ the issue will not solve the problem.
4. Citizens should be concerned⑧ and try to make their views known⑨ to their elected officials.⑩

1. ______________________
2. ______________________
3. ______________________
4. ______________________
5. ______________________
6. ______________________
7. ______________________
8. ______________________
9. ______________________
10. ______________________

Making a Complete Sentence from a Fragment That Contains a Participle

DEFINITION ➤ **Participles** are verbals, words that look like verbs but do not function as verbs in a sentence.

Two examples are

running
sitting

Participles are usually found in phrases, and as such can often create sentence fragments if not used properly. Participles often end in *-ing*, and need a verb or another group of words to form a phrase.

The man was *running* to the store.
Sitting on the bench, I saw the pigeon.

Watch out for *-ing* words. No word ending in *-ing* can be the complete verb of a sentence.

You can form a sentence from a fragment that contains a participle in any of the following ways.

Fragment: he talking in his sleep

1. Add a helping verb to the participle:

   He *is talking* in his sleep.

2. Change the participle to a different form of the verb:

   He *talks* in his sleep.

3. Use the participle as an adjective, being sure to provide a subject and verb for the sentence:

   Talking in his sleep, he muttered something about his boss.

4. Use the participle as a subject (gerund phrase):

   Talking in his sleep got him into trouble.

PRACTICE 1

Correcting the Fragment That Contains a Participle

Make four complete sentences from each of the following fragments. Use this example as your model. There can be more than one correct answer for each example. Check your answers against those in the Answer Key on p. 436.

Fragment: using the back stairway

a. He *is using* the back stairway.
b. He *uses* the back stairway.
c. *Using the back stairway,* he got away without being seen.
d. *Using the back stairway* is not a good idea.

1. climbing in the Rockies

   a. He was
   b. He climbs
   c Climbing in the Rockies was a dream come true.
   d. Climbing in the Rockies can be very dangerous.

2. playing video games

   a. He was
   b. He plays
   c. Playing video games is a lot of fun.
   d. Playing video games is a fun way to pass time.

3. going clubbing on Tuesdays

    a. She will be going clubbing on Tuesdays

    b. She goes clubbing on Tuesdays.

    c. Clubbing on Tuesdays, is what she likes to do.

    d. Clubbing on Tuesdays was her only escape.

PRACTICE 2

Recognizing the Fragment

The paragraph below contains fragments. Read the paragraph. Then write *complete* after each example that is a complete sentence. Write *fragment* after each example that is a phrase or piece of a sentence. Keep in mind that a sentence must have a subject and verb as well as express a complete thought. Check your answers against those in the Answer Key on p. 436.

> That summer, she cycled through the backcountry of southern France. Discovering early that her bike was ideal. The perfect mode of transportation. Because they are cycling fanatics. The French almost always treated her with respect and kindness. In spite of her halting attempts at the language. They would shout encouragement. As she puffed up a hill. The waitress in a café where she stopped to rest. Urged her to eat more, slipping an extra portion onto her plate.

1. That summer, she cycled through the backcountry of southern France. C
2. Discovering early that her bike was ideal. F
3. The perfect mode of transportation. F
4. Because they are cycling fanatics. F
5. The French almost always treated her with respect and kindness. C
6. In spite of her halting attempts at the language. F
7. They would shout encouragement. C
8. As she puffed up a hill. F
9. The waitress in a café where she stopped to rest. F
10. Urged her to eat more, slipping an extra portion onto her plate. F

EXERCISE

Correcting the Fragment That Contains a Participle

The following passage contains four fragments containing participles. Circle the fragments and correct them in one of the four ways shown in Practice 1. There can be more than one correct answer.

At last taking the driving test. I felt very nervous. My mother was sitting in the back seat. All my papers sitting on the front seat. The inspector got into the car and sat on my insurance form. He looked rather sour and barely spoke to me. Trying not to hit the curb. I parallel parked surprisingly well. I managed to get through all the manoeuvres. Now tensely waiting for the results.

Chapter Review Exercises

EXERCISE 1

Correcting the Fragment

Rewrite each fragment so that it is a complete sentence. There can be more than one correct answer.

1. early morning a time of peace in my neighbourhood

2. the grey mist covering up all but the faint outlines of nearby houses

3. the shapes of cars in the streets and driveways

4. to sit and look out the window

5. holding a steaming cup of coffee

6. the only sound the rumbling of a truck

7. passing on the highway a kilometre away

EXERCISE 2 Correcting the Fragment

Rewrite the paragraph in the exercise "Correcting the Fragment That Contains a Participle" on page 79. Correct the fragments in one of the following three ways. There can be more than one correct answer.

a. Join the phrase to the sentence preceding it.
b. Join the phrase to the sentence that follows it.
c. Add a subject, a verb, or both so that the sentence is complete.

EXERCISE 3 Correcting the Fragment

Each of the following passages contains a fragment. Underline the fragment, and on the lines beneath each passage, rewrite the passage so that it is composed of complete sentences. There can be more than one way to correct each fragment.

1. The moon rose high in the sky. All of us worked quickly to pitch the tent. Then making a fire.

   Revised passage: Then we made a fire.

2. Raising the drinking age to 21 saves the lives of all drivers. The drinkers and nondrinkers. Every province should raise the drinking age to 21.

   Revised passage:

3. Companies do a lot of research before they name a new product. Based on the results of a market research team. The company makes its final selection.

   Revised passage: The products name is based...

4. The day of my eighteenth birthday, the reservations made at a fine restaurant. My father came home early from work.

   Revised passage:

5. In 1930, Clint Benedict of the Montreal Maroons donned professional hockey's first facemask. It was a crude leather device intended to protect his broken nose. During the game, an opponent jammed the mask into Benedict's face. Causing further injury. Benedict tore off the mask and quit the game forever.

   Revised passage: ____

   ____

   ____

   ____

   ____

Working Together: *Editing Ad Copy*

Read the Audi advertisement illustrated below. Notice that this advertisement contains many fragments. The writing we must produce for academic or professional purposes is often very different from the kind of writing we find in advertisements and other kinds of popular writing. This kind of writing is short and snappy. Why do you think the advertiser would choose to write in this way? Rewrite the entire advertisement using only complete sentences. There can be more than one way to rewrite this advertisement.

Audi

Traction. Like a lot of things in life you take it for granted, then boom. It's taken away. And oh how you want it back. It doesn't take much. Gravel on the offramp. A soft shoulder on a rainy night.

That's why we developed quattro™ all-wheel drive for our luxury cars. Very serious grip. High performance traction. Quattro continuously distributes power between the front and back wheels, whichever has the best hold of the road. It happens instantly. And the extra traction quattro provides could be the difference between being in a collision, or avoiding a collision. So which is better, protection or traction? Get both. In an Audi quattro all-wheel drive. For more information call 1-800-668-AUDI.

Audi 90 quattro

Audi Quattro. Reprinted with kind permission of Volkswagen Canada.

CHAPTER SEVEN

7

Correcting Run-ons

QUICK QUIZ

Test yourself on your knowledge of run-ons. Some of the examples below are complete sentences; some are run-ons (two or more independent clauses inadequately separated). Write *C* if the example is correct. Write *R* if the example is a run-on. Answers to the questions are beside the quiz.

________ 1. Strong competition exists among computer companies, each carefully guards its new software designs.

________ 2. Last year, newspapers carried the story of the great video game design robbery, in fact, it sounded like a spy movie.

________ 3. A young worker for a California company wanted money to buy a sports car, so he tried to sell the secret company designs to an Asian competitor.

________ 4. The worker thought the designs were safely hidden on a disk in an airport locker, however, the police caught him and recovered the disk.

________ 5. The company pressed charges, the worker was given a suspended sentence.

Answers:
1. R
2. R
3. C
4. R
5. R

A teenager came home from school with a long face.

DAUGHTER: I had a terrible day.
MOTHER: What happened?
DAUGHTER: Well, to start with my hair looked terrible *and then* the science teacher called on me to give my oral report *and* I was counting on having another day at least to get ready for it *and* when I got to English class I realized I had left my purse in science class *and* I didn't have time to go back and get it *and* to top it off Mrs. Edmunds gave us a surprise quiz on our reading assignment.
MOTHER: *And* I thought my day was bad!

This is probably typical of many conversations you have had at one time or another. In telling about a series of events, we sometimes join the events together as if they were one long thought. A problem arises when you want to write down these events in acceptable writing form. Writing ideas down as if they are all one thought without any punctuation to help the reader is not acceptable. A sentence such as the daughter's speech above is called a **run-on**. You cannot combine independent clauses without adequate separation. A comma alone is never adequate separation.

How Many Kinds of Run-ons Are There?

The Different Kinds of Run-on Sentences

1. *The fused run-on:* two or more independent clauses that run together without any punctuation

   I met Diana again we were happy to see each other.

2. *The comma splice:* two or more independent clauses that run together with only a comma

   I met Diana again, we were happy to see each other.

3. *The "and" run-on:* two or more independent clauses that run together with a coordinating conjunction but no punctuation

   I met Diana again and we were happy to see each other and we talked for hours.

Note: A long sentence is not, in itself, a run-on sentence. The following sentence may be considered long, but it is **not** a run-on:

> I met Diana again, and despite the fact that we hadn't seen each other in years, we both felt as if we hadn't parted at all, as strange as that may seem to everyone.

How Do You Make a Complete Sentence from a Run-on?

Guide for Correcting Run-ons

1. Make two simple sentences with end punctuation:

   I met Diana again. We were happy to see each other.

2. Make a compound sentence using one of the three methods of coordination:

   I met Diana again, and we were happy to see each other.
   I met Diana again; furthermore, we were happy to see each other.
   I met Diana again; we were happy to see each other.

3. Make a complex sentence using subordination:

   When I met Diana again, we were happy to see each other.
   We were happy to see each other when I met Diana again.

EXERCISE 1

Recognizing and Correcting Run-ons

The following story is written as one sentence. Rewrite the story, making sure to correct the run-on sentences. Put a period at the end of each complete thought. You may have to omit some of the words that loosely connect two ideas, or you may want to use coordination and subordination (see Chapter 5). Remember to start each new sentence with a capital letter. More than one correct answer is possible.

Well, to start with my hair looked terrible and then the science teacher called on me to give my oral report and I was counting on having another day at least to get ready for it and when I got to English class I realized I had left my purse in science class and I didn't have time to go back and get it and to top it off Mrs. Edmunds gave us a surprise quiz on our reading assignment.

EXERCISE 2

Recognizing and Correcting Run-ons

The following story is written as one sentence. Rewrite the story, making sure to correct the run-on sentences. Put a period at the end of each complete thought. You may have to omit some of the words that loosely connect different ideas, or you may want to use coordination and subordination (see Chapter 5). Remember to start each new sentence with a capital letter. More than one correct answer is possible.

My best friend is accident-prone if you knew her you'd know that she's always limping, having to write with her left hand, or wearing a bandage on her head or ankle, last week for example she was walking down the street minding her own business when a shingle from someone's roof hit her on the head and she had to go to the emergency ward for stitches then this week one of her fingers is purple because someone slammed the car door on her hand sometimes I think it might be better if I didn't spend too much time with her you know her bad luck might be catching!

PRACTICE 1

Correcting Run-ons

Each of the following examples is a run-on. Supply four possible ways to correct each run-on. There may be more than one correct answer for each example. Check your answers against those in the Answer Key on p. 436. Use the guide on page 83 if you need help.

1. Certain Web sites offer free recorded music artists who own rights to the music are trying to stop them.

   Two simple sentences (sentences with a single subject, verb, and one complete thought):

   Certain Web sites offer free recorded music. Artists who own rights to the music are trying to stop them.

Two kinds of compound sentence (two simple sentences connected with either a comma and a coordinating conjunction, an adverbial conjunction, or a semi-colon):

a. ;
, and

b.
; therefore,

Complex sentence (use subordination):

while

2. Many people are opposed to gambling in all its forms they will not even buy a lottery ticket.

Two simple sentences:

Many people are opposed to gambling.
They will not even buy a lottery ticket.

Two kinds of compound sentence:

a. ; therefore,
;

b. ; nor will they buy a lottery ticket.
; and , and.

Complex sentence:

Because →

3. Hockey may be Canada's national sport the game can be quite brutal.

Two simple sentences:

Hockey may be Canada's national sport.
The game can be quite brutal.

Two kinds of compound sentence:

a. , but , yet
; however,

b. ______________________________

____

Complex sentence:

although ______________________________

____

4. Many young people manage to travel they find ways to do it cheaply.

Two simple sentences:

____

____

Two kinds of compound sentence:

a. ______________________________

____

b. ______________________________

____

Complex sentence:

____

____

5. The need for a proper diet is important in any health program all the junk food on the grocery shelves makes it hard to be consistent.

Two simple sentences:

____

____

Two kinds of compound sentence:

a. ______________________________

____

b. ______________________________

____

Complex sentence:

____

____

PRACTICE 2

Correcting Run-ons

Each of the following examples is a run-on. Supply four possible ways to revise each run-on. There may be more than one correct answer for each example. Check your answers against those in the Answer Key on p. 437. Use the guide on page 83 if you need help.

1. The airline has begun its new route to the islands everyone is looking forward to flying there.

   Two simple sentences:

   ____

   ____

   Two kinds of compound sentence:

   a. ______________________________

   ____

   b. ______________________________

   ____

   Complex sentence:

   ____

   ____

2. The movie begins at nine o'clock let's have dinner before the show.

   Two simple sentences:

   ____

   ____

   Two kinds of compound sentence:

   a. The movie begins at nine o'clock; therefore, let's have dinner before the show.

   b. The movie begins at nine o'clock, so lets have dinner before the show.

   Complex sentence:

   Since the movie begins at 9 o'clock, let's have dinner before the show.

3. The studio audience screamed at the contestant they wanted her to try for the big prize.

Two simple sentences:

Two kinds of compound sentence:

a.

b.

Complex sentence:

4. Maya needs new shoes she is running in the marathon.

Two simple sentences:

Maya needs new shoes.
She is running in the marathon.

Two kinds of compound sentence:

a. She is running in the marathon; therefore, Maya needs new shoes

b. Maya needs new shoes, for she is running in the marathon

Complex sentence:

Since she is running

5. My actor friend grabbed my arm she wanted to tell me about her new part in the movie.

Two simple sentences:

Two kinds of compound sentence:

a. ____

____

b. ____

____

Complex sentence:

____

____

Chapter Review Exercises

EXERCISE 1

Editing for Run-ons

Rewrite the following paragraph, correcting all run-on sentences. More than one correct answer is possible.

Commercial farming in Atlantic Canada is concentrated in the dairy, poultry, and horticultural sectors the most important crop in the region, particularly in New Brunswick and Prince Edward Island, is potatoes. In Ontario and Quebec, farming is highly diversified and includes specialty crops such as soybeans, tobacco, fruit, and vegetables. In the Prairie region, most of the country's wheat, oats, barley, rye, flaxseed, canola, mustard, and sunflowers are grown livestock raising is also very important in Canada with the majority of ranches being located in the three prairie provinces.

EXERCISE 2

Editing for Run-ons

Rewrite the following paragraph, correcting all run-on sentences. More than one correct answer is possible.

The metric system was legalized in Canada in 1871 the British Imperial system of units, based on yards, pounds, gallons, etc., continued to be used until the 1960s with rapidly expanding technology and worldwide trade, the need for an international measurement system became apparent. Britain decided to convert to the system the United States was studying a similar move. A number of Canadian businesses favoured the metric system in January 1970 the government passed legislation stating that a single, coherent measurement system based on metric units should be used for measurement purposes in this country.

EXERCISE 3 Editing for Run-ons

Correct the following run-on sentences by using the different methods you have learned. Correct the sentences in at least two different ways.

1. I had to buy a new DVD, I gave my only copy to my brother.
2. I'm taking guitar lessons, four of us want to start a band.
3. It was hot outside, I wanted to get some exercise.
4. The storm came on suddenly, we were lost.
5. There were no right answers to the questions, we tried to answer them.
6. He is a politician, he serves his community well.
7. Where is Kanata, I think it's near Ottawa.
8. When did Canada last win the World Junior Hockey Championships, I think it was a long time ago.
9. Our tour was interesting, four of us became lost in Edmonton.
10. We tried our hardest, the exam was too difficult.

EXERCISE 4 Editing for Run-ons

Correct any run-on sentences by using the different methods you have learned. Correct the run-ons in at least two different ways. If the sentence is already correct, write *C* beside the number.

1. The right answer was not at the end of the chapter, it was at the beginning of the next one.
2. I was late for school, however, the teacher wasn't in class today.
3. The pizza was cold but it was still good.
4. At the edge of the table, the marble slowed down and began to roll the other way.
5. The time was right, it was now or never.
6. Listening to the radio at dawn, I found myself singing the words to every song.
7. My teacher is dedicated to her profession, furthermore, she's the best teacher I've ever had.

Working Together: *Operation "Plot without Run-ons"*

In the telling of a story, it is tempting to use run-ons that merge the events of the story in one long sentence. Choose a movie or book you have seen or read recently and retell the plot. In about twenty minutes, write as much of the story as you can remember, being careful to write only on every other line, separating each word, and writing clearly so your classmates can read what you have written. Exchange papers and read the paper you receive in order to check for run-ons. When you have found what you believe to be a run-on, put a mark beside that sentence and be ready to read the sentence or put it on the board for class discussion.

CHAPTER EIGHT

8

Parallel Structure

QUICK QUIZ

Test yourself on your knowledge of parallel structure. The underlined portion of each sentence is not parallel with the rest of the sentence. Replace the underlined portion with the correct words, making the entire sentence parallel. Answers are in the margin.

1. While the men go out in their boats, the women and children stay in camp, cook meals and to take care of the dog teams.
2. The weather on the East Coast is often wet, windy, and the temperatures are low.
3. His office is without windows, on the fourth floor, and you have to go down a dark hallway to get there.
4. Carmelita does her work quickly, accurately, and with cheerfulness.
5. The mayor promised lower taxes, less crime, and the number of jobs would be higher.

Answers:
1. take care of the dog teams
2. cold
3. down a dark hallway
4. cheerfully
5. more jobs

What Is Parallel Structure?

DEFINITION ➤ **Parallel structure** is the balance of a series of words, phrases, or clauses within a sentence.

Which of the following sentences is better balanced?

His favourite pastimes are reading novels, listening to jazz, and to go to films.

His favourite pastimes are reading novels, listening to jazz, and going to films.

If you selected the second sentence, you made the right choice. The second sentence uses parallel structure to balance the three phrases in the series (reading, listening, and going). By giving each of the items in the series the same *-ing* structure, the sentence becomes easier to understand and more pleasant to read. You can make words, phrases, and even sentences in a series parallel:

RULE 1: **Words in a series should be the same parts of speech.**

Incorrect: The town was small, quiet, and the atmosphere was peaceful.
(The series is composed of two adjectives and one clause.)

Correct: The town was small, quiet, and peaceful.
(*Small, quiet*, and *peaceful* are adjectives.)

RULE 2: **Phrases in a series should be the same kind of phrase (infinitive phrases, prepositional phrases, verb phrases, noun phrases, participial phrases).**

Incorrect: Her lost assignment is in her closet, on the floor, and the clothes are hiding it.
(Two prepositional phrases and one clause.)

Correct: Her lost assignment is in her closet, on the floor, and under a pile of clothes.
(Three prepositional phrases beginning with *in, on*, and *under*.)

RULE 3: **Clauses in a series should be parallel.**

Incorrect: One clerk polished the antique spoons; they were placed into the display case by the other clerk.

Correct: One clerk polished the antique spoons; the other clerk placed them in the display case.

PRACTICE 1

Making Sentences Parallel

Each of the following sentences has an underlined word, phrase, or clause that is not parallel. Make the underlined section parallel. Check your answers against those in the Answer Key on p. 438.

1. My favourite armchair is lumpy, worn out, and has dirt spots everywhere.

____

____

2. She enjoys reading novels, studying the flute, and also sews her own clothes.

____

____

3. He admires teachers who make the classroom an exciting place and willingly explaining material more than once.

____

____

PRACTICE 2

Making Sentences Parallel

Each of the following sentences needs parallel structure. Underline the word, phrase, or clause that is not parallel and revise it so that its structure balances with the other items in the pair or series. There may be more than one correct answer for each sentence. An example is done for you. Check your answers against those in the Answer Key on p. 438.

Incorrect: The best leather comes from Italy, from Spain, and is imported from Brazil.

Correct: The best leather comes from Italy, from Spain, and from Brazil.

1. Winter in Edmonton is very windy and has many bitterly cold days.

2. I would prefer to fix an old car than watching television.

3. Alex is a talented athlete, a top student, and even generous to her friends.

4. The apartment is crowded and without light.

5. The dancer is slender and moves gracefully.

6. The trees were tall and had a lot of leaves.

7. My friend loves to play chess, to read science fiction, and working out at the gym.

PRACTICE 3

Making Sentences Parallel

Each of the following sentences lacks parallel structure. Underline the word, phrase, or clause that is not parallel and revise it so that its structure balances with the other items in the pair or series. There may be more than one correct answer for each sentence. Check your answers against those in the Answer Key on p. 438.

1. The dog had to choose between jumping over the fence, or he could have dug a hole underneath it.

2. She was great at swimming, canoeing, and as a rock climber.

3. As I looked down the city street, I could see the soft lights from restaurant windows, I could hear the mellow sounds of a nightclub band, and carefree moods of people walking by.

4. The singers have been on several road tours, have recorded for two record companies, and they would also like to make a movie someday.

5. They would rather order a pizza than eating homemade cooking.

6. I explained to the teacher that my car had broken down, my books had been stolen, and I left my assignment pad at home.

7. That night the prisoner was sick, discouraged, and filled with loneliness.

Chapter Review Exercises

EXERCISE 1

Making Sentences Parallel

Each of the following sentences has a part that does not work with the rest of the sentence; therefore, the sentences lack parallel structure. Find the error and correct it. There may be more than one correct answer for each sentence.

1. A new medical study of thousands of Chinese shows new connections between diet and keeping healthy.

2. The researchers found Western people have many health problems because they eat a great deal of animal protein, high-starch foods, and they buy too much take-out.

3. A Chinese person eats very few calcium products, little meat, and he or she doesn't eat bread very often.

4. They believe we should eat more vegetables, fruit, and we should exercise more.

5. The Chinese who eat the most protein also have the highest rate of serious illness such as heart disease, diabetes, and suffering from cancer.

EXERCISE 2

Making Sentences Parallel

Revise each sentence to make it parallel. There may be more than one correct answer for each sentence.

1. Most of the neighbours are friendly, considerate, and they give help.

2. She is charming and has beauty.

3. I enjoy reading, writing, and to conduct laboratory experiments.

4. Either going for a ride or to lie in the sun is my idea of a good time.

5. She got a new job with a higher salary, increased benefits, and she also works fewer hours than before.

Working Together: *Practise Making Sentences Parallel*

Read the following paragraph. Look for lack of parallel structure, and then rewrite your corrected version. When you're finished, check your answers with another student in the group or class, preferably someone with whom you would not normally sit.

I've had a lot of great summer jobs. They include desk clerk for a student residence, cashier for a busy convenience store, and I even worked as an assistant janitor in an elementary school where my boss and I had some of the best conversations I've ever had. The best summer job, however, was organizing the Miss Glace Bay Pageant. Because I'm a guy, others automatically assume the reason for this is the titillation factor associated with a beauty competition, typical of any pageant. I admit that was part of it, but not all. Other reasons for enjoying the job included auditioning talent for the entertainment component, I wrote the script for the emcee and meeting a young woman among the contestants whom I'd already met six months earlier. First, I love music: I have a huge CD collection, I frequent cafés and pubs where live music is performed, and playing piano is a favourite hobby of mine. So having a say as to who performed on the big evening was exciting beyond description. Second, I've always enjoyed writing. And writing what the emcee would say that evening gave me experience with a kind of writing I'd never tried before. But most important, when I saw Sherry with her long golden hair among the contestants on the first day of rehearsals, I knew this second meeting was no coincidence. And about a week later when she sat down next to me, laid her head on my shoulder, and "Hello, there," was whispered into my ear, I knew we'd be dating before too long. She didn't win the pageant, but she definitely won my heart. I'd had some great summer jobs, but organizing the pageant was the one that etched that summer onto the wall of my memory storehouse forever.

CHAPTER NINE

9

Pronouns

QUICK QUIZ

Test yourself on your knowledge of pronouns. In each of the following sentences, choose the correct pronouns. Answers are beside the quiz.

1. Between you and (me, I), the reason I can't go is I lost my ticket.
2. The girl I'm dating is taller than (I, me).
3. (We, Us) students are going to Cancun for the spring break.
4. Would you spare some change for my son and (I, me)?
5. (Him, He) and (me, I) spent lots of money on the weekend.

Answers:
1. me
2. I
3. We
4. me
5. He, I

Pronouns and Case

The case of a personal pronoun is determined by the function it serves in a sentence. Pronouns can function as subjects or subject complements (subjective case); as direct objects, indirect objects, or objects of prepositions (objective case); or as indicators of ownership (possessive case).

Guide to Pronoun Case

Pronouns Used as Subjects	Pronouns Used as Objects	Pronouns Used as Possessives
I	me	my (mine)
you (sing.)	you (sing.)	your (yours)
he	him	his (his)
she	her	her (hers)
it	it	its (its)
who	whom	whose
whoever	whomever	
we	us	our (ours)
you (pl.)	you (pl.)	your (yours)
they	them	their (theirs)

Use the guide to choose the correct answers in the following examples:

1. (She, Her) is singing at the concert tonight.
2. He bought those tickets for Jan and (I, me).

When you have a compound subject or object, it is easier to pick the correct pronoun if you read the sentence leaving out one of the subjects:

He bought those tickets for (I, me).

3. He sold (us, we) the best seats in the house.
4. To (who, whom) should I address the letter?
5. Her voice is much stronger than (he, him, his).

In a comparison, it is easier to pick the correct pronoun if you complete the comparison.

Her voice is much stronger than (he, him, his) voice is.

6. (Who, Whom, Whose) music was left on the piano?

Who vs. *Whom*

Who is the subjective form; *whom* is the objective form. Use *who* whenever *he, she, they, I,* or *we* could replace *who*. And likewise, use *whom* when *him, her, them, me,* or *us* could replace *whom*. (If this doesn't work, mentally rearrange the clause the way it's done in parentheses after the following examples):

To whom were you talking? (Were you talking to him?)
The next person to who I get engaged will be the one I marry. (He/she will be the next person I marry.)
The matter of who should pay was not decided. (He/she should pay.)

The rule that a subject never follows a preposition is broken here because the word *who* is also the doer of the action.

EXERCISE 1

Choosing Correct Pronoun Forms

Circle the correct pronoun in each of the sentences below.

1. Matthew and (she, her) presented the project today.
2. Between you and (I, me), I think it was outstanding.
3. Their visual materials will help (whoever, whomever) will study the project later.
4. He is usually a better speaker than (she, her).
5. (Whoever, Whomever) heard them agreed that it was an impressive presentation.
6. (Who, Whom) do you think made the best points?
7. I am not as deeply involved in my project as (they, them).
8. Their research was much more detailed than (us, our, ours).
9. The professor gave both Carolyn and (he, him) A's.
10. My partner and (I, me) will have to work harder to reach this standard.

EXERCISE 2 **Choosing Correct Pronoun Forms**

Circle the correct pronouns in the following paragraph.

When my mother and (I, me) decided to care for my very ill father at home, some of our friends objected. My sister and (they, them) said we would be exhausted and unable to handle the stress. To (who, whom) could we go for help in the middle of the night? My father, (who, whom) we believed would be happier at home, had been our first consideration. Of course, we would have benefited if my mother or (I, me) had been a nurse. However, we did have a visiting nurse available at times. We were more confident than (they, them) that we could handle the situation.

Pronoun-Antecedent Agreement

RULE 1: **A pronoun must agree in number (singular or plural) with any other word to which it refers.**

That word to which the pronoun refers is known as the **antecedent** of the pronoun. Most errors in pronoun number agreement occur when a plural pronoun is used to refer to a singular noun, and vice versa.

The following sentence contains a pronoun-antecedent disagreement in **number:**

Everyone worked on *their* final draft.

The problem in this sentence is that *everyone* is a singular word, but *their* is a plural pronoun. You may often have heard people use the plural pronoun *their* to refer to a singular subject. In fact, the above sentence may sound correct, but it is still a mistake in formal writing. Here are two approaches a writer might take to correct this sentence:

Everyone worked on *his* final draft.

Although you may encounter this approach in current writing, it is unpopular because it is widely considered a sexist construction.

Everyone worked on *his or her* final draft.

This form is technically correct, but if it is used several times, it sounds awkward and repetitious.

The best solution is to revise such a construction so that the antecedent is plural:

All the students worked on *their* final drafts.

Everyone is an **indefinite** pronoun. It may look plural, but actually, it is singular. For more on indefinite pronouns, see pp. 44–45 in Chapter 4: "Subject-Verb Agreement."

Another problem with pronoun-antecedent agreement in number occurs when a **demonstrative** pronoun (*this, that, these, those*) is used with a noun. That pronoun must agree with the noun it modifies:

Singular: this kind, that type

Incorrect: *These kind* of shoes hurt my feet.
Correct: *This kind* of shoe hurts my feet.

Plural: these kinds, those types

Incorrect: *Those type* of cars always need oil.
Correct: *Those types* of cars always need oil.

EXERCISE 1

Pronoun-Antecedent Agreement in Number

Rewrite each of the following sentences so that the pronoun agrees with its antecedent in number.

1. Everybody should believe they have choices.

2. Each of the children brought their own toys.

3. There was no one who invited us to their homes.

4. If the bird-watchers hope to see anything, one must get up early.

5. The members of the association voted on its constitution.

RULE 2: **Pronouns must also agree with their antecedents in person.** "Person" refers to the doer of the action—first person (*I*); second person (*you*); third person (*he, she, it* in the singular, *we*, *you*, *they* in the plural, among others). First-person pronouns highlight the writer and are suitable for personal writing. Second-person pronouns focus on the reader and are useful for giving instructions. Third-person pronouns emphasize the subject and are useful in informative and academic writing.

The following incorrect sentence contains a pronoun-antecedent disagreement in **person:**

> When mountain climbing, *one* must maintain *your* concentration at all times.

The sentence could be correctly rewritten as follows:

> When mountain climbing, *one* must maintain *one's* concentration at all times.
> When mountain climbing, *you* must maintain *your* concentration at all times.
> When mountain climbing, *I* must maintain *my* concentration at all times.
> When mountain climbing, *we* must maintain *our* concentration at all times.

EXERCISE 2

Pronoun-Antecedent Agreement in Person

Rewrite each of the following sentences so that the pronoun agrees with its antecedent in person.

1. I enjoy math exams because you can show what you know.

2. When I took geometry, we discovered that frequent review of past assignments helped make the course seem easy.

3. People always need to practise your skills in order not to forget them.

4. When you study for exams, one should not watch television at the same time.

5. Math is a subject we often neglect in school, but later you use it all the time.

Missing, Ambiguous, or Repetitious Pronouns

RULE: **The antecedent of a pronoun should not be missing, ambiguous, or repetitious.** The following is a sentence with a missing antecedent:

Missing antecedent: In British Columbia, they have many challenging hiking trails.
Possible revision: British Columbia has many challenging hiking trails.

In the first sentence, who is meant by *they*? If the context has not told us that *they* refers to the government or to tourist companies, for instance, then the antecedent is missing. The sentence should be rewritten in order to avoid *they*.

In the next sentence, the antecedent is ambiguous.

Ambiguous antecedent: Margaret told Lin that *she* needed to earn $1000 during the summer.
Possible revision: Margaret said that Lin needed to earn $1000 during the summer.

In the first example, *she* could refer to either Margaret or Lin. The sentence should be revised in a way that avoids this confusion.

The next example illustrates a repetitious antecedent.

Repetitious pronoun and antecedent: The newspaper article, *it* said that Earth Day, 1993, re-established humankind's commitment to the earth.
Possible revision: The newspaper article said that Earth Day, 1993, re-established humankind's commitment to the earth.

The subject should be either *article* or, if there is already an antecedent, *it*. Using both the noun and the pronoun results in needless repetition.

EXERCISE

Sentences with Proper Antecedents

Rewrite each of the following sentences so that the antecedents are not missing, ambiguous, or repetitious. More than one correct answer is possible.

1. The biologist asked the director to bring back his microscope.

2. In the report, it says that the number of science and engineering students seeking doctoral degrees has fallen considerably since the mid-sixties.

3. At the laboratory, they said the research had run into serious difficulties.

4. The testing equipment was accidentally dropped into the aquarium, and it was badly damaged.

5. You can't believe anything they say in that newspaper.

Chapter Review Exercises

PRACTICE

Making Pronouns and Antecedents Agree

Each of the following sentences contains errors with pronouns. Revise each sentence so that pronouns agree with their antecedents and there are no missing or ambiguous antecedents. There may be more than one correct answer for each sentence. Check your answers against those in the Answer Key on p. 438.

1. His father mailed him his high school yearbook.

2. No one wants their income reduced.

3. When a company fails to update its equipment, they often pay a price in the long run.

4. The graduate today has many more options open to them than ever before.

5. Everybody knows their own strengths best.

6. Each of the soccer players put effort into their game.

7. If the campers want to eat quickly, each one should help themselves.

EXERCISE

Making Pronouns and Antecedents Agree

Each of the following sentences may contain an error with pronouns. Revise each sentence so that pronouns agree with their antecedents and there are no missing or ambiguous antecedents. There may be more than one correct answer for each sentence. If a sentence is correct, mark a *C* on the lines provided.

1. The manager told Karen she was responsible for the mix-up in orders.

2. The county submitted their proposal for the bridge repairs.

3. We all rushed away from all the trees to our cars because you had to wait for the thunderstorm to stop.

4. A young person does not receive enough advice on how they should choose their career.

5. These type of watches are very popular.

6. People were taken forcibly from our homes.

____

____

7. No one ate their lunch in the cafeteria.

____

____

Working Together: *Practice with Pronouns*

Pair up with someone else in the class, preferably someone with whom you do not normally sit. Together, come up with ten sentences, each with at least three pronouns in it. Each of the three pronouns should be of different cases: subjective, objective, and possessive. Come up with at least one sentence that requires pronoun–antecedent agreement, and one other that contains potential pronoun ambiguity. Between the two of you, make sure all pronouns are correct. If you disagree on any, give the other student an explanation as to why you think yours is correct. Here is an example of a sentence that complies:

> Jacquie and **I** are faster than **they**, so **they** have to not only pay **our** way to the festival, but also give **us** spending money once **we**'re there.

I, they, they, we: subjective case
our: possessive case
us: objective case

CHAPTER TEN

10

Modifiers: Misplaced and Dangling

QUICK QUIZ

Test your knowledge of dangling and misplaced modifiers by selecting the correct sentence in each pair below. Answers are in the margin.

1. a. Sweeping the dust in the attic, the dead bugs numbered in the thousands.
   b. Sweeping the dust in the attic, I noticed the dead bugs numbered in the thousands.
2. a. Reduce speed when wet.
   b. Reduce speed when roads are wet.
3. a. While shaving in the bathroom, Grant accidentally cut his ear with his razor.
   b. While shaving in the bathroom, the razor cut Grant's ear.
4. a. To make a good impression on your employer, ensure you have a neat and clean appearance.
   b. To make a good impression on your employer, a neat and clean appearance is advisable.
5. a. Though old and shoddy, Uncle Jake made the room in the back of the house look new again.
   b. Though the room in the back of the house was old and shoddy, Uncle Jake made it look new again.

Answers:
1. b
2. b
3. a
4. a
5. b

What Are Modifiers?

DEFINITION ➤ **Modifiers** are words or groups of words that function as adjectives or adverbs.

Modifiers describe or modify other words in the sentence. If a modifier is put in the wrong place or in an ambiguous or awkward place in the sentence, the meaning will be unclear. If the modifier has no word at all to modify, the result might be confusing or even unintentionally humorous. (See #2a above.)

A modifier must be placed close to the word, phrase, or clause it modifies so that the reader can understand the intended meaning.

Below are examples of how several problems with modifiers can be revised to make the meanings clear. Study these examples carefully. After you are able to recognize them in the exercises that follow, you will begin to recognize them in your own writing as well.

What Are Misplaced Modifiers?

DEFINITION ➤ **Misplaced modifiers** are modifiers that have been placed in wrong, ambiguous, or awkward positions

There are three types of misplaced modifiers.

1. **The modifier in the wrong place**

Wrong: The salesperson sold the used car to the customer that needed extensive bodywork.

Who or what needs bodywork—the car or the customer?

Revised: The salesperson sold the customer the used car that needed extensive bodywork.

Be especially careful to put each of the following words closest to the word, phrase, or clause it modifies.

almost	exactly	just	nearly	scarcely
even	hardly	merely	only	simply

Notice how the meaning of each of the following sentences changes with the placement of the modifier *only.*

Only Charlene telephoned my brother yesterday.
Charlene only telephoned my brother yesterday.
Charlene telephoned only my brother yesterday.
Charlene telephoned my only brother yesterday.
Charlene telephoned my brother only yesterday.

2. **The awkward modifier that interrupts the flow of the sentence**

Awkward: Cheryl planned to only call my sister.

The adverb *only* could be better placed so that it would not split the infinitive *to call.*

Revised: Cheryl planned to call only my sister.

3. **The "squinting modifier"—an ambiguous modifier that could describe a word or words on either side of it**

Squinting: Cheryl having telephoned secretly appeared at the scene of the crime.

Did Cheryl telephone secretly or appear secretly?

Revised: Having secretly telephoned, Cheryl appeared at the scene of the crime.

What Are Dangling Modifiers?

DEFINITION ➤ **Dangling modifier**—a modifier in a sentence that has no word, phrase, or clause that the modifier can describe

Dangling: Working on the engine of the car, the dog barked all afternoon.

Who worked on the engine? Was it the dog?

Revised: Working on the engine of the car, I heard the dog barking all afternoon.
or
The dog barked all afternoon while I was working on the car's engine.

Chapter Review Exercises

PRACTICE

Revising Misplaced or Dangling Modifiers

Revise each sentence so there is no misplaced or dangling modifier. There may be more than one correct answer for each sentence. Check your answers against those in the Answer Key on p. 438.

1. Victor fed the dog wearing his tuxedo.

While wearing his tuxedo Victor fed the dog

2. Visiting the Vancouver Aquarium, the otters entertained us.

3. Wanting to make a good impression, my suit was conservative and well cut.

To make a good impression, I chose a suit which was conservative and well cut

4. A band was playing in the park that we had heard earlier.

5. ~~After running~~ (we ran) over the hill, the farm was visible in the valley below.

   At the top of the hill.

6. The truck caused a traffic jam, which was broken down on the highway, for kilometres.

7. Hanging from the ceiling in my bedroom, I saw three spiders.

   I saw 3 spiders hanging from my bedroom ceiling.

EXERCISE

Revising Misplaced or Dangling Modifiers

Revise each sentence so there is no misplaced or dangling modifier. There may be more than one correct answer for each sentence.

1. Leaping upstream, we fished most of the day for salmon.

2. At the age of ten, my family took a trip to Fredericton.

3. Skimming every chapter, my biology textbook suddenly made more sense.

4. Waiting at the airport, every minute seemed endless.

5. Working extra hours last week, my salary increased dramatically.

6. We watched a movie in the theatre for which we had paid five dollars.

____

____

7. Dressed as Tinkerbell, he thought she looked charming.

____

____

Working Together: *A Picture Tells a Thousand Words*

Courtesy of Su Mei Ku.

This photograph shows a family portrait from the 1930s. What do you think you can tell about these family members from their photograph?

What is the earliest photograph you have of one or more members of your own family? From stories you have been told by other members of the family, what do you know about these relatives? What do you believe you can tell about them from their photographs?

Use the next twenty minutes to write freely on this subject of your own family. You don't have to write "a thousand words," but when twenty minutes have passed, review what you have written. Look for the kinds of errors you have studied in the last few chapters. These errors include lack of subject-verb agreement, lack of pronoun-antecedent agreement, lack of parallelism, and misplaced and dangling modifiers. Then exchange papers with another member of the class and proofread that classmate's paper. Are you able to spot any of these errors in your classmate's work?

CHAPTER ELEVEN

11

Punctuation

QUICK QUIZ

Test yourself on your knowledge of commas. In each of the following sentences, place commas wherever they are needed. Answers to the questions are beside the quiz.

1. White-collar criminals dishonest company executives are being exposed in growing numbers.
2. White-collar criminals are found in industrial plants government offices and banks.
3. For example manufacturers have been caught cheating the government and well-known banks have been caught laundering money.
4. In the past white-collar criminals have not been prosecuted very vigorously by the law.
5. However some executives are now being given jail sentences for their white-collar crimes.

Answers:
1. criminals, executives,
2. plants, offices,
3. example, government,
4. past,
5. However,

The Eight Basic Rules of the Comma

Many students feel very uncertain about when to use the comma. The starting point is to concentrate on a few basic rules. These rules will cover most of your needs.

The tendency now in English is to use fewer commas than in the past. There is no one perfect set of rules on which everyone agrees. However, if you learn the eight basic rules explained in this chapter, your common sense will help you figure out what to do in other cases. Remember that a comma usually signifies a pause in a sentence. As you read a sentence out loud, listen to where you pause. This is often your clue that a comma is needed. Notice that in each of the examples for the following eight rules, you can pause where the comma is placed.

RULE 1: **Use a comma to separate parallel words, phrases, and clauses in a series.**

The sky was cloudy, grey, and ominous.
I was dreaming of running in the race, finishing among the top ten, and collapsing happily on the ground.

- A series means more than two items.
- Some writers omit the comma before the *and* that introduces the last item.

The sky was cloudy, grey and ominous.

- When an address or date occurs in a sentence, each part is treated as an item in a series. A comma follows each item even if there are only two items:

    I lived at 14 Tartan Avenue, Halifax, Nova Scotia, for many years.
    He was born on August 17, 1980, so he's a Leo.

- A comma does not follow the last item in a series unless that last item is part of an address or a date.
- A group of adjectives may not be regarded as a series if some of the words "go together." You can test this by putting *and* between each item. If it doesn't work, then don't use commas.

    I carried my *old, dark green* coat.
    In the yard was a *battered old maple* tree.
    I rode in his *new red sports* car.

PRACTICE 1

Insert Necessary Commas

In each of the following sentences, insert commas wherever they are needed. Check your answers against those in the Answer Key on p. 438.

1. Problems with the water supply of Canada the United States Europe and other parts of the world are growing.
2. Water is colourless tasteless odourless and free of calories.
3. You will use on an average day 90 L of water for flushing 120 L for bathing and washing clothes and 95 L for other uses.
4. It took 450 L of water to create the eggs you ate for breakfast 13 250 L for the steak you might eat for dinner and over 200 000 L to produce the steel used to make your car.
5. By 1970 the English–Wabigoon river system which runs through Grassy Narrows Ontario had become polluted with mercury.

RULE 2: **Use a comma along with a coordinating conjunction (joining sentences of equal rank or value) to combine two simple sentences (also called independent clauses) into a single compound sentence. (See Chapter 5 on coordination and subordination.)**

The house was on fire, but I was determined not to leave my place of safety.

- Be careful to use the comma with the conjunction only when you are combining independent clauses. If you are combining only words or phrases, no comma is used.

    The weather was hot but dry.
    He grabbed the ball and sent it flying.
    Larry was neither at third base nor at home plate.

- When clauses joined by a coordinating conjunction are short and closely connected, the comma is often omitted.

    Let's sit down and I'll dish out the food.

PRACTICE 2

Insert Necessary Commas

In each of the following sentences, insert commas wherever they are needed. Check your answers against those in the Answer Key on p. 439.

1. The most overused bodies of water are our rivers but they continue to serve us daily.
2. Canadian cities often developed next to rivers and industries followed soon after in the same locations.
3. The people of the industrial age can try to clean the water they use or they can watch pollution take over.
4. The Great Lakes are showing signs of renewal yet the struggle against pollution there must continue.
5. Most people have not been educated about the dangerous state of our water supply nor are all our members of Parliament fully aware of the problem.

RULE 3: **Use a comma to follow introductory words, expressions, phrases, or clauses.**

A. Introductory words (such as *yes, no, oh, well*)

Oh, I never thought he would do it.

B. Introductory expressions (transitions such as *as a matter of fact, finally, secondly, furthermore, consequently*). See the transitions chart on the inside back cover.

Therefore, I will give you a second chance.

C. Introductory phrases. The comma signals the end of the introductory group of words and the beginning of the sentence proper.

Long prepositional phrase: In the beginning of the course, I thought I would never be able to do the work.

Short prepositional phrases don't generally need to be followed by a comma. However, a comma is often used if the phrase ends with a date.

At night I like to watch the stars.
In 2001, a moderate earthquake hit the West Coast.

Participial phrase: Walking on tiptoe, the young mother quietly peeked into the nursery.

Verbal phrase: By walking daily, I lost weight. (Gerund)
Confident of her skills, she entered the contest. (Participle)
To be honest, I don't like it. (Infinitive)

D. Introductory dependent clauses beginning with a subordinating conjunction (see Chapter 5)

When the food arrived, we all grabbed for it.

PRACTICE 3

Insert Necessary Commas

In each of the following sentences, insert commas wherever they are needed. Check your answers against those in the Answer Key on p. 439.

1. A total solar eclipse when the moon's shadow blots out the sun completely is an outstanding cosmic event.
2. Once you see your first solar eclipse you start looking forward to the next one.
3. However witnessing this spectacle takes planning and the ability to travel to the best viewing spots.
4. In eastern Turkey on August 11 1999 a crowd of astronomers and "eclipse chasers" watched the last total eclipse of the millennium.
5. At the moment of totality people cheer clap and often cry.

RULE 4: **Use commas surrounding a word, phrase, or clause when the word or group of words interrupts the main idea.**

A. Interrupting word

We will, however, take an X-ray.

B. Interrupting phrase

Prepositional phrase: I wanted, of course, to stay.
Appositive phrase: Ann, the girl with the red hair, has a wonderful sense of humour.

C. Interrupting clause

He won't, I think, try that again.

Words, phrases, or clauses that interrupt the main idea of a sentence can be *restrictive* or *nonrestrictive*.

A **restrictive** word, phrase, or clause is essential to the meaning of the sentence and is not set off by commas from the rest of the sentence.

The man with the red hat is my father.
Author Timothy Findley said it takes failure to become a great writer.

Unless you specifically identify the man with the red hat, any number of unidentified men could be the father.

A **nonrestrictive** word, phrase, or clause is not essential to the meaning of the sentence, and *is* set off by commas from the rest of the sentence. (See more on nonrestrictive and restrictive clauses in Chapter 5, Coordination and Subordination).

Ann, who has red hair, has a wonderful sense of humour.

Some words can have more than one grammatical function.

She came to the dance; however, she didn't stay long.

In this sentence, *however* is used to combine independent clauses and therefore requires a semicolon before it.

She did, however, have a good time.

In this sentence, *however* interrupts the main idea and therefore requires a comma before it and a comma after it (comma rule #4).

Some clauses can be used in different ways.

Ann, who has red hair, has a wonderful sense of humour.

In this sentence, *who has red hair* interrupts the main idea of the sentence, and so commas are used.

The girl who has red hair is my sister Ann.

The clause *who has red hair* is part of the identity of "the girl." This clause does not interrupt the main idea but is necessary to and part of the main idea. Therefore, no commas are used.

PRACTICE 4

Insert Necessary Commas

In each of the following sentences, insert commas wherever they are needed. Check your answers against those in the Answer Key on p. 439.

1. Natural disasters I believe have not been historically significant.
2. They have, however, significantly affected the lives of many Canadians.
3. Canada's worst coal-mine disaster at Hillcrest, Alberta occurred on June 19 1914.
4. In Springhill, Nova Scotia furthermore 424 persons were killed in the mines between 1881 and 1969.
5. Avalanches, storms, and floods, which are natural disasters, have also made their marks on the face of our country.

RULE 5: **Use a comma around nouns in direct address.**

I wonder, Michaela, if you really know what you're doing.

PRACTICE 5

Insert Necessary Commas

In each of the following sentences, insert commas wherever they are needed. Check your answers against those in the Answer Key on p. 439.

1. Honey I hope you're not planning to wear that hat.
2. I wonder Samir if the game has been cancelled.
3. Dad could I borrow five dollars?
4. Can you help me doctor?
5. Ayesha is that you?

RULE 6: **Use a comma in numbers of 1,000 or larger.**

1,999
1,999,999,999

Note that in the metric system of measurement, spaces—not commas—are used in numbers of 1000 or larger. (However, numbers of four digits need not be separated.) This practice is becoming more widespread in Canada.

4000 or 4 000
38 622

RULE 7: **Use a comma to set off exact words spoken in dialogue.**

"The pen," she said, "is mightier than the sword."

The comma, as well as the period, is always placed inside the closing quotation marks, as shown in the sentence above.

PRACTICE 6

Insert Necessary Commas

In each of the following sentences, insert commas wherever they are necessary. Check your answers against those in the Answer Key on p. 439.

1. "I'm innocent" he cried "of all charges against me."
2. He mumbled "I won't incriminate myself."
3. "I was told" the defendant explained "to answer every question."
4. "This court" the judge announced "will be adjourned."
5. "The jury" said Al Tarvin of *The Star* "was handpicked."

RULE 8: **Use a comma where it is necessary to prevent a misunderstanding.**

Before eating, the cat prowled through the barn.

PRACTICE 7

Insert Necessary Commas

In each of the following sentences, insert commas wherever they are needed. Check your answers against those in the Answer Key on p. 439.

1. Kicking the child was carried off to bed.
2. To Maria Florence Suzuki was the boss from hell.
3. When you can come and visit us.
4. Whoever that is is going to be surprised.
5. Skin cancer seldom kills doctors say.

EXERCISE 1

Insert Necessary Commas

In each of the following sentences, insert commas wherever they are needed.

1. Fog-water collection is a relatively simple way to supply water to certain areas where water is scarce or polluted.

2. The collectors with screens made of a fine polypropylene mesh look like big volleyball nets.
3. The tiny water droplets which are blown sideways by the wind hit the screen and run down into a trough.
4. In El Tofo Chile 88 fog collectors supply clean water to the fishing village of Chungungo.
5. The El Tofo system on a high coastal ridge is the largest project so far.
6. Amazingly these collectors channel 13 000 litres of water per day to the village.
7. Once almost a ghost town Chungungo now boasts homes with running water and lush gardens.

EXERCISE 2 **Insert Necessary Commas**

In each of the following sentences, insert commas wherever they are needed.

1. The first games known as the British Empire Games attracted 400 competitors from eleven countries.
2. The Commonwealth Games were first held in Hamilton Ontario in 1930.
3. By 1978 during the Commonwealth Games in Edmonton nearly 1500 athletes from 41 countries competed.
4. Canada has been a leading supporter of these games which are held every four years.
5. Memorable performances feats by both Canadian and non-Canadian athletes have become a hallmark of the games.
6. In Edmonton Canadian athletes won 45 gold 31 silver and 33 bronze medals in 1978.
7. Next to the Olympics the Commonwealth Games are one of the world's best international competitions.

Other Marks of Punctuation

The Apostrophe

Use the apostrophe as follows:

RULE 1: **To form the possessive, add *'s* or just an apostrophe.**

A. Add *'s* to singular nouns:

the pen of the teacher = the teacher*'s* pen
the strategy of the boss = the boss*'s* strategy

Be careful to choose the right noun to make possessive. Always ask yourself *who* or *what* possesses something. In the phrases above, the teacher possesses the pen and the boss possesses the strategy.

As a rule, nouns that are inanimate things should not be in the possessive. Use a phrase with *of* instead.

Examples: the leg of the table (NOT the table's leg)
the smell of the sewer (NOT the sewer's smell)
the noise of the cars (NOT the cars' noise)

In common expressions that refer to time and measurements and in phrases suggesting personification, possessives are more and more acceptable:

a stone's throw
two weeks' vacation
New Year's resolution

Note these unusual possessives:

Hyphenated words: mother-in-law's advice
Joint possession: Rita and Ashley's television special
Individual possession: John's and Steve's ideas

B. Add *'s* to irregular plural nouns that do not end in *-s*.

the hats of the children = the children*'s* hats
the harness for the oxen = the oxen*'s* harness

C. Add *'s* to indefinite pronouns:

everyone*'s* responsibility
somebody*'s* wallet

Indefinite Pronouns			
anyone	everyone	no one	someone
anybody	everybody	nobody	somebody
anything	everything	nothing	something

Possessive pronouns in English (*his, hers, its, ours, yours, theirs, whose)* do *not* use an apostrophe.

Whose phone is this?
The phone is *his*.
The car is *theirs*.

D. Add only an apostrophe to regular plural nouns ending in *-s*.

the nests of the hornets = the hornet*s'* nests
the store of the brothers = the brother*s'* store

A few singular nouns ending in the *s* or *z* sound are awkward-sounding if another *s* sound is added. You may, in these cases, drop the final *s*. Let your ear help you make the decision, and be consistent with your choice.

Jones' car or Jones's car

RULE 2: **To form certain plurals in order to prevent confusion, use *'s*.**

Numbers: 100's
Letters: a's and b's
Years: 1800's or 1800s
Abbreviations: Ph.D.'s
Words referred to in text: He uses too many *and*'s in his writing.

Be sure *not* to use the apostrophe to form a plural in any case other than these.

RULE 3: **To show where letters have been omitted in contractions, use an apostrophe.**

cannot = can't
should not = shouldn't
will not = won't (the only contraction that changes its spelling)
I am = I'm
she will = she'll
it is/it has = it's

Note: The word *its* (without the apostrophe) is a possessive pronoun.

Example: The dog buried its bone.

PRACTICE 1

Using the Apostrophe

Fill in each of the blanks below using the rules you have just studied for uses of the apostrophe. Check your answers against those in the Answer Key on p. 439.

1. shirts for boys ______________ shirts
2. the house of them ______________ house
3. the bakery of Grandpa Moses ______________ bakery
4. the house of Antony and Maria (joint possession) ______________ house
5. the idea of nobody ______________ idea
6. The book belongs to him. The book is ______________.

7. in the century of 1700 — in the ________________
8. It is their choice. — ________________ their choice.
9. the nightlife of Vancouver — ________________ nightlife
10. The dress of Wendy — ________________ dress

PRACTICE 2

Using the Apostrophe

Fill in each of the blanks below using the rules you have just studied for uses of the apostrophe. Check your answers against those in the Answer Key on p. 439.

1. the voice of Don Cherry — ________________ voice
2. the flight of the geese — the ________________ flight
3. the jackets of Carol and Tess (individual possession) — ________________ jackets
4. the CD of somebody — ________________ CD
5. The drums belong to her. — The drums are ________________.
6. the terrible year of two — the terrible ________________
7. We cannot leave yet. — We ________________ leave yet.

EXERCISE 1

Using the Apostrophe

Fill in each of the blanks below using the rules you have just studied for uses of the apostrophe.

1. the ice cream of Ben and Jerry — ________________ ice cream
2. the spirit of the class — the ________________ spirit
3. the centre for women — the ________________ centre
4. the wish of everybody — ________________ wish
5. The ideas belong to them. — The ideas are ________________.
6. The student mixes up *b* and *d*. — The student mixes up his ________________.
7. I will not leave this house. — I ________________ leave this house.
8. the revenue of the company — the ________________ revenue
9. the paw of the doggie — the ________________ paw
10. the policies of Ridge School and Orchard School (individual possession) — ________________ policies

EXERCISE 2

Using the Apostrophe

Add apostrophes where necessary in the following passage:

> Doesnt anyone care about the environment? When Canadians were asked to identify the major problem facing their country today, only 3 percent cited that issue as a major concern. Economic questions have pushed environmental concerns aside. Its clear that environmental issues are something the vast majority of Canadas people care about, but theyre fading from the forefront as preserving a high standard of living becomes the focus of our concerns.

EXERCISE 3

Using the Apostrophe

Add apostrophes where necessary in the following passage:

> Many college and university students dont accept the fact that theyll be faced with a huge debt when they graduate. Many have part-time jobs, even if they cant see making careers out of these positions, and wont accept anything less than an opportunity to gain experience for future employment situations. While students attitudes are changing, however, students education is still more important than their eventual debt load.

Quotation Marks

Use quotation marks as follows:

RULE 1: **For a direct quotation**

> "Please," I begged, "don't go away."

Not for an indirect quotation:

> I begged her not to go away.

RULE 2: **For material copied word for word from a source**

> According to Statistics Canada, "Families or individuals spending 58.5 percent or more of their pre-tax income on food, clothing, and shelter are in financial difficulty."

RULE 3: **For titles of shorter works such as short stories, one-act plays, poems, articles in magazines and newspapers, songs, essays, and chapters of books**

> "A Modest Proposal," an essay by Jonathan Swift, is a masterpiece of satire.
> Mavis Gallant wrote the short story "In Youth Is Pleasure" in 1975.

Titles of longer works such as novels, full-length plays, and names of magazines or newspapers are underlined when handwritten. When word-processed or published, these titles appear in italics: *Maclean's* magazine, *Country Living*.

RULE 4: **For words used in a special way**

> "Duckie" is a term of affection used by the British, the way we would use the word "honey."

PRACTICE 1

Insert Necessary Quotation Marks

In each of the following sentences, insert quotation marks wherever they are needed. Check your answers against those in the Answer Key on p. 439.

1. The Hot House is one of the stories contained in Rosemary Sullivan's *More Stories by Canadian Women.*
2. Nellie McClung said I'll never believe I'm dead until I see it in the papers.
3. The prime minister told his caucus that they would have to settle the problem in the next few days.
4. To diss is a slang term meaning to show disrespect.
5. She read the article Whiz Kids in *The Review.*

If these five sentences were handwritten or typed, which words would have to be underlined?

The Semicolon

Use the semicolon as follows:

RULE 1: **To join two independent clauses whose ideas and sentence structure are related**

> He decided to consult the map; she decided to ask the next pedestrian she saw.

RULE 2: **To combine two sentences using an adverbial conjunction**

> He decided to consult the map; however, she decided to ask the next pedestrian she saw.

RULE 3: **To separate items in a series when the items themselves contain commas**

> I had lunch with Linda, my best friend; Mrs. Zhangi, my English teacher; and Jan, my sister-in-law.

Notice in the last example that if only commas had been used, the reader might think six people had gone to lunch.

PRACTICE 2

Using Semicolons

In each of the following sentences, insert a semicolon wherever one is needed. Check your answers against those in the Answer Key on p. 440.

1. One of the best ways to remember a vacation is to take numerous photos one of the best ways to recall the contents of a book is to take notes.

2. The problem of street crime must be solved otherwise the number of vigilantes will increase.
3. The meal was composed of bruschetta, an appetizer roast duck, the house specialty and lemon mousse, a tart dessert.
4. The bank president was very cordial however he would not approve the loan.
5. New methods of production are being used in the factories of Japan eventually they will be common in this country as well.

The Colon

Use the colon as follows:

RULE 1: **After a *complete* sentence when the material that follows is a list, an illustration, or an explanation**

A. A list

> Please order the following items: five dozen pencils, 20 rulers, and five rolls of tape.

Notice that no colon is used when there is not a complete sentence before the colon:

> The courses I am taking this semester are English Composition, Introduction to Psychology, Art Appreciation, and Survey of Canadian Literature.

B. An illustration or explanation

> She was an exceptional child: at seven she was performing on the concert stage.

RULE 2: **Following the salutation of a business letter:**

> To whom it may concern:
> Dear Madam President:

RULE 3: **In telling time**

> We will eat at 5:15.

RULE 4: **Between the title and subtitle of a book, article, essay, etc.**

> *Plain English Please: A Rhetoric*
> "Hemingway: His Foreshadowed Suicide"

PRACTICE 3

Using Colons

In each of the following sentences, insert colons wherever they are needed. Check your answers against those in the Answer Key on p. 440.

1. Two Canadian-born comedians have achieved great success in the United States Jim Carrey and Mike Myers.
2. The official has one major flaw in his personality greed.

3. The restaurant has lovely homemade desserts such as German chocolate layer cake and baked Alaska.
4. The college offers four courses in English literature Romantic Poetry, Shakespeare's Plays, The British Short Story, and The Modern Novel.
5. Arriving at 615 in the morning, Marlene brought me a sausage-and-cheese pizza, ginger ale, and a litre of ice cream.

The Hyphen

Use the hyphen as follows:

RULE 1: **Use a hyphen with two or more words that go together before the noun to act as one adjective.**

I am a second-year student.
She is a well-known actor.

If the group of words that describes the noun comes after the noun, do not use a hyphen.

Example: The actor is well known.

If the group of words contains an *-ly* adverb, do not hyphenate.

Example: The dimly lit diner closed every night at eleven.

RULE 2: **Use a hyphen at the end of a line to divide a word between syllables.** Make sure you divide the word at the right place. Check a dictionary if you're not sure. Otherwise, avoid splitting words altogether. Never split a one-syllable word.

When Farah saw her boyfriend kissing another woman, she walked away from him for good.

RULE 3: **Hyphens are used in some compound words.**
Other compound words are not hyphenated. There is no rule to determine which is which. Use a dictionary to make the right decision. Where there is disagreement between dictionaries, pick one spelling and be consistent in your own writing.

The following are word spellings upon which all dictionaries agree:

father-in-law	hairbrush
trade-in	stepmother

RULE 4: **Use hyphens with two-word numbers from twenty-one to ninety-nine.**

thirty-seven
seventy-three

RULE 5: **Use hyphens in words that contain the prefixes *self, ex,* and *all*; prefixes that are followed by proper nouns; and the suffix *elect.***

self-respect, self-confidence
ex-husband, ex-police officer
all-Canadian cast
anti-Catholic
Premier-elect Dalton McGuinty

EXERCISE

Inserting Hyphens Where Necessary

In each of the following sentences, insert a hyphen wherever it is necessary.

1. The students in third year weren't in class today, but all the second year students were.
2. Kelly caught the ball in her baseball glove despite its war torn appearance,
3. The all American company of actors was scared to come to Canada because of SARS.
4. Her low self esteem caused her to stay with her husband despite the repeated beatings he inflicted on her.
5. The widely acclaimed impressionist painter received a standing ovation before he accepted his 32 thousand dollar cheque.
6. Julia's forty four year old ex boyfriend returned all thirty three compact discs she had borrowed when she was enrolled in her postgraduate university program.
7. Faisal bought the all purpose cleaner that his mother in law recommended when he and his wife were still a happily married couple.

The Dash and Parentheses

Like the comma, both the dash and parentheses can be used to show an interruption of the main idea. The particular form you choose depends on the degree of interruption.

Use the dash for a less formal and more emphatic interruption of the main idea.

He came—I thought—by car.
She arrived—and I know this for a fact—in a pink Cadillac.
I could see you this weekend—for example, Saturday.

Use parentheses to insert extra information that some of your readers might want to know but that is not essential to the main idea. Such information is not emphasized.

Timothy Findley (1930–2002) wrote *The Wars.*

Plea-bargaining (see page 28) was developed to speed court verdicts.

PRACTICE

Using Dashes or Parentheses

In each of the following sentences, insert dashes or parentheses wherever they are needed. Check your answers against those in the Answer Key on p. 440.

1. Herbert Simon is and I don't think this is an exaggeration a genius.
2. George Eliot her real name was Mary Ann Evans wrote Silas Marner.
3. You should in fact I insist see a doctor.
4. Health Canada's Web site has suggestions to help smokers quit visit www.infotobacco.com.
5. Mass media television, radio, movies, magazines, and newspapers are able to transmit information over a wide range and to a large number of people.

Chapter Review Exercises

PRACTICE 1

Punctuation Overview

In each of the following sentences, insert marks of punctuation wherever they are needed. Check your answers against those in the Answer Key on p. 440.

1. To measure crime, sociologists have used three different techniques official statistics, victimization surveys, and self-report studies.
2. David is one of the best-loved poems of Earle Birney.
3. That show uses one thing I hate a laugh track.
4. Farley Mowat has written numerous books for adults however, he also writes very popular books for children.
5. Tuberculosis also known as consumption has been nearly eliminated by medical science.
6. The Victorian Period 1837–1901 saw a rapid expansion in industry.
7. He told me I remember the day that he would never give up.

PRACTICE 2

Punctuation Overview

In each of the following sentences, insert marks of punctuation wherever they are needed. Check your answers against those in the Answer Key on p. 440.

1. Many young people have two feelings about science and technology awe and fear.
2. Mr. Doyle the realtor Mrs. Tong the bank officer and Ivan Petroff the lawyer are the three people to help work out the real-estate transaction.
3. The book was entitled English Literature The Victorian Age.
4. My computer, she said, has been crashing all day.
5. She brought a bathing suit, towel, sunglasses, and several books to the beach.
6. The meeting to discuss a pay increase I'll believe it when I see it has been rescheduled for Friday.

7. The complex lab experiment has these two major problems: too many difficult calculations and too many variables.

EXERCISE 1

Editing for Correct Punctuation

Read the following paragraph and insert the following marks of punctuation wherever they are needed:

a. commas to separate items in a series
b. comma with coordinating conjunction to combine sentences
c. comma after introductory words, phrases, or clauses
d. commas around words that interrupt main idea
e. comma to set off spoken words
f. parentheses
g. quotation marks
h. lines under titles of full-length works of art
i. semicolon
j. apostrophe

Tom Thomson 1877–1917 is often remembered as the artist of Canada's North. He was born on August 4 1877 near Leith Ontario. During the twenties Thomson apprenticed as a machinist enrolled in business college and then spent a few years in Seattle working as an engraver. In 1906 he took art lessons and first used oil paint. His first important painting done in 1917 and titled A Northern Lake was sold for $250 a great deal of money in those days. Thomson led the vanguard of a new movement in Canadian art. One reviewer said Thomson paints a world of phenomena of colour and of form which will not be touched by another artist. Thomson drowned at Canoe Lake Algonquin Park July 8 1917. Among his many works are Ottawa by Moonlight Autumn's Garland and Jackpine.

EXERCISE 2

Editing for Correct Punctuation

Read the following paragraph and insert the following marks of punctuation wherever they are needed:

a. commas to separate items in a series
b. comma with coordinating conjunction to combine sentences
c. comma after introductory words, phrases, or clauses
d. commas around words that interrupt main idea
e. comma in numbers of 1000 or larger
f. parentheses
g. quotation marks
h. lines under titles of full-length works of art
i. semicolon
j. colon
k. apostrophe

Albert Schweitzer was a brilliant German philosopher physician musician clergyman missionary and writer on theology. Early in his career he based his philosophy on what he called reverence for life. He felt a deep sense of obligation to serve humanity. His accomplishments as a humanitarian were great consequently he was awarded the Nobel Peace Prize in 1952. Before Schweitzer was 30 he had won an international reputation as a writer on theology as an organist and authority on organ building as an interpreter of the works of Johann Sebastian Bach and as an authority on Bachs life. When he became inspired to become a medical missionary he studied medicine at the university in Strasbourg Germany. He began his work in French Equatorial Africa now called Gabon in 1913 where his first consulting room was a chicken coop. Over the years he built a large hospital where thousands of Africans were treated yearly. He used his $33 000 Nobel Prize money to expand the hospital and set up a leper colony in fact he even designed all the buildings. One of Schweitzers many famous books which you might like to find in the library is entitled Out of My Life and Thought. His accomplishments were so many music medicine scholarship theology and service to humanity.

Working Together: *Designing Punctuation Tests*

Work with a group of your classmates. Each group in the class will make up an exam to test the other students' knowledge of punctuation. From any book, choose a paragraph that uses a variety of punctuation. Have one person from the group carefully write out or type the paragraph without its punctuation. Then make enough copies so a group or the entire class can take the test. Is your test a fair one? Is it too easy or too hard? Does it cover the material studied in this chapter?

CHAPTER TWELVE

12

Capitalization

QUICK QUIZ

Test yourself on your knowledge of capitalization. Correct any errors of capitalization in the following sentences. Answers are in the margin.

1. I am hoping to go to University in British Columbia in the fall, but if I can't, I'll have more money to spend at christmas.

   ____

   ____

2. My Doctor's appointment this afternoon is with doctor Shari Mohammed.

   ____

   ____

3. The pacific ocean is beautiful at Sunset.

   ____

   ____

4. I told the umpire, "you don't know the rules of baseball any more than grandma does!"

   ____

   ____

5. Sam and i have travelled through the rockies by Train three times now, for they are absolutely breathtaking.

   ____

   ____

Answers:
1. university, Christmas
2. doctor's, Doctor (or Dr.)
3. Pacific Ocean, sunset
4. You, Grandma
5. I, Rockies, train

Many students are often confused or careless about the use of capital letters. Sometimes they capitalize words without thinking, or they capitalize "important" words without really understanding what makes them important enough to deserve a capital letter. The question of when to capitalize words becomes easier to answer when you study the following rules and carefully apply them to your own writing.

Ten Basic Rules for Capitalization

RULE 1: **Capitalize the first word of every sentence.**

RULE 2: **Capitalize the names of specific things and places.**

Specific buildings

I went to the Jamestown Post Office.
but
I went to the post office.

Specific streets, cities, states, countries

She lives on Elam Avenue.
but
She lives on the same street as my mom and dad.

Specific organizations

He collected money for the Canadian Cancer Society.
but
Janice joined more than one club at the school.

Specific institutions

The loan is from the Royal Bank of Canada.
but
The loan is from one of the banks in town.

Specific bodies of water

My uncle fishes every summer on Lake Winnipeg.
but
My uncle spends every summer at the lake.

RULE 3: **Capitalize days of the week, months of the year, and holidays. Do *not* capitalize the names of seasons.**

The second Monday in October is Thanksgiving Day.
but
I cannot wait until spring.

RULE 4: **Capitalize the names of all languages, nationalities, races, religions, deities, and sacred terms.**

My friend who is Ethiopian speaks very little English.
The *Koran* is the sacred book of Islam.

RULE 5: **In a title, capitalize the first word, the last word, and every other word *except* articles, prepositions, and coordinating conjunctions (*and, but, or, nor, yet*).**

"Recognizing Subjects and Verbs" and "Revising and Editing" are chapters in the textbook *The Canadian Writer's Workplace.*

RULE 6: **Capitalize the first word of a direct quotation.**

The teacher said, "You have been chosen for the part."
but
"You have been chosen," she said, "for the part."

Note: for is not capitalized because it is not the beginning of the sentence in quotation marks.

RULE 7: **Capitalize historical events, periods, and documents.**

the Rebellion of 1837
the Great Depression
the *Canadian Charter of Rights and Freedoms*

RULE 8: **Capitalize the words *north, south, east,* and *west* when they are used as places rather than as directions.**

He comes from the East.
but
The farm is about 40 kilometres west of Weyburn.

RULE 9: **Capitalize people's names.**
Proper names

George Hendrickson

Professional titles when they immediately precede the person's proper name

Judge Samuelson	*but*	the judge
Professor Shapiro	*but*	the professor

- Do not capitalize a title if it follows the name:

George Shapiro, professor of English

Term for a relative (like *mother, sister, nephew, uncle*) when it is used in the place of the proper name

I told Grandfather I would meet him later.

- Notice that terms for relatives are not capitalized if a pronoun, article, or adjective is used with the name.

I told my grandfather I would meet him later.

RULE 10: **Capitalize brand names.**

Band-Aid
Kleenex

Band-Aid and *Kleenex* are product names and therefore are proper nouns.

PRACTICE

Capitalization

Capitalize wherever it is necessary. Check your answers against those in the Answer Key on p. 440.

1. The italian student got a job in the school cafeteria.
2. Our train ride through the canadian rockies was fabulous.
3. The author often made references in his writing to names from the bible.
4. A student at the university of alberta was chosen for the national award.
5. My uncle's children always have a party on hallowe'en.
6. I met the president of bell canada last friday at a convention in winnipeg, manitoba.
7. The cobalt-60 cancer therapy unit was invented by a canadian, dr. donald green.
8. My niece said, "why don't you consider moving farther south if you hate the winter so much?"
9. The canadian auto workers voted not to go on strike over the new contract.
10. The book women of the klondike tells the story of the late-1890s gold rush in the north.

EXERCISE

Capitalization

Capitalize wherever it is necessary. Put in lower case any capital letters that are incorrect.

1. Some people think the Cabot trail on Cape Breton island is the most spectacular drive on the North American Continent.
2. I'm taking five courses right now, but math 101 is my favourite.
3. I love the Text called *Canadian Writer's workplace*; I've already read 20 of 28 Chapters.
4. Morris C. Shumiatcher is a Lawyer and Civil Rights Spokesperson who graduated from the University Of Calgary.
5. George Orwell wrote the novel *nineteen eighty-four* about a Government that punishes its people for thinking certain thoughts.
6. Born in Bombay, India, Writer Rohinton Mistry was raised in that City's Parsi Community.
7. The black honda accord and the white ford escape have collided at the Intersection of Chapel street and Bakersville avenue.
8. "I feel your pain," wrote rabbi Wittstein of Temple Israel of london to the muslim community, "And offer you whatever understanding, sympathy and anger I possess..."
9. Roman Polanski won an oscar for best director in 2002, but was unable to receive the award in person because if he enters the United States, he would be arrested for statutory rape.
10. Socrates was a greek teacher who is considered one of the founders of western philosophy.

Working Together: *Designing Capitalization Tests*

Work with a group of your classmates. Each group in the class will make up an exam to test the other students' knowledge of capitalization. From any book, choose a paragraph that uses a variety of capitalization. Have one person from the group carefully write out or type the paragraph without its capitalization. Then make enough copies so a group or the entire class can take the test. Is your test a fair one? Is it too easy or too hard? Does it cover the material studies in this chapter?

CHAPTER THIRTEEN

13

Unit I Review: Using All You Have Learned

Editing Sentences for Errors

In the following exercises, you will find all the types of sentence problems that you have studied thus far.

Major Sentence Errors: Fragments
Run-ons
Incorrect punctuation
Sentence parts that do not work together

PRACTICE 1

Editing Sentences for Errors

The following examples contain several types of errors studied in Unit I. If you think the example is a complete and correct sentence, mark it with a *C*. If the example has an error, correct it. More than one correct answer is possible for each example. Check your answers against those in the Answer Key on p. 441. An example is done for you.

Incorrect: A group of Roma people who now live in Ireland.

Correct: A group of Roma people now live in Ireland.

or

A group of Roma people, who now live in Ireland, make their living by repairing pots and pans.

1. Roma now living in many countries of the world.

____

____

2. The international community of scientists agree that these Roma originally came from India thousands of years ago.

____

____

3. After the original Roma people left India they went to Persia there they divided into groups.

   ____

   ____

4. One branch of Roma went West to Europe the other group decided to go East.

   ____

   ____

5. In the middle ages (476–1453), some Roma people lived in a fertile area of Greece called little egypt.

   ____

   ____

6. Roma often found it hard to gain acceptance in many countries because of their wandering lifestyle.

   ____

   ____

7. Today Roma families may be found from Canada to Chile living much as his ancestors did thousands of years ago.

   ____

   ____

PRACTICE 2 Editing Sentences for Errors

The following examples contain sentence errors studied in Unit I. If you think an example is a complete and correct sentence, mark it with a *C*. If the example has an error, correct it. More than one correct answer is possible for each example. An example is done for you. Check your answers against those in the Answer Key on p. 441.

Incorrect: Science fiction writers have imagined magic rays that can destroy entire cities, but in recent years a magic ray in the form of laser beams have become scientific fact.

Correct: Science fiction writers have imagined magic rays that can destroy entire cities, but in recent years a magic ray in the form of laser beams has become scientific fact.

1. The laser beam a miracle of modern science already has many practical uses in today's world.

   ____

   ____

2. Laser beams are narrow, highly concentrated beams of light that burns brighter than the light of the sun.

3. Scientists have found many possible military uses for the laser, but they are hoping it can be converted into constructive uses.

4. John Polanyi, Canadian winner of the 1986 Nobel Prize for chemistry, conducted early experiments on the use of lasers.

5. The possibility of making a laser was first described in 1958 and two years later in California the first laser beam was created.

6. Since they are so precise, laser beams are used in medicine to help make a specific diagnosis and to perform operations such as repairing delicate retinas and the removal of cancerous tumours.

7. The future uses of the laser seems endless, and it is up to us to decide whether we want to use this invention for war or for peaceful purposes.

EXERCISE 1

Editing Sentences for Errors

The following examples contain sentence errors studied in Unit I. If you think an example is a complete and correct sentence, mark it with a *C*. If the example has an error, correct it. More than one correct answer is possible for each example. An example is done for you.

Incorrect: Frostbite an injury to the skin and underlying tissues is a serious danger in very cold weather.

Correct: Frostbite, an injury to the skin and underlying tissues, is a serious danger in very cold weather.

1. A common threat to outdoor adventurers frostbite can strike anyone who is not adequately protected against the cold.

   ____

   ____

2. Risk factors are of three types exposure, faulty judgment, and underlying medical conditions.

   ____

   ____

3. Ice crystals in the skin possibly starting to form at –6°C.

   ____

   ____

4. Symptoms of frostbite includes: cold numbness and a feeling of clumsiness or heaviness in the affected part of the body.

   ____

   ____

5. The first thing to do is find a warm shelter and remove any wet clothing.

   ____

   ____

6. Prevention measures includes wearing proper clothing, educating yourself about weather conditions, and awareness of risk factors.

   ____

   ____

7. Frostbite injury which gets worse with time should be treated immediately.

   ____

   ____

EXERCISE 2 Making Sentence Parts Work Together

Each of the following sentences has a part that does not work with the rest of the sentence. Find the error and correct it. There may be more than one correct answer for each sentence.

1. Two Statistics Canada studies, which have been reported recently on the CBC television network, links stress and obesity now and health problems later in life.

   ____

   ____

2. Suffering from stress and obesity, the researchers found that Canadians will probably suffer major health problems as soon as six years later.

____

____

3. People who suffer from stress and obesity become a perfect candidate for health problems such as arthritis and rheumatism, chronic bronchitis or emphysema, and stomach or intestinal ulcers.

____

____

4. One study shows that for men, diseases also include heart disease, and for a woman, asthma and migraine.

____

____

5. According to one of the studies, stress in men appeared to be worse where economic issues are concerned: job loss, demotions and taking pay cuts, for example.

____

____

6. An obese adult's chance of suffering from arthritis is 60 per cent higher than an adult who is not obese.

____

____

7. They say stress goes down with age and up in low-income people.

____

____

Editing Paragraphs for Errors

EXERCISE 1 Making Sentence Parts Work Together

Read the following paragraph. Look for errors in agreement, for lack of parallel structure, and for misplaced or dangling modifiers, and then rewrite your corrected version. More than one correct answer is possible.

Cowboys became important in the United States after the American Civil War who lived on large ranches in Texas, Montana, and other western states. Canada, too, had its cowboys working on ranches on the prairies. One of the traditional names for cowboys are "cowpokes" although they prefer to be called "cowhands." The equipment for cowboys came into use because of his many practical needs. The wide-brimmed cowboy hat served as a bucket to hold water, as a sort of whip to drive cattle, and waving to other cowboys a few hills away. Cowboys began to wear tight trousers because they did not want loose pants to catch in bushes as they chased cattle. The rope is a cowboy's most important tool since they use it to catch cattle, pull wagons, tie up equipment, and even killing snakes. The famous roundup, which takes place twice a year, are important because cattle are separated, classified, and selected for market. When cowboys get together for such a roundup, they often hold a rodeo as a celebration. Rodeos give cowboys opportunities to compete in riding bareback, wrestling steer, and to rope calves. The Calgary Stampede is the modern result of these rodeos.

EXERCISE 2 Editing Paragraphs for Errors

Correct all the punctuation and grammatical errors in the following paragraph. More than one correct answer is possible.

Once upon a time whenever I tried to make my writing interesting and imaginative with all sorts of similes and metaphors and colourful language I forgot about my grammar and spelling my essays were full of sentence fragments comma splices and run-ons moreover my syntax was always scrambled even I had trouble figuring out what I had intended to say originally although I could tell that I had started with brilliant ideas help has finally arrived however since I have done all the exercises in my grammar book I now have perfect command of English grammar whereas one time I bit my nails when I handed in an assignment I worry no more no longer do I need to worry about essays being handed back bleeding to death after being savaged by some sadistic English teacher wielding his or her red pen no longer will my sleep be curtailed by hours of tedious rewrites moreover from now on I'm expecting straight As all the way.

EXERCISE 3 Editing Paragraphs for Errors

Correct all the punctuation, capitalization and grammatical errors in the following paragraphs. More than one correct answer is possible.

Sleep is one of those things you never think about. As long as you're getting your full 40 winks at night. As soon as a bout of insomnia hits though sleep is the only thing on your mind. The ancient greeks had a god of sleep called hypnos who could appear as a bird, child, or friendly warrior those images don't suggest sleep to modern people though we prefer fields of sheep and mr. sandman.

Since the greeks scientists have made much progress in unravelling the secrets of sleep but many mysteries remain. They can't explain for example exactly how we fall asleep. Or wake up. Or what dreams are. However they know a lot about insomnia and other sleep disorder. Such as narcolepsy, sudden attacks of deep sleep, sleep apnea (the sleeper stops breathing for several seconds at a time) and, sleepwalking. Which are more amusing to hear about than to experience.

Millions of people suffer from insomnia either chronically, or from time to time. They will try anything to break the curse and science and folklore offers them a carload of choices everything from warm milk and lavender sachets to sleeping pills and sleep clinics. Not that any of these things help the true insomniac of course. And, how maddening it must be for someone who hasnt slept in weeks to come across a bus passenger fast asleep sitting up. Surrounded by strangers. These innocents are like people who stay skinny without having to diet.

Working Together: *Designing Editing Tests*

Work with a group of your classmates. Each group in the class will make up an exam to test the other students' knowledge of **fragments, run-ons, lack of parallel structure, and dangling and misplaced modifiers**. From any book, choose a paragraph. After the group has deliberately made a variety of the above-listed errors in the paragraph, have one person from the group carefully write out or type the paragraph with the errors intact. Then make enough copies so a group or the entire class can take the test. Is your test a fair one? Is it too easy or too hard? Does it cover the material studied in Unit I?

UNIT TWO

The Writing Process

The Four Stages of Writing

Few people can go to a desk and write the perfect composition from scratch without giving any of it even a second look. Most people need to go about the process in stages. This chapter introduces the writing process in terms of four stages: 1) prewriting, 2) outlining, 3) the rough draft, and finally, 4) postwriting (revising, editing, and proofreading). The chapter begins with some prewriting techniques designed to generate writing ideas and ends with the part of the postwriting stage that is proofreading. Revising and editing (parts of stage four) are covered in this chapter but are examined in more depth in Chapter 18 of this unit.

Stage One: Prewriting

How many times have you heard yourself say, "I don't know what else to write"? Well, it's possible you didn't think you did at the time, but what if you really did without being aware of it? The following **prewriting techniques** are designed to retrieve your thoughts and ideas and make sense of feelings you might have so that you can start exploring them on paper. These techniques include brainstorming, freewriting, keeping a journal, and clustering. Use any, all, or none of them, whatever works for you.

Brainstorming

One of the best ways of collecting ideas is through **brainstorming.** Brainstorming is simple—all you need is some time. It is best accomplished in groups of four or more people, but numbers aren't as important as the ideas you generate.

Here's how brainstorming works:

1. Compile a list of ideas, as many of them as you can.
2. Don't criticize any idea initially. That will come later.
3. If any ideas generate objections, work on developing alternatives to the ideas rather than simply discarding them.
4. Use ideas to stimulate discussion and to generate other ideas.
5. Make sure that everyone in the group completely understands the ideas generated.
6. Put your list of ideas aside for a while in order to think about them at your leisure. This "back burner" process often generates other ideas.

When you brainstorm, allow your mind to roam freely around the topic, letting one idea lead to another, even if the ideas seem unrelated or irrelevant. Jot down every word and phrase that pops into your mind when you think about your topic.

Here is what a brainstorming process might look like.
First identify a topic:

Hockey

Then, what things come to mind when you think of this topic?

coaches	referees
Stanley Cup	new drafts
Maple Leafs	Vancouver Canucks

Now, you may want to pick out a couple of these ideas and combine them:

Maple Leafs and Stanley Cup

Expand the idea by reflecting on what you know and/or what you believe.

The Maple Leafs can't seem to win the Stanley Cup.

At this point, a question might arise:

Why can't the Leafs win the Stanley Cup?

A possible answer suggests a topic sentence for a paragraph or a thesis statement for an essay:

If they want to win the Stanley Cup, the Maple Leafs need a full-time head coach and a full-time general manager who get along with each other.

Freewriting

In freewriting, you don't have to worry about spelling, grammar, focus, or organization. You just write. Write whatever comes to mind. Let a force beyond your control guide your pen, be it your unconscious, your heart, or the spirit world. The idea here is to generate ideas for writing a composition at a later stage. In the meantime, just have fun exploding with words on paper.

Keeping a Journal

When handing in her journal at the end of a semester, a young female college student once said, "The journal was better than any man I'd ever known. It listened to absolutely everything I had to say!"

You may have kept some kind of diary in your childhood. Each entry may have started with "Dear Diary, I experienced my first French kiss today. It was sloppy but amazing..." Most diaries are logs of what goes on in the daily lives of their writers. As students get older, their diaries may evolve into journals in which the format is similar, but in which the content contains more depth and other engaging qualities. Rather than mention everything you did yesterday in last night's diary entry, for example, you might concentrate on something that struck you forcefully. It may have been a dream you had that preoccupied you all day. It may have been something in a conversation you'd overheard between two other students in front of you in a bus on the way to school. Perhaps what you had heard made you angry or sad or hopeful or, at the very least, contemplative, causing one of your friends in the cafeteria, or your professor in class, to try to shake you out of a daze.

Your Emotions Can Serve As a Guide

Think of a teacher you remember well from your past. Chances are it was someone who caused you to feel a great deal of emotion, either positive or negative. It may be a teacher who made you feel stupid, or a teacher who forced you to wear a dunce cap and to stand in the corner for three hours. Or on the more positive side, it may be a teacher who encouraged you to follow a certain path because of a talent he or she detected in you that your parents never did. Emotion is often associated with memory. The same can be said for people whom we've dated in the past. We seem to remember some girlfriends/boyfriends more than others. Those with whom we experienced strong emotions are probably the ones we tend to remember the most, no matter how long ago we were with them.

Your emotions, in this way, can be your guide when it comes to choosing the topic of your journal entries, and subsequently, your essays (if your professor gives you enough choice, that is). What moves you, after all, might cause you to want to write more and will give you more about which to write. You'll experience fewer writer's blocks, fewer occasions on which you're thinking, "I don't know what else to write."

Once you've used your emotions to help you choose the topics of your journal entries, you can take the opportunity to express these emotions in your journal. It's a place for you to sound off, so to speak. Without using too many expletives (especially four-letter swear words) at any given time, try to identify the emotion that you're feeling, for example, about the story or essay you just read for English class. Why do you think you're feeling this way? Does the story remind you of a personal experience? Do you strongly disagree with how the character dealt with his or her own situation because you would have done it very differently? What should the character have done, and why?

The journal, depending on what your professor says is necessary, doesn't have to be a response to literature all the time. If possible, try to respond in the same manner to a movie you just saw, a movie that made you very emotional. Be specific about what caused you to feel the way that you do, and then concentrate on your emotion. Again, let it guide you. Don't try to control the direction of your entry. Let your feelings take you on paper (or on your computer screen) to wherever they seem to want to take you. Try to see it as a fascinating inner journey into the unknown, a journey into your soul, or your unconscious. In fact, if you're good at it, the entire journal may become an intriguing expression of your mind, your psyche, or your personality. After all, "psyche" is Greek for the English word, "soul."

Buy a Journal That Doesn't Remind You of School

Are you a cat lover? Buy a journal with a hard cover on which there's a picture of a richly exotic Siamese cat! Or if it's cars you're into, find a journal whose cover features a picture of a sexy sports car. In any event, try to find something that you actually look forward to writing in every day or every night before you go to bed. Or take it with you in your knapsack so that you can record fresh ideas as they come to mind throughout the day. Do what works for you. Develop a relationship with your journal. (Try not to get caught talking to it out loud.) Just don't allow the journal to turn into a regular assignment that you feel forced to do just for the marks. Then it turns into meaningless drudgery, and chances are, you've let too much of life turn into this already. After all, the last thing that you should let transform into a burden is what should be, instead, a record of the journey of your mind.

If typing your entries on a computer screen is what you'd rather do, that's fine, too. Do whatever you feel most comfortable and most inspired doing. Do whatever is likely to help you cultivate that relationship, not just the one with your journal, but also the one with yourself that you'll find you are developing as you start to write on a regular basis. Writing regularly in your journal may help you not only with getting in touch with your feelings and solving your personal problems; it can also help you start writing more quickly and fluently whenever you're asked to complete a task that requires any writing at all. (See *Working Together* #3 on p. 155.)

Clustering (also known as Diagramming or Mapping)

Many students are visual learners in that they learn best by seeing something get done and not necessarily by reading or even by hearing (a lecture, tapes, etc.). The same can be said for generating ideas. Clustering is a kind of brainstorming but with the aid of a diagram. Identify a topic you either have to or want to write on. Write it in the middle of a blank page and circle it (see Figure 14.1). This topic becomes the central idea of your clustering activity. Draw a line from that circle downward, and write out another idea that is in any way related to the central topic. Don't allow yourself to think for a long time. Write down whatever comes to mind first. (What you write first does not bind you in any way to a particular outcome.) Continue to fashion a diagram in this way by building on it in several directions. Eventually, certain ideas will begin to take hold. In other words, one idea will begin to seem stronger than another depending on what is familiar and important to you at the time.

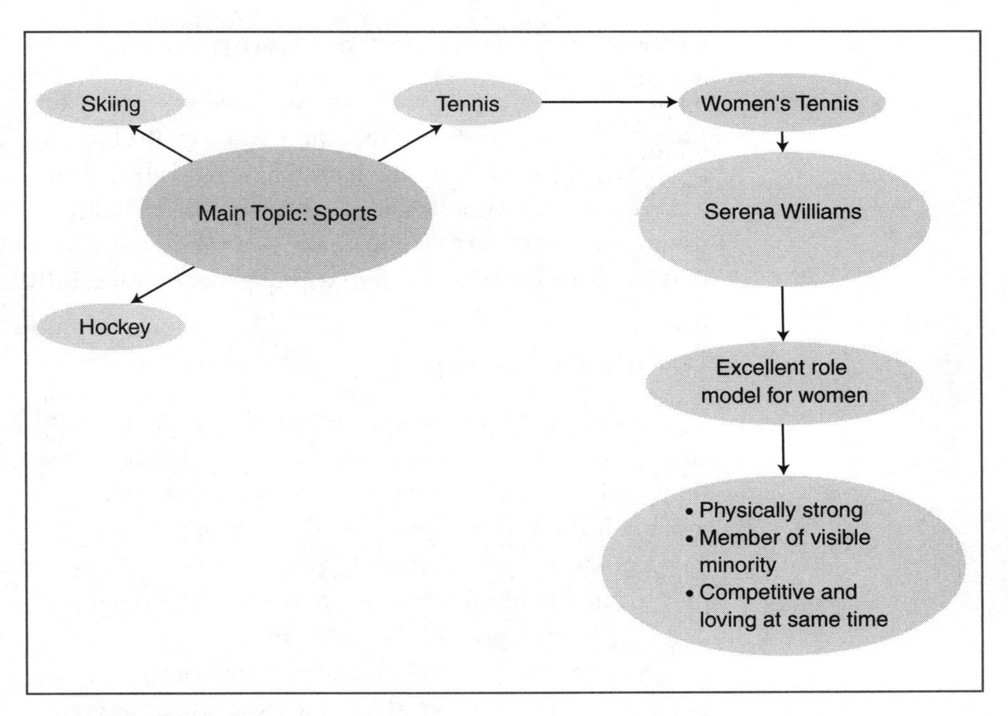

Figure 14.1: Clustering

Working from the cluster diagram, you could decide that you're interested in women's tennis, specifically in the top-ranked Serena Williams. If you feel strongly about the idea that Serena is an excellent role model for women, this might be a topic sentence for your paragraph.

Topic Sentence: Serena Williams, in her title as the No. 1 Women's Tennis Player in the World, is an excellent role model for women everywhere.

Then you might ask yourself the following question: Why is Serena an excellent role model for women?

The answer to this question might come in three parts, all of which can be used as the supporting points for your topic sentence:

Supporting points:

1. She is physically strong.
2. She's a member of a visible minority, but this has not held her back in tennis.
3. She is living proof that she can be competitive and loving all at the same time, as illustrated by her relationship with her sister.

Choosing the Topic and the Controlling Idea

Some people have no use for any of the above prewriting techniques. And that's fine. If you can come up with a topic and a controlling idea (your attitude toward the topic) right away, all the better. But remember, even if you can come up with a topic sentence without the use of prewriting techniques, these techniques can be useful for other reasons, too, such as establishing a writing routine if you have trouble getting started, dealing with personal upsets, difficulties, etc.

Use the Lists of Topics

Using the list of topics available in each chapter in Unit III on a different writing strategy (narration, description, etc.) or using ideas of your own, jot down two or three different topics that appeal to you. From this list of possibilities, select the topic you think would give you the best opportunity for writing. Which one do you feel most strongly about? Which one do you know the most about? Which one is most likely to interest your readers? Which one is best suited to being developed into a postsecondary essay?

Your next step is to decide what your controlling idea should be. What is the point you want to make about the experience? Was the experience humiliating, absurd, or hilarious?

Every Paragraph/Essay Must Be Persuasive

Where does the word "essay" come from? It comes from the French verb *essayer,* which means "to try." So what does the writer "try" to do in an essay but persuade the reader of a particular point of view no matter how "factual" the essay might seem? Even if the essay is considered more expository than argumentative, the writer still selects certain facts that he or she hopes will "persuade" the reader to see things the way the writer does. The essay, and even the single paragraph, no matter what type it happens to be, is an exercise in persuasion.

Two of the most critical elements the writer must consider in order to maximize the persuasive power of the composition are **audience** and **purpose**.

Audience

Your primary audience is, no doubt, your professor. But who else do you have in mind when you're writing your composition? If you're writing a children's story, chances are you're not going to be discussing the topic of venereal disease, nor will you be using five-syllable words. If you're writing a formal essay, you're not going to begin by saying, "I thought I'd spill a few thoughts down on some paper." Who your intended audience is, aside from the professor who will be marking your assignment, determines not only what you write, but also how you write it.

Purpose

The main reason for writing a composition at this stage in your life is probably to get a passing grade so that you can move on to the next level of English course in order to eventually graduate in your program. And the better your compositions are, the more likely you are to pass your English course. In the interest of pulling off a high-quality composition, be as mindful as you can of the specific reason for writing your particular composition.

This purpose should be crystal clear to you from the beginning. If it's not, it probably won't be clear to the reader either. First of all, is your purpose to inform, persuade, or entertain? Now that you've determined who your intended audience is, it's time you decided what you want that audience to think, do or feel. Perhaps you want your audience to do all of these things. Do you want your audience to do something or simply to understand your particular point of view toward a controversial topic? Regardless, the clearer you are on the purpose of your composition, the more effective your composition will be in the end.

Stage Two: Outlining (or Organizing)

Most texts on writing suggest elaborate outlines for paragraphs or essays, some of which seem to be as long as the paragraphs or essays themselves. Here, however, we suggest a very short outline, one that is clear and that saves you time, whether it is for a paragraph or an essay.

This outline consists of four complete sentences (sentences that appear exactly the same way within the final product).

Outline for a paragraph:

1. The topic sentence
2. The first major support sentence
3. The second major support sentence
4. The third major support sentence

Outline for an essay (of five paragraphs):

1. The thesis statement
2. The topic sentence of the second paragraph
3. The topic sentence of the third paragraph
4. The topic sentence of the fourth paragraph

Of course, by the time you've finished your composition, you may find that the wording of some or all of these sentences has changed because of improvements you've made along the way. The outline is meant to help you ensure that your composition contains persuasive power. If your outline doesn't seem logical, chances are, neither will your composition.

Stage Three: The Rough Draft

After you have applied a prewriting technique and you have organized the material into some kind of order, the time has come to write a rough draft.

A rough draft is just what its name implies: your first attempt to write your essay. The first attempt is "rough" because it will undoubtedly undergo many changes before it is finished: parts may be missing, some paragraphs will probably lack sufficient detail, and some parts may be repetitious or inappropriate. Some sentences are likely to sound awkward, and you will need to rewrite them later. The experienced writer expects all this and does not worry. All that you should try to accomplish in the rough draft is to let your mind relax and to get down on paper all of your initial ideas, according, of course, to some kind of plan as established by your work in stages one and two. These first ideas will provide the seeds that can be better developed later on.

As you work on your rough draft, you may work alone, with a group, with a peer tutor, or directly with your instructor. (An explanation of terms that relate to the paragraph can be found in Chapters 15 and 16, to the essay in Chapter 17, and to writing strategies in Chapters 21–28.) Here are some of the basic questions you should consider at this most important stage of your work:

1. Does the rough draft satisfy the conditions for paragraph or essay form? Does it have a topic sentence or thesis statement, adequate support, and a concluding sentence or paragraph? Are there at least five sentences in every paragraph that you've written, but not more than 12?
2. Does your paragraph or essay contain the writing strategy of your choice, such as narration, cause and effect, or description? Does it focus on a single event rather than on a general situation? Where does the action take place? Can the reader see it? What time of day, week, or year is it?
3. Have you put the details of the paragraph or essay in an order of a certain logic?
4. Does the paragraph or essay seem complete? Do any questions come to mind upon reading what you've written that you think should be answered here as well? Is there any material that is irrelevant and should be omitted?
5. Except for what is required in openings and closings, are there sentences or paragraphs that are repetitious?
6. Find several places where you can substitute better verbs or nouns. Add adjectives to give the reader better sensory images.
7. Can you think of a better way to begin or end your paragraph or essay?
8. Show your draft to at least two other readers, and ask for suggestions.

Armed with a first draft, you will now have something with which to work. No longer is there a blank paper staring you in the face. This accomplishment is a great relief to most writers, but remember, you are far from finished.

Stage Four: Postwriting (Revising, Editing, and Proofreading)

If you have worked hard at revising the rough draft, you will be delighted with the improvements as you write the second draft. For a detailed examination of this part of the writing process, see Chapter 18 (Revising and Editing).

Feedback is an important aid in each of the final stages of writing a paragraph/essay. A good way to help yourself see your own work more clearly is to put the writing aside for a little while, if you can. Then read what you have written aloud to someone else, or to yourself if no one else is available. You may be surprised at the number of places in your writing where you will hear the need for a change.

Revising and Editing the Rough Draft

If you have time, put aside your rough draft for a day or two. Then, when you reread it, you will look at it with a fresh mind. In this important revision stage, you should be concerned with how you have organized your ideas. At this point, do not yet worry about grammar, spelling, and punctuation.

Begin this important stage by asking these major questions:

1. Is the paragraph/essay unified? Do you stick to the topic you have announced? Go through the paragraph/essay and take out irrelevant material.
2. Do you repeat yourself? Look back over your paragraph/essay to determine whether you have given any information more than once. Even if you find you have used different words, you should delete the repeated material.
3. Does the paragraph/essay make sense? Can a reader follow your logic, your train of thought, and the course of events you describe? (Giving the rough draft to someone else to read will often answer this question for you.) If the paragraph/essay is confusing to the reader, you must find out where it goes wrong and why. Sometimes when you read your writing out loud, you will feel that one sentence has leaped to some point that doesn't follow from the sentence before.
4. For an essay, are the paragraphs roughly the same length? If you see one sentence presented as a paragraph, you know something is wrong. Aim to develop the point of each paragraph using at least five sentences. The first and last paragraphs are usually the shortest paragraphs in the essay, but they still require approximately five sentences each. Are they long enough without being too long? Check through your essay. Do you need to change the paragraphing? You may need to develop one paragraph more fully, or a one-sentence paragraph may really belong with the paragraph that comes before or after it.
5. Do you have all the components essential to a paragraph or types of paragraphs essential to an essay? For an essay, do you have the introduction with its thesis, at least three well-developed body paragraphs with transitional devices used to connect ideas, and a concluding paragraph? For a paragraph,

do you have a topic sentence that contains the topic of the paragraph and its controlling idea, strong supporting detail, and a concluding sentence?

6. Can you add more specific details? Most writing instructors agree that nearly every paper they read could be improved by adding more details, more descriptive verbs, and more sensory images to make the writing come alive. You should make sure there is sufficient detail throughout your paper, but for an essay none of the supportive detail should appear either in your introductory or concluding paragraphs.
7. Can you add dialogue or a quotation from someone?
8. Can you make the introduction, conclusion, or title more creative?

Proofreading

An important step still remains. You must check each sentence to see that it is correct, including grammar, spelling, and punctuation. In the rush to get a paper in on time, this step is often overlooked. If you take each sentence, starting with the last and going sentence by sentence backwards to the beginning, you will more easily be able to look at the sentence structure apart from the other aspects of the essay. Taking the time to look over a paper will usually result in your spotting several sentence-level errors. (As an exercise, you might want to correct errors of grammar, spelling, and punctuation in the first draft of the student essay on pages 197–198 of Chapter 18.)

Note: In many cases, your professor will not accept handwritten work, and you will be expected to submit a paper produced on a computer. Do not forget to proofread your work after it has been printed out; even if you have your paper typed for you, you are still responsible for errors. If there are not too many errors, you can make corrections neatly in ink on your printed copy before handing it in.

Proofreading

Check your second draft for

- Misspellings
- Fragments or run-ons
- Incorrect punctuation
- Consistency of voice and tense
- Verb problems
- Agreement
- Parallel structure

A checklist for the final preparation of a paragraph/essay follows.

Checklist for the Final Copy

1. Use 21.5 cm by 28 cm paper.
2. Type or write (whichever is required) on one side of the paper only.
3. Double-space.
4. Leave margins approximately 3.5 cm wide on each side of the paper.
5. Do not hyphenate words at ends of lines without consulting a dictionary for the correct division of words into syllables.
6. Centre the title at the top of the first page.
7. Put your name, the date, and the title of your paper on a separate title page, unless your professor says otherwise.
8. If you have more than one page, number them and staple or clip them together so they will not be lost.

Working Together: *Prewriting Activities*

1. Imagine yourself in the following situation: you and your classmates are guidance counsellors in a high school.You have been asked to produce a brochure that will be entitled "When a Young Person Quits School." This brochure is intended for students who are thinking of dropping out. You and the other counsellors meet to brainstorm on the topic.

   Divide into groups. Each group will brainstorm for fifteen minutes or so, and then come together again as a class. On the board make a final grouping of the ideas for this topic and discuss.
2. In groups or as a class, construct an outline for the essay to be called "When a Young Person Quits School." Use the information gathered in the brainstorming activity above. Either organize the information into main points and supporting details under those main points as it has been done above, or follow the suggestion of a brief outline under "Outlining" on page 151 in this chapter.
3. Think of a movie you've seen or a dream you've had that you have found yourself thinking about over and over again. It doesn't matter how long ago you've seen the movie or dreamt the dream because your long-term memory can be quite selective and doesn't work always on the basis of time. Even if you haven't decided to commit yourself to a journal yet, try writing a single entry in response to this movie or dream.

   Describe in writing that part of the movie or dream that you seem to be remembering over and over again. It's possible that this part you're remembering may be clamouring out to you to express it, to explore it, to somehow come to terms with it, and perhaps most importantly, to learn something from it, something important for you. After all, it's not the movie that's calling out to you. It's something in you that's doing the calling, perhaps something in your unconscious, the part programmed to tell the whole truth, and nothing but the truth about who you are, what you should be doing, where you should be going, and perhaps whom you should be seeing!

After you write about the part of the movie or dream that you remember the most, adding as much detail as you can, start to discuss how you feel. Then try to explain where those feelings are coming from. And finally, explore what that same place in your unconscious is trying to tell you about what you're supposed to learn from your preoccupation with that part of the movie or dream. You may find yourself the wiser, and the preoccupation with that part of the movie or dream may actually stop. Discuss the results of your activity with someone else in the class. Allow your partner to ask you questions about what you've just said; now it's the other person's turn to discuss his/her results with you.

CHAPTER FIFTEEN

15

The Paragraph I: Structure, Topic, and Controlling Idea

What Is a Paragraph?

DEFINITION ➤ A **paragraph** is a group of sentences that develops one main idea. A paragraph may stand by itself as a complete piece of writing, or it may be a section of a longer piece of writing, such as an essay.

No single rule will tell you how long a paragraph should be, but if a paragraph is too short, the reader will feel that basic information is missing. If the paragraph is too long, the reader will be bored or confused. An effective paragraph is always long enough to develop the main idea that is being presented. A healthy paragraph usually consists of at least five sentences and no more than ten or twelve sentences. You have undoubtedly read paragraphs in newspapers that are only one sentence long, but in fully developed writing, one sentence is usually not an acceptable paragraph.

What Does a Paragraph Look Like?

Margins, new-paragraph indication, and complete sentences are essential parts of paragraph form. Study the following paragraph from Elizabeth Pollet's "A Cold-Water Flat," to observe the standard form.

> I got the job. I worked in the bank's city collection department. For weeks, I was like a mouse in a maze: my feet scurried. Every seventh day, I received thirteen dollars. It wasn't much. But, standing beside the pneumatic tube, unloading the bundles of mail that pelted down and distributing them according to their texture, size, and colour to my superiors at their desks, I felt humble and useful.

Notice how the first line is indented. A margin of adequate width is used on each side of the text (for a manuscript page, this margin should be 3.5 cm). If another paragraph is added, make sure the first line of the second paragraph is also indented. If you follow the full-block style (no indentation of the first line of a paragraph), then make sure you skip a line between paragraphs. If you're already double-spacing, skip two lines between paragraphs. If you neither indent the first line of your paragraph nor skip an extra line between paragraphs, the reader can not be expected to know you've written two paragraphs. Figure 15.1 illustrates the structure of the paragraph.

Two Paragraph Types

TOPIC SENTENCE
REGULAR (5–7 sentences including the topic sentence)

TOPIC SENTENCE
EXTENDED (8–12 sentences including the topic sentence)

Regular or Extended Paragraphs

A **regular paragraph** has five to seven sentences. An **extended paragraph** (eight to twelve sentences) is longer because it has more supporting detail. The supporting detail of a paragraph is made up of sentences that directly support the topic sentence. These supporting sentences may be specific examples of the topic sentence, or they may be parts of an explanation.

Sample Paragraph

One of the areas in which having choice can be extremely valuable is that of friends. Like leaving home to seek greater knowledge of yourself, picking your own friends from a greater number of people can aid in your journey to seek self-knowledge. After all, if you go out with the same group of small-town friends all the time, not because you necessarily like them all that much but because they're the only ones available, this can prove quite limiting when it comes to your growth as an individual. The big city, on the other hand, offers an endless number of opportunities to meet people of like interests. You're much more likely to cultivate relationships with people who help you to grow.

Topic Sentence

A **topic sentence** includes two things: a *topic* and a *controlling idea.* The controlling idea is the attitude of the writer of the paragraph toward the topic identified in the topic sentence. A paragraph contains *one single idea*—that which is introduced in your topic sentence. The topic sentence does not always appear first in a paragraph, but until you are well practised, place the topic sentence first.

Transitions

Transitional words or phrases are used to organize the paragraph better and to make the paragraph flow more smoothly.

Stands On Its Own

Any paragraph, even if it is part of a longer work such as an essay, should be able to stand on its own, much like a sequel to a movie.

Paragraph Indication

There are only two ways **to indicate a new paragraph:**

1. **Indent** the first line of the paragraph (see sample paragraph above), or
2. Skip a line before starting the next paragraph. If you are already double-spacing your work, skip two lines, instead of one, before starting the next paragraph.

Figure 15.1: Structure of the Paragraph

Note: Any space left over at the end of the last line of a paragraph, in itself, never properly indicates the end of a paragraph. As mentioned, proper indication of a paragraph means either indenting the first line of the paragraph or skipping a line (or two, if you're already double-spacing) between paragraphs.

Working with Topic Sentences and Controlling Ideas

What Is a Topic Sentence?

DEFINITION ➤ A **topic sentence** is the sentence in a paragraph that states the main idea of that paragraph. It is the most general sentence of the paragraph. All the other sentences of the paragraph serve to explain, describe, extend, or support this main-idea sentence.

Most paragraphs you read will begin with the topic sentence. However, some topic sentences come in the middle of the paragraph; others come at the end. Some paragraphs have no stated topic sentence at all; in these cases, the main idea is implied. You are advised to use topic sentences in all your work in order to be certain that the writing has a focus and develops a single idea at a time. Whether you are taking an essay exam in a history course, doing a research paper for a sociology course, or writing an essay in a composition course, thoughtful use of the topic sentence will always bring better results. Good topic sentences help both the writer and the reader to think clearly about the main points.

Each of the two paragraphs that follow makes a separate point, which is stated in its topic sentence. In the first paragraph, the topic sentence is first; in the second, last. Read the paragraphs and notice how the topic sentence is the most general sentence; it is the main idea of each paragraph. The other sentences explain, describe, extend, or support the topic sentence.

Model Paragraph 1

> "*Turn down the volume and turn down the danger.*" That's the theme of a campaign by the Canadian Hearing Society, warning that personal stereos can be harmful to your health. The nonprofit group, which has distributed thousands of fact sheets to students, hopes to make them aware that permanent hearing loss can result from prolonged exposure to any intense noise—whether pleasant or unpleasant.

The topic sentence in this paragraph is a general statement relating sound volume to danger. It entices the reader to read the rest of the paragraph to determine the nature of the connection. The following sentences support the topic by giving an authority, the Canadian Hearing Society, as the source of the main idea, which is that playing personal stereos at high volumes can cause hearing loss—the real theme of the paragraph. These sentences reinforce the topic by restating it more specifically.

They address the paragraph to students and use the words "permanent hearing loss" to underline the danger involved.

Model Paragraph 2

Mountains of disposable diapers are thrown into garbage cans every day. Tonnes of yogurt containers, pop cans, and plastic items are discarded without so much as a stomp to flatten them out. If the old Chevy is not worth fixing, tow it off to sit with thousands of others on hectares of fenced-in junkyards. Radios, televisions, and toasters get the same treatment because it is easier and often less expensive to buy a new product than to fix the old one. Who wants a comfortable old sweater if a new one can be bought on sale? No thought is given to the fact that the new one will look like the old one after two or three washings. *We are the great "Let's junk it" society!*

All the examples in this paragraph lead up to a statement of the topic, that we are a "throwaway" society. Although the topic sentence doesn't appear until the end of the paragraph, its point gradually becomes clear as the author piles up supporting examples. When the topic is finally stated, its message has already been proven.

PRACTICE

Finding the Topic Sentence of a Paragraph

Each of the following paragraphs contains a topic sentence that states the main idea of the paragraph. Find this sentence and underline it. Check your answers against those in the Answer Key on p. 441.

1. Love is a crazy, complicated affair made trickier by the tangle of superstitions that go along with it. According to the book *Cross Your Fingers, Spit in Your Hat,* you must pull a hair from the head of the one you love to make him or her love you back. Or you can offer your loved one a glass of lemonade in which you have soaked your toenail clippings, or a bowl of soup to which you have added three drops of your blood. Once your sweetheart has devoured either of these concoctions, he or she will love you always.
2. When you remember something, your brain uses more than one method to store the information. You have short-term memory, which helps you recall recent events; you have long-term memory, which brings back items that are further in the past; and you have deep retrieval, which gives you access to long-buried information that is sometimes difficult to recall. Whether these processes are chemical or electrical, we do not yet know, and much research remains to be done before we can say which with any certainty. The brain is one of the most remarkable organs, a part of the body that we have only begun to investigate. It will be years before we start to understand all its complex processes.

How Do You Find the Topic in a Topic Sentence?

To find the topic in a topic sentence, ask yourself this question: What is the topic the writer is going to discuss? Below are two topic sentences. The first topic is underlined. Underline the topic in the second example.

Backpacking in the mountains last year was an exciting experience.

College registration can be stressful.

PRACTICE

Finding the Topic in the Topic Sentence

Find the topic in each of the following topic sentences. For each example, ask yourself this question: What is the topic the writer is going to discuss? Then underline the topic. Check your answers against those in the Answer Key on p. 441.

1. Remodelling an old house can be frustrating.
2. College work demands more independence than high school work.
3. A well-made suit has three easily identified characteristics.
4. Growing up near a museum had a profound influence on my life.
5. My favourite room in the house would seem ugly to most people.
6. A student who goes to school full-time and also works part-time has to make careful use of every hour.
7. One of the disadvantages of skiing is the expense.
8. When we met for dinner that night, I was shocked at the change that had come over my friend.
9. According to the report, current tax laws greatly benefit those who own real estate.
10. Greek restaurants, to the delight of many Canadians, can be found in most of our cities.

What Is a Controlling Idea?

Every topic sentence contains not only the topic but also a controlling idea.

DEFINITION ➤ The **controlling idea** tells us the position the writer has taken on the topic.

For example, in the topic sentence "Backpacking in the mountains last year was an exciting experience," the topic is "backpacking" and the controlling idea is that this backpacking trip was "exciting." Another person on the same trip might have had another attitude toward the trip. The person might have found the trip exhausting or boring. A single topic can therefore have any number of possibilities for development since the writer can choose from a limitless number of controlling ideas, depending on his or her attitude.

How Do You Find the Controlling Idea of a Topic Sentence?

When you look for the controlling idea in a topic sentence, ask yourself this question: What is the writer's attitude toward the topic?

In each of the following examples, the topic is underlined and the controlling idea is circled.

Sealfon's Department Store is my (favourite) store in town.

Sealfon's Department Store is (too expensive) for my budget.

PRACTICE

Finding the Controlling Idea

Below are seven topic sentences. For each sentence, underline the topic and circle the controlling idea. Check your answers against those in the Answer Key on p. 441.

1. Vigorous exercise is a good way to reduce the effect of stress on the body.
2. St. John's and Corner Brook differ in four major ways.
3. Many so-called wonder foods are less than wonderful.
4. Athletic scholarships available to women are increasing.
5. Caffeine has several adverse effects on the body.
6. Madame Benoît, a famous gourmet cook, had an amusing personality.
7. Computers will make newspapers obsolete by 2020.

Choosing Your Own Controlling Idea

Professors often assign one general topic on which all students must write. Likewise, when writing contests are announced, the topic is sometimes the same for all contestants. Since very few people have exactly the same view of or attitude toward a topic, it is likely that no two papers would have the same controlling idea. There could be as many controlling ideas as there are people to write them. The secret of writing a good topic sentence is to find the controlling idea that is right for you.

EXERCISE

Choosing Controlling Ideas for Topic Sentences

Below are two topics. For each topic, think of three different possible controlling ideas, and then write a different topic sentence for each of these controlling ideas. An example is done for you.

Topic: My mother

Three possible controlling ideas:

1. Unusual childhood
2. Silent woman
3. Definite ideas about alcohol

Three different topic sentences:

1. My mother had a most unusual childhood.

2. My mother is a very silent woman.
3. My mother has definite ideas about alcohol.

1. **Topic:** My neighbourhood

   First controlling idea: ______________________________

   First topic sentence: ______________________________

   ____

   Second controlling idea: ______________________________

   Second topic sentence: ______________________________

   ____

   Third controlling idea: ______________________________

   Third topic sentence: ______________________________

   ____

2. **Topic:** The Internet

   First controlling idea: ______________________________

   First topic sentence: ______________________________

   ____

   Second controlling idea: ______________________________

   Second topic sentence: ______________________________

   ____

   Third controlling idea: ______________________________

   Third topic sentence: ______________________________

   ____

Chapter Review Exercises

EXERCISE

Further Practice Writing the Topic Sentence

Develop each of the following topics into a topic sentence. In each case, the controlling idea is missing. First, decide on an attitude you might take toward the topic. Then use that attitude to write your topic sentence. When you are finished, underline your topic and circle your controlling idea. Be sure your topic sentence is a complete sentence and not a fragment. An example is done for you.

Topic: My brother's car accident
Controlling idea: Tragic results

Topic sentence: My brother's car accident had (tragic results) for the entire family.

1. **Topic:** Sending e-mail

   Controlling idea: ______________________________

   Topic sentence: ______________________________

   ____

2. **Topic:** Two years in the armed forces

   Controlling idea: ______________________________

   Topic sentence: ______________________________

   ____

3. **Topic:** Making new friends

   Controlling idea: ______________________________

   Topic sentence: ______________________________

   ____

4. **Topic**: Working as a waiter or waitress

   Controlling idea: ______________________________

   Topic sentence: ______________________________

   ____

5. **Topic:** Going on a diet

   Controlling idea: ______________________________

   Topic sentence: ______________________________

   ____

Working Together: *Controlling Ideas*

1. In this chapter, you have written many topic sentences in various exercises. Choose one of your best sentences to put on the board. After several students have written some of their sentences on the board, other students will underline the topics and circle the controlling ideas. If the sentences need improvements, students can write their own versions under the other sentences so the class can compare and contrast them.

2. Every topic contains numerous possibilities for controlling ideas. Take, for example, the topic of education. Each student thinks for a moment and jots down one or two controlling ideas that come to mind. Then a class member lists on the blackboard all the different controlling ideas that the members of the class have generated. Your instructor may want the class to use the remainder of the period to write a paragraph by selecting one of these controlling ideas on education.

The Paragraph II: Supporting Details

What Is a Supporting Detail?

DEFINITION ➤ A **supporting detail** is a piece of evidence used by the writer to make the controlling idea of the topic sentence convincing to the reader.

Once you have constructed your topic sentence with its topic and controlling idea, you are ready to move on to supporting your idea with details. These details will convince your readers that what you are claiming in the topic sentence is believable or reasonable.

State Facts

As you choose these supporting details, realize that readers do not necessarily have to agree with your point of view. However, your supporting details must be good enough and numerous enough to convince your readers at least to respect your position. Remember to state facts rather than opinion. You are likely not the only one who has knowledge of a particular subject, so be sure that you don't present vague assertions that leave you open to contradiction. You may have had many problems with a particular make of car that you purchased, for example, and want to write a paragraph detailing its faults. However, your reader may have had a positive experience with this same make of car, or may work for the company that built it. Respect the possible point of view of your reader.

Be Specific

Remember, too, that specific details tend to stay in readers' minds much longer than general ideas. The statement that over 34 600 males died of cancer in Canada in 2000 is much more effective and memorable than a statement saying only that cancer killed many people. Specific details also make a piece of writing more interesting to read. When the reader has concrete objects, particular people, or recognizable places to hang on to, the contents of the writing become a pleasure to read.

It is important to notice that longer paragraphs with complicated topics usually contain a large number of supporting details. The following paragraph is taken from an essay about the richness of Aboriginal peoples' languages. It begins with a good topic sentence. Then several strong details support the topic sentence.

> Languages are remarkably adaptable, easily borrowing or coining new words as circumstances change. The horse, unknown to Aboriginals when the Spanish landed, soon took on a central role among Aboriginal peoples, and words for the horse and its many uses were introduced. One device was to borrow some form of the Spanish word *caballo*. Another was to invent a descriptive term. Native people of eastern New York State used a word meaning "one rides its back"; in the western part of the state, the word for horse means "it hauls out logs." Presumably these were the first uses of horses seen in the two areas. Among the Kwakiutl of British Columbia, a steamboat was "fire on its back moving in the water." To the Tsimshian of the same area, the word for rice was "looking like maggots."

Notice that the topic sentence gives us the topic (language) and the writer's attitude toward the topic (remarkably adaptable). Each of the sentences that follow this topic sentence is a supporting detail that convinces us that the controlling idea is a reasonable attitude. The writer provides more than one example and chooses these examples from more than one group of Aboriginal people. This wide range makes the topic sentence more convincing and interesting.

Topic sentence:	Languages are remarkably adaptable, easily borrowing or coining new words as circumstances change.
First supporting detail:	The word for "horse" was adapted to meet certain situations among Aboriginal peoples.
Second supporting detail:	Spanish was adapted.
Third supporting detail:	Descriptive terms were used.
Fourth supporting detail:	The word "steamboat" was adapted by the First Nations peoples of British Columbia to serve a descriptive purpose.
Fifth supporting detail:	Another British Columbia Nation had a descriptive word for "rice."

EXERCISE

Finding the Topic Sentence and Supporting Details

For the following paragraph, write down the topic sentence and then list the supporting details.

> The time when the darkness that envelops me is most disturbing is the moment when I roll over onto my back and face the ceiling, still encased in the web of drowsiness sleep has woven, and from which it is reluctant to release me. As I become more aware of the sounds around me in the darkness, the ticking of my alarm clock draws my attention, and I look toward it to see what time this morning I have awakened. I am unable to comprehend why I can't locate its

familiar face when I know it should be there. It is at this moment that reality crashes in and reminds me, once again, that morning never comes for me anymore. Life has indeed abandoned me to the night, which is, and always will be, my constant companion. After this moment passes, I reach out into the void toward the sound of the clock. Grasping it and tracing the face that had eluded me moments ago, I sense it forfeit the time to my touch, and thus I broach another day.

Glenn David du Moulin, blind student, "Five Hours in a Life"

Topic sentence: ______________________________

____

First supporting detail: ______________________________

____

Second supporting detail: ______________________________

____

Third supporting detail: ______________________________

____

Fourth supporting detail: ______________________________

____

Fifth supporting detail: ______________________________

____

Using Examples as Supporting Details

DEFINITION ➤ An **example** is a very specific illustration or piece of evidence that supports a writer's point of view. Examples make general ideas more concrete and therefore easier to comprehend and remember.

Respect Other Points of View

When you use examples in your writing, you are trying to convince your reader that what you are saying is true and worthy of belief. At the same time, you must assume that some readers will be knowledgeable in your subject area, so be sure to respect that and make your examples as clear and concise as you can. Remember that no matter how good your examples are, they might not convince some readers, who may have education and experience you lack. So don't "preach" to the reader or consider that your point of view is the only one that is valid.

Use Specific Examples

Often, when you use examples to support your ideas, you will find yourself using further, more specific, examples to help your reader see your first examples more clearly. If you are writing about cars, for instance, you may find yourself using Ford, Dodge, Buick, and Honda to illustrate your points. However, to make your points clearer, you might refer to a Ford Tempo, a Dodge Caravan, a Buick Skylark, and a Honda Accord. The more precise your examples, the more clearly your reader will be able to see what you mean, and the more memorable your writing will be.

Examples may be given in more than one way. They may appear as lists of specific items to illustrate a particular point, or they may be written as extended examples.

DEFINITION ➤ **Extended examples** include lengthy descriptions or stories that can be an entire paragraph long.

A good piece of writing is filled with both kinds of examples that fit together to create a well-developed, convincing whole. Read the following paragraph on the terminology used in weather forecasting. As you read, look for different examples that show how listening to the weather forecast can be a challenge.

> Not only are weather forecasters often wrong with their forecasts, but they speak a language that only the most knowledgeable meteorologist can understand. For the average television viewer or radio listener, a dictionary is a necessity when listening to the weather forecast. "Watch out for the Alberta clipper, folks. It's coming this way!" seems to be part of the forecasters' lexicon in the winter. Or maybe it's the summer. In any case, what is an Alberta clipper? Are we supposed to hide under a table when it approaches? I've never understood the term, nor have I understood the significance of the dew point or a temperature inversion. How could I ever understand these terms when no one has ever defined them for me? Yet they roll off the tongues of weather forecasters as if *everyone* should know what is happening. The relative humidity mystifies me, as do troughs and ridges of pressure. I know one thing, however: if the forecast is for a sunny day, be sure to take an umbrella.

EXERCISE 1 **Finding Examples**

Analyze the paragraph above on weather forecasting. What kind(s) of examples can you find in the paragraph?

EXERCISE 2

Finding Examples

Find a newspaper or magazine article on a current topic or other subject that interests you. Examine the article for paragraphs containing lists of examples and paragraphs containing extended examples. How has the writer made the article interesting and memorable through the use of examples?

Avoid Restating the Topic Sentence

One of your most important jobs as you write a paragraph is to recognize the difference between a genuine supporting detail and a simple restatement of the topic sentence. The following is a poor paragraph with its sentences merely restating the topic sentence, which has been underlined:

> My grandmother's photograph dates from a period when she and her family came to live in St. Petersburg. I like to look at the photograph and wonder about how life was in those days. From the clothes that my grandmother is wearing in the old photograph, it looks as if she is ready for a formal occasion. It is difficult to tell, though, because the photograph is old and faded. I don't think she enjoyed formal occasions.

The supporting sentences tell the reader very little about the period in which the photograph was taken. There is no description given of the clothing or why the writer might feel that it was a formal occasion. And even though the photograph is old and faded enough that details can't be seen, the writer is assuming that his or her grandmother isn't having a good time.

By contrast, the following paragraph, from Michael Ignatieff's *The Russian Album*, has good supporting details:

> In the family album there is a photograph of my grandmother, Natasha Ignatieff, that dates from the period when she and her family came to live in St. Petersburg in the dark and cluttered apartment two blocks from the Neva river. She is dressed for a formal winter evening, a fox fur draped over her shoulders. Brussels lace [decorates] the bodice of her velvet gown, her hair [is] swept back in a tight chignon, and a twelve-strand pearl choker [hugs] her stiffly upright neck. She is thin and pale, the cheekbones of her long angular face taking the light, the eyes deep-set and dark. Her expression is guarded, and she seems at odds with the occasion. She was a private soul: in the public glare, she shrank back. She hated Petersburg society: paying courtesy calls on the wives of Paul's superiors, making curtsies and small talk and all the while feeling she was up on a high wire one step from a fall.

Ignatieff's paragraph has vivid illustrations of life in Russia during his grandmother's time. In the first place, naming her Natasha, gives a personal element to the paragraph. His description of the apartment ("dark and cluttered"), her formal wear ("fox fur," "Brussels lace," "twelve-strand pearl choker"), and her appearance ("hair [is] swept back," "thin and pale," "cheekbones of her long angular face") all contribute to the overall topic, that of the photograph mentioned in the first sentence. Rather than assuming she is not enjoying herself, the author points to concrete aspects of her features to reinforce the statement that she hated St. Petersburg society: her "guarded" expression, her "private soul," and the feeling that she was "on a high wire one step from a fall" tend to give a clarity and personality to the old picture.

PRACTICE

Avoid Restating the Topic Sentence

Each of the topic sentences below is followed by four additional sentences. Three of these additional sentences contain acceptable supporting details, but one of the sentences is simply a restatement of the topic sentence. In the space provided, identify each sentence as *SD* for supporting detail or *R* for restatement. Check your answers against those in the Answer Key on p. 441.

1. I am surprised at myself when I think how neat I used to be before I started school full-time.

_____________ a. In my closet, I had my clothes arranged in matching outfits with shoes, hats, and even jewellery to go with them.

_____________ b. I always used to take great pride in having all my things in order.

_____________ c. If I opened my desk drawer, compartments of paper clips, erasers, staples, pens, pencils, stamps, and rulers greeted me without one lost penny or safety pin thrown in out of place.

_____________ d. On top of my chest of drawers sat a comb and brush, two oval frames with pictures of my best friends, and that was all.

2. Iceland has a very barren landscape.

_____________ a. One-tenth of the island is covered with ice.

_____________ b. Not one forest with magnificent trees is to be found.

_____________ c. Nature has not been kind to the people of Iceland.

_____________ d. Three-fourths of the island is uninhabitable.

EXERCISE

Distinguishing a Supporting Detail from a Restatement of the Topic Sentence

Each of the topic sentences below is followed by four additional sentences. Three of these additional sentences contain acceptable supporting details, but one of the sentences is simply a restatement of the topic sentence. In the space provided, identify each sentence as *SD* for supporting detail or *R* for restatement.

1. In the last 30 years, the number of people living alone in Canada has increased by 400 percent.

   ____________ a. People are living alone because the number of divorces has dramatically increased.

   ____________ b. Many young people are putting off marriage until they are financially more secure or emotionally ready.

   ____________ c. More and more Canadians are finding themselves living alone.

   ____________ d. An increasing percentage of our population is in the over-65 age group, which includes many widows and widowers.

2. Writing as Sandra Field and Jocelyn Haley, Jill MacLean makes love pay the bills.

   ____________ a. Her first book, *To Trust My Love,* was published by Harlequin.

   ____________ b. Jill received a royalty cheque of about $1800 for her first book.

   ____________ c. She is the author of 36 full-fledged romance novels.

   ____________ d. Jill MacLean writes love stories under two pen names.

How Do You Make Supporting Details Specific?

Students often write paragraphs that are made up of only general statements. When you read such paragraphs, you doubt the author's knowledge and you suspect that the point being made may have no basis in fact. Here is one such paragraph that never gets off the ground.

> Doctors are terrible. They cause more problems than they solve. I don't believe most of their treatments are necessary. History is full of the mistakes doctors have made. We don't need all those operations. We should never ingest all those drugs doctors prescribe. We shouldn't allow them to give us all those unnecessary tests. I've heard plenty of stories that prove my point. Doctors' ideas can kill you.

Here is another paragraph on the same topic. This paragraph is much more interesting and convincing because the general statements throughout the essay have been changed to supporting details.

> Evidence shows that "medical progress" has been the cause of tragic consequences and even death for thousands of people. X-ray therapy was thought to help patients with tonsillitis. Now many of these people are found to have developed cancer from these X-rays. Not so long ago, women were kept in bed for several weeks following childbirth. Unfortunately, this cost many women their lives, since they developed fatal blood clots from being kept in bed day after day. One recent study estimates that 30 000 people each

year die from the side effects of drugs that were prescribed by doctors. Recently, the Centers for Disease Control reported that 25 percent of the tests done by clinical laboratories were done poorly. All this is not to belittle the good done by the medical profession, but to impress on readers that it would be foolish to rely totally on the medical profession to solve all our health problems.

This second paragraph is much more likely to be of real interest. Even if you would like to disprove the author's point, it would be very hard to dismiss these supporting details, which are based on facts and information that can be researched. Because the author sounds reasonable, you can respect him or her even if you have a different position on the topic.

In writing effectively, the ability to go beyond the general statement and get to accurate pieces of information is what counts. A writer who has a statistic, a quotation, an historical example, or a descriptive detail can use these items to clarify the theme, especially if the examples are well chosen and appropriate. Readers should go away wanting to share with the next person they meet the surprising information they have just learned.

Good writing is filled with supporting details that are specific, correct, and appropriate for the subject. Poor nonfictional writing is filled with generalizations, stereotypes, vagueness, untruths, and/or insults.

EXERCISE

Creating Supporting Details

Below are five topic sentences. Supply three supporting details for each one. Be sure each detail is specific and not general or vague.

1. Jim's entire wardrobe should be burned.

   a. ______________________________

   b. ______________________________

   c. ______________________________

2. The Internet is more valuable than television.

   a. ______________________________

   b. ______________________________

   c. ______________________________

3. Dr. Kline is an easy instructor.

   a. ______________________________

   b. ______________________________

   c. ______________________________

4. It is difficult to stop eating junk food.

   a. ______________________________

   b. ______________________________

   c. ______________________________

5. Learning another language will make your life richer.

   a. ______________________________

   b. ______________________________

   c. ______________________________

The Concluding Sentence

Some instructors will require that you add a concluding sentence to your paragraph, especially if you're writing a paragraph on its own and not as part of a larger essay; others will not. If you are required to do so, then the concluding sentence should give the paragraph a sense of closure. It should be logical and appropriate. It may or may not reiterate the topic sentence as long as it clearly is not intended to be part of the supporting detail. It also should be the last sentence in the paragraph. See the two paragraphs on pages 172–73. The first begins with "Doctors are terrible." The second one begins with "Evidence shows…" Find the concluding sentence in each paragraph. Notice that in each case, the attitude of the controlling idea of the concluding sentence seems either a bit stronger or weaker than that of the topic sentence, but that, either way, it somehow reinforces the attitude established in the topic sentence.

Working Together: *Supporting Details*

1. Divide into groups. Select one of the topic sentences on pages 173–74. Together make a list of as many supporting details or examples as you can. Then each student writes a paragraph selecting details from the list prepared by his or her group.
2. Circulate everyone's answers to the assignment within the group. Be sure to give every member of the group enough time to read through all the papers. Then discuss the various paragraphs that have been written. Even though each paragraph began with the same topic sentence and supporting details, all of the paragraphs have turned out differently. Why?

CHAPTER SEVENTEEN 17

The Essay

Writing Is a Skill

Writing is a skill. This means that a writer, no matter how experienced or inexperienced, needs to follow a certain process in order to arrive at a successful finished product. Very few writers can "dash off" a masterpiece. We sometimes think that a person is "a born dancer" or "a born writer," but the reality is that the person has worked long hours for many years to achieve his or her level of skill.

When you learned to write a well-developed paragraph in Chapters 15 and 16, you were creating something that could be a support paragraph for the essay. An essay is a longer piece of writing, usually five or more paragraphs, in which you can develop a topic in much more depth than you can in a single paragraph. The essay may also be called a composition, thesis, or paper. In most schools, such writing is an important part of almost every course, not only the English composition class.

While the essay is required in any number of courses—law enforcement, business studies, office administration, technology, social sciences, journalism, broadcasting, and the like—its purpose goes beyond fulfilling the requirements of a postsecondary-level course. Writing essays also helps prepare students for careers by providing the skills necessary to write corporate reports, evaluations, summaries, research papers, letters, memos, and job applications. While the structures of various forms of writing may vary, the essay is still the basic form of writing. Spelling, grammar, and logic, essential to the composition of an effective essay, remain paramount in all forms of writing, as does the ability to express yourself clearly.

You learned in Chapters 15 and 16 that the paragraph with its topic sentence and supporting details must have an organization that is both unified and coherent. The essay must also have these characteristics. Furthermore, since the essay develops a topic at greater length or depth, making all the parts work together becomes an added challenge. Figure 17.1 illustrates the structure of the essay.

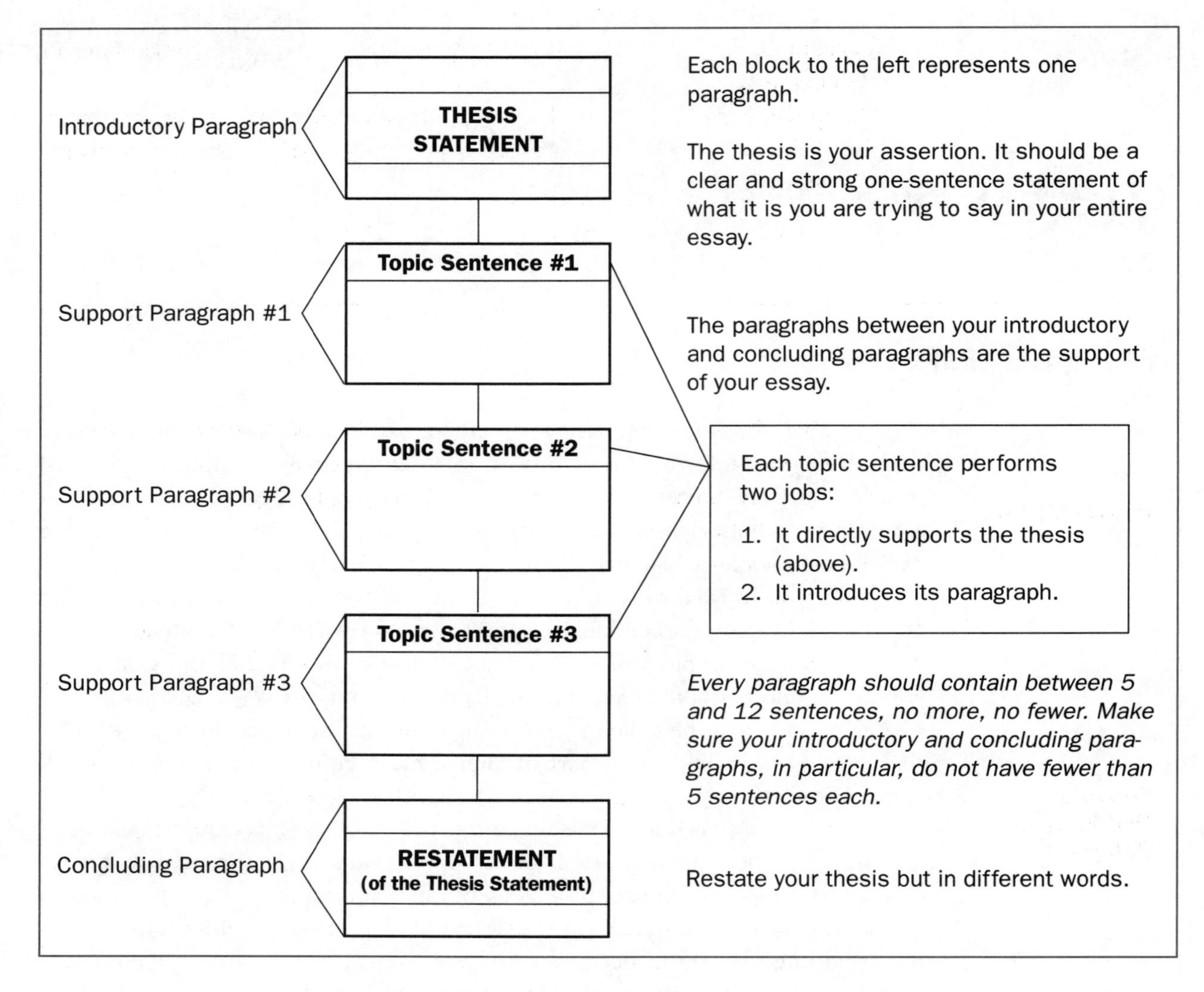

Figure 17.1: The Structure of an Essay

The Components of an Essay

Three types of paragraphs must always be present in an essay: an introductory paragraph, support paragraphs, and a concluding paragraph.

1. **The introductory paragraph is the first paragraph of the essay.** Its purpose is to be so inviting that the reader will not want to stop reading. This introduction must contain a **thesis statement.**
2. **Support paragraphs** (sometimes called body paragraphs) **provide the evidence that shows your thesis is valid.** An essay normally has at least three well-developed support paragraphs. (You have studied these kinds of paragraphs in Chapter 16.) One paragraph must flow logically into the next. This

is accomplished by the careful use of **transitional devices** (discussed later in this chapter).

3. **The concluding paragraph is the last paragraph of the essay.** Its purpose is to give the reader a sense of coming to a satisfying ending, a sense that everything has been said that needed to be said.

Figure 17.2 illustrates the components of the essay.

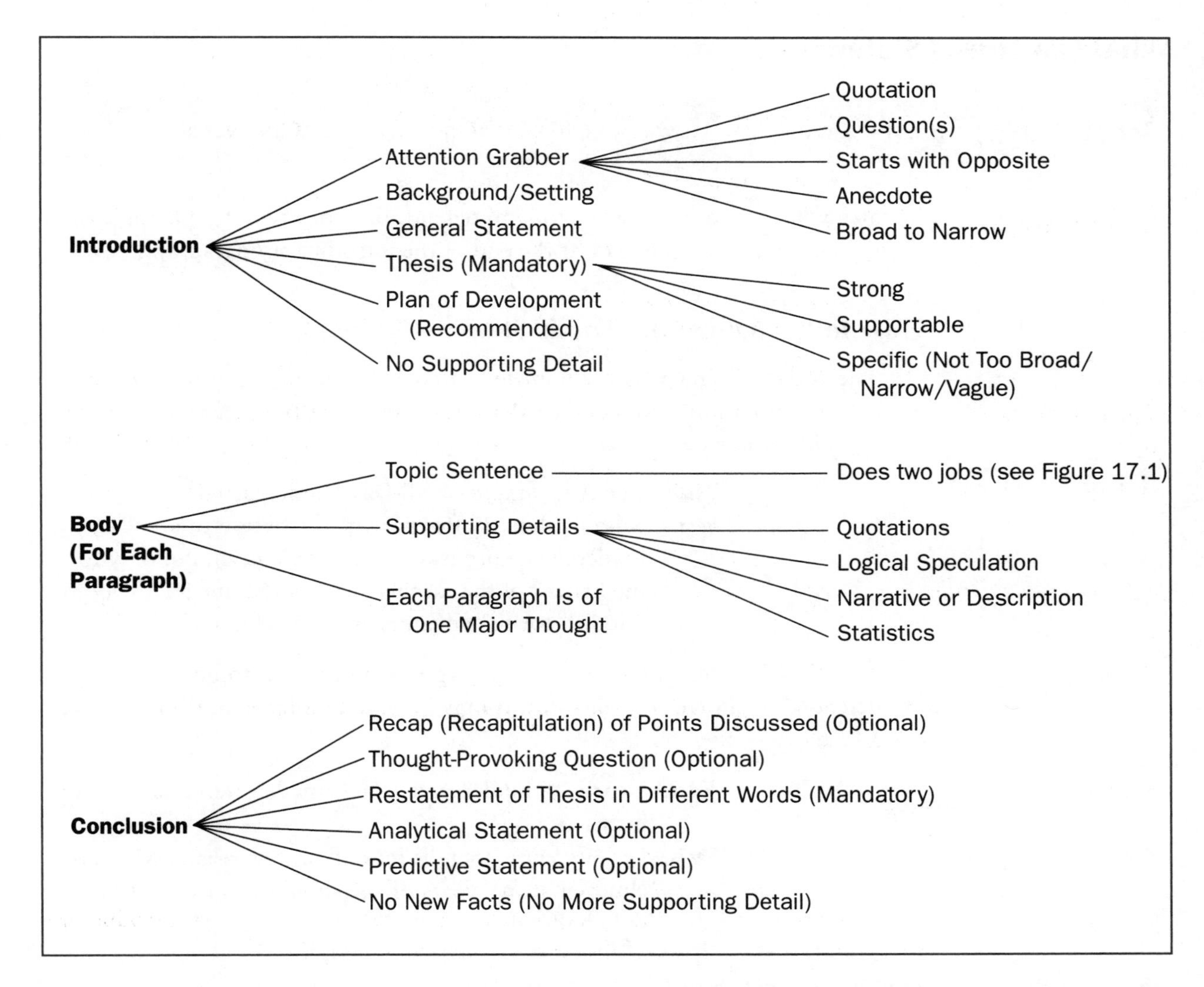

Figure 17.2: Components of the Essay

Before you begin the process of writing your own college essays, this chapter will prepare you to understand and work with these special essay features:

Thesis statement
Introductory paragraph
Transitions between body paragraphs
Concluding paragraph

What Is a Thesis Statement?

DEFINITION ➤ The **thesis** of an essay is a statement of the main idea of that essay.

It states what you are going to explain, defend, or prove about your topic. It is usually placed in the middle or at the end of the introductory paragraph.

How to Recognize the Thesis Statement

1. **The thesis statement is a complete sentence.** Students sometimes confuse a title with a thesis. Remember that titles are usually phrases rather than complete sentences.

   Title: The Advantages of All-Day Kindergarten
   Thesis: Schools should offer parents the option of an all-day kindergarten program for their children, not only for the benefit of the mother who works outside the home but also for the advantages to the children.

2. **The thesis statement presents a viewpoint about the topic that will be defended or shown in your essay. It may be based on facts, but it is not itself a fact.**

   Fact: Nearly all kindergartens in Canada offer a half day of instruction.
   Thesis: Parents know there is more than one reason why most children at five years of age should be in school for only half a day.

PRACTICE 1 **Thesis or Fact?**

Read each of the following statements. If you think the statement is a fact, mark it with an *F*. If you think the statement is a thesis, mark it with a *T*. Check your answers against those in the Answer Key on p. 442.

_______________ 1. In Canada, kindergarten is not compulsory.

_______________ 2. Children should begin learning to read in kindergarten.

_______________ 3. Putting a child into kindergarten before he or she is physically or emotionally ready can have several unfortunate effects on a child.

_______________ 4. In some European countries, children do not begin formal schooling until age seven or eight.

PRACTICE 2

Recognizing the Thesis Statement

In the space provided, identify each of the following as (1) a title, (2) a thesis, or (3) a fact that could be used to support a thesis. Check your answers against those in the Answer Key on p. 442.

_______________ 1. The personal interview is the most important step in the employment process.

_______________ 2. Looking for a job

_______________ 3. Sixty percent of all jobs are obtained through newspaper advertisements.

_______________ 4. The best time to begin learning a foreign language is in grade school.

_______________ 5. The importance of learning a foreign language

_______________ 6. By the year 2000, the number of students studying foreign languages declined dramatically.

_______________ 7. Most Canadians doing business with Japan do not know a word of Japanese.

Writing an Effective Thesis Statement

An effective thesis statement has two and sometimes three parts:

1. **It contains a topic that is not too broad:** Broad topics must be narrowed down in scope. You can do this by *limiting the topic* (changing the term to cover a smaller part of the topic) or *qualifying the topic* (adding phrases or words to the general term that will narrow down the topic).

   Broad topic: Swimming

   Limited topic: Learning to float (Floating is a kind of swimming, more specialized than the term swimming.)

   Qualified topic: Swimming for health two hours a week (The use of the phrase "for health two hours a week" narrows the topic down considerably. Now the topic concentrates on the fact that the time spent swimming and the reason for swimming are important parts of the topic.)

   There are a number of ways to narrow a topic in order to make it fit into a proper essay length, as well as make it fit your experience and knowledge.

2. **It contains a controlling idea that you can defend:** The controlling idea is what you want to show or prove about your topic; it is your attitude about that topic. The controlling idea is often an adjective, such as *beneficial, difficult*, or *maddening*.

   Learning to float at the age of 20 was a *terrifying* experience.
   Swimming two hours a week brought about a *dramatic* change in my health.

3. **Optional in a thesis statement is an indication of what strategy for development is to be used:** Often you can use words such as the following: description, steps, stages, comparison, contrast, causes, effects, reasons, advantages, disadvantages, definition, analysis, persuasion.

   Although not all writers include the strategy in the thesis statement, they must always have in mind what major strategy they plan to use to prove their thesis. Professional writers often use more than one strategy to prove the thesis. However, in this book, you are asked to develop your essays by using one major strategy at a time. By working in this way, you can concentrate on understanding and developing the skills needed for each specific strategy.

Study the following thesis statement:

> Although a date with the right person is marvellous, going out with a group can have many advantages.

Now look back and check the parts of this thesis statement.

General topic: Going out
Qualified topic: Going out in a group (as opposed to a single date)
Controlling idea: To give the advantages
Strategy for development: Contrast between the single date and the group date

EXERCISE

Writing the Thesis Statement

Below are three topics. For each one, develop a thesis statement by (1) limiting or qualifying the general topic, (2) choosing a controlling idea (what you want to explain or prove about the topic), and (3) selecting a strategy that you could use to develop that topic. An example is done for you.

General topic: Senior citizens

a. ***Limited or qualified topic:***

   Community services available to the senior citizens in my town

b. ***Controlling idea:***

   To show the great variety of programs

c. ***Strategy for development*** (narration, description, process, comparison or contrast, definition, classification, cause and effect):

Classify the services into major groups.

Thesis statement: The senior citizens of New Glasgow, Nova Scotia, are fortunate to have programs available to help them deal with health, housing, and leisure time.

1. Winnipeg (or another city with which you are familiar)

   a. Limited or qualified topic:

   ____

   b. Controlling idea:

   ____

   c. Strategy for development (narration, description, process, comparison or contrast, definition, classification, cause and effect):

   ____

   Thesis statement:

   ____

   ____

2. Shopping

   a. Limited or qualified topic:

   ____

   b. Controlling idea:

   ____

   c. Strategy for development (narration, description, process, comparison or contrast, definition, classification, cause and effect):

   ____

   Thesis statement:

   ____

   ____

3. Canadians

   a. Limited or qualified topic:

   ____

b. Controlling idea:

____

c. Strategy for development (narration, description, process, comparison or contrast, definition, classification, cause and effect):

____

Thesis statement:

____

____

The Introductory Paragraph

DEFINITION ➤ An **introduction** has one main purpose: to "grab" your readers' interest so that they will keep reading.

There is no one way to write an introduction. However, since many good introductions follow the same common patterns, you will find it helpful to look at a few examples of the more typical patterns to help you write your own introductions.

1. **Begin with a general subject that can be narrowed down to the specific topic of your essay.** Here is an introductory paragraph on astronomy, from *Universe* by W.J. Kaufmann:

   > Speculation about the nature of the universe is one of the most characteristic human endeavours. The study of the stars transcends all boundaries of culture, geography, and politics. The modern science of astronomy carries an ancient tradition of observation and speculation, using the newest tools of technology and mathematics. In the most literal sense, astronomy is a universal subject—its subject is indeed the universe.

   The specific topic of this paragraph in in the last sentence.

2. **Begin with specifics (a brief anecdote, a specific example or fact) that will broaden into the more general topic of your essay.** Here is the introduction to Miriam Waddington's "The Hallowe'en Party," an essay about a family of Russian Jews settling on a prairie farm just outside of Winnipeg:

   > The year that I was twelve my father came home one day and announced that he had bought a farm. My sister Helen and I could hardly wait to see the farm which, according to my father, consisted of 26 acres in St. Vital, just beyond the outskirts of Winnipeg. There were 20 acres of bush with buildings, and six acres of meadow beside the river. My father had dreamed of such a farm all the years he was shut up in the dark greasy

> machine shop where he earned his living. Now as I look back, I can understand my father's deep hunger for land.

The last sentence contains the topic of the story, a topic that is larger than the idea of merely buying a farm.

3. **Give a definition of the concept that will be discussed.** Here is the introduction to "Man, Woman and Child," an essay by Lydia Bailey about the rising trend toward single motherhood:

   > They are a new breed of mother—single, self-sufficient, and in their thirties. They have opted for motherhood without marriage. Some call it a return to tribal times when women raised children on their own with the help of other women. Others see it as a dangerous trend, labelling them as "the most narcissistic group of people you will ever see." Regardless of how it's perceived, statistics show that in the past few years, the number of single mothers in their thirties has increased dramatically.

4. **Make a startling statement.** Here is an example from Arthur C. Clarke's "We'll Never Conquer Space":

   > Man will never conquer space. Such a statement may sound ludicrous, now that our rockets are already 100 million miles beyond the moon and the first human travellers are preparing to leave the atmosphere. Yet it expresses a truth which our forefathers knew, one we have forgotten—and our descendants must learn again, in heartbreak and loneliness.

5. **Start with an idea or statement that is a widely held point of view.** Then surprise the reader by stating that this idea is false or that you hold a different point of view. Here is an example from "A Planet for the Taking," by David Suzuki:

   > Canadians live under the remarkable illusion that we are a technologically advanced people. Everything around us denies that assumption. We are, in many ways, a Third World country, selling our natural resources in exchange for the high technology of the industrialized world. Try going through your home and looking at the country of origin of your clothes, electrical appliances, books, car. The rare technological product that does have Canada stamped on it is usually from a branch plant of a multinational company centred in another country.

6. **Start with a familiar quotation or a quotation by a famous person,** as Frank Trippett does in this example from "Getting Dizzy by the Numbers":

   > "The very hairs of your head," says Matthew 10:30, "are all numbered." There is little reason to doubt it. Increasingly, everything tends to get numbered one way or another, everything that can be counted, measured, averaged, estimated or quantified. Intelligence is gauged by a quotient, the humidity by a ratio, pollen by its count, and the trends of

> birth, death, marriage and divorce by rates. In this epoch of runaway demographics, society is as often described and analyzed with statistics as with words. Politics seems more and more a game played with percentages turned up by pollsters, and economics a learned babble of ciphers and indexes that few people can translate and apparently nobody can control. Modern civilization, in sum, has begun to resemble an interminable arithmetic class in which, as Carl Sandburg put it, "numbers fly like pigeons in and out of your head."

7. **Give a number of descriptive images that will lead to the thesis of your essay:**

> The nuclear family is breaking up. Both parents are working and children are left on their own for long periods of time, or are sent to daycare centres. Youngsters are learning about life from television and from movies, although the life that they learn about is often far removed from the truth. The incidence of crime is increasing among children because they receive little guidance and even less teaching on the difference between right and wrong. Social, moral, and religious values are declining. These are among the reasons why the fabric of society is decaying.

The last sentence of the paragraph is the thesis statement of the essay.

8. **Ask a question that you intend to answer.** Many essays you read in magazines and newspapers use a question in the introductory paragraph to make the reader curious about the author's viewpoint. Some writing instructors prefer that students do not use this method. Check with your instructor before using this method. Here is an example of such an introduction, from "The Fatal Question," by Vivian Rakoff:

> Human beings sustained in a state of technical "life" through complex machinery present to society and medicine a terribly and increasingly familiar dilemma. All the meaning and pleasure of ordinary life are absent and there's no hope of return to a dignified existence. Who has the authority to decide that the time has come to stop the machines?

9. **Use the writing strategy of classification** (see Chapter 26) **to indicate how your topic fits into the larger class to which it belongs, or how your topic can be divided into categories that you are going to discuss.** Here is how Robert Fulford began "How the West Was Lost," an essay on the destruction of Métis and Native societies in the West:

> They may never have seen each other's faces, but the two most famous non-whites in late nineteenth-century Canada—Louis Riel and Big Bear—were linked by history and by the events of the crisis year 1885. They were dissimilar in many ways—Riel a Montreal-educated Métis who travelled widely and was three times elected to the Canadian parliament, Big Bear a Plains Cree, who knew no world beyond the Prairies. But they were also alike: both were mystics and prophets and both were charismatic leaders of peoples doomed by the westward thrust of the Canadian empire.

What Not to Say in Your Introduction

1. **Avoid telling your reader that you are beginning your essay:**

    In this essay I will discuss...
    I will talk about...
    I am going to prove...

2. **Don't apologize:**

    Although I am not an expert...
    In my humble opinion...

3. **Do not refer to later parts of your essay:**

    By the end of this essay, you will agree...
    In the next paragraph, you will see...

4. **Don't use trite expressions.** Since they have been so overused, they will lack interest. Using such expressions shows that you have not taken the time to use your own words to express your ideas. Some examples of trite expressions are

    busy as a bee
    you can't tell a book by its cover
    haste makes waste

Using Transitions to Move from One Idea to the Next

Successful essays help the reader understand the logic of the writer's thinking by using transitional expressions when needed. Transitions usually occur when the writer is moving from one point to the next. They also occur whenever the idea is complicated. The writer may need to summarize the points covered thus far; the writer may need to emphasize a point already made; or the writer may want to repeat an important point. The transition may be a word, a phrase, a sentence, or even a paragraph.

Transitions are used to form links between paragraphs and the ideas in them in the same way that transitions are used to link ideas in a sentence or within a paragraph. Paragraphs are used to show a progression of ideas within an essay, a composition, or a research paper. Here are some of the transitional expressions you might use to help the reader make the right connections. Also refer to the chart on the inside back cover of this book and notice what other transitions could be used in the categories indicated below.

1. **To make your points stand out clearly:**

the first reason	second, secondly	finally
first of all	another example	most important
in the first place	even more important	all in all
	also, next	in conclusion
	then	to summarize

2. **To present an example of what has just been said:**

    for example
    for instance

3. **To present the consequence of what has just been said:**

    therefore
    as a result
    then

4. **To make a contrasting point clear:**

    on the other hand
    but
    contrary to current thinking
    however

5. **To admit a point:**

    of course
    granted

6. **To resume your argument after admitting a point:**

    nevertheless
    even so
    nonetheless
    still

7. **To call the reader's attention to your organization:**

    Before attempting to answer these questions, let me...
    In our discussion so far, we have seen that...
    At this point, it is necessary to...
    It is beyond the scope of this paper to...

A more subtle way to link one idea to another in an essay is to repeat a word or phrase from the preceding sentence.

> I have many memories of my childhood in the Yukon. These *memories* include the aunts, uncles, grandparents, and friends I left behind when I moved to Ontario.

Sometimes instead of the actual word, a pronoun will take the place of the word.

> Like many Northerners, I've had to learn to adapt to an urban way of life. *It* hasn't been easy, but today I almost think of myself as a Torontonian.

The Concluding Paragraph

A concluding paragraph has one main purpose: to give the reader the sense of reaching a satisfying ending to the topic discussed. Students often feel they have nothing to say at the end. A look at how professional writers frequently end their essays can ease your anxiety about writing an effective conclusion. You have more than one possibility; here are some of the most frequently used patterns for ending an essay.

1. **Come full circle; that is, return to the material in your introduction.** Finish what you started there. Remind the reader of the thesis. Be sure to restate the main idea using different wording. Here is an example from the essay by Vivian Rakoff discussed earlier.

    > We are involved in an unending process of questioning and adaptation—an adaptation that, with luck, will not fall into a simple-minded rejection of the machine as the work of the devil. It is at least equally valid to see the manufacture of machines and goods as the continuous unfolding of human endowment in a cumulative history. Man the toolmaker is man expressing an ancient and important component of his true nature.

2. **Summarize by repeating the main points.** The following example of a concluding paragraph is from the essay "Inner-Peace Process" by Jenny Yuen, which appears in its entirety in Chapter 23 (pages 253–54).

    > Peace may be achieved by youth, but only if we find inner peace first. In order to effectively oppose the wars and violence in the world, we must defeat the wars within ourselves. We must triumph over rivalry and competition, negative self-images and passive support of injustice. Only then will we be prepared to take the next step: World Peace.

3. **Show the significance of your thesis by making predictions, giving a warning, giving advice, offering a solution, suggesting an alternative, or telling the results.** This example is from the essay by David Suzuki discussed previously.

    > But Canadians do value the spiritual importance of nature and want to see it survive for future generations. We also believe in the power of science to sustain a high quality of life. And while the current understanding of science's power is, I believe, misplaced, in fact the leading edges of physics and ecology may provide the insights that can get us off the current track. We need a very profound perceptual shift and soon.

4. **End with an anecdote that illustrates your thesis.** This example is from Robert Fulford's essay on the Métis and Native people (the beginning of which is on page 184).

> The criminal trials of the Indians and the Métis in the autumn of 1885 seem, in retrospect, outrageously illogical—the rebels were convicted of treason against an empire that had conscripted them as citizens without consulting them. But the North-West Rebellion also produced a trial that was merely bizarre. Shortly after the rebellion ended, an article in the Toronto *News* said that Montreal's Sixty-fifth Battalion had conducted itself during the hostilities in a way that was mutinous, reckless, disorderly, and drunken. Officers of the battalion sued, and eventually the editor of the *News*—a notorious enemy of French Canadians and the French language—was summoned to Montreal to stand trial for criminal libel. Convicted and fined $200, he emerged from the courtroom, barely escaped with his life from a howling mob of outraged Montrealers, and went home to be treated to a torchlight parade of 4000 cheering supporters in Toronto. Two years later, fed up with the stresses of daily newspaper work, the editor, Edmund E. Sheppard, founded a new periodical, *Saturday Night*.

What Not to Say in Your Conclusion

1. **Do not introduce a new point.**

    I will tell you something else...
    Additional information has come to light...
    Let me leave you with a new idea...

2. **Do not apologize.**

    I'm sorry that I can't end on a more positive note...
    If I had more space...
    I can't be sure of every point...

3. **Do not end up in the air, leaving the reader feeling unsatisfied.** This sometimes happens when the very last sentence is not strong enough.

    Maybe the problem will never be solved...
    There is no obvious solution...
    We can only hope things will get better...

Titles

Be sure to follow the standard procedure for writing your title.

1. Try to think of a short and catchy phrase (three to six words). Often writers wait until they have written a draft before working on a title. There may be a phrase from the essay that will be perfect. If you still cannot think of a clever title after you have written a draft, choose some key words from your thesis statement.
2. Capitalize the first letter of the first word, then capitalize the first letter of the other words except articles (*the, a, an*) and prepositions (such as *in, of,* and *on*).
3. Do not underline the title or put quotation marks around it when it is in a title position.
4. Centre the title at the top of the page, and remember to leave about 3 cm of space between the title and the beginning of the first paragraph.

Working Together: *Education Endangered?*

1. The cartoon on the next page uses the technique of a multiple-choice quiz to suggest reasons that education in North America is in trouble. As a class or in groups, discuss each of the four areas of concern raised by the cartoonist. Then write a five-paragraph essay (an introductory paragraph, three supporting paragraphs, and a paragraph of conclusion). Use the information you have learned in this chapter to write a good introduction and conclusion. For your supporting paragraphs, choose three of the four areas of concern shown in the cartoon and make each one the main idea for one of the support paragraphs. Be sure to make use of the ideas generated during the class discussion.

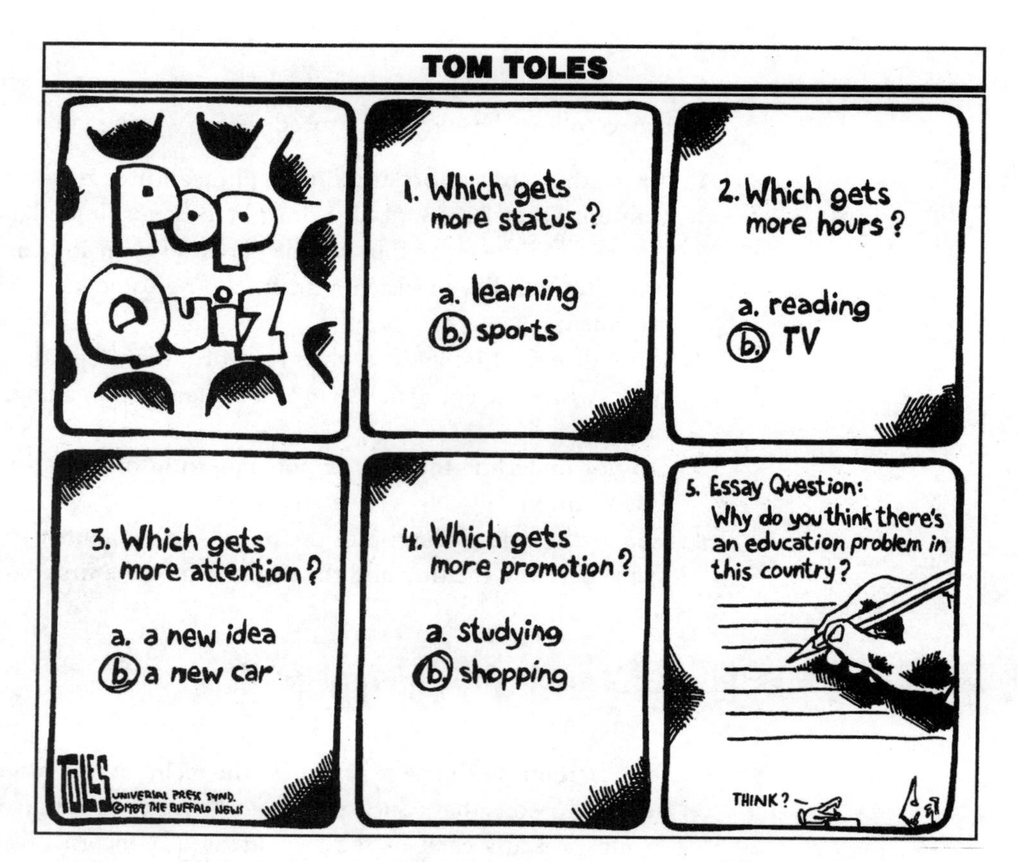

2. Divide into three groups. Each group will study the introductory and concluding paragraphs in any three of the essays in the "Readings" section of this book (Unit IV). Analyze each introduction and conclusion to decide if the author has chosen one of the patterns suggested in this chapter. Can you point to one sentence as the author's thesis statement?

Revising and Editing

The Final Stages

Revising and editing your work are necessary before word processing the final copy of your work. Of course, you'll need to proofread your final copy for typos and other mistakes you may have made, but the editing stage is the one at which you should eliminate most, if not all, of your errors.

Revising and editing are often thought of as one and the same thing. They are not. Specifically, revising is rereading your first draft very carefully and making major improvements. You might replace an entire paragraph with a new one, for example. You might cut the length of a large anecdote in half and add a smaller but completely different one. Editing, on the other hand, usually means smaller but still important changes. Revising often refers to changing the content, whereas editing often refers to improving the organization of the composition and the style of writing. Finally, proofreading refers, mostly, to correcting mistakes that might be, for example, grammatical in nature. Minor factual errors in content might also be caught at this stage.

Revising and editing can be boring jobs: few people like to spend a great deal of time on this part of the writing process. However, it's better to make major improvements and correct any mistakes at this stage than to have your professor point them out later and downgrade your work accordingly.

Too many writers finish their first draft and then start rereading to catch mistakes. Their idea is to get the editing process over with as soon as possible. If the writer misses a few little mistakes, who's going to notice? But revising and editing involve much more than rereading and hoping any mistakes jump out. It involves a well-planned approach to making improvements, finding mistakes, and discovering better ways of writing.

What you need first is a quiet place and a block of time that will allow you to complete the task in one sitting. You need to examine especially carefully those areas of spelling, grammar, or composition in which you know you have weaknesses. You will also need someone to read your material and offer a second opinion on the quality of your work when you've completed your revising and editing. But most of all, you need to follow a system. When you've finished the first draft of your work, set it aside for a day or two. Then read through the whole thing, making notes, corrections, or additions based on the checklists on pages 192–93. These checklists are adapted from *The Reluctant Writer* by Roger Mann and John Roberts.

Master Checklist for Revising and Editing

1. Check the macrocomposition: the content and the overall arrangement of ideas. (See Macrocomposition Checklist below.)
2. Check the microcomposition: the flow of thought, the sentence structure, the wording, grammar, and usage. (See Microcomposition Checklist below.)
3. Check the spelling.
4. Check the punctuation.
5. Check the manuscript form.

Macrocomposition Checklist

1. Have you provided enough background explanation at the outset for the reader to
   a. recognize the context?
   b. understand what follows?
   c. want to read further?
2. Do the ideas introduced in the beginning connect logically to a continuous line of thought that moves sensibly from introduction to discussion and ends in a conclusion? Are appropriate connecting words used?
3. Are the thoughts packaged in small chunks of information that the audience is capable of following? Will the sequence of ideas convince and enlighten the reader?
4. Is the information sufficient to do the job it is intended to do? Are there any gaps? Is all of the discussion relevant to the subject and the purpose?
5. Is the point of view toward the reader consistent throughout the text?
6. Are the time sequences logical and consistent? Check verbs for uniformity of tense and mood.
7. Is the wording concise, and are physical references precise and concrete? If you are dealing with ideas and concepts, are they adequately explained and illustrated? Is the wording geared to the presumed reading level of the reader?
8. Is the tone appropriate to the situation, the purpose, and the reader? Is it consistent throughout the text?
9. Does the conclusion fulfill the intended purpose? At the end, will the reader understand the message, agree with what you have said, and be motivated to act?

Microcomposition Checklist

Check your sentences for *grammar:*

1. Is every sentence grammatically complete, with no sentence fragments?
2. In sentences with two or more independent clauses, are the clauses grammatically parallel, and either connected by coordinating conjunctions or separated by semicolons, with no run-ons or comma splices?
3. Are subordinate clauses and verb phrases clearly related to the words they modify, with no dangling or misplaced modifiers?
4. Are the elements of each sentence consistent in grammar and in thought:
   - Do subjects agree with verbs?
   - Do pronouns agree with their antecedents and with each other in person and in number?
   - Is it clear which nouns the pronouns stand in for?
   - Are the verb tenses consistent?
   - If you have used lists, are the elements of each list grammatically parallel?
   - Is the word order appropriate and easy to follow?

(continued)

(continued)

Check your sentences for *style:*

1. Are the beginnings of your sentences varied—do some start with the subject, some with introductory phrases or clauses, and a select few with reversed word order?
2. Have you varied the clause structure of your sentences—some simple, some compound, some complex, some compound–complex?
3. Have you mixed your sentence lengths effectively—long sentences to convey information and establish a rhythm, short sentences to get important points across?

Check your *wording and usage:*

1. Have you used vocabulary suitable to the reader and the situation?
2. Are your nouns concrete, tangible, and specific?
3. Are your verbs active or passive, as is appropriate to the context?
4. Have you used adjectives and adverbs selectively and sparingly? Can you replace any adjective–noun or adverb–verb combinations with carefully selected single nouns or verbs?
5. Could you explain the reason for your choice of every word and its placement in the sentence?
6. Have you used any words that you are not entirely sure about—the spelling, the meaning, or the way the words should be used?
7. Have you used any clichés? If so, can you justify using them? If not, can you think of original expressions to replace them?
8. Have you used any idiomatic expressions? If so, are you sure you have used them correctly and appropriately?
9. Have you used jargon, such as technical terms or acronyms? Are you sure the reader will understand these terms?

Check your *punctuation:*

1. Have you used periods at the ends of sentences and after abbreviations?
2. Do question marks indicate the ends of interrogative sentences?
3. Have you used exclamation marks to emphasize especially important points or statements? (Do not overuse this device!)
4. Have you used quotation marks properly—for all direct speech, direct quotations from sources, and titles of short works?
5. Have you used, but not overused, commas to pace the reader's understanding of the text, to separate internal parts of your sentences, and to clarify potentially ambiguous word combinations?
6. Have you used semicolons to separate parts of a sentence that are grammatically distinct, or to separate items in a complex list?
7. Have you used dashes and colons correctly?

Check your *spelling, capitalization,* and *apostrophes:*

1. Have you checked the words you traditionally have trouble with?
2. Have you checked *ie* combinations, spelling changes caused by suffixes, and consonants that must be doubled or not?
3. Have you used capital letters properly—for titles, names, places, months, countries, etc.?
4. Have you used apostrophes correctly—for possessive nouns and indefinite pronouns, or for shortened forms of words?

Check your *manuscript form:*

1. Has all your source material been suitably acknowledged and documented?
2. Have you used the proper format conventions for the form you are writing—memo, letter, report, essay?

Now that the final stage of the composition has been discussed in detail, it's time to apply all the stages of the writing process to an actual sample of a student essay. You will be shown how the four steps of the writing process are applied to a specific essay as it is developed from scratch to finish. Of course, just as no two chefs or carpenters or painters approach their work in the same way, no two writers work in the same way either. In spite of this individuality, each writer goes through a surprisingly similar series of steps to reach the finished product.

Again, here are the steps in the Writing Process corresponding to their appropriate "stages" and their breakdown into more specific tasks:

Four Stages of the Writing Process

Stage One (Prewriting)

1. Getting the idea for developing a topic.
2. Gathering information (brainstorming, researching, taking notes).

Stage Two (Outlining)

3. Selecting and organizing details.

Stage Three (The Rough Draft)

4. Writing the rough draft.

Stage Four (Postwriting: Revising, Editing, and Proofreading)

5. Revising and editing the rough draft (some writers revise their work through many, many drafts before they are satisfied).
6. Writing the second draft.
7. Proofreading (grammar, spelling, style, etc.).
8. Typing or word processing the final copy.
9. Checking for errors (especially typos).

A Sample Student Essay in Progress

Stage One: Getting the Idea for Developing a Topic

A student named Allison Hickman is asked to write a personal-experience narrative essay (see Chapter 21) about fear or anxiety. She begins by making a list of the possibilities:

Taking tests
Speaking in front of a large group
Going on a date with someone for the first time
Performing on the piano
Walking alone at night
Having an argument with one's parents

Which one should Allison choose? She goes over the possibilities and discovers that when she comes to the one about the piano, she feels a tightness in her chest. Here is an experience in her life that makes her nervous just to think about it!

Furthermore, she has had several experiences performing on the piano that she thinks could make an interesting piece of writing. She feels excited because she realizes that she does indeed have many thoughts and feelings about this traumatic experience in her life.

Allison chooses a topic and controlling idea:

Topic: Performing on the piano
Controlling idea: Makes me frightened, anxious, nervous

Brainstorming the Topic

Once you have decided on a topic, you still have many choices to make. What will your controlling idea be? You might choose to tell a story, give several examples to support your thesis, define and analyze, or compare or contrast. In other words, you can choose from these different strategies the one (or any combination of them) that best suits your knowledge or experience. (See Chapters 21–28 in Unit III on Writing Strategies.)

To make these choices, writers usually need to gather some information to find out what they have to work with. If the assignment calls for your own experience, you will not need to conduct outside research—in the library or in interviews, for instance—to get information. In such a case, you can begin with the technique known as **brainstorming.** Writers use brainstorming to discover what they already know and feel about a given topic. Review the discussion of brainstorming in Chapter 14.

Here is Allison's brainstorming list.

List of Ideas That Come to Mind

stage fright
strange pianos
parents in the audience
embarrassed if I make a mistake

my shyness
Mrs. Stuart's performance classes
the performance class last year
playing the sonata
Leonard's playing
jealous

computer programming
contest in June
trills in my piece
finding time to practise in the spring

my teacher
lack of self-confidence
dread of recitals
being the oldest in the group but not the best
memorizing music
forgetting a chord in the left hand
hands and legs shaking
wanting to please my teacher
fingers get sweaty
Leonard always plays better than the rest of us
always late
feel stupid
Michelle's poor playing
some people don't appreciate classical music

Stage Two: Outlining or Organizing the Material

Allison strikes out the ideas that do not seem useful and then begins to group the other ideas that she can use. As she works with the words and phrases, she is considering what she should do with all this material. What she realizes is that she could write the essay in many ways: analyze her fears, give several examples of performances and describe her fears, or tell one special story that would reveal how she feels. She chooses the last possibility because she thinks an actual incident will be the most interesting. Furthermore, if she does this, she will have a chance to use many specific details.

She begins to work out an order. Some teachers ask students to make this order into an informal outline. She might have tried a brief four-sentence outline instead (see page 151). Here is how this student grouped her material:

Introduction
- My problems
  - shyness
  - lacking self-confidence
  - older than the others
  - not enough time to practise such long pieces
  - wanting to do well
  - difficulty memorizing
  - stage fright
  - shaky hands and legs
  - cold fingers

Supporting Details
- Coming to Mrs. Stuart's performance class
  - her personality
  - her house
  - the other students
- My performance
  - the difficulty of the sonata trills
  - runs shaky, better than I thought
  - wanting to please my teacher
- Leonard's performance
  - his appearance
  - his talent

Conclusion
- My reaction
  - feel stupid
  - disappointed
  - jealous
  - still determined

Notice how some of the ideas on the brainstorming list have been omitted or have changed slightly. Since this essay will primarily use narration, ordering is not as difficult as in some other writing. Allison will start by telling her problem, then give the story of one particular performance, and conclude with her reactions to the experience.

Stage Three: The Rough Draft

Performing on the Piano

Sometimes I wonder why I play the piano. It makes me so nervous when I have to play in front of people. I want to do well. But I can never play my best when I'm so nervous. I'm going to tell you about a typical performance I gave last February. On a Saturday afternoon I walked up the long driveway to my piano teacher's house. My hands were already shaking and my stomach felt upset. I was not looking forward to this at all. In fact, I had been dreading this moment for over a month. This day would not be the end of my terror. In the Spring I would be playing in a special contest where I would be judged and given a score.

Today, as usual, I felt my piece was not securely memorized. I never had enough time to practise. Although I wanted to please my teacher, I felt funny being nearly the oldest student in her class. I should be the best, I thought.

Now I hoped I wouldn't make a fool of myself in front of the younger kids in my teacher's class, especially that little wizard, Leonard.

He was skinny with big glasses. When he looked at you it seemed to be with a laugh. He was as great at the violin, the computer, and everything else as he was at the piano. At least I could always count on Michelle to mess up her piece. She never practised but it didn't seem to bother her. She always acted as if she was pleased with herself. At least I knew I sounded better than she did.

I was late as usual the class had begun. Mrs. Stuart was pleased to see me and she motioned to me to take a chair near the piano. The house was so nice. Filled with beautiful furniture and things on the shelves and tables.

Mrs. Stuart was kind to everyone, always trying to make us feel like "somebody." There was something about her looks and personality that made everybody who knew her like her. She had dark eyes and brown hair, was not too tall, and never seemed to wear makeup.

Before I knew it, it was my turn. Everyone was watching me.

I said what piece I was going to play and sat down. Starting was always the worst. This piece had hard trills and runs and I was really scared. I counted to ten, took a deep breath, and began.

It went better than I thought. The trills weren't so great, my runs were shaky, but at least I got through it without forgetting any part. What a relief when it was over.

My teacher seemed pleased. She says a few nice words and then moves on to the next student. People were beginning to get tired of sitting. One little girl yawned. Then it was Leonard's turn. He got up and announced that he was going to play the same piece as me. My heart started to beat faster. I was really upset. This little kid was going to play my piece.

You can guess what happened. He played better than me. The teacher praised him to the sky and I ended up feeling like a jerk. Why should I even bother to play piano when there are kids like Leonard?

Stage Four: Revising and Editing the Rough Draft

Here is the same essay. This time, marginal comments have been added by the student's writing instructor to aid in revision. No corrections of punctuation, spelling, or grammar have been made yet. At this stage, the student should focus on the organization and content. As the student works with the text, she may correct some of the grammar errors when she rewrites, deletes, or adds material.

A more creative title?

Performing on the Piano

Student has another idea for an introduction.

This is the end of the Introduction. Should begin a new paragraph.

Sometimes I wonder why I play the piano. It makes me so nervous when I have to play in front of people. I want to do well. But I can never play my best when I'm so nervous. I'm going to tell you about a typical performance I gave last February. ¶ On a Saturday afternoon I walked up the long driveway to my piano teachers house. My hands were already shaking and my stomach felt upset. I was not looking forward to this at all. In fact, I had been dreading this moment for over a month. This day would not be the end of my terror. In the Spring I would be playing in a special contest where I would be judged and given a score.

Paragraph 2 is too short.

Today, as usual, I felt my piece was not securely memorized. I never had enough time to practise. Although I wanted to please my teacher, I felt funny being nearly the oldest student in her class. I should be the best, I thought.

Paragraph 3 is too short. Belongs to paragraph 2.

Now I hoped I wouldn't make a fool of myself in front of the younger kids in my teacher's class, especially that little wizard, Leonard.

Needs to be a new paragraph.

He was skinny with big glasses. When he looked at you it seemed to be with a laugh. He was as great at the violin, the computer, and everything else as he was at the piano. ¶ At least I could always count on Michelle to mess up her piece. She never practised but it didn't seem to bother her. She always acted as if she was pleased with herself. At least I knew I sounded better than she did.

Be more specific.

I was late as usual the class had begun. Mrs. Stuart was pleased to see me and she motioned to me to take a chair near the piano. The (house was so nice.) Filled with beautiful furniture and things on the shelves and tables.

Be more specific.

Mrs. Stuart was kind to everyone, always trying to make us feel like "somebody." There was (something) about her looks and personality that made everybody who knew her like her. She had dark eyes and brown hair, was not too tall, and never seemed to wear makeup.

Use a quotation here.

Before I knew it, it was my turn. Everyone was watching me. I said what piece I was going to play and sat down. Starting was always the worst. This piece had hard trills and runs and I was really scared. I counted to ten, took a deep breath, and began.

Paragraph too short. Give more detail.

It went better than I thought. The trills weren't so great, my runs were shaky, but at least I got through it without forgetting any part. What a relief when it was over.

Use a quotation here.

My teacher seemed pleased. She says a few nice words and then moves on to the next student. People were beginning to get tired of sitting. One little girl yawned. Then it was Leonard's turn. He got up and announced that he was going to play the same piece as me. My heart started to beat faster. I was really upset. This little kid was going to play my piece.

Slang—not appropriate. Give more thought to your reactions.

You can guess what happened. He played better than me. The teacher praised him to the sky and I ended up feeling like a (jerk.) Why should I even bother to play piano when there are kids like Leonard?

Preparing the Final Copy

If you have worked hard in revising and editing the rough draft, you will be delighted with the improvements as you write the final copy.

At this stage of the writing process, it is time to proofread and to use the "Checklist for the Final Copy," which can be found on page 155 in Chapter 14.

A Student Essay in Progress: The Final Copy

Sonata in C Major, Opus 35
by Allison Hickman

Have you ever been to a children's piano recital? The little seven-year-olds walk eagerly up to the piano, play their 30-second piece that is 16 bars long, feel very pleased with themselves, and walk back to their seats to wait for everyone else to finish. All they are thinking about is the cookies and punch. I, on the other hand, sit pale and still, twisting my hands, dreading the moment when I must take my place at the piano. I must play well. What if I don't play well? What if I make a mess? The thought of forgetting the piece or stumbling through a difficult passage in front of an audience is unnerving. My experience last month at a class recital still makes me shudder.

It was a bleak Saturday afternoon in February. I trudged up the long driveway to my piano teacher's house. My hands were already shaking, and my stomach felt upset. I had been dreading this moment all week. I had to perform my contest piece in front of my teacher and 15 other talented students. Later in the spring, I would be performing the same piece for a judge who would give me a score.

Today, as usual, I felt my piece was not securely memorized. I never had enough time to practise. Even though I practised one hour a day, I really needed to spend at least two hours to get the Mozart sonata that I was playing in good shape. To make matters worse, I was the oldest student. This made me feel that I should be the best even though I knew that several of the others had been playing much longer than I had. Now, I could only hope I didn't make a fool of myself in front of the younger kids in my teacher's class. They never seemed to make any mistakes when they played, especially that little Leonard.

Leonard was a skinny little kid with a mat of black hair slicked smoothly back against his egg-shaped head. His thick glasses made him look like the stereotype of a brainy kid. When he looked at anyone, it was always with a look of amusement. I guess he knew his grey matter was far superior to whatever was in the rest of our heads! He was as good in computer programming, creative writing, and chemistry as he was at the piano. He had been taking lessons for only three years and was already playing pieces at an advanced level. What's more, I heard his mother complaining once that Leonard didn't spend much time at the piano. The worst part of performing in the same room with Leonard was his age. He was only nine!

Now, a student like Michelle made me feel better about myself. I could always count on her to break down in the middle of her piece. She seldom practised. Nevertheless, she was content to do what she could. At least I knew I sounded better than she sounded.

I entered the large Victorian house through the back door as the sound of a familiar Bach prelude drifted out from the heavy doors of the music room. As usual, I was late. I took off my shoes and crept noiselessly into the room, where I slipped into an armchair near the door.

Oh, if only I could sit here and just listen. My eyes wandered across the large room filled with beautiful antique furniture and treasures from around the world. In the far corner stood the black ebony grand piano. How much more beautiful its tone was than the old spinet on which I practised. Children ranging in age from five to twelve sat motionless in the rows of sturdy wooden folding chairs set up across a large Oriental rug.

Mrs. Stuart looked over and smiled, seeming to know how nervous I was. She had tried for years to assure me of my talent, yet I still tended to doubt it—particularly on these occasions. Mrs. Stuart was not your typical overbearing piano instructor. She was kind and always encouraging. She was in her mid-thirties, yet appeared younger. Her face was free of makeup, yet her high cheekbones and large dark eyes seemed not to need it. She radiated a warmth that was felt by all of her students.

As soon as the music ceased, I was jolted back into the reality of my situation. I was next. I approached the piano cautiously, feeling the eyes of the younger children riveted upon me. "Uhm…this piece is a Mozart sonata," I murmured quietly. Filled with difficult runs and countless trills, it was the kind of piece that could easily fall apart, especially when the performer is nervous. I counted to ten in an attempt to calm my nerves, and with one deep breath, I began.

To my surprise, I played the first movement smoothly, hardly missing a note. In the second movement, I made a small memory slip, but I managed to keep going. The third movement gave me some trouble. My fingers didn't seem to be able to move fast enough for the trills. I had to slow down. I missed two of the hard runs. Finally, I reached the last notes of the sonata, heaved a great sigh of relief, and stood up from the bench.

"Beautiful, Allison. I think that was the best I've heard you play this piece. By April you will sound more secure." The reassuring voice of Mrs. Stuart broke the silence, and I started to relax. The younger students were beginning to get restless. One girl yawned, and two boys in the back were poking at each other. Then it was Leonard's turn.

Leonard marched up to the piano with the posture of a West Point cadet. In a high, somewhat nasal voice, he announced, "This afternoon I will perform the Mozart Sonata in C Major, Opus 35."

My heart started to beat faster. I was disgraced! Leonard was going to play my piece. How could Mrs. Stuart have given us both the same piece?

Of course all of my hopes were shattered as he began to play. The sound of the music took everyone by surprise. I stared at my teacher in disbelief. I could hardly recognize this as the same piece. The evenness of the trills, the beauty of the melody, the flawless technique on the runs—I had to admit the piece was more beautiful than I had imagined. I was thrilled and devastated. The piece was gorgeous, but my performance had been mediocre, and I felt discouraged.

So now I ask myself, "What keeps me going back to the piano? How can all this misery be worth it?" Well, the answer seems clear to me, now more than ever. It's the thrill of hearing a beautiful piece. And it's the challenge of my re-creating that beauty.

Working Together: *Improving Employment Cover Letters*

Identify an employment position you might want to apply for upon graduation from your program. Take twenty minutes to write the first draft of an employment cover letter (three to four paragraphs long) responding to a make-believe posting for the position you've identified. Your letter should discuss three qualifications you have as they match three requirements of the job. Once you've written your first draft, exchange letters with a student in your group or class. Take ten minutes to revise and edit that person's letter before giving it back. Discuss the results with that person, and then with the rest of the group or class. Do you agree with the changes made to your letter? What have you learned from the revision and editing process?

CHAPTER NINETEEN 19

Writing in Response to Reading

Some English departments put more emphasis on the reading component than others when it comes to learning how to write better. Sometimes, English courses require all composition to be in response to reading. Regardless of the extent to which you'll be instructed to do this, the better your skills in this area of learning become, the more successful you'll be as a student in general. At the very least, you will be expected to know how to paraphrase and summarize. Eventually, you'll be expected to engage in analysis—a much more sophisticated response to reading.

The ability to **paraphrase and summarize** well is perhaps one of the most useful skills you will learn. Paraphrasing and summarizing are techniques for rewriting something you have read; they require putting in your own words the main idea or ideas of the original text. They are especially useful techniques when studying and writing research essays because they develop and demonstrate your understanding of the material you have read. When writing a research assignment, the techniques of paraphrasing and summarizing are important in making a coherent document out of your various sources. Translating ideas and information into your own words also helps you remember them better, because in order to summarize, you must have a complete understanding of what you have read. You probably will not forget something once you understand it.

Paraphrasing

DEFINITION ➤ **Paraphrasing** is the process of taking another writer's work and putting it into your own words. A paraphrase can be as long as or even longer than the original.

An effective **paraphrase** follows not only the line of reasoning in the original source but also the sequence of ideas or evidence as well. You paraphrase in an essay when it is important that every sentence of the original work be conveyed to your reader. Paraphrasing is typically done for shorter passages that are about a paragraph or two in length. Don't worry, your instructor won't ask you to paraphrase a whole book!

Writing a Successful Paraphrase

1. **Read the passage and define all unfamiliar or technical terms.** Write all unfamiliar terms and their definitions on a separate sheet of paper.
2. **Reread the passage, paying closer attention to the content and the order in which the ideas develop.** Make sure you have a clear understanding of the passage you are reading before you begin paraphrasing it.
3. **Begin converting the language of the passage into your own words, sentence by sentence.** Look for synonyms of words used in the passage. Alter sentence structure and vocabulary until you are conveying the original ideas in your own voice. If the original uses the first person (*I*), change it to the third person (*he* or *she*).
4. **Write out your paraphrase in full sentences of your own.** Remember not to use more than three words at a time from the original.
5. **Edit for spelling and grammar.**

EXERCISE 1

Writing Paraphrases

Use your own words or phrases to express the following. Answers will vary.

1. utterly

   ____

2. therefore

   ____

3. never before seen

   ____

4. A picture is worth a thousand words.

   ____

5. Every cloud has a silver lining.

   ____

6. A penny saved is a penny earned.

   ____

7. No pain, no gain.

   ____

8. He's like a wolf in sheep's clothing.

   ____

9. Haste makes waste.

   ____

10. The apple doesn't fall far from the tree.

____

The sample paragraph below is followed by unacceptable and acceptable paraphrases.

Original:

"Reality-based" TV programs, which have become very popular recently, appear to capture spontaneous events on film. However, most viewers are not aware that much of the action that transpires on these programs is staged. People who appear on these shows are often selected because producers think they will appeal to the audience, and directors often script important pieces of dialogue at critical moments during production. Therefore, relationships that develop between participants on these shows are often as contrived as those between characters on a TV sitcom or a soap opera.

Unacceptable:

"Reality-based" TV shows, which have become popular recently, seem to depict spontaneous events on film. Most people, however, do not know that a lot of the action that takes place on these programs is staged. The people on shows like these are often selected because the producers believe they will appeal to viewers, and directors frequently write important pieces of dialogue at crucial moments during the filming of the show. Therefore, relationships that develop are frequently as phony as those between personalities on TV sitcoms or soap operas.

This is an unsuccessful paraphrase because the underlined structure and phrasing are almost identical to the original. In fact, much of the structure and phrasing has not changed at all from the original.

Acceptable:

The popularity of "reality-based" TV shows is founded on the belief that live events are being filmed, but many viewers do not know that much of what they see is made purposely dramatic. Producers of these shows often choose participants because they believe viewers will find them attractive, and the shows' directors often have them acting from scripts to heighten the drama. Thus, participants create relationships that are no more real than those we see on other TV shows, such as sitcoms or soap operas.

This passage is an example of good paraphrasing. The writer has taken the main idea of the original paragraph and restated it using his or her own words. All of the original details and examples appear, but they have been reworded and the sentences restructured.

Plagiarism: A Serious Offence

Students who write unacceptable paraphrases can be accused of plagiarism. Plagiarism is a form of intellectual theft. It occurs when a student uses the ideas or words of another person *without giving credit to the original source or author.* You can avoid plagiarism by ensuring that credit for work other than your own is cited. When you paraphrase a passage, be sure to inform your reader about who the original author is and where the original work appeared.

Plagiarism often results in a mark of zero on an assignment. If this is a major assignment, one case of plagiarism can result in the overall failure of a course. Plagiarism is not only contrary to school policy; it is also against the law. If you are not sure about how to avoid being accused of plagiarism, ask your professor for advice.

EXERCISE 2

Paraphrasing a Paragraph

The following passage was excerpted from an article entitled "A Dead End for Humanity," by Wade Davis. Write a paraphrase of this paragraph. The passage contains 79 words, so your paraphrase should be about the same length.

> Of the 6000 languages spoken today, fully half are not being taught to children. Effectively, these languages are already dead. By the end of the twenty-first century linguistic diversity may be reduced to as few as 500 languages. A language, of course, is not simply vocabulary and grammar; it is a flash of the human spirit, the vehicle by which the soul of a culture comes into the material realm. Each language represents a unique intellectual and spiritual achievement.

The Globe and Mail (December 28, 2000)

Summarizing

DEFINITION ➤ Like a paraphrase, a **summary** is written in your own words, but it is a condensed version of an original source.

We practise summarization all the time in our day-to-day lives. When telling friends about a movie, you don't repeat the story or dialogue from beginning to end. Instead, you will probably relate the main points in the plot or things about the movie that captured your interest.

A summary states the main idea of a passage. The purpose of a summary is to shorten the original piece of writing, providing only important information and eliminating nonessential points. A summary allows the reader to understand the main facts and ideas in the original without actually having to read the entire passage.

A summary should be no more than one-third the length of the original passage. As in a paraphrase, the words you use should be your own. You should not use more than three words at a time from the original.

Tips on Writing a Successful Summary

1. **Read the passage and identify the topic sentence and controlling idea.** Underline the sentence that you think best expresses the main point of the passage. Rewrite this sentence in your own words.
2. **Identify and eliminate minor supporting ideas.** Specific facts or examples may be important in developing a main idea, but they are not to be included in a summary.
3. **Write out the major supporting details in full sentences of your own.** Use as few words as possible and remember not to use more than three words at a time from the original.
4. **Count the words.** Make sure the total is no more than one-third the original.
5. **Reread your summary.** Make sure that the meaning of the passage is conveyed clearly and that your sentences work together.
6. **Edit for spelling and grammar.**

EXERCISE 1

Writing Summaries

Find single words to replace the following phrases. Answers will vary.

1. conduct a discussion of ______________________
2. perform an analysis of ______________________
3. create a reduction in ______________________
4. make a discovery of ______________________
5. engage in the preparation of ______________________
6. make an assumption of ______________________
7. give consideration to ______________________
8. is dependent on ______________________
9. reach a conclusion about ______________________
10. take an action on ______________________

The following passage is quoted in its entirety and then summarized:

Wired 'n' Wealthy

How wired is *your* province? It's no coincidence that the three provinces with the highest average household incomes—British Columbia, Alberta and Ontario—also have the highest rate of Internet use at home. According to a survey by Statistics Canada, almost five million Canadian households—or 42 percent of the population—had at least one member who used the Internet regularly in 1999, at either home, school, or work. British Columbia, Alberta, and Ontario all topped that average. In about 3.4 million households—or 29 percent of the population—at least one member logs on from home. That's up sharply from the 16 percent of homes that were wired in 1997. Internet use rises in direct proportion to income: the richest households are five times as likely to be wired as the lowest-income groups. Along with the well-established use of the Internet for recreation, StatsCan reports that 19 percent of the survey respondents use the Web to buy goods and services, 54 percent use it to seek medical and health information, and 28 percent use it for electronic banking. One in five households uses the Internet at home for self-employment reasons, and one in four for employer-related use.

(198 words)

Maclean's (December 18, 2000)

Acceptable Summary:

The three provinces with the highest average incomes per household—British Columbia, Alberta and Ontario—also have the highest rate of home Internet use. A survey reported that almost half of Canadian households use the Internet regularly, and a significant increase in the number of households wired for Internet use has been seen. While higher-income households are more likely to be wired, all levels of Canadian society now count on the Internet to some extent for personal services.

(78 words)

EXERCISE 2

Summarizing a Paragraph

Summarize the following passage, reducing it to approximately one-third of its original length:

Canadian society in the twenty-first century is very different from that of early Canadians, and not just because we have televisions and VCRs. Two hundred years ago, people lived half as long as they do today, and families had twice as many children. In general, all Canadians are living longer, which means not only is our working life extended, but we can expect to retire from work and live another 15 to 20 years to enjoy the fruits of our labours. Canadians born in 1700 had an average life expectancy of 30 to 35 years due to poor diet, disease, and accidents. By 1831, four generations had passed, and there had been a slight improvement in life expectancy, with males expecting to live to age 40 and females to 42. During the next four generations, major medical breakthroughs and public health education eliminated a number of infectious diseases and reduced infant mortality, so that Canadians' life spans were almost double what they were a little more than a century previously. But while Canadians can expect a long and healthy life, with many living well into their seventies or eighties, the average life span will not increase indefinitely. While we can expect to live longer than the Canadians of the 1700s, we can't expect to live forever.

EXERCISE 3

Summarizing an Article

John Cleland and Thérèse Zarb wrote this 435-word article. Write a 100-word summary of it.

Steer Away from Road Rage

According to a Steel Alliance-Canada Safety Council survey last year, drivers in B.C. are more likely than those in other regions to tailgate and change lanes without signalling. Ontario drivers are more likely to drive through a yellow light turning red, and steal parking spaces.

Road aggression is not a new phenomenon. It gained attention when the media recharged it by coining the term "road rage." According to Claudia Palucci, media and public affairs specialist for CAA Central Ontario, "what was rude and careless driving before, now has a sexy new term [road rage]. But aggressive driving hasn't suddenly appeared on our roadways; it was always there." In public opinion surveys, Canadians perceive an increase in roadway aggression despite a lack of objective data to confirm this.

***

Although systematic observational studies are lacking, traffic researchers have suggested several factors that increase the likelihood of aggressive driving.

"Driving is tailor-made to engender anger," says Dr. Lorne Korman, clinical psychologist and head of the Anger and Addictions Program at the Centre for Addiction and Mental Health in Toronto. He explains that the inherent goal of driving is to get from point A to point B, and reality dictates that there will always be obstacles along the path: other automobiles, pedestrians, road signs, and construction. The more congested our roads become, the more thwarted we feel on the way toward our goal. For many, this interference amounts to personal violation. And it is when we feel violated, says Dr. Korman, that we react with anger. Angry drivers seem to attribute the situational barriers to other drivers' deliberate interference. Furthermore, drivers are less likely to inhibit this aggression because "driving is life and death. You are moving fast, you have to make fast decisions, and your body is aroused physiologically."

Dr. Korman also believes that the deluge of car chases and smashes in the media contributes to our feeling of empowerment and recklessness behind the wheel; the automobile becomes an aggressive tool rather than a means of transportation.

***

Due to the anonymity of driving, we are more likely to express our annoyance in our car than on the sidewalk. We believe that we can get away with an anti-social act because we are not face-to-face and do not know our opponent. Escape is easy when we rely on the protection and speed of our automobile.

Finally, we can roll out the usual suspects believed to fuel dangerous driving. We transport our personal and professional stress with us in our cars. Combine that with a "me-first," rat-race mentality and we may find ourselves skidding toward a head-on collision with aggression.

Wellness Options (February–March 2001)

Analyzing and Critiquing

Eventually, your professor will ask you not only to repeat what someone else has already written, but to agree or disagree and explain the reasons why. If you look at Unit IV of this text, you'll notice several questions at the end of each reading, questions that are classified in four groups. This first of four groups is called "Comprehension Questions." These are questions that require some paraphrasing and summarizing. They require that you recall or look back at what you've read and that you repeat, in one way or another, what the author has written.

"Questions for Discussion" and "Questions about Form," on the other hand, require more thinking on your part. They require analysis and argumentation. You, at times, will have to support or refute what the author has written. One skill you will develop in this area is usually referred to as critical thinking. It is often a requirement in courses across the curriculum at the postsecondary level, a requirement that can only help you in any workplace.

Working Together: *Summarizing Opposing Points of View*

Form groups of three or four. Look in your local newspaper for feature articles on controversial topics that are of concern to many Canadians, such as the effects of global warming or genetic engineering. Try to find one article that looks at the problem from one perspective, and another article that takes an opposing view. For instance, find an article that supports high-speed police chases and another that takes the view that high-speed police chases are too dangerous. Each person then writes a summary of one of these articles, making sure that the opposing points of view are clearly indicated. You might use this information to discuss ways in which the media attempt to influence the attitudes of Canadians.

CHAPTER TWENTY 20

Writing under Pressure

How to Write Well under Pressure

Most people prefer to do their writing when they have the time to develop their subject, but it often happens that you do not have the chance to write and revise as you would like. Certainly, in your later work life, you will often be required to write to tight deadlines. Even now, you sometimes have to write under pressure. For example, you may be given a last-minute assignment that must be done right away, or what is even more likely, you may have to produce an in-class written examination for a course you are taking.

No matter what the circumstances are, you want to be able to do the best writing you can with the time you are given. For example, if you are given an essay question for a final examination in a course, your first step should *not* be to begin writing. Instead, you should take a few moments to analyze the question you have been given. What does the question require you to do? Is there more than one part to the question? Does the professor want you to *define* a term or *compare* two historical figures or *narrate* the story of your search for the right part-time job? Furthermore, how many points is the question worth? How much time do you have to spend on the question?

Study the following sample essay question to determine exactly what is being asked for:

> Describe the rise of the feminist movement in the 1960s in Canada. Be specific.

If this were one of five short-essay questions on a final examination, the following answer would probably be adequate. The answer would be in the form of a paragraph.

> The late 1960s saw, in Canada as throughout the Western world, the emergence of a new women's movement. This new feminism rejected all limits to the equality of women's rights and showed that equality in daily life could not be obtained through simple legal, political, or institutional modifications. Discovering that "sisterhood is powerful," women from Vancouver to Halifax began forming groups. The Vancouver Women's Caucus was organized in 1968. The Montreal Women's Liberation Movement was founded in 1969, and the Front de libération des femmes du Québec published a feminist

manifesto in 1970. At first, some were consciousness-raising groups, but others quickly turned to concrete action, providing access to abortion services, health centres, militant theatre, daycare, shelters for battered women, and rape crisis centres, and they began agitating for equal pay. By the end of the 1960s, Canada had begun to adjust to the rebirth of a major social movement.

Strategies for Answering Timed In-Class Essay Questions

1. Read the question twice. How many points is it worth? Decide how much time you should spend answering it.
2. What is the method of development asked for?
3. From key words in the question, compose your thesis statement.
4. Answer the question using several specific details (include names and dates of important facts).
5. Check the question again to be sure you have answered all parts of the question. (A question can have more than one part.)

Frequently Used Terms in Essay Questions

There are five popular methods of developing an answer to an essay question: definition, comparison or contrast, narration, summary, and discussion. The following terms used in essay questions will tell you which method the instructor is asking for.

Define: A definition is the precise meaning of a word or term. When you define something in an essay, you usually write an *extended definition*, in which you select an appropriate example or examples to illustrate the meaning of a term.

Compare or Contrast: When you *compare* two items, you point out the similarities between them. When you *contrast* two items, you point out the differences. Sometimes you may find yourself using both comparison and contrast in an essay.

Narrate: To *narrate* is to tell a story by carefully relating a sequence of events. The events are usually (but not always) given in chronological order.

Summarize: When you *summarize*, you supply the main ideas of a longer piece of writing. A summary, as described in the *Harbrace College Handbook*, is a concise restatement, shorter than the source. When you summarize or paraphrase, avoid copying the actual words, and avoid imitating the writer's style or sentence structure. Restate in your own words what has been stated previously.

Discuss: This is a general term that encourages you to analyze a subject at length. Inviting students to *discuss* some aspect of a topic is a widely used method of asking examination questions.

Of course, answering an essay question correctly depends largely on the work you have done to prepare for the test. To study for an essay exam, you should try to anticipate questions your professor is likely to ask. Then prepare the information you need to have in order to answer these questions. Unlike the multiple-choice or true/false test, the essay examination requires you to have absorbed the material so well that you can give it back in your own words.

PRACTICE

Methods of Development

Each of the following college essay questions deals with the topic of computers. Use the preceding list of frequently used terms to help you decide which method of development is being called for in each case. Check your answers against those in the Answer Key on p. 442.

1. Tell the story of the first time you encountered a computer. Did you first see a computer at school, at work, or in a friend's home? What was your reaction to this technology? What did you learn about computers at this first encounter?

   Method of development: ______________________________

2. Point out the similarities and differences between computer use in the home and at school. In how many ways are these uses similar? In how many ways are they different?

   Method of development: ______________________________

3. Analyze the present role of computers in society.

   Method of development: ______________________________

4. List and explain the uses of computers in school, at work, and at home.

   Method of development: ______________________________

5. Write a condensed account of the history of computers, from the time they were invented up to the present day.

   Method of development: ______________________________

EXERCISE

Methods of Development/Parts of a Question

Each of the following is an example of an essay question. In the spaces provided after each question indicate (a) what method of development (definition, comparison or contrast, narration, summary, or discussion) is being called for, and (b) how many parts there are to the question. This indicates how many parts there will be in your answer. An example is done for you.

> ***Example:*** What does the term sociology mean? Include in your answer at least four different meanings the term sociology has had since this area of study began.

Method of development: definition
Number of parts to the question: four

1. Compare the reasons Canada entered the Korean War with the reasons it entered World War II.

   Method of development: ____________________

   Number of parts to the question: ____________________

2. Briefly trace the history of spacecraft exploration of Mars from the Viking missions of the 1970s to the launch of the Mars Odyssey in 2001. Include in your answer evidence for and against the presence of water on Mars.

   Method of development: ____________________

   Number of parts to the question: ____________________

3. Contrast marriage customs in India with those in Canada.

   Method of development: ____________________

   Number of parts to the question: ____________________

4. Explain the three effects of high temperatures on space vehicles as they re-enter the earth's atmosphere.

   Method of development: ____________________

   Number of parts to the question: ____________________

5. What was the complete process of building the transcontinental railway? Include in your answer six different aspects of the construction, from laying the rails across the Canadian Shield to the effects of the Riel Rebellion.

   Method of development: ____________________

   Number of parts to the question: ____________________

Using the Thesis Statement in Essay Questions

One of the most effective ways to begin an essay answer is to write a thesis statement. Your thesis statement should include the important parts of the question and should also give a clear indication of the approach you intend to take in your answer. Writing your opening sentence in this way gives you a real advantage: as your professor begins to read your work, it is clear *what* you are going to write about and *how* you are going to treat your subject.

For example, suppose you were going to write an essay on the following topic:

> A woman prime minister could handle the demands of the most stressful job in the country.

An effective way to begin would be to write the following thesis sentence:

> I agree that a woman prime minister could handle the demands of the most stressful job in the country.

The reader would then know that this was the topic you had chosen and would also know how you intended to approach this topic.

EXERCISE

Writing Thesis Statements

Rewrite each of the following essay questions in thesis statement form. Read each question carefully and underline the important words or phrases in it. Then decide on the approach you would take in answering that question. An example has been done for you.

Essay question: How does one learn another language?
Thesis statement: The process of learning another language is complicated but usually follows four distinct stages.

1. Essay question: Discuss the effects of raising the legal driving age to eighteen.

   Thesis statement: ______________________________

   ____

   ____

2. Essay question: Why or why not should the Canadian government support young artists?

   Thesis statement: ______________________________

   ____

   ____

3. Essay question: What is the value of being able to speak two languages in Canada?

   Thesis statement: ______________________________

   ____

   ____

4. Essay question: What are three reasons schools should spend less time on optional subjects and more time on the basics such as English and mathematics?

   Thesis statement: ____

   ____

   ____

5. Essay question: Is it harmful or beneficial to adopt a child from one culture and raise that child in another culture?

   Thesis statement: ____

   ____

   ____

6. Essay question: What are the effects of free trade on Mexico?

   Thesis statement: ____

   ____

   ____

7. Essay question: In what ways can the Canadian government discourage people from smoking?

   Thesis statement: ____

   ____

   ____

8. Essay question: In what ways is regionalism relevant in today's global world?

   Thesis statement: ____

   ____

   ____

9. Essay question: Discuss the quotation "One picture is worth a thousand words."

   Thesis statement: ____

   ____

   ____

10. Essay question: Are some forms of advertising harmful, and, if so, should harmful advertising be banned?

    Thesis statement: ____

    ____

    ____

Working Together: *Guess the Professor's Questions*

The following passage on the consequences of the shift of human society from nomadic to agricultural is taken from *Biology*, by Helena Curtis:

> Whatever its causes, the change to agriculture had profound consequences. Populations were no longer nomadic. Thus they could store food not only in silos and granaries, but in the form of domesticated animals. In addition to food stores, other possessions could be accumulated to an extent far beyond that previously possible. Even land could be owned and accumulated and passed on by inheritance. Thus the world became divided into semi-permanent groups of haves and have-nots, as it is today.
>
> Because the efforts of a few could produce enough food for everyone, the communities became diversified. People became tradesmen, artisans, bankers, scholars, poets, all the rich mixture of which a modern community is composed. And these people could live much more densely than ever before. For hunting and food-gathering economies, two square miles, on the average, are required to provide enough for one family to eat.
>
> One immediate and direct consequence of the agricultural revolution was an increase in populations. A striking characteristic of hunting groups is that they vigorously limit their numbers. A woman on the move cannot carry more than one infant along with her household baggage, minimal though that may be. When simple means of birth control—often just abstention—are not effective, she resorts to abortion or, more probably, infanticide. In addition, there is a high natural mortality, particularly among the very young, the very old, the ill, the disabled, and women at childbirth. As a result, populations dependent on hunting tend to remain small.

1. After you have studied the selection, construct an essay question that a professor in a biology or anthropology course could ask as part of a midterm or final examination. At the same time, your present instructor could also make up a question based on the selection. When everyone has finished, your instructor could read his or her question first. Is it the question you had expected? How many students in the class came close to the instructor's choice of question?

2. After the instructor's question and the students' questions have been discussed, use the following checklist to analyze each question.
   a. Does the question seem to be fair? (Some questions might be too vague or too general to be a proper test of what the student has learned.)
   b. How many parts does the question have?
   c. Does the question call for a specific method of development (for example, definition and analysis)?
   d. What are the key terms that should be used in the answer?
   e. What would be an effective opening sentence for the answer?

UNIT THREE

Writing Strategies

CHAPTER TWENTY-ONE

21

Narration

What Is Narration?

DEFINITION ➤ **Narration** is the oldest and best-known form of verbal communication. It is, quite simply, the telling of a story.

Every culture in the world, past and present, has used narration to provide entertainment as well as information for the people of that culture. Since everyone likes a good story, the many forms of narration, such as novels, short stories, soap operas, and full-length movies, are always popular.

Developing Paragraphs: Narration

The following narrative paragraph, taken from an essay by Al Purdy titled "The Iron Road," tells the story of Purdy's trip westward in 1937, the height of the Great Depression, when he was looking for work. In this passage, Purdy has been caught illegally riding a freight train by the railway police, and he is imprisoned in a caboose.

> When returned to my prison-on-wheels, I felt panic-stricken. I was only seventeen, and this was the first time I'd ventured far away from home. I examined the caboose-prison closely, thinking: two years. Why, I'd be nineteen when I got out, an old man! And of course it was hopeless to think of escape. Other prisoners had tried without success, and windows were broken where they'd tried to wrench out the bars. And the door: it was wood, locked on the outside with a padlock, opening inward. It was a very springy door, though. I could squeeze my fingertips between sill and door, one hand at the top and the other a foot below. That gave me hope, blessed hope, for the first time. My six-foot-three body was suspended in air by my hands, doubled up like a coiled spring, and I pulled. The door bent inward until I could see a couple of daylight inches between door and sill. Then Snap! and screws fell out of the steel hasp outside. I fell flat on my back.

Working with Narration: Using Narration to Make a Point

At one time or another, you have met a person who loves to talk on and on without making any real point. This person is likely to tell you everything that happened in one day, including every cough and sideways glance. Your reaction to the seemingly needless and endless supply of details is probably one of fatigue and hope for a quick getaway. This is not narration at its best! A good story is almost always told to make a point: it can make us laugh, it can make us understand, or it can change our attitudes.

When Al Purdy tells the story of his escape from the caboose, he is careful to use only those details that are relevant to his story. For example, the way the door is constructed is important. Had it not been wooden and springy, he might never have been able to get his fingertips in and force an opening. He might have had to spend two years in prison. Then Purdy would have had a different story to tell.

What is Purdy's point in this paragraph? The excerpt is part of an essay about Purdy's experiences during the Depression, and specifically, in this part, about the dangers of travelling illegally by train during that time, which many thousands of people had to do, illegal and dangerous or not. On its surface, then, the story is merely about a trip, although an unusual one. Being imprisoned in the caboose, however, might be metaphorical: the caboose in which Purdy was imprisoned might represent the life of hopeless despair caused by unemployment that he and thousands of others were imprisoned in, and Purdy's escape was the escape from despair toward the hope that a trip to the West could bring, with its opportunities for a better life.

EXERCISE

Using Narration to Make a Point

Each of the following examples is the beginning of a topic sentence for a narrative paragraph. Complete each sentence by providing a controlling idea that could be the point for the story.

1. During my trip to the East Coast, I was surprised by ______________________

   ____

2. When I couldn't get a job, I realized ______________________________

   ____

3. After going to the movies every Saturday for many years, I discovered ________

   ____

4. When I arrived at the room where my business class was to meet, I found ____

   ____

5. When my best friend got married, I began to see that ____________________

   ____

Coherence in Narration: Placing Details in Order of Time Sequence

Ordering details in a paragraph of narration usually follows a time sequence. That is, you tell what happened first, then next, and next, until finally you get to the end of the story. An event could take place in a matter of minutes or over a period of many years.

In the following paragraph, the story takes place in a single day. The six events that made the day a disaster are given in the order in which they happened. Although some stories flash back to the past or forward to the future, most use the natural chronological order of the events.

> My day was a disaster. First, it had snowed during the night, which meant I had to shovel before I could leave for work. I was mad that I hadn't gotten up earlier. Then I had trouble starting my car, and to make matters worse, my daughter wasn't feeling well and said she didn't think she should go to school. When I eventually did arrive at school, I was 20 minutes late. Soon I found out the secretary had forgotten to type the exam I was supposed to give my class that day. I quickly had to make another plan. By three o'clock, I was looking forward to getting my paycheque. Foolish woman! When I went to pick it up, the woman in the office told me that something had gone wrong with the computers. I would not be able to get my cheque until Tuesday. Disappointed, I walked down the hill to the parking lot. There I met my final defeat. In my hurry to park the car in the morning, I had left my parking lights on. Now my battery was dead. Even an optimist like me had the right to be discouraged!

PRACTICE

Coherence: Placing Details in Order of Time Sequence

Each of the topics below is followed by six supporting details. These supporting details are listed in random order. Order the events according to time sequence by placing the appropriate number in the space provided. The first one is done for you. Check your answers against those in the Answer Key on p. 442.

1. The driving test

___2___ She had her last lesson with Mr. Panakos on Saturday morning.

___5___ As she ate breakfast Monday morning, Daniela read the driver's manual one more time because she knew it was her last chance to review.

___1___ Daniela's driving test was scheduled for Monday morning.

___3___ On Sunday afternoon her father gave her some advice on what to be careful of when she took her road test.

___6___ As her mother drove her to the motor vehicle bureau, Daniela tried to relax and not think about the test.

4	The night before her test, Daniela had phone calls from two friends who wished her good luck.

2. Making up my mind

______	By the time I saw the dean for final approval of the change, I knew I had made the right decision.
______	When I registered for my new courses for the next semester, I knew that I was doing what I should have done all along.
______	I spent the summer of my second year thinking about the career I really wanted to follow.
______	I suppose the experience taught me that you should always make a change in your life after you have thought it through completely.
______	When I finally did decide to change majors, my friends acted as though I had decided to change my citizenship.
______	When I told my favourite professor about my change of mind, he was very supportive, even though I had begun my major with him.

Transitions

Once you have determined the sequence of events for your paragraph, you must then be able to move smoothly from detail to detail. Transitional words and phrases connect thoughts within a sentence, between sentences, and among paragraphs. They can appear anywhere in a sentence or paragraph. Transitions can be used to show relationships such as time (*first of all, next, finally*), comparison (*similarly, just like, also*), contrast (*despite, however, otherwise*), and more.

After a ten-hour delay we *finally* got to board the plane.
I left home too late and *just like* last time, I got a speeding ticket.
Despite the high ticket price, the concert sold out.

Notice how these words and phases show the logical connection between ideas.

An extensive list of transitional words and phrases categorized by their function is found on the inside back cover of this book and in Chapter 17: "The Essay."

Writing the Narrative Paragraph Step by Step

To learn a skill with some degree of ease, it is best to follow a step-by-step approach so that various steps can be worked on one at a time. This will ensure that you are not missing a crucial point or misunderstanding a part of the whole. There are other ways to go about writing an effective paragraph, but here is one logical method you can use to achieve results.

Steps for Writing the Narrative Paragraph

1. Study the given topic, and then plan your topic sentence with its controlling idea.
2. List the events that come to mind when you think about the topic you have chosen.
3. Choose the five or six most important events from your list.
4. Put your final list in order.
5. Write at least one complete sentence for each of the events you have chosen from your list.
6. Write a concluding statement that gives some point to the events of the story.
7. Finally, copy your sentences into standard paragraph form.

Step-by-Step Example of Writing a Narrative Paragraph

The following example starts with a suggested topic and then uses the seven steps above to work through each stage of the writing process.

Topic: At one time or another, most people have to buy a car. Often it's not the type of car purchased that leads to a story, but the process of buying it. Write a narrative paragraph about buying a car (or some other expensive item, such as a stereo).

1. Topic sentence: Because my classes were at different campuses, and because I lived quite a distance from the college, I decided to buy a car.
2. Make a list of events.
   a. Tired of waiting for the bus
   b. Budget—gas, insurance, licence, repairs, financing
   c. Car loan
   d. Newspaper ads—dealerships
   e. Want ads
   f. Comparison shopping
3. Circle the five or six events you believe are the most important for the point of the story.
4. Put your final choices in order by numbering them.
5. Using your final list, write at least one sentence for each event you have chosen.
   a. I was tired of waiting for the bus on cold and rainy days, and being late for class when the bus was late didn't impress my professors.
   b. My budget didn't allow me to purchase a new car, especially when I calculated the price of gasoline, insurance, repairs, licensing, and finance charges.

c. My bank manager was very helpful when it came to arranging a car loan, but even though the payments were spread out over a long period of time, it was still an expensive proposition.
d. I looked in the newspaper for ads from car dealerships, trying to decide whether I'd be better off buying from a dealer, with at least a minimal warranty on the car, or from a private seller.
e. Comparison shopping was a long and tedious, but necessary, process.

6. Write a concluding statement: I finally bought a car, although it wasn't what I really wanted because of my financial situation. At least I don't have to wait for the bus any more.
7. Copy your sentences into standard paragraph form.

Because my classes were at different campuses, and because I lived quite a distance from the college, I decided to buy a car. I was tired of waiting for the bus on cold and rainy days, and being late for class when the bus was late didn't impress my professors. My budget didn't allow me to purchase a new car, especially when I calculated the price of gasoline, insurance, repairs, licensing, and finance charges. My bank manager was very helpful when it came to arranging a car loan, but even though the payments were spread out over a long period of time, it was still an expensive proposition. I looked in the newspaper for ads from car dealerships, trying to decide whether I'd be better off buying from a dealer, with at least a minimal warranty on the car, or from a private seller. Comparison shopping was a long and tedious, but necessary, process. I finally bought a car, although it wasn't really what I wanted because of my financial situation. At least I don't have to wait for the bus anymore.

EXERCISE

Writing the Narrative Paragraph Step by Step

The following exercise will guide you through the construction of a narrative paragraph. Start with the suggested topic. Use the seven steps and the example on pages 225–26 to help you work through each stage of the writing process.

Topic: Recount the plot of a book you have read recently or a movie you have seen within the last few weeks.

1. Topic sentence: ______________________________

____

2. Make a list of events.

a. ______________ f. ______________

b. ______________ g. ______________

c. ______________ h. ______________

d. ______________ i. ______________

e. ______________ j. ______________

3. Circle the five or six events you believe are the most important for the point of the story.
4. Put your choices in order by numbering them.
5. Using your final list, write at least one sentence for each event you have chosen.

   a. ______________________________

   ____

   b. ______________________________

   ____

   c. ______________________________

   ____

   d. ______________________________

   ____

   e. ______________________________

   ____

   f. ______________________________

   ____

   g. ______________________________

   ____

6. Write a concluding statement.

   ____

   ____

7. Copy your sentences into standard paragraph form.

   ____

   ____

   ____

   ____

   ____

   ____

   ____

   ____

   ____

   ____

On Your Own: Writing Narrative Paragraphs from Model Paragraphs

The Story of How You Faced a New Challenge

Model Paragraph

I hate to be late. So, when I began my new job, I was determined to be on time for my first day. I awoke early, had a leisurely breakfast, and gave myself lots of time to get through the traffic. I entered my new office building and sat down at my new desk a good fifteen minutes before starting time. My boss noticed me, smiled, and came over to my desk. "I'm glad you're early," she said. "In fact, you're a week early. You start *next* Monday."

ASSIGNMENT

Narrative Paragraph

Write a paragraph telling the story of a day or part of a day in which you faced an important challenge of some kind. It could have been a challenge you faced in school, at home, or on the job. The preceding paragraph is an example of such an experience.

SUGGESTED TOPICS

1. The day I started a new job
2. Becoming a member of a sports team
3. The morning of my big job interview
4. Facing a large debt
5. Sharing the telephone
6. The day I started driving lessons
7. Losing

Writing the Narrative Essay

Writing a narrative essay, as opposed to a narrative paragraph, gives you the opportunity to write a longer story with more detail. Try to structure your essay in such a way that it appears organized even though you're writing a narrative—probably the most informal of essay strategies.

You might, for example, devote each support paragraph to a single event or a different character in your story. At the very least, make sure that some sort of shift has taken place, one that warrants a new paragraph. Don't fall into the trap of starting a new paragraph simply because the old one is getting too long.

For an in-depth look at the essay and its standard format (for all writing strategies in this unit), see Chapter 17: "The Essay." Also review Chapter 14: "The Four Stages of Writing," which can be applied to both the paragraph and the essay.

The essay you will write will be a narrative essay, in which you will tell a story about yourself. Because the experience happened to you, you are the expert on the topic. As you read the model essays in this chapter, and as you study how a narrative essay is constructed, you will be preparing to write your own essay based on your personal experience.

The following narrative essay was a winning entry in Centennial College's Student Writing Contest (2001–2002):

Model Essay: Transparent Silhouette

by Akis Stylianou

On many lonely nights when I am too far from home to remember where home is and too beat to care where I lay my head, I have often heard an echo or seen a reflection that reminded me of a woman I knew. A silhouette through the window reflects the image of a petite yet shapely figure with long strands of silken hair falling over her shoulders. The wind whistling through the trees calls her name, taking me to another place where I can delay my misery.

We met early in life as classmates in elementary school. She used to stand alone in the schoolyard, surrounding herself with the walls she had built. It was a few years later before I could find the strength to enter those walls and discover her world. She told me she came from a broken home with an alcoholic mother and an abusive father. Being the only child, she was often the target of their frustration and rage, though she constantly dreamt of escaping her parents. By the time we reached our teens, she was running out of ways to numb her pain, and, soon after, she left home to live on the streets. Caring as much as I did, it tore me apart knowing there was nothing I could do to help.

She met the wrong kind of people and got involved with their crowds. She did many things she would come to regret, but, if the price was fitting, she was willing to sacrifice herself. My role as her friend was never to judge the path she had chosen; thus, friendship was never compromised. Most people considered her character unethical and immoral. However, she could smile with relief because she had finally escaped from the chains that weighed her down in the past.

One night, she was working as a dancer in a sleazy downtown bar when one of her customers began boasting about his position as an adult film producer. He told her that she had the look he was interested in. Soon after, she started acting, and her status as an adult film star rocketed. Before her twenty-fifth birthday, she had a brand new sports car, a beautiful apartment in the heart of the city, and a bank account holding her six-figure salary. On one occasion, we met at a restaurant for dinner. As she entered the room, all eyes were on her, as if they were in a hypnotic state. The men wanted to be with her, and the women were jealous of her graceful presence. Behind all her jewelry, fur coat and expensive clothing, I could still see the frightened, bruised little girl I cared about. She pretended it didn't bother her, but beneath her polished exterior, I could see inside she wanted to explode.

That was the last chance I had to see her before her body was found lying lifeless in an empty apartment. The police said it was a burglary that went wrong and resulted in a homicide. She taught me to accept the good with the bad. After the rain falls, I walk the streets where she once lived, and the dried up puddles remind me of her permanent tears.

Analyzing the Writer's Strategies

1. What do you think is the writer's thesis?
2. What is the writer's tone?
3. What is the meaning of the essay's title?
4. How do you think the writer feels about his friend?
5. How did the writer foreshadow the ending of the essay?
6. Why did the writer foreshadow the ending?

ASSIGNMENT

Narrative Essay

Choose one of the following topics and write a narrative essay of at least five paragraphs to develop that topic.

SUGGESTED TOPICS:

1. My worst classroom experience
2. A parent who would not listen
3. My first ____________________
4. When I tried to convince someone to hire me for a job
5. My experience with an aggressive salesperson
6. A day when nothing went right
7. A misunderstanding with a friend
8. Trouble at the workplace
9. A day that changed my life
10. A major disappointment
11. How my nervousness made matters worse
12. A perfect evening
13. The best summer of my life
14. An embarrassing experience
15. Learning something surprising about myself

For helpful hints on the following subjects, all of which will assist you in developing your narrative essay, see Chapter 14:

Brainstorming
Choosing the Topic and the Controlling Idea
Outlining
The Rough Draft
Revising the Rough Draft
Proofreading
Checklist for the Final Copy

Working Together: *"The Story of the Tortoise and the Hare"*

1. Aesop is believed to have been a Greek slave of some 2500 years ago. He wrote over 200 fables, which have become part of our literary heritage. Below is one of Aesop's most famous fables, often called "The Story of the Tortoise and the Hare."

    > A tortoise and a hare disagreed about which one of them was faster, so they decided to settle the dispute by having a race. The hare was so confident of his ability to move swiftly that after running awhile, he decided to take a nap by the side of the road. The tortoise was very aware of his own slow movement, and so he went steadily along the road. He did not stop until he had passed the sleeping hare and so won the race.
    >
    > Moral: A slow and steady person often beats a person who has great natural abilities but who does not make use of them.

    Sometimes a writer's purpose is to teach a lesson. Notice how Aesop points out a moral lesson to his readers. You might enjoy creating a fable of your own with a moral lesson added at the end. Your fable might also use animals, but you could set the action of your fable in a modern town or city. You might discuss with your classmates some of the social or personal concerns that might be the subject of a particular fable. For example, you might want to teach a lesson about human ambition or greed. Your narration might make a very good story to read to the children in your family. What lesson would you like them to learn?

2. A parlour game that is amusing is telling a story by creating it on the spot. One person begins with a sentence that sets the scene. Then it is continued sentence by sentence as each person takes a turn. Do this for perhaps twenty minutes. Elect one student in charge of putting the sentences on the board. Then discuss the outcome. In what ways is the narrative a success? What are its weaknesses?

3. In this chapter, each student is invited to write a narrative essay. Divide into groups and share the narrative essays in your group. Attach a sheet of paper to each essay in which you critique the essay by answering two questions:
   a. In your opinion, what is one aspect of the essay that you believe is very strong?
   b. In your opinion, what is one aspect of the essay that still needs improvement?

CHAPTER TWENTY-TWO

22

Description

What Is Description?

Description is one of the basic building blocks of good writing. When you are able to write an effective description of a person, an object, a place, or even an idea, you are in control of your writing. Good description also makes you able to control what your reader sees and does not see.

The key to writing a good description is the choice of the **specific details** you will use. Specific details make your descriptions real and help your reader remember what you have written. A careful writer always pays special attention to specific details in any piece of writing.

A second important aspect of good description is the use of **sensory images.**

DEFINITION ➤ **Sensory images** are details that relate to your sense of sight, smell, touch, taste, or hearing.

Example: The deafening screams and relentless yelling of the children on the school bus drove its driver mad.

When you appeal to at least some of the five senses in your descriptive writing, your reader will be able to relate directly to what you are saying. Sensory images also help your reader remember what you have written.

A third important aspect of good description is the order in which you place the details you have chosen. The combination of specific details, sensory images, and the order in which you present these details and impressions will help your reader form a **dominant impression** of what you are describing.

Developing Paragraphs: Description

The following example of a descriptive paragraph shows all of the elements of a good description. As you read this description of a typical neighbourhood delicatessen, note the specific details and the sensory images the writer uses. After you have read the description, ask yourself what dominant impression the writer wanted us to have of the place.

The delicatessen was a wide store with high ceilings that were a dark brown colour from many years of not being painted. The rough wooden shelves on both sides of the store were filled from floor to ceiling with cans of fruits and vegetables, jars of pickles and olives, and special imported canned fish. A large refrigerator case against one wall was always humming loudly from the effort of keeping milk, cream, and several cases of pop and juice cool at all times. At the end of the store was the main counter with its gleaming white metal scale on top and its cold cuts and freshly made salads inside. Stacked on top of the counter beside the scale today were baskets of fresh rolls and breads that gave off an aroma that contained a mixture of onion, caraway seed, and pumpernickel. Behind the scale was the friendly face of Mr. Rubino, who was in his store seven days a week, fourteen hours or more each day. He was always ready with a smile or a friendly comment, or even a sample piece of cheese or smoked meat as a friendly gesture for his "growing customers," as he referred to us kids in the neighbourhood.

Working with Description: Selecting the Dominant Impression

When you use a number of specific sensory images as you write a description, you should do more than simply write a series of sentences that deal with a single topic. You should also create a dominant impression in your reader's mind. Each individual sentence that you write is part of a picture that becomes clear when the reader finishes the paragraph.

For example, when you describe a place, the dominant impression you create might be of a place that is warm, friendly, or comfortable; or it could be a place that is formal, elegant, or artistic. When you write a description of a person, your reader could receive the dominant impression of a positive, efficient person who is outgoing and creative, or of a person who appears to be cold, distant, or hostile. All the sentences should support the dominant impression you have chosen.

Here is a list for you to use as a guide as you work through this chapter. Picking a dominant impression is essential in writing the descriptive college paragraph.

Selecting the Dominant Impression

Possible Dominant Impressions for Descriptions of Places

crowded	cozy	inviting	cheerful	dazzling
romantic	restful	dreary	drab	uncomfortable
cluttered	ugly	tasteless	unfriendly	gaudy
stuffy	eerie	depressing	spacious	sunny

Possible Dominant Impressions for Descriptions of People

creative	angry	independent	proud	withdrawn
tense	shy	aggressive	generous	sullen
silent	witty	pessimistic	responsible	efficient
snobbish	placid	bumbling	bitter	easygoing

EXERCISE

Selecting the Dominant Impression

Each of the following places could be the topic for a descriptive paragraph. First, the writer must decide on a dominant impression. Fill in each blank to the right of the topic with an appropriate dominant impression. Use the list on page 234 if you need help. The first one is done for you.

Topic	**Dominant Impression**
1. The college pub on pub night	loud
2. A park at dusk	______________
3. The room where you are now sitting	______________
4. The variety store nearest you	______________
5. The college bookstore in September	______________
6. An overcrowded waiting room	______________
7. The kitchen in the morning	______________

Revising Vague Dominant Impressions

Certain words in the English language have become so overused that they no longer have any specific meaning for a reader. Careful writers avoid these words because they are almost useless in descriptive writing. Here is a list of the most common overused words:

good, bad
nice, fine, okay
normal, typical
interesting
beautiful

The following paragraph is an example of the kind of writing that results from the continued use of vague words:

> I had a typical day. The weather was nice and my job was interesting. The food for lunch was okay; supper was really good. After supper I saw my girlfriend, who is really beautiful. That's when my day really became fun.

Notice that all of the details in the paragraph are vague. The writer has told us what happened, but we cannot really see any of the details that are mentioned. This is because the writer has made the mistake of using words that have lost much of their meaning. Replacing the vague words in the paragraph will create an entirely different impression:

> I had an event-filled day that was typical of the type of day I've been enjoying lately. The weather on this summer day was perfect for late June,

and the challenge of my job in the health-care field made me feel that this warm and sunny day was made just for me. I had a delicious lunch in a tiny Italian restaurant, and a supper to excite the taste buds at a cozy Greek restaurant that just oozed atmosphere. After supper, I met my girlfriend, who has a warm sense of humour and who is a partner in a major law firm down the street from where I work.

The following exercise will give you practice in recognizing and eliminating overused words.

EXERCISE

Revising Vague Dominant Impressions

In each of the spaces provided, change the underlined word to a more specific dominant impression. An example is done for you.

Vague: The tablecloth was beautiful.
Revised: The tablecloth was of white linen with delicate blue embroidery.

1. The sunset was beautiful. ______________________
2. The water felt nice. ______________________
3. Horseback riding was fun. ______________________
4. The traffic was bad. ______________________
5. The hotel lobby was typical. ______________________
6. The main street is interesting. ______________________
7. The dessert tasted good. ______________________

Working with Description: Sensory Images

One of the basic ways all good writers communicate experiences to their readers is by using sensory impressions. We respond to writing that makes us *see* an object, *hear* a sound, *touch* a surface, *smell* an odour, or *taste* a flavour. When a writer uses one or more of these sensory images in a piece of writing, we tend to pay more attention to what he or she is saying, and we tend to remember the details of what we have read.

For example, if you come across the word *door* in a sentence, you may or may not pay attention to it. However, if the writer tells you it was a *brown wooden* door that was *rough to the touch* and *creaked loudly* when it opened, you would hardly be able to forget it. The door would stay in your mind because the writer used sensory images to make you aware of it.

The following sentences are taken from the description of Mr. Rubino's delicatessen that you read on page 234. Notice how in each sentence the writer uses at least one sensory image to make the details of that sentence remain in our minds. The physical sense the writer is appealing to by the use of one or more sensory images is indicated after the sentence.

1. A large refrigerator case against one wall was always humming loudly from the effort of keeping milk, cream, and several cases of pop and juice cool at all times.

   Physical sense: hearing

2. Stacked on top of the counter ... were baskets of fresh rolls and breads that gave off an aroma that contained a mixture of onion, caraway seed, and pumpernickel.

   Physical sense: smell

3. He was always ready with ... a sample piece of cheese or smoked meat as a friendly gesture....

   Physical sense: taste

When you use sensory images in your own writing, you will stimulate your readers' interest and create images in their minds that they will remember.

Coherence in Description: Putting Details in Spatial Order

In descriptive paragraphs, the writer often chooses to arrange supporting details according to space. With this method, you place yourself at the scene and then use a logical order such as moving from nearby to farther away, right to left, or top to bottom. Often you move in such a way that you save the most important detail until last in order to achieve the greatest effect.

In the paragraph about the delicatessen on page 234, the writer first describes the ceilings and walls of the store, then proceeds to the shelves and large refrigerator, and ends by describing the main counter of the deli with its owner, Mr. Rubino, standing behind it. The ordering of details has been from the outer limits of the room to the inner area, which is central to the point of this paragraph. A description of a clothes closet might order the details differently. Perhaps the writer would begin with the shoes standing on the floor and finish with the hats and gloves arranged on the top shelf, an arrangement that goes from the ground up.

Here is a paragraph from Thierry Mallet's *Glimpses of the Barren Lands*, a description of his travels through the Canadian Arctic:

> Our camp had been pitched at the foot of a great, bleak, ragged hill, a few feet from the swirling waters of the Kazan River. The two small green tents, pegged down tight with heavy rocks, shivered and rippled under the faint touch of the northern breeze. A thin wisp of smoke rose from the embers of the fire.

Notice that the writer begins with a description of the landscape, then gives a description of the camp, and ends with a picture of the small fire. We are able to follow the writer through the description because there is a logic or plan. No matter which method of spatial order you choose in organizing details in a descriptive paragraph, be sure the results allow your reader to see the scene in a logical order.

PRACTICE

Coherence: Putting Details in Spatial Order

Each of the following topic sentences is followed by descriptive sentences that are out of order. Put these descriptive sentences in order by placing the appropriate number in the space provided. Check your answers against those in the Answer Key on p. 442.

1. The young woman was a teen of the eighties.
   (*Order the material from top to bottom.*)

   ________ She wore an oversized sweater that she had borrowed from her father.

   ________ Her shoes were white tennis sneakers.

   ________ Her dangling earrings, which were red and green, matched her outfit.

   ________ Her short blond hair was clean and feathered attractively.

   ________ Her jeans, which were the latest style, had a faint paisley print.

2. The locker room was in chaos.
   (*Order the material from near to far.*)

   ________ Immediately to my right I saw Pat and Chris slapping each other with towels.

   ________ Behind the pair, a row of locker doors banged open and shut.

   ________ I squeezed past a noisy group crowding the doorway.

   ________ At the back, the rest of the team was hugging and congratulating our hero in celebration of her winning goal.

Writing the Descriptive Paragraph Step by Step

To learn a skill with some degree of ease, it is best to follow a step-by-step approach so that various steps can be worked on one at a time. This will ensure that you are not missing a crucial point or misunderstanding a part of the whole. There are other ways to go about writing an effective paragraph, but what follows is one logical method you can use to achieve results.

Steps for Writing the Descriptive Paragraph

1. Study the given topic, and then plan your topic sentence, especially the dominant impression.
2. List at least ten details that come to mind when you think about the topic.
3. Choose the five or six most important details from your list. Be sure these details support the dominant impression.
4. Put your final list in order.
5. Write at least one complete sentence for each of the details you have chosen from your list.
6. Write a concluding statement that offers some reason for describing this topic.
7. Finally, copy your sentences into standard paragraph form.

EXERCISE

Writing the Descriptive Paragraph Step by Step

The following exercise will guide you through the construction of a descriptive paragraph. Start with the suggested topic. Use the seven steps to help you work through each stage in the writing process.

Topic: A person you admire

1. Topic sentence: ____________________

____

2. Make a list of possible supporting details.

a. ____________ f. ____________

b. ____________ g. ____________

c. ____________ h. ____________

d. ____________ i. ____________

e. ____________ j. ____________

3. Circle the five or six details you believe are the most important for the description.
4. Put your choices in order by numbering them.
5. Using your final list, write at least one sentence for each detail you have chosen.

a. ____________________

____

b. ____________________

____

c. ____________________

____

d. ____________________

e.

f.

g.

6. Write a concluding statement.

7. Copy your sentences into standard paragraph form.

On Your Own: Writing Descriptive Paragraphs from Model Paragraphs

Description of a Person

In the following model paragraph, from Alistair MacLeod's story "The Lost Salt Gift of Blood," the author describes his mother in Nova Scotia.

Model Paragraph

My mother ran her house as her brothers ran their boats. Everything was clean and spotless and in order. She was tall and dark and powerfully energetic. In later years, she reminded me of the women of Thomas Hardy, particularly Eustacia Vye, in a physical way. She fed and clothed a family of seven children, making all of the meals and most of the clothes. She grew miraculous gardens and magnificent flowers and raised broods of hens and ducks. She would walk miles on berry-picking expeditions and hoist her skirts to dig for clams when the tide was low. She was fourteen years younger than my father, whom she had married when she was 26, and had been a local beauty for a period of ten years. My mother was of the sea as were all of her people, and her horizons were the very literal ones she scanned with her dark and fearless eyes.

ASSIGNMENT

Descriptive Paragraph

Describe a person—preferably one you have observed more than once. If you saw this person only once, indicate the details that made him or her stay in your mind. If you choose to describe a person with whom you are familiar, select the most outstanding details that will help your reader have a single, dominant impression.

SUGGESTED TOPICS:

1. A loyal friend
2. A local musician
3. A cab driver
4. A fashion model
5. A gossipy neighbour
6. A police officer
7. An aerobics instructor

Writing the Descriptive Essay

Like the topic sentence of a descriptive paragraph, the thesis of a descriptive essay identifies what is being described and contains the overall impression the author has of the topic. Each support paragraph might deal with one component of that which is being described. The following is a brief outline of a descriptive essay:

Thesis: The 100-year-old house was definitely haunted.

Topic Sentence #1: First of all, every time people entered any room in the house, something seemed to be out of place contrary to the owner's insistence that she never changes a thing.

Topic Sentence #2: Secondly, visitors constantly scurry out of the house in a fright claiming later they've sighted at least one ghost.

Topic Sentence #3: Scariest of all are the stories about visitors to the house constantly hearing what seems like moaning coming from the walls, as if the walls are filled with sick people struggling to break free.

For an in-depth look at the essay and its standard format (for all writing strategies in this unit), see Chapter 17: "The Essay." Also review Chapter 14: "The Four Stages of Writing," which can be applied to both the paragraph and the essay.

The following descriptive essay was a winning entry in Centennial College's Student Writing Contest (2001–2002):

Model Essay: A Profile of Daphne

by Alexandra Savage-Ferr

The first time I saw her sitting amidst the Gypsy caravans, I knew this was a woman I had to meet. After all, we shared a love—a love of books, a love of secret, special places, and a love of the caravans we read and dreamt about in childhood. Daphne designs and builds unique living spaces based upon English Gypsy wagons at her home in the Durham Region of Ontario.

Using the frame and wheels of old farm wagons and the occasional antique CP baggage cart, she custom-builds wooden living spaces that writers and dreamers will truly appreciate. Each caravan is uniquely hand painted and decorated with themes from literature, such as Robin Hood's Sherwood Forest and Kenneth Grahame's *The Wind in the Willows.*

Today, surrounded by sun-drenched maples, this skilled craftswoman in sweater and jeans, ponytail a-flying, leads me from one work of art to the next, while a grey, shaggy dog—a rescued stray—prances about in circles of dappled sunlight. Several brightly coloured Gypsy caravans are dotted about the six-acre wooded estate located just north of Uxbridge.

Gypsies, also known as Roma or Romany Gypsies, have their origins in India over a thousand years ago. As they entered southeastern Europe at the end of the 13th century, it was thought that they were from Egypt. They were called 'Gyptians, which is how they became known as "Gypsies."

Learning woodworking as a child, using miniature tools alongside her father building boats, Daphne discovered more than just carpentry skills. Inside her rustic country home, the walls are lined floor-to-ceiling with row upon row of books, many of which belonged to her father. No fewer than six copies of *The Secret Garden*, and the entire set of Baum's *Oz* tales—first editions, of course—are friends. This literary multitude seems as much alive as the two cats that preen themselves before the fire. Fantasy abounds as I gaze over antique photographs, carousel horses, and a brimming bag of apples picked during an early morning snowfall. She serves me Russian Caravan Tea and cuts thick slabs of sugary confection.

After building various theatre props over the years for the Scugog Choral Society and others, the old adage rang true: If you want one, build one. Conjuring magic for the stage, Daphne gazed into the crystal ball of her imagination and translated her visions into a real-life living space. Now she builds caravans for others with their own visions. "I'm interested in the ones who say, 'Wouldn't it be perfect for me?' because there's imagination there," she says. "They see it as their own spot."

These caravans are not intended for traveling, however. Rather, they are meant to be a dreaming, reading, and writing spot remote from the house, sequestered from interruptions and distractions. Since building her own personal retreat, she has crafted several more—the most recent one being commissioned as a unique guestroom for a Port Perry bed and breakfast.

Her own caravan roosts at the top of a hill overlooking the pond. "In the morning, the bulrushes are full of blackbirds," she relates. Indeed, the birds are singing now as our feet crunch through the hoarfrost-covered leaves. This earthy woman with carpenter's hands beckons me inside. I climb a small set of wooden steps and enter through the narrow Dutch door.

Inside, we are cozily sheltered from a sudden hailstorm pinging on the metal roof. Personal treasures, like sprites, peek from every nook and cranny. A crazy quilt travels the length of the platform bed beneath a window overlooking tangled briar. A hanging lantern, cherished books, photographs, and blessed gifts from her children hum with joyful verse. "This is my special place," she whispers.

I knew why I had to meet her, there by the gypsy caravans. I *knew* she had the secret. She'd had it all along.

Analyzing the Writer's Strategies:

1. What part of speech enriches the descriptive value of this piece more than any other?
2. Give some examples from this piece of this particular part of speech.
3. What is the object of the description in this essay? Could it be argued there are two? Why or why not?
4. In Paragraph 6, the writer uses double quotation marks and single quotation marks. Explain their usage.
5. The last paragraph mentions "the secret." What "secret" did the writer know Daphne had all along?

ASSIGNMENT

Descriptive Essay

Choose one of the following topics and write a descriptive essay of at least five paragraphs to develop that topic.

SUGGESTED TOPICS:

1. The best job I ever had
2. The career of my dreams
3. My favourite aunt or uncle
4. My pet _______________
5. My first car

6. The ideal mate
7. The most embarrassing date
8. The best dance club
9. My best friend
10. The best meal I ever had
11. The worst restaurant I've ever eaten in
12. My favourite music
13. My tattoos and/or piercings
14. The worst hospital I've ever been in
15. The best float in a certain parade

To help you work through the stages of the writing process, see the following subjects in Chapter 14. All of them can assist you in developing your descriptive essay:

Brainstorming
Choosing the Topic and the Controlling Idea
Outlining
The Rough Draft
Revising the Rough Draft
Proofreading
Checklist for the Final Copy

Working Together: *The Hunt for a Roommate*

The following personal advertisement appeared in a local newspaper:

> Young man seeks neat, responsible roommate to share off-campus apartment for next academic year. Person must be a nonsmoker and respect a vegetarian who cooks at home. Furniture not needed, but CD player would be welcome!

Finding the right roommate in a college or university residence, finding the right person with whom to share an apartment, or finding the right long-term companion may be difficult. People's personal habits have a way of causing friction in everyday life. Divide into groups for a brief discussion of the kinds of problems one finds in sharing the same space with another person.

1. Imagine that you must write a paragraph or two in which you provide a character description of yourself for an agency that will match you up with a roommate. As you write, be sure you include information about your hobbies, habits, attitudes, and any other personal characteristics that could make a difference in the kind of person the agency will select for you.
2. Imagine that you must write a paragraph or two in which you provide a character sketch of the person you would like the agency to find for you.

Process

What Is Process?

DEFINITION ➤ **Process** is the method that explains how to do something or that shows how something works. There are two kinds of process writing: **directional** and **informational**.

A process that is directional actually shows you, step by step, how to do something. For example, if you want to show someone how to brew a perfect cup of coffee, you would take the person through each step of the process, from selecting and grinding the coffee beans to pouring the finished product. Instructions on a test, directions on how to get to a wedding reception, or a recipe for your favourite spaghetti sauce are a few examples of the kinds of process writing you see and use regularly. You can find examples of directional process writing everywhere you look: in newspapers, magazines, and books, as well as on the containers and packages of products you use every day.

On the other hand, *a process that is informational tells you how something is or was done, for the purpose of informing you about the process.* For example, in a history course, it might be important to understand how the process of Confederation joined Upper and Lower Canada. Of course, you would not use this process yourself. The purpose is for information.

Developing Paragraphs: Process

The following paragraph, from Mary Finlay's *Communication at Work*, is an example of directional process writing, and describes the several steps you need to follow when determining the length of an oral presentation.

> Ascertain how long your presentation is expected to take. Normally, a speech is delivered at about 150 words a minute. Make sure that your material is adequate for the time allotted. Of course, this does not mean that a ten-minute oral report will be as dense as a 1500-word essay. Rehashing points you have already made in order to fill up your time is a sure-fire way to annoy and frustrate your listeners. Leave time for questions and feedback. If

there is none, don't fill in the time by answering the questions nobody asked. This suggests that you are having second thoughts about the organization and planning of your report.

The following paragraph provides an example of informational process writing, giving an overview of the process leading up to Canadian Confederation:

> Confederation, the political union of British North America, didn't happen overnight. Starting as a topic of discussion among politicians before the 1860s, it began to take shape after 1864 with a conference in Charlottetown to discuss the possibility of a union, followed by a second conference at Quebec the same year. Details were hammered out at yet another conference in London, England, in 1866, leading to the passage of the *British North America Act* in March 1867, and resulting in the formation of the Dominion of Canada on July 1, 1867.

Working with Process: Don't Overlook Any of the Steps

The writer of the process essay is almost always more of an authority on the subject than the person reading the essay. In giving directions or information on how something is to be done or was done, it is possible to leave out a step that you think is so obvious that it is not worth mentioning. The reader, on the other hand, does not necessarily fill in the missing step, as you did. An important part of process writing, therefore, is understanding your reader's level of ability. All of us have been given directions that, at first, seemed very clear. However, when we actually tried to carry out the process, something went wrong. A step in the process was misunderstood or missing. The giver of the information either assumed we would know certain parts of the process or didn't stop to think through the process completely. The important point is that directions must be complete and accurate. Here is one further consideration: If special equipment is required in order to perform the process, the directions must include a clear description of the necessary tools.

EXERCISE

Is the Process Complete?

In each of the following two processes, try to determine what important step or steps have been omitted. Try to imagine yourself going through the process using only the information provided.

How to Prepare for an Essay Exam

1. Read the relevant chapters as they are assigned, well in advance of the test.
2. Take notes in class.
3. If the teacher has not described the test, ask him or her what format the test will take.
4. Get a good night's sleep the night before.
5. Bring any pens or pencils that you might need.

6. Arrive at the classroom a few minutes early in order to get yourself settled and to keep yourself calm.

Missing step or steps: ______________________________

____

____

How to Plan a Wedding

1. Make an appointment with the minister or other authority involved, to set a date for the wedding.
2. Discuss plans with both families as to the budget available for the wedding; this will determine the size of the reception and where it is to be held.
3. Reserve the banquet hall as much as eight months in advance.
4. Choose members of the wedding party and invite them to participate in the ceremony.
5. Begin to choose the clothing for the wedding party, including your own wedding gown or tuxedo.
6. Enjoy your wedding!

Missing step or steps: ______________________________

____

____

Coherence in Process: Order in Logical Sequence

When you are writing about a process, it is important to make sure not only that the steps in the process are complete, but also that they are given in the right sequence. For example, if you are describing the process of cleaning a mixer, it is important to point out that you must first unplug the appliance before you remove the blades. The importance of this step is clear when you realize that neglecting it could cost someone a finger. Improperly written instructions could cause serious injuries or even death.

PRACTICE

Coherence: Order in Logical Sequence

The following steps describe the process of setting up a filing system that works. Number the steps in their proper sequence in the blanks to the left. Check your answers against those in the Answer Key on p. 442.

__________ When your mind begins to blur, stop filing for that day.

__________ Now label a file folder and slip the piece of paper in.

__________ Gather together all materials to be filed so that they are all in one location.

_______ Alphabetize your file folders and put them away into your file drawer, and you are finished for that session.

_______ Add to these materials a wastebasket, folders, labels, and a pen.

_______ Pick up the next piece of paper and go through the same procedure, but ask yourself whether this new piece of paper might fit into an existing file, rather than one with a new heading.

_______ Pick up an item from the top of the pile and decide whether this item has value for you. If it does not, throw it away. If it does, go on to the next step.

_______ Finally, to maintain your file once it is established, riffle through each file folder you consult, and pick out and throw away the deadwood.

_______ If the piece of paper is worth saving, ask yourself the question "What is this paper about?"

Transitions for Process

Writers of process, like writers of narration, usually order their material by time sequence. Although it would be tiresome to use "and then" for each new step, a certain number of transitions are necessary for the process to read smoothly and be coherent. Here is a list of transitions frequently used in process writing.

Transitions		
the first step	while you are ...	the last step
in the beginning	as you are ...	the final step
to start with	next	finally
to begin with	then	at last
first of all	the second step	eventually
	after you have ...	

Refer again to the chart of transitional words and phrases on the inside back cover of this book and in Chapter 17, and to the temporal and spatial (time and space) methods of ordering paragraphs in Chapters 21 and 22.

EXERCISE

Using Transitions to Go from a List to a Paragraph

Select one of the two processes outlined in the first exercise in this chapter, on pages 246–47. Change this list into a process paragraph that uses enough transitional devices to make the paragraph coherent and flowing.

Writing the Process Paragraph Step by Step

To learn a skill with some degree of ease, it is best to follow a step-by-step approach so that various steps can be worked on one at a time. This will ensure that you are not missing a crucial point or misunderstanding a part of the whole. There are other ways to go about writing an effective paragraph, but here is one logical method you can use to achieve results, which in itself is a process.

Steps for Writing the Process Paragraph

1. Write a topic sentence.
2. List as many steps or stages in the process as you can.
3. Eliminate any irrelevant points; add equipment needed or special circumstances of the process.
4. Put your final list in order.
5. Write at least one complete sentence for each of the steps you have chosen from your list.
6. Write a concluding statement that says something about the results of completing the process.
7. Finally, copy your sentences into standard paragraph form.

EXERCISE

Writing the Process Paragraph Step by Step

The following exercise will guide you through the construction of a process paragraph. Start with the suggested topic. Use the seven steps to help you work through each stage of the writing process.

Topic: How to burglar-proof your home

The incidence of break-and-enter crimes increases yearly, and many people are concerned about their homes when they are away on vacation. Give advice to a homeowner on how to protect a house against burglary.

1. Topic sentence: ______________________________

____

2. Make a list of possible steps.

a. ______________ f. ______________

b. ______________ g. ______________

c. ______________ h. ______________

d. ______________ i. ______________

e. ______________ j. ______________

3. Circle the five or six steps you believe are the most important to complete the process.
4. Put your final choices in order by numbering them.

5. Using your final list, write at least one sentence for each step you have chosen.

   a. ______________________________

   ____

   b. ______________________________

   ____

   c. ______________________________

   ____

   d. ______________________________

   ____

   e. ______________________________

   ____

   f. ______________________________

   ____

   g. ______________________________

   ____

6. Write a concluding statement.

   ____

   ____

7. Copy your sentences into standard paragraph form.

   ____

   ____

   ____

   ____

   ____

   ____

   ____

   ____

   ____

   ____

On Your Own: Writing Process Paragraphs from Model Paragraphs

Directional: How to Care for Your Health

Concern for health and physical fitness is enjoying great popularity, bringing in big profits to health-related magazines, health clubs, health-food producers, and sports equipment manufacturers. The following paragraph tells us how to get a good night's sleep.

Model Paragraph

The process of getting a good night's sleep depends on several factors. First, the conditions in your bedroom must be correct. Be sure the room temperature is around 18°C and the room is as quiet as possible. Next, pay attention to your bed and how it is furnished. A firm mattress is best, and wool blankets are better than blankets made of synthetic material. Similarly, a firm pillow is best; one that is too soft can cause a stiff neck and lead to a night of poor sleep. Also, keep in mind that what and how you eat are part of the process of preparing for bed. Do not go to bed hungry, but do not overeat, either. Avoid candy bars or cookies; the sugar they contain acts as a stimulant. Finally, do not go to bed until you are sleepy; do something relaxing until you are tired.

ASSIGNMENT 1

Process Paragraph

Write a paragraph in which you give the major steps in some area of caring for your physical or mental health.

SUGGESTED TOPICS:

1. How to plan a daily exercise program
2. How to choose a sport that is suitable for you
3. How to live to be 100
4. How to pick a doctor
5. How to make exercise and dieting fun
6. How to stop smoking
7. How to deal with depression

Informational: How to Accomplish a Task

The following paragraph describes how an insect builds a nest.

Model Paragraph

The insect known as the hunter wasp goes through a regular procedure when it builds a nest. First, it digs a small tunnel into the earth. Then it goes in search of a cicada, a large insect that resembles a cricket. After stinging and paralyzing the cicada, the hunter wasp brings it to the tunnel, lays an egg on the helpless insect, and seals the tunnel. The hunter wasp then leaves. When the egg hatches, the larva uses the cicada as a source of food.

ASSIGNMENT 2

Process Paragraph

Write a paragraph in which you show how an important task is accomplished. The task may be something that is frequently done by humans or that occurs in the world of nature.

SUGGESTED TOPICS:

1. How cheese is made
2. How to burn a CD
3. How people obtain a divorce
4. How to get a driver's licence
5. How yeast causes bread to rise
6. How a bill becomes a law
7. How planets are formed

Writing the Process Essay

Any process paragraph easily can be turned into a process essay by simply increasing the amount of detail in all of the steps. Follow the essay structure as it is shown in Chapter 17, and devote each support paragraph to a single step in the process.

EXERCISE

When Process Goes Wrong

It is your sister's birthday. You have bought her a gift that you must first put together. Carefully following the instructions, you try to assemble the item, but something is wrong. It does not work. Either you have not followed the instructions properly, or the instructions themselves are not clear. All of us have found ourselves in this situation at one time or another. It takes careful thought to write about a process. The writer must not assume the reader knows more than he or she is likely to know.

Answer the following questions in further exploration of this topic.

1. Think of a time when you had to put something together but were not given adequate directions. What did you do?
2. When people write instructions or give directions, what do they usually neglect to keep in mind?
3. Recall a time when you had to explain a process to someone. Perhaps you had to show someone how to get somewhere or had to write a detailed description of how to do a science experiment. What was the process? Was it hard to explain? Why or why not?
4. What was your worst experience with trying to follow a process? You could have been trying to work something out yourself or follow someone else's directions. How did you overcome your difficulty?

For an in-depth look at the essay and its standard format (for all writing strategies in this unit), see Chapter 17: "The Essay." Also review Chapter 14: "The Four Stages of Writing," which can be applied to both the paragraph and the essay.

Much of the instruction in this book is based on a process. Chapter 21, for instance, outlined the process of writing a narrative paragraph or essay. Another process we are all familiar with is that of assembling a bookcase or other item from printed instructions. Still another process may deal with how to bring about an important change. In the following essay, for example, Jenny Yuen discusses the process she believes is necessary to undertake on a more personal level before young people can expect "to change the world."

Model Essay: Inner-Peace Process

by Jenny Yuen

Humanity seems to seek violence and conflict. It is important to recognize that no exterior force will assist the human race in attaining peace. We must do it ourselves. Without fundamental personal change, however, it is simply not feasible for youth to have a significant role in developing a society that is capable of achieving world peace. In order for youth to play this role, we must change the mentalities that make it impossible. If we wish to accomplish worldwide peace, we must first learn to achieve an inner peace through a number of steps.

The first step to achieving inner peace is to learn to value affirmation that is not won through competition with one another. If we continue to criticize the minor differences of each other, it always will be difficult to work together. We must learn to focus on our own personal goals instead of judging ourselves against the goals of others. If we put effort into our objectives, we can accomplish them. By our earned merit, we can then determine our own self-identity. To empower ourselves, we must stop treating others as inferiors, just to make ourselves feel good. When we gloat about high-test marks in order to show off how intelligent we are, we make our peers feel inferior by comparison. And everyday, students mock others because of the different clothing they wear. Each person has his/her own features, which make each person unique. Affirmation won through this kind of rivalry and competition is invalid.

The second step we must take is to endeavour to create a positive self-image uninfluenced by media-driven expectations. The media expect youth to buy into the values of the typical postmodern family. They expect us to want to own large houses with white picket fences, to work "nine-to-five" jobs and to raise "2.5" children. We must abolish the ironically twinned assumptions that today's youth are the sexy, beautiful, perfect consumers and/or that today's youth are inherently rebellious, irresponsible failures. The film *Fight Club* depicts today's youth as a generation lacking in focus with only the goals of a consumption-driven society to guide us. It conveys that "we are the middle children of history, with no purpose or place. We have been raised by television to believe that we'll be millionaires and movie gods and rock stars—but we won't be. And we're very, very pissed off." Surely, we must not allow such messages to define us, so that we end up doubting our own abilities. We can create a mature self-image by making independent decisions and accepting their consequences.

The final step to achieving inner peace is to create power for ourselves. To empower ourselves, we must always be willing to champion the victims of injustice. We must not avoid protecting the weak and vulnerable. We must stop hiding from situations just because we know we might not conquer. We must deal with conflict caused by injustice, prejudice and bias. We must be open-minded and tolerant to different cultures, and we must openly and loudly defend their rights even when such defense seems not to have direct impact on us.

Peace may be achieved by youth, but only if we find inner peace first. In order to effectively oppose the wars and violence in the world, we must defeat the wars within ourselves. We must triumph over rivalry and competition, negative self-images and passive support of injustice. Only then will we be prepared to take the next step: World Peace.

Analyzing the Writer's Strategies

1. Is this process essay more directional or informational?
2. What method did the writer use for the introduction? (See pages 182–85.)
3. What method did she use for the conclusion? (See pages 187–88.)
4. How many steps are there to the process as the writer described it?
5. Where, at each step of the process, does the writer give specific examples to make each part of the process clear?

ASSIGNMENT

Process Essay

Choose one or more of the following topics, and write a process essay of at least five paragraphs to develop that topic.

SUGGESTED TOPICS:

1. How to give a speech
2. How to do well in a job interview
3. How to plan a backpacking trip
4. How to buy a used computer
5. How to study for a test
6. How to choose the right college

7. How to redecorate a room
8. How to buy clothes on a limited budget
9. How to learn to sing
10. How to make new friends

Writing the Process Essay: How to...

Thousands of books and articles have been written that promise to help us accomplish some goal in life: how to start a business, how to cook, how to lose weight, how to install a shower, how to assemble a bicycle. In the essay you are about to write, you have the opportunity to describe how you once went through a process to achieve a goal of some kind.

To help you work through the stages of the writing process, see the following subjects in Chapter 14. All of them can assist you in developing your process essay:

Brainstorming
Choosing the Topic and the Controlling Idea
Outlining
The Rough Draft
Revising the Rough Draft
Proofreading
Checklist for the Final Copy

Working Together: *Campus Woes*

1. The class as a whole discusses and lists some of the problems on their particular campus today. Then the class divides into groups of three or four, each group choosing one of the problems identified. After discussion, each group draws up a list of steps that need to be taken in order to improve the situation.
2. Each group chooses a secretary. The group uses the list to create sentences that will go into a letter to be sent to the appropriate college or university official suggesting the process that could be followed to solve the problem. The secretary will write the finished letter. Be sure there is an introductory paragraph that presents the problem and a conclusion that thanks the official for his or her attention.

3. Imagine you're Abby. Read the letter to the right and answer the questions that follow it.

   If you were the one to advise this person, what would you tell her to do? Explain the process she should follow in order to solve her problem.

   In order to better answer this question, the class could divide into groups to consider the following questions:

   a. Should she confront the man who is harassing her?
   b. Should she go to her supervisor? Should she have told her co-workers about the problem?
   c. Should she share her problem with the man she is dating?
   d. Should she avoid the problem and quit her job?
   e. How important is evidence for a person in this situation? How and when should she gather documentation for a possible formal action?
   f. Does she need a lawyer? Does she need to consider the consequences of a formal action?

> **DEAR ABBY**
>
> Dear Abby: I am doing my co-op at a cable television company as a computer operator. Lately, every morning when I sign in on my computer, I find suggestive messages from the man I relieve from the night shift.
>
> I am a single mother. I am also dating another man and have no interest in this co-worker. Should I report him to my supervisor? Someone in my office suggested that I file a sexual harassment charge.
>
> —Harassed

4. Sexual harassment is not the only problem workers or students might face. In a brief discussion with your classmates, list some other common complaints workers or students might have. Are there steps that need to be followed in order to successfully resolve all such problems? Following the class discussion, write your own paragraph/essay describing the steps you feel are necessary to deal with such situations.

CHAPTER TWENTY-FOUR

24

Comparison or Contrast

What Is Comparison or Contrast?

Comparison and contrast are two related methods of explaining subjects.

DEFINITION ➤ When we use **comparison**, we emphasize the similarities between two subjects. When we use **contrast,** we emphasize the differences between two subjects. It is best to use one or the other, but not both, when writing a paragraph or essay.

We sometimes use the word *comparison* to refer both to similarities and differences between people or things, but it is more exact to use *comparison* for similarities and *contrast* for differences. For example, if you were to write about twin sisters you know, and how close they are in appearance and personality, the similarities you noted would make up a comparison. On the other hand, if you wanted to emphasize some important differences between the two sisters, the result would be a contrast.

We use comparison or contrast in a variety of ways every day. We talk about what a boyfriend and girlfriend have in common; we put similar products side by side in the store before we decide to buy one of them; we listen to two politicians on television and think about the differences between their positions before we vote for one of them; and we read college and university catalogues and talk to our friends before we decide which school to attend.

Developing Paragraphs: Comparison or Contrast

Working with Comparison or Contrast: Choosing the Two-Part Topic

The problem with writing a good comparison or contrast paragraph usually centres on the two-part topic. This demands very careful attention to the topic sentence. While you must be careful to choose two subjects that have enough in common to make them comparable, you must avoid choosing two that have so much in common that you cannot possibly handle all the comparable points in one paragraph or even ten paragraphs. For example, a student trying to compare the French word *chaise* with the English word *chair* might be able to come up with only two sentences of material. With only a dictionary to consult, the student is unlikely to find enough material for several points of comparison. On the other hand, contrasting Canada with Europe would present such an endless supply of points to compare that the student would tend to give only general facts that the reader would already know. When the subject is too broad, the writing is often too general. A better two-part topic might be to compare travelling by train in Europe with travelling by train in Canada.

Once you have chosen a two-part topic that you feel is not too limiting and not too broad, you must remember that a good comparison or contrast paragraph should devote an equal or nearly equal amount of space to each of the two parts. If a writer is interested in only one of the topics, the paragraph may end up being very one-sided.

Here's an example of a one-sided contrast:

> While Canadian trains go to only a few towns, are infrequent, and are often shabby and uncomfortable, the European train is much nicer.

The following example is a better-written contrast that gives attention to both topics:

> While Canadian trains go to only a few large cities, run very infrequently, and are often shabby and uncomfortable, European trains go to virtually every small town, are always dependable, and are clean and attractive.

PRACTICE

Evaluating the Two-Part Topic

Study the following topics and decide which are too broad for a paragraph and which are suitable as topics for a paragraph of comparison or contrast. Mark your choice in the appropriate space to the right of each topic. The first two are done for you. Check your answers against those in the Answer Key on p. 442.

Topic	Too Broad	Suitable
1. Australia and England	✓	
2. Indian elephants and African elephants		✓
3. Canadian wine and French wine		✓
4. Wooden furniture and plastic furniture		✓
5. Wood and plastic	✓	
6. Photography and oil painting	✓	

Two Methods: Point-by-Point and Block

The first method for ordering material in a paragraph or an essay of comparison or contrast is known as the **point-by-point method.** When you use this method, you compare a point of one topic with a point of the other topic. For example, here is a paragraph in which the writer uses the point-by-point method to compare the difficulties of being a freelance editor with those of working as an editor on staff at a magazine.

> Now, of course, I knew that it was going to be as difficult making an income as a freelance editor as it was as an editor on staff at the magazine, if not more so. I would be at home hustling editing contracts via telephone, while everyone else spent their mornings at the office gabbing over endless cups of coffee. I sometimes resented having to work so hard to make a living, while my old colleagues on staff sat in meetings, went to conferences, and attended company luncheons. But I never envied them on their way to work on cold, dark winter mornings. And I wondered how many of them would have gladly switched places with me as I worked outside on my patio in the summer, while they looked longingly out their office windows.

Notice how, after the opening topic sentence, the writer uses half of each sentence to describe a freelance editor's experience and the other half of the same sentence to describe the experience of an editor who works for a magazine. This technique is effective in such a paragraph, and it is most often used in longer pieces of writing in which many points of comparison are made. This method helps the reader keep the comparison or contrast carefully in mind at each point.

The second method for ordering material in a paragraph of comparison or contrast is known as the **block method**. When you use this approach, you present all of the facts and supporting details about your first and second topics separately. Here, for example, is another version of the paragraph above, this one written using the block method:

> Now, of course, I knew that it was going to be as difficult making an income as a freelance editor as it was as an editor on staff at the magazine, if not more so. I spent my mornings hustling editing contracts on the telephone, and I sometimes resented having to work so hard to earn a living. On the other hand, I didn't envy my old colleagues on their way to work on cold, dark winter mornings. They could spend as much time as they wanted to gabbing over coffee and going to meetings, conferences, and company luncheons; but I wonder how many of them would have gladly switched places with me as I worked outside on my patio in the summer?

Notice how the first half of this version presents almost all of the details about the freelance editor, while the second half presents all of the information about the editor on staff. This method is often used in shorter pieces of writing, where it is possible for the reader to keep in mind blocks of information.

Looking at the above two paragraphs in outline form will help you see the shape of their development.

Point-by-Point Method (sometimes referred to as the "Slice" Method)

Topic sentence: Now, of course, I knew that it was going to be as difficult making an income as a freelance editor as it was as an editor on staff at the magazine, if not more so.

First point, first topic: I would be at home hustling editing contracts via telephone...

First point, second topic: ...while everyone else spent their mornings at the office gabbing over endless cups of coffee.

Second point, first topic: I sometimes resented having to work so hard to earn a living...

Second point, second topic: ...while my old colleagues on staff sat in meetings, went to conferences, and attended company luncheons.

Third point, first topic: But I never envied them on their way to work on cold, dark winter mornings.

Third point, second topic: And I wondered how many of them would have gladly switched places with me as I worked outside on my patio, while they looked longingly out their office windows.

Block Method (sometimes referred to as the "Chunk" Method)

Topic sentence: Now, of course, I knew that it was going to be as difficult making an income as a freelance editor as it was as an editor on staff at the magazine, if not more so.

First topic, points one, two, and three: I spent my mornings hustling editing contracts on the telephone and I sometimes resented having to work so hard to earn a living. On the other hand, I didn't envy my old colleagues on their way to work on cold, dark, winter mornings.

Second topic, points one, two, and three: On the other hand, I didn't envy my old colleagues on their way to work on cold, dark winter mornings. They could spend as much time as they wanted to gabbing over coffee and going to meetings, conferences, and company luncheons; but I wonder how many of them would have gladly switched places with me as I worked outside on my patio in the summer?

You will want to choose one of these methods before you write a comparison or contrast assignment. Although the block method is most often used in shorter writing assignments, such as a paragraph, you will have the chance to practise the point-by-point method as well.

PRACTICE

Recognizing the Two Methods

Each of the following passages is an example of comparison or contrast. Read each paragraph carefully and decide whether the writer has used the point-by-point method or the block method. Indicate your choice in the spaces provided after each example. Also indicate whether the piece emphasizes similarities or differences. Check your answers against those in the Answer Key on p. 442.

1. Female infants speak sooner, have larger vocabularies, and rarely demonstrate speech defects. (Stuttering, for instance, occurs almost exclusively in boys.) Girls exceed boys in language abilities, and this early linguistic bias often prevails throughout life. Girls read sooner, learn foreign languages more easily, and, as a result, are more likely to enter occupations involving language mastery. Boys, in contrast, show an early visual superiority. They are also clumsier, performing poorly at tasks such as arranging a row of beads, but excel at other activities calling for total body coordination. Their attentional mechanisms are also different. A boy will react to an inanimate object as quickly as he will to a person. A male baby will often ignore the mother and babble at a blinking light, fixate on a geometric figure, and, at a later point, manipulate it and attempt to take it apart.

   __________ Point-by-Point __________ Block

   __________ Similarities __________ Differences

2. It is hard to decide who are the better inventors, Canadians or Martians. Canadians have invented wonderful devices that have made a significant contribution to their civilization, but then so have the Martians. Canadians invented the chain saw, the paint roller, the power mower, and the zipper. But Martians are no slouches, having come up with the intergalactic spaceship, the long-range power blaster, and the moon-dust mobile home. Of course, not all Canadian inventions have been stellar successes; consider, for example, the cast-iron airship, the reverse cooking stove, and the patent medicine carrot cure-all. But neither have Martians hit a winner every time: who can forget the ill-fated interplanetary bicycle, the invisible mirror, or the boomerang rocket? In the ingenuity department, you'd have to say it's a tie.

   __________ Point-by-Point __________ Block

   __________ Similarities __________ Differences

EXERCISE 1

Using the Point-by-Point and Block Methods

Choose one of the paragraphs from the above practice, and rewrite it using the opposite method for comparison or contrast. For instance, if a paragraph uses the point-by-point method, rewrite it using the block method.

EXERCISE 2

Using the Point-by-Point and Block Methods

Use the lists on the next page to write a paragraph comparing or contrasting life in the city with life in the suburbs. Review the lists provided and add to them any of your own ideas. Omit any you do not wish to use. Then, selecting either the block method or the point-by-point method, write a comparison or contrast paragraph.

Topic sentence: If I could move back to the city from the suburbs, I know I would be happy.

The following points provide details that relate to living in the city and living in the suburbs:

Topic I **Advantages of the City**	**Topic II** **Disadvantages of the Suburbs**
A short ride on the bus or subway gets you to work.	Commuting to work in the city is often long and exhausting.
Less time spend commuting leaves more time to get involved in the community.	More time commuting means less time to get involved in neighbourhood activities.
Variety is more stimulating.	Sameness of people and streets is monotonous.
Familes and single people.	Mostly families.
Local shopping for nearly everything.	Mostly highway shopping.
Mingle with people walking in the neighbourhood daily.	Little walking, use cars to go every where.

Notice that the maker of these lists focused only on the disadvantages of the suburbs in contrast to the city. No mention, for instance, has been made of crime or noise. You could also present the contrast from the point of view of someone who prefers the suburbs.

Working for Coherence: Using Transitions

A number of words and phrases are useful to keep in mind when writing the comparison or contrast paragraph. Some of them are used in phrases, some in clauses.

Common Transitions

Transitions for Comparison	**Transitions for Contrast**	
similar to	on the contrary	though
similarly	on the other hand	unlike
like	in contrast with	even though
likewise	in spite of	nevertheless
just like	despite	however
just as	instead of	but
furthermore	different from	otherwise
moreover	whereas	except for
equally	while	and yet
again	although	still
also		
too		
so		

Notice the different uses of *like* and *as*:

***Like* is a preposition and is used in the prepositional phrase "like me."**

My sister is just *like* me.

***As* is a subordinate conjunction and is used in the clause below with a subject and a verb.**

My sister sews every evening, *as* does her oldest daughter.

See the chart on the inside back cover of this book and Chapter 17: "The Essay" for additional transitions.

Writing the Comparison or Contrast Paragraph Step by Step

To learn a skill with some degree of ease, it is best to follow a step-by-step approach so that various skills can be worked on one at a time. This will ensure that you are not missing a crucial point or misunderstanding a part of the whole. There are other ways to go about writing an effective paragraph, but here is one logical method you can use to achieve results.

Steps for Writing the Comparison or Contrast Paragraph

1. Study the given topic, and then plan your topic sentence, especially the dominant impression.
2. List all your ideas for points that could be compared or contrasted.
3. Choose the three or four most important points from your list, and put them in order.
4. Decide whether you want to use the point-by-point method or the block method of organizing your paragraph.
5. Write at least one complete sentence for each of the points you have chosen from your list.
6. Write a concluding statement that summarizes the main points, makes a judgment, or emphasizes what you believe is the most important point.
7. Finally, copy your sentences into standard paragraph form.

EXERCISE

Writing the Comparison or Contrast Paragraph Step by Step

The following exercise will guide you through the construction of a comparison or contrast paragraph. Start with the suggested topic. Use the seven steps to help you work through each stage of the writing process.

Topic: Compare or contrast going to work with going to college immediately after high school.

1. Topic sentence: ______________________________

   ____

2. Make a list of possible comparisons or contrasts.

   a. ____________ f. ____________

   b. ____________ g. ____________

   c. ____________ h. ____________

   d. ____________ i. ____________

   e. ____________ j. ____________

3. Circle the three or four comparisons or contrasts that you believe are most important, and put them in order.
4. Choose either the point-by-point method or the block method.
5. Using your final list, write at least one sentence for each comparison or contrast you have chosen.

   a. ______________________________

   ____

   b. ______________________________

   ____

   c. ______________________________

   ____

   d. ______________________________

   ____

   e. ______________________________

   ____

   f. ______________________________

   ____

   g. ______________________________

   ____

6. Write a concluding statement.

   ____

   ____

7. Copy your sentences into standard paragraph form.

____

____

____

____

____

____

____

____

____

____

On Your Own: Writing Comparison or Contrast Paragraphs from Model Paragraphs

Comparing or Contrasting Two Places

The following paragraph contrasts the East Coast and a major urban centre as they appear to a person who has been to both places.

Model Paragraph

Both the East Coast and the big city where I live leave distinct impressions, but it's the East Coast to which I am undeniably partial. When I was riding a bus between Louisbourg and Sydney, Nova Scotia, an old man waved the bus down, boarded, and handed the driver a large fish to pay for his fare. In the city, exact change is the rule on the bus, and that only in coin of the realm. In St. John's, Newfoundland, I found that some nightclubs and bars remained open until the last customer had left, and that the best time was had when patrons brought their own musical instruments and set up some Down East foot-stompin' music. Back home, you sit, behave yourself, and drink your beer, or out you go. Incidentally, the best pizza I ever had was from a small shop on the St. John's waterfront, with a Volcano pizza from Windsor, Ontario, a close second. The cardboard pizzas from the fast-food joints in Toronto and Montreal don't even rate. On the other hand, my favourite hamburger came from Montreal, and nothing can beat Prince Edward Island for seafood. Do I sound biased toward the East? If you're not from the East, take your next vacation there. You'll see what I mean.

ASSIGNMENT

Comparison or Contrast Paragraph

Write a paragraph in which you compare or contrast two places you know, either from personal experience or from your reading.

SUGGESTED TOPICS:

1. Two neighbourhoods
2. Two towns or cities
3. Two vacation spots
4. Two provinces
5. Two countries
6. Two streets
7. Two colleges or universities

The Comparison or Contrast Essay

In a comparison or contrast essay, the thesis statement (like the topic sentence in a paragraph) identifies what is being compared or contrasted and what the author's overall feeling toward the comparison or contrast is (controlling idea).

Example: The Honda Civic beats the Toyota Corolla in many respects.

If you're using the block method, the second paragraph of the essay might be used for everything you want to say about the Honda, while the third paragraph contains everything you want to say about the Toyota (as it contrasts with everything you've said in the previous paragraph about the Honda).

A four-paragraph essay would be appropriate if you are using the block method for your comparison or contrast essay. The last paragraph of your four-paragraph essay, of course, would contain a restatement of your thesis but in different words (see Chapter 17: "The Essay").

If, on the other hand, you're using the point-by-point method, the second paragraph of the essay would compare or contrast both the Honda and the Toyota based on the first of, ideally, three points. The third paragraph of the essay would deal with the second of three points, and so on. With the point-by-point method, provided you are discussing your findings on the basis of three points, it would be appropriate to go back to a standard five-paragraph essay, rather than the four-paragraph essay recommended for the essay in which you might have chosen the block method.

For an in-depth look at the essay and its standard format (for all writing strategies in this unit), see Chapter 17: "The Essay." Also review Chapter 14: "The Four Stages of Writing," which can be applied to both the paragraph and the essay.

The following essay explores the differences between living in a small town and living in a big city, according to its author. Compare and contrast this essay with the model paragraph on a similar topic earlier in this chapter (page 265).

Model Essay: City Life Beats the Small-Town Blues

by Zack Goodman

Growing up in a small town has its perks. You might have fewer friends than you have in the big city, but you tend to keep them closer. The East Coast small-town author Hugh MacLennan once said that a writer who grows up in a small town has a greater knowledge of human intimacy even if that intimacy dries up at the age of 40. Well, not everybody agrees with either of those points. In fact, city life can offer just as much intimacy if not more than small-town life can. Life is better in the big city, and it all comes down to one general reason: more choice.

One of the areas in which having choice can be extremely valuable is that of friends. Like leaving home to seek greater knowledge of yourself, picking your own friends from a greater number of people can aid in your journey to seek self-knowledge. After all, if you go out with the same group of small-town friends all the time, not because you necessarily like them all that much but because they're the only ones available, this can prove quite limiting when it comes to your growth as an individual. The big city, on the other hand, offers an endless number of opportunities to meet people of like interests. You're much more likely to cultivate relationships with people who help you to grow.

If you're the type of person who enjoys learning about other cultures and meeting people of many different ethnicities, you're much more likely to do both of these things in a big city. People from all over the world prefer the big city to which to emigrate because they might already have relatives there, or at least some sort of community similar to the one they've left in their country of origin. They might not have to learn English right away to get along because there are enough people with whom they can speak in their native tongue, and in general, the big city can afford more resources to make them more comfortable. In a small town, you might have to get used to a group of people of one origin, maybe even a community in which there is only one religion. If this is what you want, there's no problem. But if you consider yourself a citizen of the world, a one-ethnicity town might be pretty boring after a while.

And finally, if you're a person who enjoys the arts, the small town probably won't be able to hold a candle to the arts community of a big city. A small town might have one cinema that shows maybe three different movies at any one time. A big city can have more than 100 theatres showing at least a hundred different movies, and not all mainstream film, but independent film, B-movies, foreign film (do Canadian movies qualify as foreign films in

Canada?) and second-run movies for those who missed them the first time around. But movies are only one form of entertainment in the big city on any given night. There's the Broadway musical, the independent stage theatre, ballet, modern dance, cabaret, poetry reading, cafés and night clubs with live music including jazz, house, Latin, retro, hip-hop (you ask for it; the big city's got it), street festivals in the summer, outdoor skating and indoor tennis in the winter, and so on and so on. A small town may have some of this some of the time, but a big city is more likely to have most of it most of the time.

A small town has its advantages; that's true. The cost of living is lower. The streets are probably safer at night. And it might even be easier to meet someone special. But if you're an arts lover who enjoys the company of people from all over the world, and you're interested in cultivating friends who help you to grow spiritually and not just to get drunk on a Saturday night, city life is tough to beat.

Analyzing the Writer's Strategies

1. An essay of comparison usually emphasizes the similarities between two subjects, while an essay of contrast usually emphasizes the differences. With this in mind, is the essay you have just read an essay of comparison or contrast? Why?
2. Does the writer use the point-by-point method or the block method in writing this essay?
3. Does the writer provide an equal number of details that relate to both the small town and the big city?
4. Specifically, how does the writer demonstrate the superior nature of the big city?

Writing the Comparison or Contrast Essay

Every time you go to the grocery store or look in your closet to decide what to wear, you are involved in making comparisons or contrasts. When you have to make a big decision in life, usually the problem involves weighing the advantages and disadvantages of one choice against the advantages and disadvantages of another choice. Should you go to college or get a job? Should you get married now or wait another year? Should you tell that person how upset you are by what he or she did? In all cases, you must compare the two choices to see which seems to be the better one. Making a decision is not easy, just as writing a good comparison or contrast essay is not easy. You have to consider two topics rather than one.

ASSIGNMENT

Comparison or Contrast Essay

Choose a topic from below and write a comparison or contrast essay of at least five paragraphs to develop that topic.

SUGGESTED TOPICS:

Compare or contrast:

1. High school classes with college classes
2. Life in a city with life in a rural area
3. Two movies (the acting, the cinematography, the quality of the story)
4. A friend from your childhood with a present friend
5. Two similar items you have owned (e.g., cars, bicycles, radios)
6. Seeing a play with seeing a movie
7. Two vacation spots
8. Two apartments or houses where you have lived
9. Researching in a library with researching on the Internet
10. Cooking dinner at home with eating out

For helpful hints on the following subjects, all of which will assist you in developing your comparison or contrast essay, see Chapter 14:

Brainstorming
Choosing the Topic and the Controlling Idea
Outlining
The Rough Draft
Revising the Rough Draft
Proofreading
Checklist for the Final Copy

Working Together: *To Compare or Contrast—That Is the Question*

In a group of three to five students, decide among yourselves which two movies, fashion items, concerts or advertisements you'd like to compare or contrast. Make sure that everyone in your group has seen both items. Decide whether you're going to compare or contrast the two items you've identified. Then try to reach a consensus about your overall conclusion before you begin to compare or contrast the items on the basis of at least three points. Discuss your results with the rest of the class. Was it easy to reach consensus on everything? What did you learn by the process? Did most groups end up comparing or contrasting?

CHAPTER TWENTY-FIVE

25

Definition

What Is Definition?

Definition is one of the most useful forms of writing. The ability to provide accurate definitions is crucial to ensuring your audience understands your words and ideas. Most of the essays you will write in college or university will require you to define terms.

When you are asked to give a definition, you are usually asked to explain what a word means. You will often need to define terms in your writing when they are very technical or would otherwise be unfamiliar to your reader. For example, not many people would know what a contusion is, so the writer of a health-sciences report may want to explain that a contusion is another word for a bruise. In fact, defining a term or concept is often an effective way to begin an essay. Thus, the writer of an essay on discrimination may first want to provide a definition of the term before describing examples of discrimination.

There may also be situations where you want to give a more personal meaning to a common term. For instance, you may think that you have a clear idea of what the word *success* means. By talking with your classmates about their definitions of success, however, you'll see that each has a different mental picture of what success looks like. For some a successful person may have lots of money. For others success may mean achieving a personal goal, such as competing in the Olympics. For still others, success means having a happy family life. Personal definitions are useful in writing because they cast new light on ordinary terms and make us question our conceptions about our day-to-day lives.

DEFINITION ➤ A **definition** is an explanation of the meaning or significance of a word or term. The starting point for a good definition is to group the word into a larger **category** or class. (See Chapter 26 on classification.)

For example, the trout is a kind of fish; a doll is a kind of toy; a shirt is an article of clothing. Here is a dictionary entry for the word *family*.

> **family** (fam′e -le, fam′le) *n., pl.* **-lies.** *Abbr.* **fam.** 1. The most instinctive, fundamental social or mating group in man and animal, especially the union of man and woman through marriage and their offspring; parents and their

children. 2. One's spouse and children. 3. Persons related by blood or marriage; relatives; kinfolk. 4. Lineage; especially, upper-class lineage. 5. All the members of a household; those who share one's domestic home.

To what larger category does the word *family* belong? The family, according to this entry, is a kind of *social group*.

DEFINITION ➤ Once the word has been put into a larger class, its **definition** gives the **identifying characteristics** that make the word different from other members in the class.

What makes a *trout* different from a *bass*, a *doll* different from a *puppet*, a *shirt* different from a *sweater*? Here a definition can give examples. The first dictionary definition of *family* identifies the family as a married man and woman and their children. Four additional meanings suggest some variations.

When you write a paragraph or an essay that uses definition, the dictionary entry is only the beginning. In order for your reader to understand a difficult term or idea, you will need to expand this definition into what is called **extended definition**. It is not the function of a dictionary to go into great depth. It can provide only the basic meanings and synonyms.

DEFINITION ➤ **Extended definition** seeks to analyze a concept in order to give the reader a more complete understanding.

For instance, you might include a historical perspective. When or how did the concept begin? How did the term change or evolve over the years, or how do different cultures understand the term? You will become involved in the connotations of the word. Extended definition, or **analysis** as it is sometimes called, uses more than one method to arrive at an understanding of a term.

Developing Paragraphs: Definition

The following paragraph, taken from *Sociology: An Introduction* by John E. Conklin, is the beginning of a chapter on the family. The author's starting point is very similar to the dictionary entry.

> In every society, social norms define a variety of relationships among people, and some of these relationships are socially recognized as family or kinship ties. A *family* is a socially defined set of relationships between at least two people who are related by birth, marriage, or adoption. We can think of a family as including several possible relationships, the most common being between husband and wife, between parents and children, and between

people who are related to each other by birth (siblings, for example) or by marriage (a woman and her mother-in-law, perhaps). Family relationships are often defined by custom, such as the relationship between an infant and godparents, or by law, such as the adoption of a child.

The author began this definition by putting the term into a larger **class:** *family* is one type of social relationship among people. The writer then identifies the people who are members of this group. Family relationships can be formed by marriage, birth, adoption, or custom, as with godparents. The author does not stop here. The extended definition explores the functions of the family, conflicts in the family, the structure of the family, and the special characteristics of the family.

EXERCISE 1

Working with Definition: Class

Define each of the following terms by placing it in a larger class. Keep in mind that when you define something by class, you are placing it in a larger category so that the reader can see where it belongs. Use the dictionary if you need help. The first example is done for you.

Chemistry is one of the branches of science that deals with a close study of the natural world.

1. A *motorcycle* is ______________________________
2. *Poetry* is ______________________________
3. *Democracy* is ______________________________
4. *Sugar* is ______________________________
5. A *viola* is ______________________________
6. *Mozzarella* is ______________________________
7. A *novel* is ______________________________

EXERCISE 2

Working with Definition: Distinguishing Characteristics

Using the same terms as in Exercise 1, give one or two identifying characteristics that differentiate your term from other terms in the same class. An example is done for you.

Chemistry studies the structure, properties, and reactions of matter.

1. A *motorcycle* ______________________________

____

____

2. *Poetry* ______________________________

____

____

3. *Democracy* ______________________________

____

____

4. *Sugar* ______________________________

____

____

5. A *viola* ______________________________

____

____

6. *Mozzarella* ______________________________

____

____

7. A *novel* ______________________________

____

____

EXERCISE 3

Working with Definition: Example

Help define each of the following terms by providing one example. Well chosen, appropriate examples help to clarify writing. An example is done for you.

Term: Chemistry

Example: Chemistry studies elements such as hydrogen. This element is the simplest in structure of all the elements, with only one electron and proton; it is colourless, highly flammable, the lightest of all gases, and the most abundant element in the universe.

1. *Love*

____

____

____

2. A *constellation*

____

____

____

3. *Terrorism*

____

____

____

4. *Comic-book heroes*

____

____

____

5. *Equality*

____

____

____

6. *Envy*

____

____

____

7. A *volcano*

____

____

____

Writing the Definition Paragraph Step by Step

To learn a skill with some degree of ease, it is best to follow a step-by-step approach so that the various aspects of the skill can be worked on one step at a time. This will ensure that you are not missing a crucial point or misunderstanding a part of the whole. There are other ways to go about writing an effective paragraph, but the following is one logical method you can use to achieve results.

Steps for Writing the Definition Paragraph

1. Write a topic sentence that identifies what you are going to define.
2. List all the possible concepts for your extended definition.
3. Eliminate inappropriate concepts from your list.
4. Put your final list in order.
5. Write at least one complete sentence for each of the concepts that you have chosen from your list.
6. Write a concluding statement that summarizes the important parts of your definition.
7. Finally, copy your sentences into standard paragraph form.

EXERCISE

Writing the Definition Paragraph Step by Step

The following exercise will guide you through the construction of a definition paragraph. Start with the suggested topic. Use the seven steps above to help you work through each stage of the writing process.

Topic: Intelligence

We often equate intelligence with being "smart" or with having above-average ability in some area. Yet we likely all know some rather intelligent people who don't act very smart, or who are very absent-minded. We could also have a pet that is "intelligent." What is intelligence as you understand it?

1. Topic sentence: ______________________________

____

2. Make a list of possible concepts.

a. ______________ f. ______________

b. ______________ g. ______________

c. ______________ h. ______________

d. ______________ i. ______________

e. ______________ j. ______________

3. Eliminate any concepts that are not appropriate.
4. Put your final list in order.
5. Using your final list, write at least one sentence for each of the concepts you have chosen.

a. ______________________________

____

b. ______________________________

____

c. ______________________________

____

d. ______________________________

____

e. ______________________________

____

f. ______________________________

____

g. ______________________________

____

6. Write a concluding statement.

____

____

7. Copy your sentences into standard paragraph form.

____

____

____

____

____

____

____

____

____

____

On Your Own: Writing Definition Paragraphs from Model Paragraphs

Definition of Who or What You Are: Distinguishing Characteristics

The following paragraph, taken from Richard Wright's novel *The Weekend Man*, defines the author's image of himself.

Model Paragraph

What is a weekend man, you ask? A weekend man is a person who has abandoned the present in favour of the past or the future. He is really more interested in what happened to him 20 years ago or in what's going to happen to him next week than he is in what's happening to him today. If the truth were known, nothing much happens to most of us during the course of our daily passage. It has to be said. Unless we are test pilots or movie stars, most of us are likely to wake up tomorrow morning to the same ordinary flatness of our lives. This is really not such a bad thing. It is probably better than fighting off a sabre-tooth tiger at the entrance to the cave. But we weekend men never leave well enough alone. First off, we must cast about for a diversion. A diversion is anything that removes us from the ordinary present. Sometimes we divert ourselves into our own pasts. This is more likely to happen as we grow older. I am only 30, for instance, but in the course of an average day I sometimes shake my head a dozen times to keep from sinking into my own past. Diverting oneself into the past would not be so bad if it didn't bring on the "nostalgies." But, of course, it does, and a severe case of the "nostalgies" can often as not leave a person worse off than he was before.

ASSIGNMENT

Paragraph of Definition

Some of us are dreamers, and some of us are idealists; we all have distinguishing characteristics within the larger class of human being. Using the above paragraph as a model, and perhaps one of the following suggested topics, write a paragraph of definition of who or what you are.

SUGGESTED TOPICS:

1. Happy-go-lucky
2. Creative
3. A friend to all
4. A comedian
5. Reserved
6. Studious
7. Cynical

Developing an Essay of Definition

The thesis in this type of essay, of course, identifies what is being defined. It also should provide a good but general definition. Then each support paragraph deals with an explanation of a different component or aspect of what has been defined in the first paragraph.

For example, see the essay on the next page by Jenny Yuen on sexual addiction entitled "Love Hurts." The first support paragraph (the second paragraph of the essay) deals with the question as to how common the addiction is. The third support paragraph deals with a particular example. The fifth support deals with the notion that attending twelve-step program meetings may not be enough to control this addiction, and so on.

No one support paragraph should deal with more than one component or aspect of that which is being defined. But once the support paragraph has identified the component to be discussed in its first sentence (the topic sentence of that paragraph), the author, of course, can go ahead and add various sorts of supporting details (including examples) to support the topic sentence.

For an in-depth look at the essay and its standard format (for all writing strategies in this unit), see Chapter 17: "The Essay." Also review Chapter 14: "The Four Stages of Writing," which can be applied to both the paragraph and the essay.

Model Essay: Love Hurts

by Jenny Yuen

For love and sex addicts, Valentine's Day may not be simply roses and candy, but rather a traumatic reminder that love hurts. Feb. 14 may bring back painful memories of past breakups, or trigger the need to go out and find a "special someone" who may not turn out to be all that special. Sexual and love addiction is the continuing pattern of unwanted compulsive romantic behaviour that has a negative impact on the addict's personal, social and/or economic standing.

Sex and love addiction are more common than you might imagine, says Rob Hawkings, a psychotherapist at Bellwood Health Services in North York, Ontario. These addictions are also very complex disorders in which the victims may not realize that their behaviour falls into the "addict" category. How can you tell whether you have "normal" relationship problems or that you're in love with love and sex? (See questionnaire at bottom.) The answer is another question: Are you in control? But having self-control is much easier said than done. "We look for a pattern of out-of-control behaviour, whether that's with pornographic material or flirting or continually getting into romantic involvements in a serial kind of way or giving into simultaneous multiple [relationships]," says 51-year-old Hawkings, a recovering alcoholic and sex addict, himself, who has been working in the field for a decade.

Although the demographic of addicts varies, most of the people who attend the 12-step meetings are males in their late 20s to late 50s. Still, there are no definite statistics of how much of the Canadian population is affected by sexual and love addiction, although Hawkings says more patients would be checking into Bellwood for therapy if they realized it is a problem.

Judy, 37, tormented herself with obsessive sexual fantasies for four years. She had constant fantasies about extra-marital relationships, and suffered from sexual anorexia, trying to avoid her problems so she wouldn't have to deal with them. "I was in a marriage, and I started thinking about men outside my marriage so much that it was affecting my work life. I hate to use the word obsession,...but I found myself powerless over my thoughts."

While Bellwood is new at the sex addiction game, SLAA (or Sex and Love Addicts Anonymous), also known as The Augustine Fellowship, has been working worldwide with addicts for more than 20 years. SLAA champions the Alcoholics Anonymous 12-step program as an efficient treatment program for sufferers of sex and love addiction. Currently, SLAA has more than 1200 meeting locations throughout the world, open to all who believe they may have a problem. People who believe they may suffer from love and sexual addiction may come in anonymously and tell their stories and listen to others.

Although Bellwood avidly encourages its sex addiction patients to attend these meetings, Hawkings says 12-step programs are not enough. Bellwood's program includes life-skills coaching to help addicts deal with communication and feelings. In some special cases, Bellwood prescribes medication for sex addicts. "There are situations where there are some people who need a carefully-prescribed anti-depressant," says Hawkings, who is careful not to recommend addictive medication such as Valium. "We sometimes get people coming in who have real psychiatric problems as well as addictions going on."

The question still remains: Can the love and sex addict be cured? "The classic stereotype is AA, where people are recovering for the rest of their lives, but for the rest of their lives need not forget they're alcoholics," Hawkings says. By and large, that is the case with sexual addiction. People are always going to be susceptible to using the sexual-addictive fix that they might have used in the past when they were under stress. "One thing we work very hard on in recovery is managing the stress in their lives."

Judy was fortunate enough to alter her sexual behaviours into healthier ones because of the SLAA program. "I felt freedom right away. I was really fortunate," Judy says. "You don't graduate from [a 12-step program]. They call it being 'restored to sanity,' but a better way to put it is we now have a choice over our decisions."

***

The following is a questionnaire to help determine if you are a sex and/or love addict. If you answer yes to most of these questions, you may be.

- Do you still see someone, even though you know the relationship has a destructive effect on you?
- Do you feel like you *have* to have sex?
- Do you have sex regardless of the consequences?
- Do you feel you lack dignity and wholeness?
- Is your life unmanageable because of your sexual or romantic behaviour?

Contact Information:

- SLAA Coxwell branch (416) 486-8201 or Toll-free 1-800-977-4325
- Bellwood Health Clinic: Rob Hawkings, sex psychotherapist, (416) 495-0926, ext. 107 or toll-free 1-800-387-6198
- Dr. Patrick Carnes' Website: www.sexhelp.com
- Pia Mellody's Website: www.piamellody.com

Analyzing the Writer's Strategies

1. What is the central thing being defined in this essay?
2. In what ways is sexual addiction like alcoholism? In what ways is it different?
3. What surprises you the most in this piece by Jenny Yuen?
4. What do you think is the main purpose of this essay? Why?

ASSIGNMENT

Essay of Definition

Choose one of the topics below, or take one of your own, and write an essay of definition of at least five paragraphs to develop that topic.

SUGGESTED TOPICS:

1. Definition of love
2. Definition of Buddhism or other religion
3. Definition of your favourite martial art
4. Definition of a particular disease or medical condition
5. Definition of "global warming"
6. Definition of "the greenhouse effect"
7. Definition of a political treaty such as the Kyoto Accord
8. Definition of a term in your particular field of study
9. Definition of a particular endangered species of animal
10. Definition of "impressionism" or other kind of painting theory

For helpful hints on the following subjects, all of which will assist you in developing your essay of definition, see Chapter 14:

Brainstorming
Choosing the Topic and the Controlling Idea
Outlining
The Rough Draft
Revising the Rough Draft
Proofreading
Checklist for the Final Copy

Working Together: *What Does the Cover Mean to You?*

One could argue that to interpret a picture is to define it. Look at the cover of this book, and come to a one-sentence conclusion as to what you think it means to you. This one-sentence conclusion becomes your topic sentence/thesis statement for your paragraph/essay of definition. Once you've done this, look at the various components of the picture, and pick three that make the biggest impression on you. Discuss these three parts as points that support your one-sentence interpretation.

Then exchange papers with someone else in your group/class. Discuss the results with the group/class. Are there several interpretations? Are there certain universal points that everybody has made? Do any or all of the interpretations relate to the study of writing?

CHAPTER TWENTY-SIX

26

Classification

What Is Classification?

DEFINITION ➤ **Classification** is the placing of items into separate categories for the purpose of helping us think about these items more clearly. This can be extremely useful and even necessary when large numbers of items are being considered.

In order to classify things properly, you must always take the items you are working with and put them into **distinct categories**, making sure that each item belongs in only one category. For example, if you were to classify computers into imported computers, Canadian-made computers, and used computers, this would not be an effective use of classification because an imported computer or a Canadian-made computer could also be a used computer. When you classify, you want each item to belong in only one category.

A classification should also be **complete**. For example, if you were to classify computers into the two categories of new and used, your classification would be complete because any item can be only new or used.

Developing Paragraphs: Classification

In the following paragraph, the writer classifies different kinds of neighbours:

> To me, there are only two kinds of neighbours: those with cats and those without cats. I refuse to get along with cat owners, regardless of how pleasant either the cats or their owners happen to be. I take great exception to having cats on my property, fighting with each other in the middle of the night, dirtying my flower beds, and chasing the birds that come to my feeder. I don't have a great deal to say to neighbours who let their cats out at night to get into my garbage, and when I point out the mess that these cats leave, I'm told, "There's no law against it." As far as those neighbours who don't have cats are concerned—they can borrow my lawn mower any time.

In this paragraph, the writer presents two distinct types of neighbours—cat owners and those who don't own cats. These are the only types that have any significance for the writer. The writer's classification is complete because it covers the entire range of neighbours—there are, in the writer's opinion, no other types of neighbours. This is a useful classification because many of us have neighbours with cats; perhaps you are that neighbour.

EXERCISE 1 Working with Classification: Finding the Basis for a Classification

For each of the following topics, pick three different ways that topic could be classified. You may find the following example helpful.

Topic: Ways to choose a vacation spot.

Basis for classification: By price (first class, medium price, economy), by its special attraction (the beach, the mountains, the desert, etc.), by the accommodations (hotel, motel, cabin, trailer)

1. **Topic:** Cellular phones

   Ways to divide the topic: ______________________________

   ____

2. **Topic:** Houses

   Ways to divide the topic: ______________________________

   ____

3. **Topic:** Neighbourhoods

   Ways to divide the topic: ______________________________

   ____

4. **Topic:** News sources

   Ways to divide the topic: ______________________________

   ____

5. **Topic:** Medicines

   Ways to divide the topic: ______________________________

   ____

6. **Topic:** Snack foods

   Ways to divide the topic: ______________________________

   ____

7. **Topic:** Relatives

   Ways to divide the topic: ______________________________

   ____

EXERCISE 2

Working with Classification: Making Distinct Categories

First pick a basis for classifying each of the following topics. Then break the topics into distinct categories. Divide the topic into as many distinct categories as you think the classification requires.

Keep in mind that when you divide your topic, each part of your classification must belong to only one category. For example, if you were to classify cars, you would not want to make sports cars and international cars two of your categories because several kinds of sports cars are also international cars. You may find the following example helpful.

Topic: Wine
Distinct categories: red, white, rosé (by colour)
or
Distinct categories: French, Australian, Italian, Canadian, Chilean, etc. (by national origin)

1. Clothing stores

   Distinct categories: ______________________________

   ____

2. Television commercials

   Distinct categories: ______________________________

   ____

3. Olympic sports

   Distinct categories: ______________________________

   ____

4. Writers

   Distinct categories: ______________________________

   ____

5. Coffee

   Distinct categories: ______________________________

   ____

6. Mail

   Distinct categories: ______________________________

   ____

7. Art forms

   Distinct categories: ______________________________

   ____

Writing the Classification Paragraph Step by Step

To learn a skill with some degree of ease, it is best to follow a step-by-step approach so that various aspects of the skill can be worked on one at a time. This will ensure that you are not missing a crucial point or misunderstanding a part of the whole. There are other ways to go about writing an effective paragraph, but here is one logical method you can use to achieve results.

Steps for Writing the Classification Paragraph

1. Write a topic sentence, stating the basis of the classification. Use either comparison/contrast or definition.
2. List all the possible categories in your classification.
3. Eliminate inappropriate categories from your list.
4. Put your final list in order.
5. Write at least one complete sentence for each of the categories you have chosen from your list.
6. Write a concluding sentence that emphasizes the basis of the classification.
7. Finally, copy your sentences into standard paragraph form.

EXERCISE

Writing the Classification Paragraph Step by Step

This exercise will guide you through the construction of a classification paragraph. Start with the suggested topic. Use the seven steps to help you work through each stage of the writing process.

Topic: Games

We play games as children. Some of these we continue to play as adults, and we play different types of games, as well. We are even accused of "playing games"—mind games—from time to time. There are board games, mind games, electronic games; how many other categories of games can you think of?

1. Topic sentence: ______________________________

   ____

2. Make a list of possible categories.

a. ______________________ f. ______________________

b. ______________________ g. ______________________

c. ______________________ h. ______________________

d. ______________________ i. ______________________

e. ______________________ j. ______________________

3. Eliminate any categories that are not appropriate.
4. Put your final list in order.
5. Using your final list, write at least one sentence for each category you have chosen.

a. ____

____

b. ____

____

c. ____

____

d. ____

____

e. ____

____

f. ____

____

g. ____

____

6. Write a concluding statement.

____

____

7. Copy your sentences into standard paragraph form.

____

____

____

On Your Own: Writing Classification Paragraphs from Model Paragraphs

The following model paragraphs are examples of effective classification writing. Whether you are classifying relationships, the media, activities, occupations, or any other topic, you must plan your paragraph keeping in mind the following points: Does the classification help to organize the material? Are you sure the classification is complete and that no item could belong to more than one category? Is there some purpose for your classifying the items as you did? (For example, will it help someone make a decision or understand a concept?)

Classifying Relationships

In the model paragraph that follows, the writer classifies the very different relationships he has with his parents.

Model Paragraph

Perhaps because my parents have been divorced for many years, my relationship with each of them has gone in quite different directions. My mother is a buddy now, a role she has assumed more and more as I've grown older. She asks my opinion about clothes and jobs, and I can tell her about my most outrageous friends without fear of her judging them, although she might raise an eyebrow. My dad is my mentor, totally focused on encouraging me to make what he considers smart college, career, and even social choices. He's introduced me to people who might be helpful later on and taught me how not to embarrass myself in the presence of even the most exalted CEO. With him, I don't mention my friends much, except for Jeremy, who is my dad's idea of a good influence.

ASSIGNMENT

Classification Paragraph

Pick a topic from the list below, and write a paragraph in which you classify relationships.

SUGGESTED TOPICS:

1. Friends
2. Classmates or colleagues at work
3. Girlfriends/boyfriends
4. Pets
5. Teachers
6. Bosses
7. Casual acquaintances

Developing an Essay of Classification

The thesis statement of a classification essay, like the topic sentence of the classification paragraph, identifies what is being classified. In the essay, it's important to devote each support paragraph to a single type within the discussion of classification. For example, the essay below classifies people into four groups according to what psychiatrist M. Scott Peck considers an evolution of spirituality. The first support paragraph (the second paragraph of the essay) deals only with the least spiritually evolved group (the first group). Because there are four groups being classified, it would be most appropriate to have a six-paragraph essay as opposed to the standard five, which many professors insist upon or at least strongly recommend.

For an in-depth look at the essay and its standard format (for all writing strategies in this unit), see Chapter 17: "The Essay." Also review Chapter 14: "The Four Stages of Writing," which can be applied to both the paragraph and the essay.

Model Essay: The Evolution of Spirituality

by Margo Fine

Psychiatrist and prolific author M. Scott Peck is probably most famous for his book *The Road Less Traveled,* which has appeared on the New York Best-Seller's List for more than 25 years. Peck entitled a sequel to this book *Further Along the Road Less Traveled*—a title that is appropriate if unoriginal. It is in this book, however, that Peck discusses a model of spiritual evolution into which, he says, every single person can be fit according to a particular classification system. Peck classifies people into four groups according to the extent to which they have spiritually evolved: the first group being the least evolved and the fourth being the most.

The first group is made up of people who are governed by their emotions. These are the quintessential charmers of the model. How nice they are, and therefore, how well they treat others, depend on whether they want something at that particular time. As soon as they get what they want, they're gone, or they're not so nice anymore: narcissism and greed are most apparent in this group. Their responses to people are generally unpredictable as these responses depend solely on these people's emotions. There is little or no self-examination or self-evaluation here.

The second group up from the bottom can quite aptly be called the "organizational clingers." These people are aware of the fact that left to their own devices, they would be completely governed by their own emotions like those in the first group. People in the second group inherently know this would prove disastrous. To avoid such a consequence, they opt to cling to an organization of some sort, one that promises to take care of them, one that offers a sense of protection and belonging but also discipline by means of a strict code of conduct. This organization prevents them from depending on their emotions for answers to their important questions. Organized religion is often the structure to which people in this group cling. In fact, Peck would put most religious fundamentalists (of any religion) in this category.

The third group up from the bottom (and therefore, the second from the top) is the group that seems to react quite vehemently to the second group (especially to religious fundamentalists). These are the secularists. These people are often very well educated in the sciences or the arts, and they are often politically active or motivated. People in this group often pride themselves on being free thinkers, especially when they compare themselves to people in the second group. However, they, themselves, depend on a structure, however less rigid than those in the second group, for answers to their important questions. After all, the sciences, especially, are dependent upon laws and knowledge of the natural world—the world people can only perceive with any or all of their five senses, the part of existence that we can see and hear, etc. Despite their self-declaration of being the free thinkers of the world, it is often they who dismiss the idea that there is an order to the universe that is not explainable by science or that can not be proven by anything empirical.

It is the fourth group that is most spiritually evolved, says Peck. These people, like their counterparts in the third group, are often very well educated. And although they probably call themselves secularists, they can probably be better described by the word "seekers," or perhaps "mystics." Like Albert Einstein, they may be highly regarded for their achievements in the secular world, but at the same time, they know there is more to life than that which we can see and hear or perceive with any of our five senses. People in the fourth group are very much aware of the importance of intuition, or an inner voice and the idea that something else is at work in the universe that can not be explained by science that makes a great deal of sense whether we can understand it or not. They are not necessarily quick to call it God or Allah or a cosmic consciousness, but whatever it is, it is definitely in the realm of the supernatural. But unlike those in the second group, people in the fourth group are not satisfied with any one set of holy books or especially any one set of interpretations that a single religion can offer in its explanation of a higher power.

It's difficult to avoid value judgments (especially in the case of the first group) in this classification system of spiritual evolution, but Peck notes that the system is only a model. Most people are, most often, a combination of two or more of these groups, but he says every individual is usually more strongly associated with one group as opposed to any other. To which group does each of your friends/family belong? With which group do *you* identify? Life is constantly changing, and our spiritual evolution is no exception, says Peck. If you don't think you're in the fourth group, don't despair: self-awareness and self-examination are already indicators of upward movement.

Analyzing the Writer's Strategies:

1. Do you agree with Peck's classification system? Why or why not?
2. How do you think, based on the above essay, Peck would define "spirituality"?
3. Does the author of the above essay agree with Peck's classification system? What evidence is there to suggest the author does agree? Is there evidence to the contrary?

ASSIGNMENT

Essay of Classification

Choose one of the topics below or pick one of your own, and write a classification essay of at least five paragraphs to develop that topic.

SUGGESTED TOPICS:

1. Different kinds of beer or wine
2. Different types of music
3. Different swimming strokes
4. Different genres of cinema
5. Different models of Honda (or any other make of car)
6. Different hairstyles
7. Different types of student
8. Different types of fashion
9. Different kinds of first dates (blind, set-up, Internet, etc.)
10. Pick a typical classification system within your field of study

For helpful hints on the following subjects, all of which will assist you in developing your classification essay, see Chapter 14:

Brainstorming
Choosing the Topic and Controlling Idea
Outlining
The Rough Draft
Revising the Rough Draft
Proofreading
Checklist for the Final Copy

Working Together: *Brainstorming for Classification*

Brainstorming can be wonderfully helpful when several people put their heads together. Divide into groups and brainstorm on one of the classification topics given below. After the members of each group have thought of everything they can, come together as a class, and put your classifications on the board. Compare and contrast them. What makes one more successful than another? Can you use each other's material?

Suggested Topics for Brainstorming:

1. Fads
   What is a fad? Classify as many different types of fads as you can.
2. Friendship
   What is friendship? Classify as many different types of friendships as you can.
3. Causes of car accidents
   What are the causes of car accidents? Classify as many different types of causes as you can.
4. Sports events
   What are the different kinds of sports events? Classify as many different types of sports events as you can.
5. Alcoholic beverages
   What are the different kinds of alcoholic beverages? Classify as many different types of alcoholic beverages as you can.

Your professor may now ask each student to write his or her own paragraph/essay using this material.

CHAPTER TWENTY-SEVEN **27**

Cause and Effect

What Is Cause and Effect?

People have always looked at the world and asked the questions "Why did this happen?" and "What are the results of that event?" Ancient societies created beautiful myths and legends to explain the origin of the universe and our place in it, while modern civilization has emphasized scientific methods of observation to find the cause of a disease or to determine why the planet Mars appears to be covered by canals. When we examine the spiritual or physical mysteries of our world, we are trying to discover the connections or links between events. In this chapter, we will refer to connections between events as **causal relationships**.

Causal relationships are part of our daily lives and provide a way of understanding the cause, result, or consequence of a particular event. The search for cause or effect is a bit like detective work. Probing an event is a way of searching for clues to discover what caused an event or what result it will have in the future.

For example, we might ask the question "Why did the car break down just after it came back from the garage?" as a way of searching for the cause of the car's new problem. Or we might ask, "What will be the side effects of a certain medicine?" in order to determine what effect a particular medicine will have on the body. This search for connections can be complex. Often the logical analysis of a problem reveals more than one possible explanation. Sometimes the best one can do is find *possible* causes or *probable* effects.

Developing Paragraphs: Cause and Effect

Two Types of Cause and Effect Paragraph or Essay

A cause and effect paragraph or essay always explains why something happened. But there are two types of cause and effect paragraph or essay: In the **first type**, the *cause* is identified in the topic sentence (for a paragraph) or thesis statement (for an essay); the supporting detail, however, is made up of several *effects*. In the **second type**, the *effect* is identified in the topic sentence or thesis statement, and the supporting detail, this time, is made up of several *causes*.

DO NOT try to deal with causes *and* effects of an event in the supporting detail of a single cause and effect paragraph or essay.

The Topic Sentence of a Cause and Effect Paragraph

The **topic sentence** of a cause and effect paragraph should reveal whether the paragraph will focus on causes or effects. For example, the following topic sentence uses the word *factors* to indicate that causes are about to follow:

> Several factors contributed to my decision to lose weight.

Losing weight is the effect, but the causes in the paragraph are about to follow.

On the other hand, this next topic sentence begins with the cause first and subsequently that a number of *effects* are about to follow:

> Losing weight had a number of positive effects on my life.

Supporting Detail of a Cause and Effect Paragraph

Again, the supporting detail of this type of paragraph contains either causes or effects, but **not both**.

Importance of Logic

In a good cause and effect paragraph, a cause must lead to an effect, not just precede the effect. That's why writing a cause and effect paragraph requires analysis to determine that a logical connection exists between events. For example, the fact that a person walked under a ladder just before he got hit by a car does not prove cause and effect. His walking under a ladder merely preceded the car's hitting him. To suggest that walking under a ladder caused him to get hit by a car is to use **faulty logic**. The reader of a cause and effect paragraph is meant to understand the relationship between a cause and its effects.

Avoid These Common Errors in Logic

1. Do not confuse coincidence or chronological sequence with evidence.
2. Look for underlying causes beneath the obvious ones and for far-reaching effects beyond the ones that first come to mind. Often what appears to be a single cause or a single effect is a much more complex problem.

Here is an example of a possible error in logic:

> Every time I try to write an essay in the evening, I have trouble getting to sleep. Therefore, writing must prevent me from sleeping.

In this case, writing may indeed be a stimulant that prevents the person from sleeping. However, if the person is serious about finding the cause of insomnia, he or she must observe whether any other **factors** may be to blame. For instance, if the person is drinking several cups of coffee while writing each evening, this could be a more likely cause of the person's wakefulness.

The following paragraph is an example of a good cause and effect paragraph.

The Causes of My Car Accident

There were a number of factors that caused my car accident on Deerfoot Trail last week. First, the weather was horrible that night. It was dark, and the rain made it even harder to see where I was going. The rain also made the roads very slippery, which meant that controlling my car was more difficult than usual. There was another factor that made my car difficult to control that night. I was returning home with a very heavy concrete birdbath for our backyard. When I slammed on my brakes and turned the steering wheel to avoid getting hit, the weight in my trunk shifted and caused the back end of my small car to swing around. Perhaps the most important factor was negligence. The driver of a black sports car was speeding and driving erratically. Rather than slow down when I changed into his lane ahead of him, he sped up, swerved and cut directly in front of me. I had to slam on my brakes and turn my steering wheel sharply to avoid hitting him. As a result, my car spun around in a complete circle in the middle of the highway. I wound up in a ditch on the side of the road, a little shaken but realizing things could have ended much worse.

PRACTICE 1

Looking for the Causal Relationship

Study each of the following situations. In each case, if the sequence of events is merely coincidental or chronological, put a *T* for time in the space provided. If the relationship is most likely causal, put a *C*. Be prepared to explain your answers in class. Check your answers against those in the Answer Key on p. 442.

__________ 1. Every time I carry my umbrella, it doesn't rain. I am carrying my umbrella today; therefore, it won't rain.

__________ 2. We put the fertilizer on the grass. A week later the grass grew two inches and turned a deeper green.

__________ 3. On Tuesday morning, I walked under a ladder. On Wednesday morning, I walked into my office and was told I had lost my job.

__________ 4. The child was born with a serious kidney condition. Seven days later, the child died.

__________ 5. Tar and nicotine from cigarettes damage the lungs. People who smoke cigarettes increase their chances of dying from lung cancer.

________ 6. A political scandal was exposed in the city on Friday. On Saturday night, only 24 hours later, a power blackout occurred in the city.

________ 7. Very few tourists came to the island last year. The economy of the island declined last year.

PRACTICE 2

Separating the Cause from the Effect

In the following practice exercise, there is an action or event above a group of related sentences. Put a *C* next to those sentences that are causes and an *E* next to those details that are effects. Check your answers against those in the Answer Key on p. 442.

1. Quitting smoking

________ a. Smoking costs a lot of money.

________ b. There are fewer public places that allow smoking now.

________ c. My terrible cough is gone.

________ d. I have gained 5 kg.

________ e. It bothered my friends and family.

________ f. I have found that my food tastes better.

2. Buying a new car

________ a. I got a great deal on financing.

________ b. My old car was unreliable.

________ c. I have less money every month because I have to pay more for insurance and gas.

________ d. My popularity at school has increased.

________ e. I was tired of having to take the train whenever I wanted to visit my family.

________ f. I was embarrassed to drive my rusted old car.

EXERCISE

Separating the Cause from the Effect

In each sentence, separate the cause, problem, or reason from the effect, solution, or result. Remember, the cause is not necessarily given first.

1. More than half of the mothers with children under one year of age work outside the home, which has resulted in an unprecedented need for daycare in this country.

   Cause: ____

   ____

Effect: ____

____

2. By 2000, two-thirds of all preschool children and four out of five school-age children had working mothers, facts that led to increased strain on our system of daycare.

   Cause: ____

   ____

   Effect: ____

   ____

3. In one national survey, over half the working mothers reported that they had either changed jobs or cut back on their hours in order to be more available to their children.

   Cause: ____

   ____

   Effect: ____

   ____

4. Many mothers who work do so only when their children are in school, while other mothers work only occasionally during the school year because they feel their children need the supervision of a parent.

   Cause: ____

   ____

   Effect: ____

   ____

5. Many mothers experience deep emotional crises as a result of their struggle to meet both the financial obligations of their home and their own emotional needs as parents.

   Cause: ____

   ____

   Effect: ____

   ____

Working for Coherence: Using Transitions

Several transitions and expressions are particularly useful when writing about causes or effects. You will need to feel comfortable using these words and expressions, and you will need to know what punctuation is required.

Common Transitions

Common Transitions for *Cause:*
because
caused by
results from
the reason is that ...+ a complete sentence
since

Common Transitions for *Effect:*
accordingly
as a result, resulted in
consequently
for this reason
so, so that
then, therefore, thus

Other transitional words and phrases can be found in Chapter 17: "The Essay" and on the inside back cover of this book.

EXERCISE 1

Using Transitional Words and Expressions of Cause

Use each of the following words or phrases in a sentence that demonstrates your understanding of its use for expressing cause relationships.

1. to be caused by ______________________________
____
2. because (of) ______________________________
____
3. resulted from ______________________________
____
4. the reason is that + complete sentence ______________________________
____
5. since ______________________________
____

EXERCISE 2

Using Transitional Words and Expressions for Effect

Use each of the following words or phrases in a complete sentence to demonstrate your understanding of how the word or phrase is used to point to an effect.

1. accordingly ____________________

____

2. as a result ____________________

____

3. results in ____________________

____

4. consequently ____________________

____

5. for this reason ____________________

____

6. so ____________________

____

7. therefore ____________________

____

Writing the Cause or Effect Paragraph Step by Step

To learn a skill that has so many different aspects, it is best to follow a step-by-step approach, so that one aspect can be worked on at a time. This will ensure that you are not missing a crucial point or misunderstanding a part of the whole. There are other ways to go about writing an effective paragraph, but here is one logical method you can use to achieve results.

Steps for Writing the Cause or Effect Paragraph

1. After you have chosen your topic, plan your topic sentence.
2. Brainstorm by jotting down all possible causes or effects. Ask others for their thoughts. Research if necessary. Consider long-range effects or underlying causes.
3. Choose the three or four best points from your list.
4. Decide on the best order for these points. (From least important to most important is one way to organize them.)
5. Write at least one complete sentence for each of the causes or effects you have chosen from your list.
6. Write a concluding statement.
7. Finally, copy your sentences into standard paragraph form.

EXERCISE 3 Writing the Effect Paragraph Step by Step

This exercise will guide you through the effect paragraph. Start with the suggested topic. Use the seven steps to help you work through each stage of the writing process.

Topic: What are the effects when students have part-time jobs after classes?

1. Topic sentence: ____________________

 ____

2. Make a list of possible effects. (Consider long-range effects.)

 a. ____________ f. ____________

 b. ____________ g. ____________

 c. ____________ h. ____________

 d. ____________ i. ____________

 e. ____________ j. ____________

3. Cross out any points that may be illogical, merely coincidental, or the result of only time sequence.
4. Put your list in order.
5. Using your final list, write at least one sentence for each of the effects you have found.

 a. ____________________

 ____

 b. ____________________

 ____

 c. ____________________

 ____

 d. ____________________

 ____

 e. ____________________

 ____

 f. ____________________

 ____

 g. ____________________

 ____

6. Write a concluding statement.

____

____

7. Copy your sentences into standard paragraph form.

____

____

____

____

____

____

____

____

____

____

On Your Own: Writing Cause and Effect Paragraphs from Model Paragraphs

The Causes of a Social Problem

The following paragraph looks at possible reasons for placing an elderly relative in a nursing home.

Model Paragraph

Industrialized societies have developed homes for the elderly who are unable to care for themselves. In spite of much criticism, these homes have a growing percentage of our nation's elderly. Why do some people feel forced into placing parents into a nursing home? The most immediate cause is that following some serious illness, there is often no place for the elderly person to go where he or she can be cared for. In the family of today, it is often the case that both partners work outside the home, so no one is home during the day to care for the person. Hiring a nurse to be in the home every day is beyond the budget of nearly every family. Even when a family member can be home to care for the elderly person, the problems can be overwhelming. The older person can be too heavy for one or even two to manage. Bathing, particularly, can be dangerous in these circumstances. In addition, many elderly people have to be watched very carefully because of their medical condition. Many families do not have the proper training to meet these needs. Finally, elderly people who may be senile and difficult can often intrude on a family's life to the point that a caregiver may never be able to leave the house or get a proper night's rest. Perhaps a better system of visiting nursing care could help some families keep their loved ones in their homes longer.

ASSIGNMENT 1

Cause and Effect Paragraph (Causes)

Pick a topic from the list below, and write a paragraph about the causes of a social problem that is of concern to you.

SUGGESTED TOPICS:

1. The causes of homelessness
2. The causes of prostitution
3. The causes of teenage pregnancy
4. The causes of college or university drop-outs
5. The causes of workplace theft
6. The causes of tax cheating
7. The causes of panhandling

The Causes of Disaster

The following model paragraph looks at the causes for the loss of life in the sinking of a supposedly unsinkable ship on its maiden voyage over eighty years ago.

Model Paragraph

One of the most tragic events of the twentieth century was the sinking of the British ship *Titanic* in the Atlantic Ocean on April 15, 1912, with the loss of over 1500 lives. The immediate cause of this terrible loss of life was a large iceberg that tore a 300-foot gash in the side of the ship, flooding five of its watertight compartments. Some believe that the tragedy took place because the crew members did not see the iceberg in time, but others see a chain of different events that contributed to the tragedy. First was the fact that the ship was not carrying enough lifeboats for all of its passengers: it had enough boats for only about half of the people on board. Furthermore, the ship's crew showed a clear lack of concern for the third-class or "steerage" passengers, who were left in their cramped quarters below decks with little or no help as the ship went down. It has often been said that this social attitude of helping the wealthy and neglecting the poor was one of the real causes of the loss of life that night. Indeed, some of the lifeboats that were used were not filled to capacity when the rescue ships eventually found them. Finally, the tragedy of the *Titanic* was magnified by the fact that some ships nearby did not have a radio crew on duty and therefore missed the distress signals sent by the *Titanic*. Out of all this, the need to reform safety regulations on passenger ships became obvious.

ASSIGNMENT 2

Cause and Effect Paragraph (Effects)

Select a community or area disaster that you have personally experienced or heard about. This could include a severe climatic condition or a manufactured disaster. Instead of writing a paragraph about the disaster's causes such as in the above paragraph, point out the effects it had on you or the people involved.

SUGGESTED TOPICS:

1. The effects of an earthquake
2. The effects of a power blackout on a major city or town
3. The effects of a flood or other extensive water damage on a home or community
4. The effects of a chemical spill on land or offshore
5. The effects of a transit strike on a community
6. The effects of a major fire on a downtown block
7. The effects of the terrorist attack on 9/11.

Developing the Cause and Effect Essay

Like in the cause and effect paragraph, the essay, too, should focus only on either causes or effects, but not both. And it should be self-evident from the thesis statement of your essay which one that particular essay will be discussing.

Again, the thesis appears somewhere between the middle and the end of the first paragraph. And each support paragraph deals with one cause or one effect, depending on which type of essay you've chosen to write.

Bear in mind that all three causes or all three effects should directly support your thesis, whatever it is. If not, you must make some adjustments. Whether you change your thesis or support paragraphs (perhaps only one support paragraph needs to be reworked), it is up to you. At this stage, you may want to make whatever changes require the least amount of time, especially if you're writing the essay in class and you're writing under the pressure of a rigid time limit.

For an in-depth look at the essay and its standard format (for all writing strategies in this unit), see Chapter 17: "The Essay." Also review Chapter 14: "The Four Stages of Writing," which can be applied to both the paragraph and the essay.

Model Essay I: Whose Choice Is It, Anyway?

by Donald Pianissimo

It is so easy to think that the decisions you make are your own choices. But when you consider the events leading up to those decisions, it may not be so easy to claim the decisions as your own. My decision to go into journalism was, I thought, something I had chosen completely on my own without external influence. But when I think of three particular events in my life before leaving high school, I begin to think my say in the matter was minimal at best. I begin to think I was simply following a path that had already been laid out for me.

My mom used to serve in the medical profession as a nurse, and she confided in me long after I'd dropped chemistry in high school that she always wanted me to be a doctor. My dad, although a writer, never called himself a journalist; journalism was not the kind of writing he preferred to do. But perhaps I underestimated his influence on my choice to enter a writing career. In fact, it was he who encouraged me to publish an article in a local magazine when I was only nine years old. I still remember his editing my work. I also remember the thrill of my anticipation of seeing my name in print. It was the first taste of being published I would get, and it wouldn't be the last.

A second incident is as vivid in my memory as the first. In Grade 8, the first English teacher who would truly inspire me with his passion for teaching announced to the class one day that there were three essays he had marked that were worthy of recognition. He asked three students to read their essays out loud in front of the entire class, and I was one of them. He made me feel I had a gift, a gift worth sharing.

And finally, by the time I'd gotten to high school, a classmate and I were asked by a teacher to co-edit the school newspaper. I never thought I would have so much fun. Better still, the paper was a hit with the other students. Our high school hadn't seen so successful a student newspaper in years. I couldn't help but love the popularity that came with it, too.

I envied those students who knew they wanted to be doctors, or lawyers or engineers since the time they could talk. I just figured I wasn't so blessed with such an ardent and focused career desire. By the time I'd graduated from high school, I chose to enter a field of study for my postsecondary education based on one of my most enjoyable pastimes: writing for an audience. Journalism seemed the logical choice. What didn't occur to me until much later was that my choice seemed the logical conclusion of a number of monumental events in my young life. Were they random events, or were they meant to lead me in a certain direction? Your guess is as good as mine.

Analyzing the Writer's Strategies:

1. Does the writer support the idea of free will, or the idea of fate?
2. Is there evidence in this essay to suggest support for one or the other?
3. How much does the author attribute his choices to the influence of parents and teachers?
4. What is the author's thesis?
5. Is the thesis adequately supported?

Exploring the Topic:

1. How did you decide to enter your current field of study? Was it free will or fate?
2. Does reading this essay make you think twice about whether or not you made the choice to enter your field of study totally independently of outside influence?

ASSIGNMENT

Cause and Effect Essay

Choose one of the topics from the following list, or one of your own, and write a cause and effect essay of at least five paragraphs to develop that topic.

SUGGESTED TOPICS:

1. The causes of war
2. The causes of failing a course
3. The causes of breaking up with a boyfriend/girlfriend
4. The causes of addiction (alcohol, drugs, sex, relationship, etc.)
5. The causes of lying
6. The effects of lying
7. The effects of parents who don't show their children affection
8. The effects of poverty in the home
9. The effects of fame
10. The effects of dating a real "hottie"

For helpful hints on the following subjects, all of which will assist you in developing your cause and effect essay, see Chapter 14:
Brainstorming
Choosing the Topic and the Controlling Idea
Outlining
The Rough Draft
Revising the Rough Draft
Proofreading
Checklist for the Final Copy

Working Together: *Identifying Causes*

Listen while the following analysis of the causes for the decline of Central America's Mayan culture is read aloud to the class. The class should then divide into groups. Work with your group to list the immediate and the underlying causes for the decline of Mayan civilization. One person from each group will then read the group's complete list of immediate and underlying causes to the class. After a complete listing is agreed upon, make a judgment as to how positive scientists are about the underlying causes of this historical phenomenon.

Model Essay II: Anything but Peaceful

by Zack Goodman

In the last few years, scholars have made great strides in translating the Mayas' previously indecipherable writing system. From the emerging texts and from recent excavations has emerged a new, at times bewildering, picture of the Maya civilization at its peak, from A.D. 250 to 900. Great as their cultural and economic achievements manifestly were, they had anything but a peaceful society.

Indeed, the latest feeling among scholars is that the increasing militarism of Maya society may have undermined the ecological underpinnings of the economy. Some of them speculate that siege warfare concentrated population in urban centres, caused desperate farmers to abandon previously successful practices of diversified agriculture, and led to overexploitation of the forest.

Dr. Arthur A. Demarest, an archaeologist who directs an ambitious Maya dig in Guatemala, has said that the evidence from stone art and texts points to the surprising conclusion that "the Maya were one of the most violent state-level societies in the New World, especially after A.D. 600."

Various writings and artifacts, Dr. Demarest says, indicate continual raiding and warfare between the elites of adjacent city-states and also the practice of ritual bloodletting and human sacrifice. The prestige of ruling dynasties, and hence their power, seemed to depend on their success in battle and the sacrifice of prisoners of war. Dr. Linda Schele, a Maya scholar, wrote in an issue of *Natural History* magazine, "We don't know if the early Maya went to war mainly to acquire territory, take booty, control conquered groups for labour, take captives for sacrifice in sanctification rituals, or a combination of these."

Whatever the specific goal, archaeologists think that for centuries the wars were limited to ritualized conflicts between the elite troops of two rulers. The losing ruler was sometimes decapitated with great ceremony, as depicted in Maya art.

CHAPTER TWENTY-EIGHT

28

Argumentation

What Is Argumentation?

So far, your purpose in many writing assignments in this text has been to describe, narrate, or explain by using various writing strategies for development. Still another purpose in writing is to argue.

DEFINITION ➤ **Argumentation** is an attempt to change the reader's present viewpoint, or at least to convince her or him that your viewpoint is a valid one.

Every time you write a paper for a course, you are trying to persuade your professor that what you are presenting is the correct view of the subject matter. You might want to show, for example, that Canadian airlines are among the safest in the world, or that the crime novel is becoming Canada's favourite form of fiction. As you approach such types of assignments, you need to be aware of each part of the argumentative process so that you will be able to use it effectively in your own writing.

You could view all writing as persuasive, since one of the writer's main goals is to get the reader to see, think, and believe in a certain way. Although "persuasiveness" is a quality of *all* paragraph/essay writing strategies (narration, classification, etc.), **argumentation** is considered a separate writing strategy altogether. **Formal argumentation** follows certain guidelines. If you have ever been a member of a debating team, you have spent a good deal of time studying this special form. How to recognize techniques of argument and use them in your own writing is the subject of this chapter.

Writing the Argumentative Paragraph

In all of the previous chapters in this unit, more emphasis was placed on the development of the paragraph than on the essay. With respect to the writing strategy of argumentation, the opposite will be done here. The most effective arguments are those supported by several points that are treated rather thoroughly. For this reason, an argumentative essay would probably be a more effective piece of writing than an argumentative paragraph so long as the points are thoughtful, well expressed, and directly supportive of your overall assertion or argument. However, that is not to say that a good argumentative paragraph can not be written. Of course, it can. If you do attempt to write such a paragraph, just remember to establish your argument in the form of a topic sentence that is clear and strong, and make sure your supporting details are the strongest evidence in support of your argument you can find.

Guide to Writing the Argumentative Essay

1. **State a clear thesis.** Use words such as *must, ought,* and *should.*

   Marijuana should be legalized for medical uses.
   Canada must reform its prison system.
   All information on the Internet should be free.

2. **Use examples.** Well-chosen examples are the heart of any essay. Without them, the writing is flat, lifeless, and unconvincing. Providing a good example for each of your main points helps make a much stronger argument. Examples help your reader *see* what you are talking about.
3. **Use opinions from recognized authorities to support your points.** One of the oldest methods of supporting an argument is to use one or more authorities to support your particular position. People usually believe what well-known experts claim. You should use carefully chosen experts to help make your position on a topic more persuasive. However, be sure that your authority is someone who is respected in the area you are discussing. For example, if you are arguing that we must end the nuclear arms race, your argument will be stronger if you quote a respected scientist who can accurately predict the consequences of a nuclear war. A famous movie star giving the same information might be more glamorous and get more attention, but he or she would not be as great an authority as the scientist.
4. **Answer your critics in advance.** When you point out beforehand what your opposition is likely to say in answer to your argument, you are writing from a position of strength. You are letting your reader know that you are aware that there is another side to the argument you are making. By pointing out this other side and then answering its objections in advance, you are strengthening your own position.
5. **Point out the results.** Help your reader see what will happen if your argument is (or is not) believed or acted upon as you think it should be. You should be specific and rational when you point out results, making sure that you avoid exaggeration of any kind. For example, if you argue against the possession of handguns, it would be an exaggeration to say that everyone is going to be murdered if the opposition's point of view is listened to instead of yours.

For an in-depth look at the essay and its standard format (for all writing strategies in this unit), see Chapter 17: "The Essay." Also review Chapter 14: "The Four Stages of Writing," which can be applied to both the paragraph and the essay.

The following essay by Leanne C. Southall is about the relationship between attitudes and oppression against women. As you read the essay, look for the major parts of an effective argument: strong thesis, carefully chosen examples, quotations from authorities, answers to the opposition, and predictions. Can you find any weaknesses in the argument?

Model Essay I: Individuals Must Spur Change

by Leanne C. Southall

***Note:** This piece was written in the form of a letter to the editor written in response to an article published in the* Hamilton Spectator *on July 19, 2001. The article outlined the proposed regulations put forward by Turkey's Health Minister that female nursing students must undergo "virginity testing" to proceed with their training. These regulations are being proposed "to ensure that nursing schools are not encouraging prostitution." The letter was sent on July 30, prior to the events of September 11, 2001.*

Once again, attitudes toward females in a fundamentalist religious realm are perpetuating women's oppression. Regulations proposed by Turkey's health minister, Osman Durmus—stating that women training to be nurses must prove their virginity—are a discriminatory offence. He has suggested that nursing students who have ever been sexually active may lead schools to become places for prostitution. His statement implies that sexually active women are immoral. Since Durmus issued the directive, Turkish newspapers have reported that he has been told by government leaders to take a vacation.

But this situation is just one of many restrictions on women around the world. Essentially, being a woman anywhere may be reason enough for targeting. In countries such as India and Jordan, daughters can be viewed as property; "honour killings" are tolerated if a woman shames her family. Recently, in Iran, where girls are forced to cover their heads and bodies from age 9, ten prostitutes were murdered. A special investigation ensued, and the deputy governor-general for law enforcement explained, "They were little and unimportant." In Pakistan, where 80 per cent of women are subjected to domestic violence, there is emerging a pattern of husbands dumping kerosene on their wives, lighting a match, and claiming their death to be a stove accident. Acid attacks are now being seen in hospitals. Reasons for getting rid of wives may include a suspicion of other sexual partners, a dowry considered too small or a woman's failure to get pregnant. (Incidentally, a woman's testimony was once only half the weight of a man's in Pakistan). Female genitalia mutilation is still a harmful custom in various countries around the world; some 4000 girls in Africa are to undergo this ritual in October.

In Afghanistan's past twenty years of war, women and girls have been beaten, raped, abducted and sold into prostitution. Since Taliban rule began in 1994, women are not permitted to work or attend school and must not make noise when they walk. They are not to leave their homes unless accompanied by a male relative, and certainly not without their restrictive burqua [a black veil that cloaks a woman's body from head to toe, leaving a small meshed window for her eyes to see through]. Their windows are painted black, ensuring that they cannot be seen from the street. In the United States, women are excluded from leading congregations because "Southern Baptists, by practice as well as conviction, believe leadership is male," as explained by Drafting Committee Chairman Reverend Adrian Rogers.

And what about Canada? Each of us should evaluate how our attitudes toward women affect lives. A mere 4 per cent of sexual assault charges result in convictions. The court process resembles a second violation, where her medical records and previous charges can be subpoenaed and her credibility is put on trial. Women still earn less than men in the same jobs. The only exception may be fashion modeling, which demonstrates the emphatic value we place on a woman's beauty, versus intelligence or contribution.

Judged far too quickly are single moms supported by social programs. Provinces have tightened eligibility for social assistance and designed policies that lead single mothers into the labour market. However, with licensed daycare costs as high as $7000 per year and limited regulated spaces available, help is far beyond the means of many single moms. Consequently, 56 per cent of single-parent families headed by women are poor.

If violence toward women reflects societal attitudes, sexism is all too alive in Canada. Some 51 per cent of Canadian women report having experienced physical or sexual violence. In 1998, more than 90,000 women and children used emergency abuse shelters across Canada. While not every woman has experienced violence, there is virtually no one who has not feared it.

Globally, we must adopt a system that embraces gender equality within political, economic and social spheres. Working toward that day, as individuals, let us each be aware of our attitudes and the part we can play to improve the status of women around the world.

Analyzing the Writer's Strategies

Because Leanne C. Southall's essay deals with a controversial topic, some people may take exception to some of the points she makes. However, the writer combines the results of several nations' experiences and those of Canada to persuade us to change our attitudes where appropriate.

1. In your own words, what is Southall's thesis statement? Which sentence, in particular, is *her* thesis statement?

2. What is her strongest supporting detail? Why? What is her weakest supporting detail? Why?
3. What does she want her readers to do?

Even more controversial, perhaps, is the following essay on euthanasia: the killing of dying patients. Try to keep an open mind as you read it regardless of your views. Listen to the arguments. Which ones are weak? Which ones are strong? Is there anything you need to know more about before you can make an informed decision?

Model Essay II: It's Time We Helped Patients Die

by Dr. Howard Caplan

For three years, the husband of one of my elderly patients watched helplessly as she deteriorated. She'd burst an aneurysm and later had an astrocytoma removed from her brain. Early in the ordeal, realizing that she'd never recover from a vegetative state, he'd pleaded with me to pull her nasogastric tube.

I'd refused, citing the policy of the convalescent hospital. I told him I could do it only if he got a court order. But he couldn't bring himself to start such proceedings, although the months dragged by with no signs of improvements in his wife's condition. He grieved as her skin broke down and she developed terrible bedsores. She had to have several courses of antibiotics to treat the infections in them, as well as in her bladder, which had an indwelling catheter.

Finally I got a call from a lawyer who said he'd been retained by the family to force me to comply with the husband's wishes.

"I'm on your side," I assured him. "But you'll have to get that court order just the same."

I went on to suggest—though none too hopefully—that we ask the court to do more than just let the patient starve to death. "If the judge will agree to let her die slowly, why won't he admit that he wants death to happen? Let's ask for permission to give her an injection and end her life in a truly humane manner."

The lawyer had no answer except to say, "Aw, come on, Doc—that's euthanasia!"

Frankly, I'd have been surprised at any other reaction. Although most states have enacted living-will laws in the past decade, none has yet taken the next logical step—legalizing euthanasia. But I believe it's time they did. Ten years of practice in geriatrics have convinced me that a proper death is a humane death, either in your sleep or being *put* to sleep.

I see appropriate patients every day in the extended-care facilities at which I practice. About 50 of the 350 people under my care have already ended their biographical lives. They've reached the stage in life at which there's no more learning, communicating, or experiencing pleasure. They're now simply existing in what is left of their biological lives.

Most of these patients are the elderly demented. A typical case is that of a woman in her eighties or nineties, who speaks only in gibberish and doesn't recognize her family. She has forgotten how to eat, so she has a feeding tube coming from her nose. She is incontinent, so she has an indwelling catheter. She can no longer walk, so she is tied into a wheelchair. She's easily agitated, so she gets daily doses of a major tranquilizer. Why shouldn't I, with the concurrence of her family and an independent medical panel, be allowed to quickly and painlessly end her suffering?

I think of another patient, a woman in her fifties, with end-stage multiple sclerosis, unable to move a muscle except for her eyeballs and her tongue. And younger patients: I have on my census a man in his early forties, left an aphasic triplegic by a motorcycle accident when he was nineteen. For nearly a quarter of a century, while most of us were working, raising children, travelling, reading, and otherwise going about our lives, he's been vegetating. His biographical life ended with that crash. He can't articulate—only make sounds to convey that he's hungry or wet. If he were to become acutely ill, I would prefer not to try saving him. I'd want to let pneumonia end it for him.

Of my remaining 300 patients, there are perhaps 50 to 100 borderline functional people who are nearing the end of their biographical lives and—were euthanasia legal—would probably tell me: "I'm ready to go. My bags are packed. Help me."

Anyone who's had front-line responsibility for the elderly has been asked if there wasn't "something you can give me" to end life. Such requests are made by patients who clearly see the inevitability of their deterioration and dread having to suffer through it. For these people, there is no more pleasure, let alone joy—merely misery. They want out.

What is their fate? Chances are they'll be referred for psychiatric consultation on the grounds that they must be seriously depressed. The psychiatrist, usually decades younger than the patient, does indeed diagnose depression and recommends an antidepressant.

But if such patients lived in the Netherlands, odds are they'd get assistance in obtaining a release from the slow dying process to which our modern technology condemns them. While euthanasia is not yet legal there, it's openly practised. On a segment of the CBS show *60 Minutes* not long ago, I heard a Dutch anesthesiologist describe how doctors in his country help 5000 terminal patients slip away peacefully each year. Isn't that a promising indication of how well euthanasia would work in this country?

I realize that there are those who vigorously oppose the idea. And there are moral issues to confront—how much suffering is too much, the one-in-several-million chance that a person given no hope of improving will beat the odds. But it's time for society to seriously reconsider whether it is immoral to take the life of someone whose existence is nothing but irreversible suffering.

Euthanasia ought to be treated the same way the abortion issue has been treated: people who believe it a sin to take a life even for merciful reasons would not be forced to do so. What I'm pleading for is that doctors and their patients at least have the choice.

I doubt that we'll get congressional action on such an emotionally charged issue during my lifetime. Action may have to come at the state level. Ideally, legislatures should permit each hospital and each nursing home to have a panel that would approve candidates for euthanasia. Or it might be more practical to have one panel serve several hospitals and nursing homes in a geographic area. Made up of one or two physicians and a lawyer or judge, plus the attending doctor, the panel would assess the attending's findings and recommendations, the patient's wishes, and those of the immediate family. This would ensure that getting a heart-stopping injection was truly in the patient's best interests, and that there was no ulterior motive—for example, trying to hasten an insurance payout. Needless to say, members of the board would be protected by law from liability claims.

Then, if the patient had made it known while of sound mind that under certain circumstances he wanted a deadly substance administered, the process would be easy for everyone. But in most cases, it would be up to the attending to raise the question of euthanasia with the patient's relatives.

I'd start with those who've been part of the patient's recent life. If there are relatives who haven't seen the patient for years, it really shouldn't be any of their business. For instance, I'd try involving a son who's just kept in touch by phone. I'd say to him, "If you really want to stop this from happening, then you'd better come out here to see firsthand what's going on."

However, if he said, "Well, I can't really get away, Doctor, but I violently disagree," my answer would be, "Well, not violently enough. Everyone here can see what shape your mother's in. We're quite sure what she'd want if she could tell us, and we're going to help her."

Before any of this can happen, though, there's going to have to be widespread public education. The media will have to do a better job of discussing the issues than it has with living wills. Among my patients who are nearing death, there aren't more than a half-dozen with living wills attached to their charts. Patients' families often haven't even heard of them, and even when large institutions encourage families to get these things taken care of while the patient is still alert, it's hardly ever done.

Not knowing about living wills, unaware of no-code options, many families plunge their loved ones—and themselves—into unwanted misery. How many rapidly deteriorating patients are rushed from a nursing home to a hospital to be intubated, simply because that's the facility's rigid policy? How many families impoverish themselves to keep alive someone who's unaware of himself and his surroundings?

Every day in my professional life, I encounter illogical, irrational, and inhumane regulations that prevent me, and those with whom I work, from doing what we know in our souls to be the right thing. Before high technology, much of this debate was irrelevant. There was little we could do, for example, when a patient arrested. And what we could do rarely worked.

But times have changed. Now we have decisions to make. It helps to understand that many of the elderly infirm have accepted the inevitability—and, indeed, the desirability—of death. We who are younger must not mistake this philosophical position for depression. We need to understand the natural acceptance of death when life has lost its meaning.

About 28 percent of our huge medicare budget is spent providing care during the last year of life. Far too little of that money goes to ensure that dying patients' last months are pain-free and comfortable. Far too much is wasted on heroic, pain-inducing measures that can make no difference. It's time to turn that ratio around—and to fight for the right to provide the ultimate assistance to patients who know their own fight to prolong life is a losing one.

Analyzing the Writer's Strategies

Because Dr. Caplan deals with a very sensitive subject, many people might find his position to be dangerous and even frightening. Even before we examine his essay, the title of the piece gains our attention. It's likely to shock both those for and those against euthanasia because of its bluntness.

The fact that the author is a doctor, in itself, might persuade the reader to accept whatever he says as true. But what if another doctor as familiar with dying patients as the author were to argue *against* euthanasia? Would you then have to consider the arguments more carefully? Do we, at times, trust authority too blindly?

To support his position on euthanasia, Caplan refers to the case of the Netherlands where euthanasia, although officially illegal, has become an acceptable policy of medical practice as long as certain rules are followed. Rachel Nowak, however, reported the following facts in "The Dutch Way of Death" in the book *Moral Philosophy for Modern Life* by Anthony Falikowski, which Caplan does not acknowledge in his essay:

> At least a third of the 5000 or so Dutch patients, who each year receive lethal doses of drugs from their doctors, do not give their unequivocal consent. About 400 of those patients never even raise the issue of euthanasia with their doctors. Moreover, of those who willingly opt for euthanasia, only about 5 per cent do so because of unbearable pain. A much higher proportion, about a third, do so partly for fear of becoming dependent on others.

Nowak adds that each year, doctors have acknowledged that about 1300 patients are given an increased dose of painkillers, "not to alleviate their pain but to shorten their lives." Does this weaken or strengthen Caplan's point about medical policy in the Netherlands? Does this additional evidence about euthanasia affect his overall argument?

Exploring the Topic

1. Did you support euthanasia before discovering this piece in *The Canadian Writer's Workplace*? Does this section change your views at all? Explain.
2. What does Caplan mean by a "biographical life"? What part of life might Caplan not be taking into consideration in his argument? Is his understanding of life too limited?
3. Consider the point the author made about a son not having the right to contribute to the decision of his mother's fate (of living or dying) because the son says he cannot make it to a meeting. Is this a good or bad argument? Explain.
4. Why does he begin his essay with an example of a dying patient? Does this part appeal to the reader's sense of reason or emotion? Is this an effective way to start? Is it fair? Is it responsible? Explain.

ASSIGNMENT

Argumentative Essay

Choose one of the ten topics below and write an essay of at least five paragraphs. Argue for or against the topic of your choice. Use the following five points, discussed earlier in this chapter, as a guide for your writing.

1. Write a strong thesis statement.
2. Provide examples for each of your reasons.
3. Use at least one authority to support your thesis.
4. Admit that others have a different point of view.
5. Indicate the results or your predictions in the conclusion.

SUGGESTED TOPICS:

1. Capital punishment
2. Censorship of books or movies
3. Same-sex marriages
4. Human cloning
5. Gun control
6. Stricter immigration laws
7. Prayer in the public schools
8. Single-parent adoption
9. Abortion
10. Control of pornography

Many, many more topics for both argumentative paragraphs and essays are provided under the heading of *Writing Ideas,* which can be found at the end of the section of questions immediately following each major reading in Unit IV. Questions under the heading *Questions for Discussion* (also after each major reading in Unit IV) might also be deemed suitable argumentative writing topics.

For helpful hints on the following subjects, all of which will assist you in developing your argumentative essay, see Chapter 14:

Brainstorming
Choosing the Topic and the Controlling Idea
Outlining
The Rough Draft
Revising the Rough Draft
Proofreading
Checklist for the Final Copy

Working Together: *The Ongoing Debate on Euthanasia*

Below are several pieces of information on the controversial topic of **euthanasia** (or assisted suicide). Discuss with a group of your peers the question of who should make the life-and-death decisions in such matters. Use the following research as the basis for your discussion and, perhaps, your own essay on the topic. You may choose to rely on as many facts as you want, or you may adapt the opinions to agree with your own way of thinking. As you study the list, try to decide in which of your paragraphs you would use each of the facts or opinions you are given.

1. Nearly 4000 Canadians commit suicide every year.
2. The idea of suicide has been rejected by society for many centuries.
3. Some societies discourage suicide by enacting strict laws against it.
4. Euthanasia is an act of charity when there is no hope that the sick person will ever enjoy a healthy life.
5. In British Columbia, doctors assisted Sue Rodriguez to end her life when she felt she could no longer live with dignity during her terminal illness.
6. As our technical ability to extend life increases, the pressure on us to make life-and-death decisions also increases.
7. "Suicide," the German poet Goethe said, "is an incident in human life which, however much disputed and discussed, demands the sympathy of every man, and in every age must be dealt with anew."
8. In Saskatchewan, Robert Latimer killed his severely disabled daughter to end her suffering.
9. If we had laws that encouraged euthanasia, we would not have the lives of such people as Helen Keller to show the world what disabled people can do.
10. The general reaction to euthanasia will change as people realize that life should not always go on no matter the cost.
11. The Canadian Medical Association does not support euthanasia.
12. The worst tragedy in life is to live without dignity.

13. People often make "living wills" stating that they should be allowed to die naturally.
14. Years ago, people seldom spoke openly about suicide; now there are organizations that openly advocate it.
15. A very common form of euthanasia occurs when parents and doctors agree not to give disabled newborn children needed medical attention, eventually leading to their deaths.
16. All life has dignity and euthanasia threatens that dignity.
17. Society pressures its members to look "normal," and euthanasia legalizes the rejection of the "abnormal."

UNIT FOUR

IV

Readings

Many schools subscribe to the philosophy that reading and writing are inseparable components in the process of improving one's writing skills. The readings that follow include works of nonfiction, fiction, and poetry, all Canadian, and all written by seasoned writers. Many of these will not represent specific essay models as described earlier in this book, but as is often the case, a single essay written by a professional writer can contain a mixture of different modes and styles. These readings have been selected in the hope that they will inspire discussion and written responses from students.

✦ ✦ ✦

Don Juan/Doña Juana

Rosemary Sullivan

Professor of English at the University of Toronto, Rosemary Sullivan is also a novelist and writer of nonfiction. The following piece is taken from her book called *Labyrinth of Desire*, which offers a collection of perspectives on different aspects of love and sex. The term "Don Juan" (from the mythological story of a man who is a lover of thousands of women) is often considered a good thing. Sullivan, however, reveals what lies beneath the term and in the depths of the psyche of the person "honoured" with the title. She also shows that the term should by no means be restricted to men.

1 In the age-old cliché, a man will fight over a woman as if she were the prize trophy. But a woman will compete against another woman for the prize in a ruthless, predatory way.

2 Anyone who has been involved in a triangular affair knows how this works. Neither our own motives nor our man's are examined. The other woman is the enemy. She must be defeated.

3 What kind of man precipitates such **acrimony**? Traditionally, the man who indulges in multiple lovers is a Don Juan **archetype**, a narcissist. And what characterizes a **narcissist** is that the only real relationship he is capable of is one with himself.

4 The novelist Leon Whiteson once remarked that most men who play this role do so to cover their fear of intimacy. "SIN for men," he explained, "is Safety In Numbers." Having many women is a guarantee against having to deal intimately with one individual woman. It's a perfect device for protecting the bottom line: *I need no one*. As soon as such a man allows himself to acknowledge need, he opens himself to betrayal. How can he trust that he will not be abandoned?

5 The bad luck for women is that we often find men who fit the Don Juan archetype to be so attractive. They fall impulsively into erotic relationships, and we women immediately get ourselves busy searching out the heart within these transparently sensitive men. We do not recognize that their whole strategy is to

keep us unsettled: now you know him, now you don't. This kind of man can't deal with women candidly because to do so would compromise his power. And for us, the not-knowing, the continual shift in his affections, leaves us in a state of constant anxiety and self-doubt.

6 These affairs can only degenerate into very unpleasant **Tantalus** games. The dynamic is thoroughly destructive, a push/pull dance of misinterpretation. Nights of hysteria without sleep. Days plotting what to say. Then the accusatory barbs. A woman will find herself trivialized, undermined. She turns into the very thing she hates most: the **supplicating** female.

7 So much of obsessive love takes place in the head. We spend our time desperately trying to understand the other's perspective. It's as if we have failed a test we had no idea we were taking. We want to justify ourselves, to have our interpretation heard. We are left with lingering feelings of failure and guilt. We haven't the least clue what's going on.

8 I have been speaking as if there were no female equivalent to Don Juan, but of course there is a Doña Juana, though she hasn't been so named. She is variously called the *femme fatale*, the seductress, the siren, the vamp, *la Belle Dame Sans Merci*.

9 One of her most fascinating **incarnations** is as Scarlett O'Hara in the 1939 film *Gone With the Wind*. Scarlett is petulant, childish, totally limited in her feelings, and seemingly irresistible to men. She collects men as trophies for her beauty, using them for her own ends. She admits to having no real feeling for them and complains about the need to pretend she does. As a type, her power is incomprehensible to women. She is so transparent, can't men see through her?

10 But the quality of the seductress that is irresistible to men is her combination of vulnerability and willfulness. She has a passionate energy, an infectious appetite for life (Scarlett's favorite expletive is "great balls of fire"), but she trades on her helplessness. Probably men are flattered, but not fooled. They secretly admire her strength, which is, paradoxically, so unfeminine. One lover complains, with relish, that she cut her teeth on his heart.

11 Scarlett is ruthless, self-absorbed and manipulative. As the film makes clear, war brings out the best in her—her indomitable will to survive. She lies, cheats, and even steals her sister's fiancé to keep the family estate intact. At war's end, knowing there will be a building boom, she sets up her own lumber business and is as brutal as any man, replacing slave labor with that of convicts on starvation rations.

12 But while the Don Juan is often admired by other men for his swordsmanship (that old metaphor for sexual conquest), the vamp is vilified by other women for throwing herself after men, for making a spectacle of herself, and so forth. She becomes an outsider, and the only one to whom she might be vulnerable is an outsider like herself.

13 In *Gone With the Wind*, Rhett Butler is the outsider, and Scarlett's twin. He says they're made for each other—they're both selfish and ruthless, but, as he once remarks, at least they have the guts to look life in the face.

14 The vamp, like the Don Juan, is always the basis for a cautionary tale and both must get their comeuppance. By the end of the film, Scarlett discovers she really loves Rhett Butler, but it's too late. His cavalier dismissal of her final plea to stay is the stuff of legend. And he's a smart man not to give in. To do so would be foolish. He knows Scarlett's misfortune is to love only the one who resists her. After all, he's a Don Juan himself.

15 These days we are less prescriptive in our notions of sexual propriety, and so the seducers and seductresses are not nearly so coy in their behavior. And anyway, at some point most of us play at erotic games of seduction and many of us are even promiscuous. But the game of sexual conquest can still involve a cautionary tale.

16 To play at sex hardens the heart. *Why can't I meet anyone who feels anything?* we say. *Why can't I meet anyone who responds?* Yet sometimes what we are meaning is the exact opposite: *Why can't I let myself go, and love?*

Glossary

acrimony: Extreme bitterness of temper; ill feeling.

archetype: (In Jungian psychology) an inherited primitive mental image.

narcissist: Anyone who has excessive interest in one's own appearance, comfort, abilities, importance, etc. (from the Greek mythological character Narcissus).

Tantalus: Greek mythological king doomed in the lower world to stand in water that always receded when he tried to drink it.

supplicating: Asking humbly and earnestly, as by prayer.

incarnations: Persons or things serving as the type or embodiment of a quality or concept.

Comprehension Questions

1. How does Sullivan define "narcissist"?
2. What does the novelist Leon Whiteson say is the reason certain men have multiple lovers?
3. Why are women, according to Sullivan, so attracted to Don Juan types?

Questions about Form

1. Take a look at the last paragraph of the piece. Is this an appropriate paragraph for the end? Why or why not?
2. *Gone with the Wind* is a particularly old movie (released in 1939, before most of the readers of this text were born). Why do you think Sullivan refers to it here?

Questions for Discussion

1. In paragraph 8, Sullivan refers to the many labels of the female version of Don Juan. Discuss what you think is the relationship between a *Doña Juana* and what you know of a *femme fatale*.

2. Despite the indisputable similarities between the characteristics of the Don Juan and the female counterpart, do you think the male of this type is still looked upon more positively than the female as Sullivan suggests? Why or why not?

3. Consider the last paragraph of this piece. Is this problem common today? Discuss.

4. Based on the entry in the above glossary for "Tantalus," what do you think Sullivan means when she refers to "Tantalus games"?

Writing Ideas

1. Write a paragraph/essay of cause and effect discussing either the causes or the effects of being a Don Juan/Doña Juana.

2. Much of Sullivan's piece deals with the reasons for which the Don Juan/Doña Juana type of person makes the worst kind of dating/mating partner to have. Write a paragraph/essay on the reasons such a person would make an ideal dating/mating partner, instead. If you have to add a sarcastic tone to your composition, so be it. On the other hand, if you believe such a person would, in fact, make an ideal partner, then, of course, there's no need for the sarcasm.

✦ ✦ ✦

HIDDEN LESSONS

David Suzuki

World-famous host of CBC's *The Nature of Things*, scientist David Suzuki was born in Vancouver in 1936. He's written approximately thirty books, ten of which explain nature to children. He lectures internationally and writes a syndicated newspaper column. His lifelong pursuit is literally to save the planet, and to this end, among countless other things, he has written the following piece, which first appeared in Toronto's *The Globe and Mail*.

1 In spite of the vast expanse of wilderness in this country, most Canadian children grow up in urban settings. In other words, they live in a world conceived, shaped and dominated by people. Even the farms located around cities and towns are carefully groomed and landscaped for human convenience. There's nothing

wrong with that, of course, but in such an environment, it's very easy to lose any sense of connection with nature.

2 In city apartments and dwellings, the presence of cockroaches, fleas, ants, mosquitoes or houseflies is guaranteed to elicit the spraying of insecticides. Mice and rats are poisoned or trapped, while the gardener wages a never-ending struggle with ragweed, dandelions, slugs and root-rot. We have a modern **arsenal** of chemical weapons to fight off these invaders and we use them **lavishly**.

3 We worry when kids roll in the mud or wade through a puddle because they'll get "dirty." Children learn attitudes and values very quickly and the lesson in cities is very clear—nature is an enemy, it's dirty, dangerous or a nuisance. So youngsters learn to distance themselves from nature and to try to control it. I am astonished at the number of adults who **loathe** or are terrified by snakes, spiders, butterflies, worms, birds—the list seems endless.

4 If you reflect on the history of humankind, you realize that for 99 per cent of our species' existence on the planet, we were deeply embedded in and dependent on nature. When plants and animals were plentiful, we flourished. When famine and drought struck, our numbers fell accordingly. We remain every bit as dependent upon nature today—we need plants to fix photons of energy into sugar molecules and to cleanse the air and replenish the oxygen. It is folly to forget our dependence on an intact **ecosystem**. But we do whenever we teach our offspring to fear or detest the natural world. The urban message kids get runs completely counter to what they are born with, a natural interest in other life forms. Just watch a child in a first encounter with a flower or an ant—there is instant interest and fascination. We condition them out of it.

5 The result is that when my 7-year-old daughter brings home new friends, they invariably recoil in fear or disgust when she tries to show them her favorite pets—three beautiful salamanders that her grandfather got for her in Vancouver. And when my 3-year-old comes wandering in with her treasures—millipedes, spiders, slugs and sowbugs that she catches under rocks lining the front lawn—children and adults alike usually respond by saying "yuk."

6 I can't overemphasize the tragedy of that attitude. For, inherent in this view is the assumption that human beings are special and different and that we lie outside nature. Yet it is this belief that is creating many of our environmental problems today.

7 Does it matter whether we sense our place in nature so long as we have cities and technology? Yes, for many reasons, not the least of which is that virtually all scientists were fascinated with nature as children and retained that curiosity throughout their lives. But a far more important reason is that if we retain a spiritual sense of connection with all other life forms, it can't help but profoundly affect the way we act. Whenever my daughter sees a picture of an animal dead or dying, she asks me fearfully, "Daddy, are there any more?" At 7 years, she already knows about extinction and it frightens her.

8 The yodel of a loon at sunset, the vast flocks of migrating waterfowl in the fall, the indomitable salmon returning thousands of kilometres—these images of

nature have inspired us to create music, poetry and art. And when we struggle to retain a handful of California **condors** or whooping cranes, it's clearly not from a fear of ecological collapse, it's because there is something obscene and frightening about the disappearance of another species at our hands.

9 If children grow up understanding that we are animals, they will look at other species with a sense of fellowship and community. If they understand their ecological place—the **biosphere**—then when children see the great virgin forests of the Queen Charlotte Islands being clearcut, they will feel physical pain, because they will understand that those trees are an extension of themselves.

10 When children who know their place in the ecosystem see factories spewing poison into the air, water and soil, they will feel ill because someone has violated their home. This is not mystical mumbo-jumbo. We have poisoned the life support systems that sustain all organisms because we have lost a sense of ecological place. Those of us who are parents have to realize the unspoken, negative lessons we are conveying to our children. Otherwise, they will continue to desecrate this planet as we have.

11 It's not easy to avoid giving these hidden lessons. I have struggled to cover my dismay and queasiness when Severn and Sarika come running in with a large wolf spider or when we've emerged from a ditch covered with leeches or when they have been stung accidentally by yellowjackets feeding on our leftovers. But that's nature. I believe efforts to teach children to love and respect other life forms are priceless.

Glossary

arsenal: Place for storing weapons; collection.

lavishly: Giving or spending generously.

loathe: Abhor; detest.

ecosystem: System made up of a community of animals, plants, and bacteria and its interrelated physical and chemical environment.

condors: Very large vultures of the South American Andes.

biosphere: All the living organisms of the earth.

Comprehension Questions

1. What are the causes, according to Suzuki, of our disdain for nature?
2. Does Suzuki think more of us should live in rural areas and not the city? Explain.
3. What is Suzuki's attitude toward the way most of us think of animals?
4. What does Suzuki mean when he mentions "a spiritual sense of connection with all other life forms" in paragraph 7?

Questions about Form

1. How does Suzuki open the piece and therefore get your attention?
2. What writing strategy does Suzuki seem to use to organize most of his article?
3. Why is paragraph 6 the shortest paragraph of the essay?
4. What is the purpose of paragraph 5, in which Suzuki refers to his daughters and their "pets"?

Questions for Discussion

1. What do you think Suzuki is hoping to accomplish with this essay? Will he succeed? Why or why not?
2. Is paragraph 6 likely to meet with controversy among its readers? Why or why not?
3. Do movies generally help or hurt Suzuki's cause of sensitizing people to the environment? Examples of movies for discussion might include *ANTZ, Jurassic Park, The Fly, Arachnophobia, Gorillas in the Mist, Lassie, Flipper, Cujo,* etc.
4. What are your feelings toward the "less palatable" parts of the environment? In light of Suzuki's message, do you think anyone's attitude in this area can be changed? Explain.
5. It's tragic, according to Suzuki, that many human beings believe they're more special than animals. Does Suzuki undermine his argument by not mentioning how many human beings believe they're better than *other human beings*? How do we sensitize human beings to the pain of animals when we have a hard enough time sensitizing people to the pain of other people? Discuss.

Writing Ideas

1. What could most people do, without too much effort, to reverse these "hidden lessons" that Suzuki writes about in this piece? Write a paragraph/essay of process to this effect.
2. Have you ever lived in a non-urban setting? Write a comparison/contrast paragraph/essay contrasting urban living with rural living as they relate to the environment.

✦ ✦ ✦

In Praise of Old Women

Marya Fiamengo

Brought up and schooled in British Columbia, Marya Fiamengo is the child of Yugoslavian parents. She has taught literature at the University of British Columbia, and she's written several books of poetry, including *White Linen Remembered*. Much of her work has been included in anthologies and has been studied by students of high school, college, and university.

1 Yes, **Tadeusz Rozewicz,** I too
prefer old women.
They bend over graves
with flowers,
they wash the limbs of the dead,
they count the beads of their rosaries,
they commit no murders
they give advice
or tell fortunes,
they endure.

2 In Poland, in Russia,
in Asia, in the Balkans,
I see them shawled, kerchiefed,
bent-backed, work-wrinkled.

3 But Tadeusz,
have you been to America?

4 Where we have no old women.
No **Stara Babas,**
no haggard Madonnas.

5 Everyone, Tadeusz, is young in America.
Especially the women
with **coifed** blue hair
which gleams like the steel
of jets in the daytime sky.
Smooth-skinned at sixty,
second debuts at fifty
renascent
they never grow old in America.

6 And we have in America
literate, sexually liberated women
who wouldn't touch a corpse
who confuse **lechery** with love,
not out of viciousness
but boringly
out of confusion, neurosis, identity crises.

7 Tadeusz,
I go to the cemetery
with my mother
one of us stoically old,
the other aging,
and I tell you, Tadeusz,
I will grow old in America.
I will have no second debut.
I will raise my son on old battles,
Kossovo, Neretva, Thermopylae,
Stalingrad and Britain
and I will wrinkle adamantly in America.

8 I will put salt in the soup
and I will offer bread and wine
to my friends,
and I will stubbornly praise old women
until their thin taut skins
glow like Ikons ascending on escalators
like Buddhas descending in subways,
and I will liberate all women
to be old in America
because the highest manifestation of
Hagia Sophia
is old and a woman.

Glossary

Tadeusz Rozewicz: Contemporary Polish poet.

Stara Babas: Old women (term common to several Slavic languages).

coifed: Styled.

renascent: Showing new strength or vigour.

lechery: Excessive indulgence of sexual desires.

Hagia Sophia: Holy Wisdom (Greek).

Comprehension Questions

1. What is Fiamengo contrasting in her poem?
2. What does Fiamengo mean by what she says in the fourth stanza: "…we have no old women"?
3. What are some of the differences between the two items Fiamengo is contrasting?
4. What does it mean when the poet says "I will wrinkle adamantly in America" (last line, seventh stanza)? Why do you think she feels this way?

Questions about Form

1. Why is Fiamengo speaking to someone called Tadeusz Rozewicz instead of directly to the reader? Why do you think she has chosen this particular person with whom to speak?
2. What does *"Hagia"* in *Hagia Sophia* (second-last line) look like in English? Contrast this answer with what *"Hagia Sophia"* really means. What does this discrepancy suggest? And how does it contribute to your understanding of the poem?

Questions for Discussion

1. In one sentence, what seems to be Fiamengo's message? Do you agree with it? Why or why not?
2. Approximately how old do you think Fiamengo was when she wrote this poem? Why might she have written it at this time in her life?
3. Is this poem likely to provoke some strong emotions in anyone? Who? What emotions and why?
4. What do you think Fiamengo hopes to accomplish by writing this poem? Is she likely to achieve her goal? Why or why not?

Writing Ideas

1. Write a paragraph/essay on the reasons there are, as the poet suggests, "no old women in America." Include toward the beginning of your composition what you believe "there are no old women in America" means.
2. In the last stanza of her poem, Fiamengo declares, "…I will liberate all women / to be old in America…" Write a paragraph/essay in which you suggest how all women in America can "liberate" themselves in this way.

✦ ✦ ✦

Heart of Loneliness

Jean Vanier

Noah's Ark was a place of refuge and new beginnings. While in France, Jean Vanier founded an organization called L'Arche after the ark of the Old Testament. L'Arche is an international network of communities for people of intellectual disabilities. The son of former governor general of Canada Georges Vanier, Jean Vanier has written several books, one of which is *Becoming Human*, out of which the following piece has been taken. Loneliness may seem like a bad thing to most, but with the acknowledgment of certain principles, says Vanier, loneliness can be like Noah's Ark, a place that offers refuge and new beginnings.

1 A sense of loneliness can be covered up by the things we do as we seek recognition and success. This is surely what I did as a young adult. It is what we all do. We all have this drive to do things that will be seen by others as valuable, things that make us feel good about ourselves and give us a sense of being alive. We only become aware of loneliness at times when we cannot perform or when imagination seems to fail us.

2 Loneliness can appear as a faint dis-ease, an inner dissatisfaction, a restlessness in the heart.

3 Loneliness comes at any time. It comes in times of sickness or when friends are absent; it comes during sleepless nights when the heart is heavy, during times of failure at work or in relationships; it comes when we lose trust in ourselves and in others. In old age, loneliness can rise up and threaten to overwhelm us. At such times, life can lose its meaning. Loneliness can feel like death.

4 When people are physically well, performing creatively, successful in their lives, loneliness seems absent. But I believe that loneliness is something essential to human nature; it can only be covered over, it can never actually go away. Loneliness is part of being human, because there is nothing in existence that can completely fulfill the needs of the human heart.

5 Loneliness in one form is, in fact, essential to our humanity. Loneliness can become a source of creative energy, the energy that drives us down new paths to create new things or to seek more truth and justice in the world. Artists, poets, mystics, prophets, those who do not seem to fit into the world or the ways of society, are frequently lonely. They feel themselves to be different, dissatisfied with the status quo and with mediocrity; dissatisfied with our competitive world where so much energy goes into **ephemeral** things. Frequently, it is the lonely man or woman who revolts against injustice and seeks new ways. It is as if a fire is burning within them, a fire fuelled by loneliness.

6 Loneliness is the fundamental force that urges mystics to a deeper union with God. For such people, loneliness has become intolerable but, instead of slipping into **apathy** or anger, they use the energy of loneliness to seek God. It pushes them towards the absolute. An experience of God quenches this thirst for the absolute but at the same time, paradoxically, whets it, because this is an experience that

can never be total; by necessity, the knowledge of God is always practical. So loneliness opens up mystics to a desire to love each and every human being as God loves them.

7 Loneliness, then, can be a force for good. More frequently, however, loneliness shows other, less positive faces. It can be a source of apathy and depression, and even of a desire to die. It can push us into escapes and **addictions** in the need to forget our inner pain and emptiness. This apathy is how loneliness most often shows itself in the elderly and in those with disabilities. It is the loneliness we find in those who fall into depression, who have lost the sense of meaning in their lives, who are asking the question born of despair: What is left?

8 I once visited a psychiatric hospital that was a kind of warehouse of human misery. Hundreds of children with severe disabilities were lying, neglected, on their cots. There was a deadly silence. Not one of them was crying. When they realize that nobody cares, that nobody will answer them, children no longer cry. It takes too much energy. We cry out only when there is hope that someone may hear us.

9 Such loneliness is born of the most complete and utter depression, from the bottom of the deepest pit in which the human soul can find itself. The loneliness that engenders depression manifests itself as chaos. There is confusion, and coming out of this confusion there can be a desire for self-destruction, for death. So, loneliness can become agony, a scream of pain. There is no light, no consolation, no touch of peace and of the joy life brings. Such loneliness reveals the true meaning of chaos.

10 Life no longer flows in recognizable patterns. For the person engulfed in this form of loneliness there is only emptiness, anguish, and inner agitation; there are no **yearnings**, no desires to be fulfilled, no desire to live. Such a person feels completely cut off from everyone and everything. It is a life turned in upon itself. All order is gone and those in this chaos are unable to relate or listen to others. Their lives seem to have no meaning. They live in complete confusion, closed up in themselves.

11 Thus loneliness can become such uncontrolled anguish that one can easily slip into the chaos of madness.

Eric

12 Let me tell you some stories, from my own experience, of the damage loneliness can create. I met Eric for the first time in 1977. He was in the children's ward of the local psychiatric hospital, 40 kilometres from the l'Arche community in Trosly, France. He was blind and deaf, as well as severely intellectually disabled; he could neither walk nor eat by himself. He came to l'Arche at the age of sixteen, full of tremendous needs, anguish, and fears. He often sat on the ground and whenever he felt someone close by, would stretch out his arms and try to clutch that person and to climb up on them. Once he had succeeded in getting someone to hold him, his actions would become wild: he would lose control, struggling to be held and, at the same time, jumping up and down. Holding Eric under these

conditions became intolerable for anyone and, inevitably, it ended in a struggle, trying to get rid of him as he fought to remain held. He was someone who seemed to be living in immense anguish.

13 Anguish is inner agitation, a chaotic, unfocused energy. Anguish breaks sleep and other patterns and brings us to a place of confusion. To be lonely is to feel unwanted and unloved, and therefore unloveable. Loneliness is a taste of death. No wonder some people who are desperately lonely lose themselves in mental illness or violence to forget the inner pain.

14 Eric was a terribly lonely young man. He needed to be loved but his needs were so great that no one person could fulfill them. It took a long time in l'Arche before he found some inner peace. Little by little, as he learned to trust those around him, he discovered he was loved.

Pierre

15 By way of contrast, Pierre was the seventh child in a family of thirteen, a man who had spent seven years in prison. I met him in Montreal. He had run away from home when he was twelve years old because he felt unnoticed and unwanted by his family. So, for a long time he lived with gangs on the street. In his heart, Pierre was a lonely man who felt lost. He had nowhere to go, no meaning in his life. He needed a friend, a teacher, someone who could help him find himself and a sense of purpose.

16 When he was sixteen Pierre committed a crime, which I believe was a cry for help. He went to jail for it. While he was there, he fell in love with a woman who regularly visited the prison. They got married and his life took on new meaning; he finally had someone and something to live for. It was the beginning of his process of becoming human, and it happened because he felt loved …

17 In Eric and Pierre, there were chaos and disorder. Yet in the midst of the chaos there was a way out. Are not all our lives a movement from order to disorder, which in turn evolves into a new order?

Order and Disorder

18 In human beings, there is a constant tension between order and disorder, connectedness and loneliness, evolution and revolution, security and insecurity. Our universe is constantly evolving; the old order gives way to a new order and this in its turn crumbles when the next order appears. It is no different in our lives in the movement from birth to death.

19 Change of one sort or another is the essence of life, so there will always be the loneliness and insecurity that come with change. When we refuse to accept that loneliness and insecurity are part of life, when we refuse to accept that they are the price of change, we close the door on many possibilities for ourselves; our lives become lessened, we are less than fully human. If we try to prevent, or ignore, the movement of life, we run the risk of falling into the inevitable depression that must accompany an impossible goal. Life evolves; change is constant. When we try to prevent the forward movement of life, we may succeed for a

while but, inevitably, there is an explosion; the **groundswell** of life's constant movement, constant change, is too great to resist.

20 And so empires of ideas, as well as empires of wealth and power, come and go. To live well is to observe in today's apparent order the tiny anomalies that are the seeds of change, the harbingers of the order of tomorrow. This means living in a state of a certain insecurity, in anguish and loneliness, which, at its best, can push us towards the new. Too much security and the refusal to evolve, to embrace change, leads to a kind of death. Too much insecurity, however, can also mean death. To be human is to create sufficient order so that we can move on into insecurity and seeming disorder. In this way, we discover the new.

21 Those who have the eyes to see this new order, as it arises, will often be considered too revolutionary, too modern, too **liberal**. Dictators everywhere have clamped down on movements for liberation; those who lead are always so certain that anarchy will arise if they do not govern with a firm hand. In reality, leaders are frightened of sharing or losing power. They too are frightened of change. They want to control everything. Those who see the coming new order will frequently be alone, persecuted.

Five Principles

22 But how do we learn to read the signs of evolution and to see where it is going? We can only help the new to evolve if we have certain clear principles. Here are five principles that have helped me.

23 **First:** all humans are sacred, whatever their culture, race, or religion, whatever their capacities or incapacities, and whatever their weaknesses or strengths may be. Each of us has an instrument to bring to the vast orchestra of humanity, and each of us needs help to become all that we might be.

24 **Second:** our world and our individual lives are in the process of evolving. Evolution is a part of life but it is not always easy to determine the good and the bad in something that is evolving.... It is a question of loving all the essential values of the past and reflecting on how they are to be lived in the new. These values include openness, love, wholeness, unity, peace, the human potential for healing and redemption, and, most important, the necessity of forgiveness ...

25 **Third:** maturity comes through working with others, through dialogue, and through a sense of belonging and a searching together. In order to evolve towards greater maturity and wholeness, we humans need a certain security; only when we have attained this can we advance in insecurity with others towards the new.

26 **Fourth:** human beings need to be encouraged to make choices, and to become responsible for their own lives and for the lives of others. We need to be encouraged to evolve in order to become mature, and to break out of the shell of self-centredness and out of our defence mechanisms, which are as oppressive to others as they are to ourselves. In other words, we humans need to be rooted in good earth in order to produce good fruit. But for this we need to freely risk life in order to give of ourselves.

27 **Fifth:** in order to make such choices, we need to reflect and to seek truth and meaning. Reality is the first principle of truth. To be human means to remain

connected to our humanness and to reality. It means to abandon the loneliness of being closed up in illusions, dreams, and ideologies, frightened of reality, and to choose to move towards connectedness . . .

28 Each one of us needs to work at searching for truth, not be afraid of it. We need to strive to live in truth, because the truth sets us free, even if it means living in loneliness and anguish at certain moments.

29 We must not try to return to the past, but instead launch out into the future—to understand each other and what it means to be human, to understand what is happening in the world—in order to become more fully human and to work for peace and unity. It is only as we begin to integrate such a sense of reality more fully into our being, as we thirst for that which gives meaning to our lives, that we discover the fundamental meaning of loneliness: a cry, often a painful cry of anguish, for more respect and love of others, to be even more enfolded in truth, held in God. Such a cry could bring a new wholeness to humanity.

Glossary

ephemeral: Lasting for only a short time.

apathy: Lack of concern or interest; indifference.

addictions: Processes of being dependent on as compulsive habits. Activities such as gambling, smoking, sex, shopping, eating, etc. become addictions when they are done *compulsively*.

yearnings: Strong emotional longings.

groundswell: Increasingly forceful presence.

liberal: Open-minded; generous.

Comprehension Questions

1. Why is loneliness essential to our humanity, according to Vanier?
2. What is the relationship, according to Vanier, between loneliness and God?
3. What did Eric and Pierre have in common that led to their loneliness?
4. What is the relationship between loneliness and addictions, violence, and other forms of self-destruction, according to the author?

Questions about Form

1. This piece begins with a discussion of what society considers a disease and ends with five principles that Vanier considers a sort of antidote. Discuss the effectiveness of this format.
2. Why does Vanier include the cases of two young men?

Questions for Discussion

1. Compare this piece to the one entitled "Bad Girls" by Shari Graydon (also in Unit IV). Is there a cause–effect relationship between the loneliness that Vanier describes and the violence that takes place among teens that Graydon describes?
2. Do you think it's possible to be lonely if you're surrounded by people? Why or why not? What in Vanier's piece supports your answer to this question?
3. What are the possible meanings of the title of this piece?

Writing Ideas

1. Write a paragraph/essay on how one might go about solving his/her own problem of loneliness in a practical way, but by considering Vanier's five principles of evolution.
2. What are the causes predominant in North American urban culture that contribute to loneliness? Write a cause and effect paragraph/essay discussing these causes.

✦ ✦ ✦

CANADA, MY CANADA

Tomson Highway

Celebrated novelist and award-winning playwright Tomson Highway is a Cree Native from Brochet, in northern Manitoba. He holds three honorary degrees and is a member of the Order of Canada. This piece by Highway is quite flattering of our nation. How would you expect a member of an aboriginal group to view Canada today? When you finish reading the following piece by Highway, compare or contrast your answer to this question with your observation of Highway's article.

1 Three summers back, a friend and I were being hurtled by bus through the heart of Australia, the desert flashing pink and red before our disbelieving eyes. It seemed never to end, this desert, so flat, so dry. The landscape was very unlike ours—scrub growth with some exotic cacti, no lakes, no river, just sand and rock forever. Beautiful, haunting even—*what the surface of the moon must look like*, I thought as I sat in the dusk in that almost empty bus.

2 I turned to look out the front of the bus and was suddenly taken completely by surprise. Screaming out at me in great black lettering were the words CANADA NO. 1 COUNTRY IN THE WORLD. My eyes lit up, my heart gave a heave, and I felt a **pang** of homesickness so **acute** I actually almost hurt. It was all

I could do to keep myself from leaping out of my seat and grabbing the newspaper from its owner.

3 As I learned within minutes (I did indeed beg to borrow the paper), this pronouncement was based on information collected by the United Nations from studies comparing standards of living for 174 nations of the world. Some people may have doubted the finding, but I didn't, not for an instant.

4 Where else in the world can you travel by bus, automobile or train (and the odd ferry) for ten, 12 or 14 days straight and see a landscape that changes so spectacularly: the Newfoundland coast with its white foam and roar; the red sand beaches of Prince Edward Island; the graceful curves and slopes of Cape Breton's Cabot Trail; the rolling dairy land of south-shore Quebec; the maple-bordered lakes of Ontario, the haunting north shore of Lake Superior; the wheat fields of Manitoba and Saskatchewan; the ranch land of Alberta; the mountain ranges and lush rain forests of the West Coast. The list could go on for pages and still cover only the southern section of the country, a sliver of land compared with the North, the immensity of which is almost unimaginable.

5 For six years in a row now the United Nations has designated Canada the No. 1 country in which to live.

6 We are so fortunate. We are water wealthy and forest rich. Minerals, fertile land, wild animals, plant life, the rhythm of four distinct, undeniable seasons—we have it all.

7 Of course, Canada has its problems. We'd like to lower the crime rate, but ours is a relatively safe country. We struggle with our health-care system, trying to find a balance between **universality** and affordability, but no person in this country is denied medical care for lack of money. Yes, we have our concerns, but in the global scheme of things we are well off.

8 Think of our history. For the greater part, the pain and violence, tragedy, horror and evil that have scarred forever the history of too many countries are largely absent from our past. There's no denying we've had our trials, but they pale by comparison with events that have shaped many other nations.

9 Our cities are gems. Take Toronto, where I have chosen to live. My adopted city never fails to thrill me with its racial, linguistic and cultural diversity. On any ordinary day on the city's streets and subway, in stores and restaurants, I can hear the muted ebb and flow of 20 different tongues. I can feast on food from different continents, from Greek souvlaki to Thai mango salad, from Italian **prosciutto** to Jamaican jerk chicken, from Indian lamb curry to Chinese lobster.

10 And do all these people get along? Well, they all enjoy a life of relative harmony, co-operation and peace. They certainly aren't terrorizing, torturing and massacring one another. They're not igniting pubs, cars and schools with explosives that blind, cripple and maim. And they're not killing children with machetes, cleavers and axes. Dislike—**rancour**, even—may exist here and there, but not, I believe, hatred of the blistering intensity we see elsewhere.

11 Is Canada a successful experiment in racial harmony and peaceful **coexistence**? Yes, I would say so—and proudly.

12 When I, as an aboriginal citizen of this country, find myself thinking about all the people we've received into this beautiful homeland of mine, when I think of the millions to whom we've given safe haven, following agony, terror, hunger and great sadness in their own home countries, well, my little Cree heart just puffs up with pride. And I walk the streets of Canada, the streets of my home, feeling tall as a maple.

Glossary

pang: Sudden and brief pain, physical or emotional.

acute: Severe and sharp.

universality: The quality of not being restricted to a privileged few.

prosciutto: Spicy Italian ham served in thin slices.

rancour: Continuing and bitter hatred.

coexistence: Living side by side.

Comprehension Questions

1. What in the newspaper sparked Highway's interest? Upon what were the findings in the newspaper story based?
2. What does Highway say is the most important thing about Canada that makes it great?
3. What problems in Canada does Highway admit to, and how does he defend Canada in spite of them?

Questions about Form

1. In paragraph 1, Highway uses italics for the words "what the surface of the moon must look like." Why do you think he uses italics here? What is his tone? What effect is he looking for? Does he achieve this effect?
2. If this is a piece about Canada, why does Highway start out by talking about Australia?

Questions for Discussion

1. In paragraph 8, Highway refers to the history of Canada as being quite tame when compared to that of other countries. Compare or contrast this comment to the message Rita Joe is sending in her poem "I Lost My Talk," on page 353. What do you make of the fact that both of these writers are Native Canadian?

2. Do you agree with Highway when he says Canada is a "successful experiment in racial harmony and peaceful coexistence"? Why or why not?
3. At any time throughout this piece, do you expect Highway to mention the fact that Canada has not always been kind to aboriginal peoples, or that the governments of the past have even committed genocide against his people? Why do you think he doesn't? Would it help to be told this piece appeared before in a journal called *The Imperial Oil Review*? Why or why not?
4. In paragraphs 9 and 10, Highway refers to the multicultural mix of Toronto, in particular, and Canada, in general. Compare or contrast his attitude to that of Neil Bissoondath in "Selling Illusions," which begins on page 371.
5. Paragraph 10 uses some rather harsh language. What countries do you think Highway might be referring to by the examples he uses?
6. Look up poems by the American poet Walt Whitman. Is there a poem whose title is similar to Highway's title of this piece? Account for the similarity.

Writing Ideas

1. In a paragraph/essay, compare or contrast Canada with any other one country in the world with which you are very familiar.
2. Is Canada one of the best places in the world to live? In a paragraph/essay, explain why or why not.

✦ ✦ ✦

My Body Is My Own Business

Naheed Mustafa

Wearing the hijab, says Naheed Mustafa, is a requirement of her Muslim faith. But in this piece, her faith in this respect seems far from blind. She argues that wearing the hijab, contrary to popular belief, liberates her. Mustafa works as an editor in Toronto.

1 I often wonder whether people see me as a radical, fundamentalist Muslim terrorist packing an AK-47 assault rifle inside my jean jacket. Or maybe they see me as the poster girl for oppressed womanhood everywhere. I'm not sure which it is.

2 I get the whole gamut of strange looks, stares and covert glances. You see, I wear the *hijab*, a scarf that covers my head, neck and throat. I do this because I am a Muslim woman who believes her body is her own private concern.

3 Young Muslim women are reclaiming the *hijab*, reinterpreting it in light of its original purpose—to give back to women ultimate control of their own bodies.

4 The **Koran** teaches us that men and women are equal, that individuals should not be judged according to gender, beauty, wealth or privilege. The only thing that makes one person better than another is her or his character.

5 Nonetheless, people have a difficult time relating to me. After all, I'm young, Canadian born and raised, university-educated—why would I do this to myself, they ask.

6 Strangers speak to me in loud, slow English and often appear to be playing **charades.** They politely inquire how I like living in Canada and whether or not the cold bothers me. If I'm in the right mood, it can be very amusing.

7 But why would I, a woman with all the advantages of a North American upbringing, suddenly, at 21, want to cover myself so that with the *hijab* and the other clothes I choose to wear, only my face and hands show?

8 Because it gives me freedom.

9 Women are taught from early childhood that their worth is proportional to their attractiveness. We feel compelled to pursue **abstract** notions of beauty, half realizing that such a pursuit is futile.

10 When women reject this form of oppression, they face ridicule and contempt. Whether it's women who refuse to wear makeup or to shave their legs or to expose their bodies, society, both men and women, have trouble dealing with them.

11 In the Western world, the *hijab* has come to symbolize either forced silence or radical, **unconscionable** militancy. Actually, it's neither. It is simply a woman's assertion that judgment of her physical person is to play no role whatsoever in social interaction.

12 Wearing the *hijab* has given me freedom from constant attention to my physical self. Because my appearance is not subjected to public scrutiny, my beauty, or perhaps lack of it, has been removed from the realm of what can legitimately be discussed.

13 No one knows whether my hair looks as if I just stepped out of a salon, whether or not I can pinch an inch, or even if I have unsightly stretch marks. And because no one knows, no one cares.

14 Feeling that one has to meet the impossible male standards of beauty is tiring and often humiliating. I should know, I spent my entire teenage years trying to do it. I was a borderline bulimic and spent a lot of money I didn't have on potions and lotions in hopes of becoming the next Cindy Crawford.

15 The definition of beauty is ever-changing; **waifish** is good, waifish is bad, athletic is good—sorry, athletic is bad. Narrow hips? Great. Narrow hips? Too bad.

16 Women are not going to achieve equality with the right to bare their breasts in public, as some people would like to have you believe. That would only make us party to our own **objectification.** True equality will be had only when women don't need to display themselves to get attention and won't need to defend their decision to keep their bodies to themselves.

Glossary

Koran: Holy book of Muslims.

charades: Games in which somebody acts out a word or phrase and players guess its meaning.

abstract: Not concrete; conceptual; hard to put into words.

unconscionable: Extremely unethical; morally wrong.

waifish: Skinny.

objectification: Act of treating like an object or "piece of meat."

Comprehension Questions

1. According to Mustafa, what does the Koran teach about equality?
2. How does the issue of attractiveness make it difficult to achieve equality between the sexes?
3. According to the author, what in the Western world has the hijab come to represent? What does it represent in reality, instead, according to Mustafa?

Questions about Form

1. Why does Mustafa begin her piece by referring to herself?
2. Most of Mustafa's paragraphs in this piece are extremely short, unlike those of a proper academic essay. Does the fact that this piece was written for *The Globe and Mail* (1993) offer a clue as to why it was written this way? Explain.

Questions for Discussion

1. If a woman is not a practising Muslim but sympathizes with Mustafa's reasons for wearing a hijab, what could she do besides wear a hijab?
2. In the last paragraph, Mustafa says baring their breasts will only make women "party to our own objectification." What does this mean? Do you agree? Why or why not?
3. Many people would argue that sexual attraction is an intrinsic part of falling in love with someone. If this is true, how does one fall in love if another doesn't reveal his/her (especially her) sexuality by wearing revealing clothes?
4. Mustafa refers to the "tiring" and "humiliating" male standards of beauty in paragraph 14. What are women's standards of attractiveness in men? Are they just as tiring and humiliating? What does this article suggest about stereotyping?

5. Look at the very last line of the article. Mustafa ponders a time when true equality between the sexes will be had. Has that time arrived? Cite evidence from life in Canada that supports your answer.

Writing Ideas

1. Write a paragraph/essay of cause and effect focusing on the causes of inequality between the sexes in North American culture. When you have finished your rough draft, decide whether you've assigned more blame to women or to men or equally to both.

2. Is attention the same as respect? If a woman gets attention because of the way she is dressed, does that mean she's going to win respect, too? Write a paragraph/essay answering the above question and supporting your answer. Feel free to refer to Mustafa's piece for further support of your topic sentence/thesis statement regardless of your point of view.

✦ ✦ ✦

THE JADE PEONY

Wayson Choy

Born and raised in Vancouver's Chinatown, Wayson Choy originally wrote "The Jade Peony" as the story that appears below. It eventually evolved into a full-fledged novel by the same name, for which he won the Trillium Award. He was subsequently nominated for the Governor General's Award for his memoirs, *Paper Shadows*. Currently living in Toronto, Choy has recently retired from teaching Communications at Humber College, but he still teaches for the internationally acclaimed Humber School for Writers.

1 When Grandmama died in 1940 at eighty-three, our whole household held its breath. She had promised us a sign of her leaving, final proof that her life had ended well. My parents knew that without any clear sign, our own family fortunes could be altered, threatened. Stepmother looked every day into the small cluttered room the ancient lady had occupied. Nothing was touched; nothing changed. Father, thinking that a sign should appear in Grandmama's garden, looked at the frost-killed shoots and cringed: *No, that could not be it.*

2 My two older teenage brothers and my sister, Liang, were embarrassed by my parents' behaviour. What would white people in Vancouver think of us? We were Canadians now, *Chinese-Canadians*, a hyphenated reality that our parents could never accept. So it seemed, for different reasons, we were all holding our breath, waiting for *something*.

3 I was nearly seven when Grandmama died. For days she had resisted going into the hospital ... *a cold, just a cold* ... and instead gave constant instructions to Stepmother on the boiling of ginseng root mixed with bitter extract. At night, between racking coughs and deadly silences, Grandmama had her back and chest rubbed with heated camphor oil and sipped a bluish decoction of an herb called Peacock's Tail. When all these failed to abate her fever, she began to arrange the details of her will. This she did with Father, confessing finally: "I am too stubborn. The only cure for old age is to die."

4 Father wept to hear this. I stood beside her bed: she turned to me. Her round face looked darker, and the gentleness of her eyes, with the thin, arching eyebrows, seemed weary. I brushed a few strands of grey, brittle hair from her face; she managed to smile at me. Being the youngest, I had spent nearly all my time with her and knew that she would be with me forever. Yet when she spoke, and her voice hesitated, cracked, the sombre shadows of her room chilled me. Her wrinkled brow grew wet with fever, and her small body seemed even more **diminutive**.

5 "You know, Little Son, whatever happens I will never leave you," she said. Her hand reached out for mine. Her palm felt plush and warm, the slender, old fingers bony and firm; so magically strong was her grip that I could not imagine how she could ever part from me. Ever.

6 Her hands *were* magical. Long, elegant fingers, with impeccable nails, a **skein** of fine barely visible veins, and wrinkled skin the colour of light pine. Those hands were quick when she taught me, at six, simple tricks of juggling, learnt when she was a village girl in southern Canton; a troupe of actors had stayed on her father's farm. One of them, "tall and pale as the whiteness of petals," fell in love with her, promising to return. "My juggler," she said, "he never came back to me from Honan ... perhaps the famine ..." In her last years, his image came back into her life. He had been a magician, an acrobat, a juggler, and some of the things he taught her she had absorbed and passed on to me through her stories and games.

7 Most marvellous for me was the quick-witted skill her hands revealed in making windchimes for our birthdays: windchimes in the likeness of her lost friend's parting present to her, made of bits of string and the precious jade peony, a carved stone the size of a large coin, knotted with red silk to hang like a pendant from the centre, like the clapper of a sacred bell. This wondrous gift to her had broken apart years ago, in China, but Grandmama kept the jade pendant in a tiny red silk envelope, and kept it always in her pocket, until her death.

8 Hers were not ordinary, carelessly made chimes, such as those you now find in our Chinatown stores, whose rattling noises drive you mad. But the making of her special ones caused dissension in our family, and some shame. Each one that she made was created from a treasure trove of glass fragments and castaway costume jewellery. The problem for the rest of the family lay in the fact that Grandmama looked for these treasures wandering the back alleys of Keefer and Pender Streets, peering into our neighbours' garbage cans, chasing away hungry, nervous cats and shouting curses at them.

9 "All our friends are laughing at us!" Second Brother Jung said at last to Father, when Grandmama was away having tea at Mrs. Lim's.

10 "We are not poor," First Brother Kiam declared, "yet she and Sek-Lung poke through garbage as if—" he shoved me in frustration and I stumbled against my sister "—they were beggars!"

11 "She will make Little Brother crazy!" Sister Liang said. Without warning, she punched me sharply in the back; I jumped. "You see, look how *nervous* he is!"

12 I lifted my foot slightly, enough to swing it back and kick Liang in the shin. She yelled and pulled back her fist to punch me again. Jung made a menacing move towards me.

13 "Stop this, all of you!" Father shook his head in exasperation. How could he dare tell the Old One, his ageing mother, that what was appropriate in a poor village in China was shameful here? How could he prevent me, his youngest, from accompanying her? "She is not a beggar looking for food. She is searching for—for ..."

14 Stepmother attempted to speak, then fell silent. She, too, was perplexed and somewhat ashamed. They all loved Grandmama, but she was *inconvenient*, unsettling.

15 As for our neighbours, most understood Grandmama to be harmlessly crazy, others conceded that she did indeed make lovely toys, but for what purpose? *Why?* they asked, and the stories she told to me, of the juggler who had smiled at her, flashed in my head.

16 Finally, by their cutting remarks, the family did exert enough pressure that Grandmama no longer openly announced our expeditions. Instead, she took me with her on "shopping trips," ostensibly for clothes or groceries, while in fact we spent most of our time exploring stranger and more distant neighbourhoods, searching for splendid junk: jangling pieces of a broken vase, cranberry glass fragments embossed with leaves, discarded glass beads from Woolworth necklaces. We would sneak them all home in brown rice sacks, folded into small parcels, and put them under her bed. During the day when the family was away at school or work, we brought them out and washed the pieces in a large black pot of boiling lye and water, dried them carefully, and returned them, sparkling, to the hiding place under her bed.

17 Our greatest excitement occurred when a fire gutted the large Chinese Presbyterian Church, three blocks from our house. Over the still-smoking ruins the next day, Grandmama and I rushed precariously over the blackened beams to pick out the stained glass that glittered in the sunlight. Her small figure bent over, wrapped against the autumn cold in a dark blue quilted coat, she happily gathered each piece like gold, my spiritual playmate: "There's a good one! *There!*"

18 Hours later, soot-covered and smelling of smoke, we came home with a carton full of delicate fragments, still early enough to smuggle them all into the house and put the small box under her bed.

19 "These are special pieces," she said, giving the box a last push, "because they come from a sacred place."

20 She slowly got up and I saw, for the first time, her hand begin to shake. But then, in her joy, she embraced me. I buried my face in her blue quilted coat, and for a moment, the whole world seemed perfect.

21 One evening, when the family was gathered in their usual places in the parlour, Grandmama gave me her secret nod of warning: a slight wink of her eye and a flaring of her nostrils. There was *trouble* in the air. Supper had gone badly, school examinations were approaching. Father had failed to meet an editorial deadline at the *Chinese Times*.

22 A huge sigh came from Sister Liang. "But it is useless, this Chinese they teach us!" she lamented, turning to First Brother Kiam for support.

23 "I agree, Father," Kiam began. "You must realize that this Mandarin only confuses us. We are Cantonese speakers ..."

24 "And you do not complain about Latin, French or German in your English school?" Father rattled his newspaper, a signal that his patience was ending.

25 "But Father, those languages are *scientific*." Kiam jabbed his brush in the air for emphasis. "We are now in a scientific, logical world."

26 Father was silent. He wanted his children to have both the old ways and the new ways.

27 Grandmama went on rocking quietly in her chair. She complimented Stepmother on her knitting, made a remark about the "strong beauty" of Kiam's brushstrokes, which, in spite of himself, immensely pleased him.

28 "*Daaih ga tohng yahn*," Grandmama said. "We are all Chinese." Her firm tone implied that this troubling talk about old and new ways should stop.

29 "What about Sek-Lung?" Second Brother Jung pointed angrily at me. "He was sick last year, but this year he should have at least started Chinese school, instead of picking over garbage cans!"

30 "He starts next year," Father said, in a hard tone that immediately warned everyone to be silent. Liang slammed her book shut.

31 The truth was, I was sorry not to have started school the year before. I knew going to school had certain privileges. The fact that my lung infection in my fifth and sixth years gave me a reprieve only made me long for school the more. Each member of the family took turns on Sunday, teaching me. But Grandmama taught me most. Tapping me on my head, she would say, "Come, Sek-Lung, we have *our* work," and we would walk up the stairs to her small crowded room. There, in the midst of her antique shawls, the ancestral calligraphy and multi-coloured embroidered hangings, beneath the mysterious shelves of sweet-smelling herbs and bitter potions, we would continue making windchimes.

32 "I can't last forever," she declared, when she let me in on the secret of the chime we had started this morning. "It will sing and dance and glitter." Her long fingers stretched into the air, **pantomiming** the waving motion of her ghost chimes. "My spirit will hear its sounds and see its light and return to this house to say goodbye to you."

33 Deftly, she reached into the carton she had placed on the chair beside me. She picked out a fish-shaped amber piece, and with a long needlelike tool and a steel

ruler, she scored it. Pressing the blade of a cleaver against the line, she lifted up the glass until it cleanly snapped into the exact shape she required. Her hand began to tremble, the tips of her fingers to shiver, like rippling water.

34 "You see that, Little One?" She held her hand up. "That is my body fighting with Death. He is in this room now."

35 My eyes darted in panic, but Grandmama remained calm, undisturbed, and went on with her work. I got out the glue and uncorked the jar for her. Soon the graceful ritual movements of her hand returned to her, and I became lost in the magic of her task: she dabbed a secret mixture of glue on one end and skilfully dropped the braided end of a silk thread into it. This part always amazed me: the braiding would slowly, *very* slowly, unwind, fanning out like a prized fishtail. In a few seconds, as I blew lightly over it, the clear, homemade glue began to harden, welding to itself each separate silk strand.

36 Each jam-sized pot of glue was treasured; each large cork stopper had been wrapped with a fragment of pink silk. We went shopping at the best stores in Chinatown for the perfect square of silk she required. It had to be a deep pink, blushing towards red. And the tone had to match, as closely as possible, her precious jade carving, the small peony of white and light-red jade, her most lucky possession. In the centre of this **semitranslucent** carving, no more than an inch wide, was a pool of pink light, its veins swirling out into the petals of the flower.

37 "This colour is the colour of my spirit," Grandmama said, holding it up to the window so I could see the delicate pastel against the broad strokes of sunlight. She dropped her voice, and I held my breath at the wonder of the colour. "This was given to me by the young acrobat who taught me how to juggle. He had four of them, and each one had a centre of this rare colour, the colour of Good Fortune." The pendant seemed to pulse as she turned it: "Oh, Sek-Lung! He had white hair and white skin *to his toes!* It's true—I saw him bathing." She laughed and blushed, her eyes softened at the memory. The silk had to match the pink heart of her pendant, for the colour was magical for her: it held the unravelling strands of her memory.

38 Six months before she died, we began to work on her last windchime. Three thin bamboo sticks of varying length were steamed and bent into circlets; twenty exact lengths of silk thread, the strongest kind, were cut and braided at both ends and glued to pieces of the stained glass. Her hands worked on their own command, each hand racing with a life of its own: cutting, snapping, braiding, knotting. Sometimes she breathed heavily, and her small body, growing thinner, sagged against me. *Death*, I thought, *is in this room*, and I would work harder alongside her. For weeks, Grandmama and I did this every other evening, a half-dozen pieces each time. The shaking in her hand grew worse, but we said nothing. Finally, after discarding a hundred, she told me she had the necessary twenty pieces. But this time, because it was a sacred chime, I would not be permitted to help her tie it up or have the joy of raising it.

39 "Once tied," she said, holding me against my disappointment, "not even I can raise it. Not a sound must it make until I have died."

40 "What will happen?"

41 "Your father will then take the centre braided strand and raise it. He will hang it against my bedroom window so that my ghost may see it, and hear it, and return. I must say goodbye to this world properly or wander in this foreign land forever."

42 "You can take the streetcar!" I blurted, suddenly shocked that she actually meant to leave me. I thought I could hear the clear **chromatic** chimes, see the shimmering colours on the wall: I fell against her and cried, and there in my crying I knew that she would die. I can still remember the touch of her hand on my head, and the smell of her thick woollen sweater pressed against my face. "I will always be with you, Little Sek-Lung, but in a different way … You'll see."

43 Weeks went by, and nothing happened. Then one late September evening, Grandmama was preparing supper when she looked out our kitchen window and saw a cat—a long, lean white cat—jump into our garbage pail and knock it over. She ran out to chase it away, shouting curses at it. She did not have her thick sweater on and when she came back into the house, a chill gripped her. She leaned against the door: "That was not a cat," she said, and the odd tone of her voice caused Father to look with alarm at her. "I cannot take back my curses. It is too late." She took hold of Father's arm. "It was all white and had pink eyes like sacred fire."

44 Father started at this, and they both looked pale. My brothers and sister, clearing the table, froze in their gestures.

45 "The fog has confused you," Stepmother said. "It was just a cat."

46 But Grandmama shook her head, for she knew it was a sign. "I will not live forever," she said. "I am prepared."

47 The next morning she was confined to her bed with a severe cold. Sitting by her, playing with some of my toys, I asked her about the cat: "Why did Father jump when you said the cat was white with pink eyes? He didn't see it, you did."

48 "But he and Stepmother know what it means."

49 "What?"

50 "My friend, the juggler, the magician, was as pale as white jade, and he had pink eyes." I thought she would begin to tell me one of her stories, a tale of **enchantment** or wondrous adventure, but she only paused to swallow; her eyes glittered, lost in memory. She took my hand, gently opening and closing her fingers over it. "Sek-Lung," she sighed, "*he* has come back to me."

51 Then Grandmama sank back into her pillow and the embroidered flowers lifted to frame her wrinkled face. She placed her hand over mine, and my own began to tremble. I fell fitfully asleep by her side. When I woke up it was dark and her bed was empty. She had been taken to the basement of St. Paul's Hospital, where the sick Chinese were allowed to stay. I was not permitted to visit her.

52 A few days after that, Grandmama died of the complications of pneumonia. Immediately after her death, Father came home. He said nothing to us but walked up the stairs to her room, pulled aside the drawn lace curtains of her window, and lifted the windchimes to the sky.

53 I began to cry and quickly put my hand in my pocket for a handkerchief. Instead, caught between my fingers, was the small, round firmness of the jade peony. In my mind's eye I saw Grandmama smile, and heard, softly, the pink centre beat like a beautiful, cramped heart.

Glossary

diminutive: Remarkably small; tiny.

skein: A cluster resembling a loosely coiled bundle of yarn.

pantomiming: Using gestures and facial expressions to convey meaning.

semitranslucent: Less than transparent.

chromatic: In music, ascending or descending by semitones.

enchantment: Charmed or bewitched by magic spells; filled with delight.

Comprehension Questions

1. Describe the relationship between Grandmama and Sek-Lung.
2. What two worlds are being represented in this story? Which characters represent each of them?
3. The juggler gives gifts of two types to Grandmama: those one can see, and those one cannot. Give examples of each.

Questions about Form

1. How does the story open? Why does the author choose to begin this way? Should the author have followed more of a chronological order of events, instead? Why or why not?
2. Choy writes this story, but who is telling it? Is it being told in first person or in third? Is this an effective way to tell it? Why or why not?

Questions for Discussion

1. Why do Grandmama and Sek-Lung get along as well as they do?
2. What is the jade peony? What does it represent or symbolize? Why does Choy use this for the title of his story?
3. What do you think the story suggests about the notion of death? Refer to evidence in the story that would support your answer.
4. In paragraph 14, Choy writes, "They all loved Grandmama, but she was *inconvenient*, unsettling." What does this mean? Why is "inconvenient" in italics?

Writing Ideas

1. Write a paragraph/essay on the difficulty you experienced living between two different worlds similar to those compared and contrasted in "The Jade Peony."
2. Why is it grandparents often have better relationships with their grandchildren than parents do with their children? Write a paragraph/essay answering this question. Refer to the story once in your composition, and draw from personal experience as well.

✦ ✦ ✦

Leaving the Cave

John Artibello

Plato's classic work, *The Republic,* is an account of a conversation in which the philosopher Socrates and a few of his friends are trying to lay out a plan for a perfect society. It seems we cannot understand what makes society work well without understanding what it means to be human and, especially, what makes people happy. According to Socrates, who is the main speaker in the book, human happiness depends on becoming enlightened, illustrated by the famous myth called "The Allegory of the Cave." John Artibello, a philosophy professor and self-declared seeker, who has been influenced by such thinkers as Jean Vanier and Marshall McLuhan, interprets this myth in his article that follows.

1 So, what's the secret? What makes us happy? Is it money, success, self-confidence, relationships, God? As long as we are human, we face the questions: How can I get it all together? How can I find what I need?

2 As we all know, the answers to these questions do not come easily. In fact, some people claim that if you are really taking these questions seriously, you are probably thinking too much. As the words of the song say, "We're here for a good time, not a long time ..."

3 None of us can be blamed for suspecting that the really big questions are probably unanswerable. So, if that is the case why not take the road of least resistance? Relax, chill. If anybody asks the tough questions (say on a first date, or in some crazy English class), just smile and say, "Ignorance is **bliss**!"

4 The philosopher Socrates would never have agreed with the idea that ignorance is bliss. In fact, he would have insisted that ignorance or what he called "unenlightenment" is actually the cause of personal unhappiness, depression, social breakdown and even war. As Socrates puts it, *"The unexamined life is not worth living."* That is, if you are not thinking about your life, it might be impossible to *really live.*

5 Fancy that! A person who claims *you are what you think*! But "thinking" for Socrates is not like going into the library to do your homework. It is more like a process of waking up, and it begins when you start to question all of the conventional, generally accepted ideas and values of the society in which we live.

6 People often say that human growth is a painful process. According to Socrates, the source of the pain is our tendency to prefer "comfortable **illusions**" to the hard realities and challenges that we all must face to become fully human. The central theme of the "**Allegory** of the Cave" is disillusion, and there is a great reward for the pain of moving away from the half-truths of common sense. As you move closer and closer to the real world, you draw closer and closer to your real Self.

7 In Socrates' story of the Cave, we are introduced to a series of powerful but troubling images. According to the philosopher, people who are unenlightened have very little self-knowledge and they are like people who live their whole lives in a darkened cave without ever discovering what is outside the cave. In fact, they don't even know that there is an "outside." Their dark cave and the shadows on the wall of the cave are their "reality." Their lives are, therefore, lives of complete illusion. This is the beginning of Socrates' ancient parable:

8 Here is a myth to illustrate the extent to which our nature may be enlightened or unenlightened. Imagine the condition of people living in a sort of cavernous chamber, with an entrance open to the light and a long passage all down the cave. Here they have been since childhood, chained by the leg and also by the neck, so that they cannot move and can only see what is in front of them because the chains will not let them turn their heads. At some distance higher up is the light of a fire burning behind them; and between the prisoners and the fire is a track with a parapet built along it, like the screen at

> a puppet show, which hides the performers while they show their puppets over the top.
>
> 9 Now behind this parapet imagine people carrying artificial objects, including figures of men and animals in wood or stone or other materials, which project above the parapet. Naturally, some of these persons will be talking, others silent.
>
> 10 ... Of course if the prisoners were talking, they would suppose their words to refer only to those passing shadows which they saw and not to the real objects which are the causes of the shadows.

11 Although this imagery is over two thousand years old, it resonates when we think, for example, of people "chained" to their televisions, watching an endless parade of chaotic but amusing images. Of course, the deeper question is, what does it all mean?

12 At this stage of the story, Socrates is describing the lives of people who try to find happiness in material things. If you are a "material girl" or a "material boy," chances are you live pretty much on the surface of life ("the shadows"). Happiness consists in looking good, having a nice car, nice clothes, and a life based on the images and truths of popular magazines and television "reality" shows. This kind of life is for Socrates equivalent to a kind of slavery. Life is at bottom unsatisfying because it is based on a lie: the message of the advertisers, which is "Don't accept yourself as you are; there is something wrong with you. You need more stuff to be happy. You need more illusion to be real."

13 Of course, the person who begins to see through the superficial messages of materialism is beginning a process of enlightenment, of coming out of the cave. This is what happens in the next part of the story.

> 14 Now consider what would happen if their release from the chains and the healing of their unwisdom should come about in this way. Suppose one of the prisoners was set free and forced suddenly to stand up, turn his head, and walk toward the light and the objects before the fire.
>
> 15 ... What do you think he would say if someone told him that what he had formerly seen was meaningless illusion, but now being somewhat closer to reality and turned towards more real objects, he was getting a truer view? ... Would he not be perplexed and believe that the objects now shown him to be not so real as what he formerly saw?
>
> 16 ... And if he were to look at the fire itself, would not his eyes ache, so that he would try to escape and turn back to the more comfortable shadows? ...
>
> 17 ... And suppose someone were to drag him forcibly up the steep and rugged ascent and not let him go until he hauled him up into the sunlight, would he not suffer pain and vexation at such treatment, and, when he had come into the light find his eyes so full of radiance that he could not see a single one of the things that he was now told were real?
>
> 18 ... Now imagine what would happen if he went down again to take his former seat in the cave. Coming suddenly out of the sunlight, his eyes would

be filled with darkness. He might be required once more to deliver his opinion on those shadows, in competition with the prisoners who had never been released, while his eyesight was still dim and unsteady; and it might take some time to get used to the darkness. They would laugh at him and say that he had gone up only to come back with his sight ruined.

19 The story shows the transition from looking at the "shadows" on the wall to looking at the "fire" to being hauled up into the "sunlight." These are very important symbols. The shadows represent the material world, the fire represents knowledge, and the sunlight represents goodness or morality. The ascent to the things in the "upper world," where the sunlight dwells, represents the upward journey of the mind to the world of spiritual meaning behind the physical things we see everyday. This is a metaphor for the learning process. Socrates further notes that, in the world of knowledge, the last thing to be perceived and only with great difficulty is the essential nature of Goodness (the sun). This means that our knowledge of reality is ultimately moral: when we look past the outward and obvious aspect of things, we will learn to distinguish the good from what "appears" to be good. All of our material things are thought to be essential to the

good life, but after studying things more closely, we may need to change our minds.

20 So getting out of the cave involves a kind of learning that transforms us. Once we develop a deep knowledge of the world, we develop a deeper connection to it, and this is ultimately what makes us fully alive. The contrast between watching "shadows on the wall" and seeing the sun and the objects of nature (outside the cave) is meant to awaken our interest in connecting to the *real world* and to saying no to the crass commercialized world of our everyday experience. When our knowledge has called into question how we live, we are living what Socrates calls the "examined life," a life really worth living. An examined life and a passionate engagement with ideas are much more interesting than a life of working like a slave to pay for a superficial materialism and the accompanying depression that seems to be **epidemic** these days in North America.

21 Perhaps "living in the cave" is **symbolic** of a modern situation like this: think of a person riding a subway on the way to school. She does not usually read on the subway because books are pretty boring. She is attracted by an ad for a new pair of jeans. She sees herself in the shapely model wearing the clothes. The come-on is "if you don't have these jeans, you won't be happy." If you buy into the message of the ad, you are buying into a whole philosophy of life, which is that "life is about *having*, rather than *being*." And, "if you want to be beautiful, *buy, buy, buy.*"

22 Of course, at this stage of your life, you don't know much about what is behind the images and the material objects you enjoy so much. You don't care, for example, that the people who make your jeans and sweaters are working for three or four dollars a day somewhere in the Third World. Your ideas of morality are pretty basic as well. Really bad people are terrorists and suicide bombers, but they live mostly in other countries. Living in the shadows is a metaphor for our tendency to immerse ourselves in superficial things as a way to avoid deeper and potentially threatening ideas and issues.

23 Some people, however, can't help asking tough questions. Why, for example, as our society becomes technologically more powerful, do individuals feel more and more powerless? Are all of the goods and gadgets that we work so hard to get making our lives more meaningful? To answer these questions, we need to get past "the shadows"; we need to break the chains and turn towards the light. This process of enlightenment, of moving into the light, is impossible apart from the search for truth, which in terms of the story, results in our understanding not just *how* things work (technology) but *why* things and people behave as they do (philosophy).

24 Consider a modern example of what the cave might represent: someone who is "in the cave" is like a person who owns a car without knowing what effect it has on the environment. If asked what makes the car work, this person says, "Just turn on the ignition, put her in gear, and off you go." If the car breaks down, the owner has no idea how to fix it. But someone who decides to take a course in auto mechanics or engineering is "breaking the chains" of **ignorance**

and attempting to look at the "real objects" involved in the working of the car: things like the engine, the transmission, the spark plugs, alternator, and the burning of the fossil fuel without which there would be no cars, no highways, no drive-in movies and probably no wars in the Middle East! When your study has taken you "outside the cave," or to "the real world," you see the political, environmental and moral aspects of cars. A person who "sees the sun" (outside the cave) can put it all together. The person sees the bigger picture. The car that you love to drive is connected to a larger, more complex reality involving the politics of oil and the destruction of the environment, and as we all know, that can't be good!

25 In the story of the Cave, Socrates is saying that humans are confronted with a fundamental option: reality or illusion. He suggests that the journey to your true self begins by going deeper and deeper into the world to find its true beauty and meaning. The philosophers will tell you that learning is the key, especially when you *explore* what really interests you. When you love to learn, it is because you are finding yourself in your study. The journey is endless, as are the rewards. As T.S. Eliot says,

26 We shall not cease from exploration
And the end of all our exploring
Will be to arrive where we started
And know the place for the first time.

Glossary

bliss: Great joy or happiness.

illusions: Mistaken perceptions.

allegory: Story in which people, things, and happenings have a hidden or symbolic meaning.

epidemic: Prevalent and spreading among many individuals in a community at the same time (said especially of a human contagious disease).

symbolic: Of something that stands for or represents another thing.

ignorance: Lack of knowledge or education; unawareness (of).

Comprehension Questions

1. What do most people, according to Artibello, think happiness consists of?
2. What takes place in the cave (in Plato's myth) that relates to the material world?
3. What does Artibello cite as a modern example of what the cave symbolizes?

4. What is the difference, according to Artibello, between an ignorant person who owns a car, and an enlightened person who has a deeper knowledge of cars? How does morality relate to this contrast?

Questions about Form

1. What effect or effects do the illustrations that accompany this article have on you?
2. Some of the "Allegory of the Cave" is taken directly from a translation of Plato's *Republic.* Would it have made any difference if Artibello had simply paraphrased these parts?
3. The "Socratic Approach" is one of asking deep, thought-provoking questions. In paragraph 23, for example, Artibello asks two questions that he does not proceed to answer directly. Do you think there is a reason for this? If so, what?

Questions for Discussion

1. Artibello is interpreting Plato to mean that, to be fully alive, we need to prefer the world of ideas to the world of "material things" such as cars, clothes, etc. Is it possible that the "material girl or boy" cannot be whole or happy? Discuss the role of ideas in the good life.
2. In the conclusion of the article, the concept of a "fundamental" or life option is introduced. Discuss the role of fundamental options and turning points in life. In what sense do these options involve a movement from illusion to reality?
3. Plato is known as an idealist philosopher. That is, he was critical of the physical world because it passes away while the deeper things like the ideals of truth, virtue, and beauty are eternal. What images in the story of the cave reinforce this position? Do you agree with this idea? Explain.
4. If you were to lead an examined life, what would you need to do? Would you have to make changes to your lifestyle or in what you are studying? Discuss.

Writing Ideas

1. Write a paragraph/essay on what you think it means for people in general to lead examined lives. How would their lives have to change?
2. Now that you've read and perhaps discussed the article, write a paragraph/essay of definition explaining what "leaving the cave" means to you. What are some of your own examples of what "leaving the cave" represents?

Further Reading and Research

1. In a book entitled *Plato not Prozac!* Lou Marinoff explores the relationship between what we think and how we feel. He is exploring an ancient idea that

being passionate about thinking, especially about deep and interesting issues (such as the meaning of life), is what keeps us sane.

2. Great philosophical ideas are often conveyed in stories, poems, and myths. Read T. S. Eliot's "The Waste Land," and compare the imagery of the poem to the imagery of the cave.
3. Iris Murdoch is one of the world's great interpreters of Plato. Her novel *The Philosopher's Pupil* is a fictional account of a philosopher's journey to "the dark side."
4. One source of beautiful poems about the journey to the light is Mary Oliver's *New and Selected Poems* (Beacon Press, 1992). See especially "The Journey" and "Wild Geese."

✦ ✦ ✦

I Lost My Talk

Rita Joe

Rita Joe is a Micmac Native, and her writings are about aboriginal people. She was born on a reservation in Wycocomagh on Cape Breton Island in Nova Scotia. At the age of 12, after both her parents had died, she placed herself in an Indian residential school in Shubenacadie, Nova Scotia. Rita Joe is an acclaimed poet with several collections to her name, including *Lnu and Indians We're Called* (1991). She became a member of the Order of Canada in 1990.

1 I lost my talk
The talk you took away.
When I was a little girl
At **Shubenacadie** school.

2 You snatched it away:
I speak like you
I think like you
I create like you
The scrambled **ballad,** about my word.

3 Two ways I talk
Both ways I say,
Your way is more powerful.

4 So gently I offer my hand and ask,
Let me find my talk
So I can teach you about me.

Glossary

Shubenacadie: A town in Nova Scotia.

ballad: A popular song, generally of a personal or political nature.

Comprehension Questions

1. What do you think Rita Joe is saying in the first stanza of her poem?
2. What does "scrambled ballad" mean? Might it have more than one meaning?
3. What does the author mean by the word *word* in the ninth line?

Questions about Form

1. What is the difference in tone between the first line of the poem and the very last line? How might this contribute to an interpretation of the poem's theme?
2. What do you think might be the reason for the repetition in the second stanza?
3. How would you describe the type of language being used here? Does it contribute to an overall deliberate effect? Why or why not?

Questions for Discussion

1. What do you know of Canadian history that relates to this poem? What might have been the reasons the school authorities did what they did?
2. Does the knowledge that Rita Joe placed herself in the school at Shubenacadie affect your interpretation of her poem? Why or why not?

Writing Ideas

1. Do some research on what Canadian school authorities did to assimilate Native Canadians, and take a position either for or against this action in a paragraph/essay.
2. In a cause and effect paragraph/essay, discuss the repercussions of one's voice being denied. You may want to talk more specifically of a child whose voice is not taken seriously, or of women whose voice is silenced in certain cultures, or of North American Blacks who have been marginalized and/or discriminated against ever since the days of slavery, etc.
3. Besides the obvious difference between this work by Rita Joe and the piece by Tomson Highway, which begins on page 333 (they are two different genres), are there any other differences? In a paragraph/essay, compare or contrast the two works.

✦ ✦ ✦

Rats

W. Frank Epling

Named Outstanding Teacher of the Year in Psychology at the University of Alberta, Frank Epling taught behaviour analysis to approximately 1000 students a year. He died in 1998 at the age of fifty-four. He was known as a creative researcher whose ideas continue to permeate the scientific community. In this piece, Epling takes a novel approach to the controversial subject of animal rights.

1 I am an animal researcher, and I work with rats. Now, for most people, the rat is an animal that does not **elicit** great sympathy. In fact, most people would hit a rat with a shovel if it dared to run across their basement floor. Of course, in Alberta, rats do not run across basement floors because the province is "rat free" and proud of it. This is not, however, exactly correct because some rats manage to sneak in from British Columbia and Saskatchewan, and I have some in my laboratory. Nonetheless, the Alberta Rat Patrol does an excellent job, and only very sneaky rats survive the border crossing. Since most of these are new arrivals and don't have a home, the Alberta winter usually gets what the Rat Patrol misses.

2 There are good rats and there are bad rats. I know this sounds absurd but stick with me and I will explain. Some time ago I was preparing a twelve-page written document that was an **ethics** justification for some proposed research with rats. I had to make certain that my rats got the very best food, shelter, and medical care. I also had to convince the local committees that I had the overall welfare of my rats foremost in my mind. This proposal took several days to write. The reason for all this is that I have good rats. Good rats live in laboratory cages.

3 Following the second day of work on my ethics proposal, I went home, opened a beer, put up my feet and flipped on the tube. *Fifth Estate* or *W5* was on, I don't remember which. Also, I can't recall the first news item but I certainly can the second—it was about the Alberta Rat Patrol. On this show, the dedicated people of the Rat Patrol were keeping the cities, fields, and houses of Alberta rat free. This was not a fun time for those creatures who tried to invade the province. The documentary focused on the Alberta/Saskatchewan border. There are lots of rats in Saskatchewan. Well, let me tell you, the members of the Rat Patrol were shooting, hitting, and poisoning rats; these were bad rats. Bad rats do not live in laboratory cages.

4 There are other ways to be a bad rat. Rats that escape from their cages are not protected by ethics proposals. As soon as their feet hit the laboratory floor they become pests and are subject to traps, poison, and so on. Shotguns are not used because of damage to walls, noise, and the possibility of shooting a student or researcher. Believe me though, these rats are not held in high esteem. This is particularly true in Alberta because they could get out of the building and infest our rat-free province.

5 Another way that rats lose their good status is to be food. There are animals, like some very large snakes, that will not eat unless their prey items are alive. In order to keep these animals, they must be fed. Food is not protected by ethics committees.

6 All of this makes me wonder why I am spending a significant amount of time writing ethics proposals for rats, rather than doing research with them. Don't misunderstand me. I happen to like rats and I do not advocate mistreating them. I am against the use of these animals for testing cosmetics and for repeating research where the findings are well established and rats are made to suffer. I am, however, convinced that research with rats (and other animals) can lead to findings that promote human welfare, and I am in favour of doing that research. In order to understand why I am spending a fair amount of time writing ethics proposals for my rat research, it is necessary to consider the animal rights movement.

7 Over the past fifteen years, this movement has steadily grown in number of members, and it has received increasing attention from the press. So called "animal activists" belong to a variety of organizations and they range from moderate to extreme in their views. I think it is fair to say, though, that all animal activists think that cute furry animals are nice animals—even when they are pests or food. Rats have two strikes against them, bad press and a long hairless tail. Also, the black plague did not help their cause. This prejudice for some animals and against others is curious. Not very many people are concerned about the live lobsters found at supermarkets. I think this is because the lobster is very tasty and looks vaguely like a large underwater insect. On the other hand, baby seals look cute, warm, cuddly, and helpless. Thus, the seal but not the lobster gets sympathy. Returning to my point, the animal rights movement has created a public concern for the welfare of animals, and some of this has reached hysterical and absurd proportions.

8 A few of the more extreme views include stopping all medical research with animals, replacing animal subjects with humans, including animals in the United States Bill of Rights, recognizing **specism** as a prejudice similar to racism and so on. I don't know about you, but I can't imagine a rat, a lobster, or even a seal with the rights of free speech, assembly, and the pursuit of happiness. How would they know they had these rights? Also what happens when one animal, say a lion, **infringes** on a deer's right to life? All in all, these views seem a bit "whacky" to me but they are taken seriously by some people.

9 One tactic of the more extreme animal activists has been overt violence and intimidation. Some individuals have joined paramilitary animal rights movements. This is an odd development since it is the only revolutionary movement I know of where none of the members are the creatures whose rights are being fought for. Nonetheless, these people are serious, and they have bombed the houses of animal researchers, released laboratory animals, vandalized labs, threatened to inject meat products with poison, organized and promoted letter writing campaigns to stop legitimate research, and harassed reputable scientists with threatening letters and phone calls.

10 I don't know how many of my fellow citizens are members of, or in sympathy with, the animal rights movement; but I suspect not very many. This speculation is based on the number of steaks on display at my local grocery and the notable lack of concern for pit bull dogs in Edmonton. So, why all the fuss?

11 A few years ago, the *Edmonton Sun* called and wanted to interview me and several other animal researchers. We were encouraged to participate in this interview in order to "promote the benefits of animal research." Anyway, we had one of the best run and closely supervised facilities in Canada. The reporter and a photographer showed up and asked questions about my projects, photographed my rats, thanked me for giving them time, and left. I looked forward to local fame.

12 A week or so later, the *Sunday Sun* carried the article. I was not famous. They had so garbled my name that you could not tell whose research they were talking about. This was very fortunate (or perhaps intentional to prevent a civil suit). The first page of the Sunday supplement had a full-page picture of a monkey sitting in a restraining chair looking like it had just had a tooth pulled by a student dentist. None of the people interviewed by the *Sun* worked with monkeys and I recognized the picture. The photograph was a famous one that has appeared in antivivisectionist magazines and advertising campaigns for "save the animals." I don't know why the same picture is used over and over, but it is.

13 Articles like this portray animal researchers as modern day versions of **Dr. Mengele**. It would seem that we can't wait to torture animals in order to arrive at conclusions everybody knows already. We have not received "good press." I could present a case for doing animal research but I would digress from the point I am trying to make. Writing ethics proposals that defend research with animals that are **arbitrarily** defined as good is bizarre.

14 As I have said, there are good and bad rats. At least in Alberta, it appears there are going to be bad rats for some time to come. Being a bad rat seems to depend on "the luck of the draw." Since bad rats are not considered worthy of ethics protection, I could use them in my research. There is, however, a problem. I could ask for bad rats but they would automatically become good when they were placed in cages in my laboratory. To appreciate this, it is necessary to understand a few things about universities and public relations.

15 The people who run universities tend to place great value on "positive press": "negative press" is very much discouraged. This makes sense; the public supports universities and if they don't like what is going on they may withdraw their support. Animal activists would like to stop all animal experiments, and they search for an opportunity to provide unfavorable press. Forcing scientists to justify the ethics of their animal research helps protect the university from this publicity. There are, however, unfortunate side effects. Large sums of money are spent on animal care staff who police laboratories. Time is wasted on writing ethics proposals, sitting on ethics committees, and waiting for ethics approval. This and more for an animal most citizens would stomp on if given the chance.

16 I am probably more concerned about the welfare of rats than most people. I have known many rats over the years and I have liked more than a few. I am in favor of kind treatment for rats and other animals that are used in scientific research. I do think, however, that a consideration of good and bad rats and lobsters and seals points to a confusion of ethics. So what can I do? Not much, write a commentary like this and then put in another two days writing another ethics proposal. Rats!

Glossary

elicit: Draw out; evoke (an admission, response, etc.).

ethics: Science of morals in human conduct.

specism: Assumption of human superiority over animals.

infringes: Trespasses; affects something so as to limit or restrict it.

Dr. Mengele: A ruthless Nazi doctor who performed experiments mostly on Jewish inmates of death camps during the Holocaust in World War II. Many of these experiments resulted in the victims' sterility or death.

arbitrarily: Based on the unrestricted will of a person.

Comprehension Questions

1. What does Epling mean when he says, "Good rats live in laboratory cages" at the end of paragraph 2?
2. How does Epling feel the press handled the story for which he was interviewed, and why?

Questions about Form

1. Why does Epling begin his article by identifying what he does for a living?
2. Although an "Alberta rat control program" does exist, there is no group of people in Alberta known officially as the "Rat Patrol." Why do you think Epling places such emphasis on this made-up label?

Questions for Discussion

1. In paragraph 12, Epling says he doesn't know why the picture of the monkey keeps getting used over and over. Based on the rest of his article, what reasons might he give on further speculation?
2. What do you think, in your own words, is Epling's thesis? What is the sentence in the piece that comes closest to your answer? Do you agree with this thesis? Why or why not?
3. Why does Epling call his article "Rats"? Are there at least two meanings here?

Writing Ideas

1. Do you favour the testing of rats for medical research purposes? Write a paragraph/essay supporting your stand. Refer to Epling's article in further support of your argument.
2. Does your attitude toward specism determine whether you favour animal research or not? Where does this attitude come from? Discuss your answers in a paragraph/essay.

✦ ✦ ✦

Gretzky in Eighty-Four

Mordecai Richler

Most famous of Mordecai Richler's novels are the award-winning *The Apprenticeship of Duddy Kravitz* and the more recent *Barney's Version*. Known for his courageous content and biting style, the Montreal-born Richler, who died in 2001, could always be counted on to tell it like it is. This persuasive essay on our own heroic No. 99, the Great Gretzky, reveals what it is this hockey boy wonder had that earned even Richler's respect.

1 Nineteen eighty-four. Edmonton. One day in March, at Barry T's Roadhouse out there on tacky 104th Street—wedged between welding shops and cinder-block strip joints and used-car lots—the city's amiable sportswriting **fraternity** gathered for its annual award luncheon. The writers were going to present Wayne Gretzky with their Sports Professional of the Year Award again. "I'll bet he tells us it means more to him than the Stanley Cup," one of the writers said.

2 "Or the Hart."

3 "Or his contract with General Mills. What do you think that's worth, eh?"

4 Bill Tuele, director of public relations for the Oilers, joined our table. "Does flying really scare Gretzky that much?" I asked.

5 "Nah. It doesn't scare him *that* much," Tuele said. "It's just that if we go bumpety-bump, he staggers off the plane with his shirt drenched."

6 Gretzky, who was running late, finally drifted into Barry T's. A curiously bland twenty-four-year-old in a grey flannel suit, he graciously accepted his plaque. "Any time you win an award, it's a thrill," he said. "With so many great athletes in Edmonton, I'm very honoured to win this." Then, his duty done, he retreated to a booth to eat lunch. And in Western Canada, where civility is the rule, he was not immediately besieged by reporters with notebooks or tape recorders. They left him alone with his overdone roast beef and curling, soggy french fries.

7 There had been a game the night before, the slumping Edmonton Oilers ending a five-game losing streak at home, edging the Detroit Red Wings, 7–6,

only their second victory in their last eight outings. Even so, they were still leading the league. Gretzky, juggling his crammed schedule, had fit me in for an interview at the Northlands Coliseum at 9 a.m. Increasingly caught up in the business world, he told me he had recently read ***Iacocca*** and was now into ***Citizen Hughes***. Though he enjoyed watching television soap operas and had once appeared on *The Young and the Restless* himself, he never bothered with fiction. "I like to read fact," he said. "I'm so busy, I haven't got the time to read stories that aren't real."

8 After the interview, there was a team practice and, following the sportswriters' lunch, he was scheduled to shoot a television commercial, and then there was a dinner he was obliged to attend. The next night, there was a game with Buffalo. It would be the seventieth for the Oilers in the regular NHL schedule but the seventy-second for Gretzky, who had played in two Canada Cup games immediately before the NHL season. There were a further ten games to come in the regular season and, as it turned out, another eighteen in the playoffs before the Oilers would skate to their second consecutive Stanley Cup.

9 But, at the time, Gretzky, understandably, was in a defensive mood, aware that another undeniably talented club, the Boston Bruins, led by Bobby Orr and Phil Esposito, had promised better than they had paid, faltering more than once in the playoffs. "We've already been compared to the great Boston team of the early seventies, which won only two cups but they still say should have won four," Gretzky said.

10 I asked Gretzky if he didn't consider the regular NHL schedule, which more than one **wag** has put down as the longest exhibition season in sport, to be insufferably long and meaningless. After all, it ran to 840 games, from September to April, and when it was over only five of the then twenty-one teams had been cut from what knowledgeable fans appreciated as the real season—the Stanley Cup playoffs. "Well," he said, "this city's not like New York, where there are lots of things to do. In Edmonton in February, we're the only attraction."

11 When I asked Peter Pocklington, the owner of the Oilers, about the seemingly endless season, he protested, "We're the only show in town. Coming to see Gretzky is like going to watch Pavarotti or Nureyev. What else are you going to do in Edmonton in the middle of the winter? How many beers can you drink?"

12 The capital of Alberta is a city you come from, not a place to visit, unless you have relatives there or an interest in an oil well nearby. On first glance, and even on third, it seems not so much a city as a jumble of a used-building lot, where the spare office towers and box-shaped apartment buildings and cinder-block motels discarded in the construction of real cities have been abandoned to waste away in the cruel prairie winter.

13 If Canada were not a country, however fragmented, but, instead, a house, Vancouver would be the solarium-cum-playroom, an afterthought of affluence; Toronto, the counting room, where money makes for the most glee; Montreal, the salon; and Edmonton, Edmonton, the boiler room. There is hardly a tree to be seen downtown, nothing to delight the eye on Jasper Avenue. On thirty-below-

zero nights, grim religious zealots loom on street corners, speaking in tongues, and intrepid hookers in miniskirts rap on the windows of cars that have stopped for traffic. There isn't a first-class restaurant anywhere in town. For all that, Edmontonians are a truly admirable lot. They have not only endured great hardships in the past but also continue to suffer an **abominable** climate as well as isolation from the cities of light. And, to some degree, like other westerners, they thrive on resentments against the grasping, self-satisfied East, which has exploited their natural resources for years, taking their oil and gas at cut prices to subsidize inefficient Ontario and Quebec industries.

14 Insults, injuries.

15 For as long as Edmontonians can remember, the biggies were elsewhere. Though they had contributed many fine hockey players to the game, they could only hear about their feats on radio or later see them on television. Hockey was *their* game, damn it, *their* national sport, but New York, Chicago, Detroit, and Boston were in the NHL long before the league's governors adjudged Edmonton not so much worthy as potentially profitable. But in 1984, Canada's hockey shrines were either in decline, as was then the case in Montreal, or in total disrepute, as in Toronto. In those glory days, if easterners wanted to see the best player in the game more than twice a season, if they wanted to catch a dynasty in the making, why, then, they had to pack their fat coats and fur-lined boots and head for Edmonton, home of the Stanley Cup champions and the Great Gretzky himself.

16 In March 1984, Gretzky the commodity was soaring to new heights of fame and fortune; Gretzky the most famous player ever was struggling, justifiably fatigued.

17 In a five-week period, Gretzky had been on the cover of *Sporting News*, two Canadian hockey magazines, and *Sports Illustrated* (for the fifth time), and he had shared a *Time* cover with Larry Bird of the Boston Celtics. He had tested his scoring skills against no less a goalie than George Plimpton, and he had been the subject of an article in the *Saturday Evening Post* and an interview in *Playboy*. He had, Gretzky told me, been criticized for submitting to the *Playboy* interview, accused of endorsing pornography. But, as he put it, "You can't please everybody." Actually, the engaging truth is that his interview with *Playboy* was a triumph of small-town Canadian rectitude over that magazine's appetite for salacious detail.

18 PLAYBOY: How many women have been in your life?

19 GRETZKY: Vickie Moss was my first girlfriend. I never dated anyone else.

20 PLAYBOY: Do you have *any* vices?

21 GRETZKY: Oh, yeah, I'm human. I do have a bad habit of swearing on ice. I forget that there are people around the rink. It's a problem. I hope I'm heading in a direction where I can correct it, but I don't know if I will be able to.

22 Gretzky was what athletes are supposed to be, but seldom are—McIntosh-apple wholesome, dedicated, an inspirational model for young fans. He was an **anachronism,** rooted in an age when a date wasn't a disco, then your place or

mine, but rather a movie, then maybe a banana split at the corner soda fountain. He had owned a Ferrari for four years but had never had a speeding ticket. He still phoned home to Brantford, Ontario, to report to his father three times a week. He struck me as nice, very nice, but incapable of genuine wit or irreverence, like, say, Rug McGraw. What he did tell me, his manner appropriately solemn, was that he felt it was his responsibility never to refuse to sign an autograph: "For that person, that kid, it could be the greatest thing that ever happened to him."

23 Gretzky worked hard, incredibly hard, both for the charities he supported and for himself. He was boffo sales stuff. The hockey stick he endorsed, Titan, leaped from twelfth to first place in sales in thirty-six months. Gretzky also pitched for Canon cameras, Nike sportswear, General Mills Pro Stars cereal, Mattel toys, Travellers Insurance, and American Express. These endorsements were handled by Michael Barnett of CorpSport International out of handsomely appointed offices in an old, converted Edmonton mansion. There was a large portrait of Gretzky in action on a wall in the reception room as well as the essential LeRoy Neiman; and a placard with a quotation from Ralph Waldo Emerson: "Make the most of yourself, for that is all there is of you."

24 CorpSport International represented other athletes, but for the past four years, Gretzky, who then earned an estimated $1 million annually in endorsements—about the same as his salary—had been the major preoccupation of its thirty-four-year-old president. Barnett, a former minor-league hockey player himself, was in daily contact with Gretzky's lawyer as well as the firm that handled his investments. "Though Wayne listens to all his advisers," Barnett said, "he makes his own business and investment decisions. We get some three dozen personal appearance requests for him a month, but he will only speak for charities. Pro Stars cereal advertises the Wayne Gretzky Fan Club on four million boxes. It costs seven bucks a year to be a member, and for that you get four annual Wayne Gretzky newsletters as well as this set of photographs.

25 "There have been seven unauthorized biographies," Barnett continued. "Wayne gets between two to five thousand fan letters a month. Vickie Moss's mother handles that for him."

26 Mattel has marketed a Wayne Gretzky doll ("For avid fans, his out-of-town uniform, jogging suit, and tuxedo are also available"), which has led to cracks about the need for a Dave Semenko doll to beat up any kid who roughs up the Gretzky doll.

27 Late at night, even as he talked business with Barnett, Gretzky autographed coloured photographs of himself. Mattel supplied the photographs, which included its logo, but Gretzky, according to Barnett, paid the postal charges, about $2,000 monthly. Barnett also pointed out that, since the Oilers took their first Stanley Cup on May 19, 1984, Gretzky had only six weeks off the ice before joining the Canada Cup training camp, playing in that series, and then moving directly into the NHL season.

28 And in March, things weren't going well. Gretzky was playing without his usual intensity. I asked saucy, streetwise Glen Sather, president, general manager, and coach of the Oilers, if he was guilty of overplaying Gretzky. "Wayne," he said, "plays something like twenty-two minutes a game. He thrives on work. The more ice time he gets, the better he is."

29 Yet Gretzky hadn't had a two-goal game since February 19 or scored a hat trick for two months. He would, however, finish the 1984–85 season with 208 points (73 goals, 135 assists). This marked the third time he had scored more than 200 points in his six seasons in the NHL. A truly remarkable feat, this, when you consider that no previous player in league history had managed it even once.

30 Records.

31 The Official Edmonton Oilers 1984–85 Guide lists a modest three records under the heading, "NHL Individual Records Held or Co-Held by Edmonton Oilers (excluding Wayne Gretzky)," and there follows a stunning full page of Wayne Gretzky's contribution to the NHL records. Paraphrasing the guide, here are Gretzky's statistics:

32 "No. 99, centre: height, 6′0″; weight, 170 lbs.; born, Brantford, Ontario, Jan. 26, 1961; shoots, left. He is not the fastest or the most graceful skater in hockey, neither does he boast the hardest shot. But he now holds 38 NHL records."

33 Of course, he would, as was his habit, set or tie even more records in the 1985 playoffs, as well as win the Conn Smythe Trophy for most valuable player in that series. But back in March 1984, all I asked him was, did he feel a 100-goal season was possible?

34 "Sure, it's possible," Gretzky said. "Somebody will do it. The year I got ninety-two, everything went my way." But he had begun to feel the pressure. "Yesterday you got two goals in a game, tomorrow the fans want three." He has said he would like to retire at the age of thirty, after fifteen years in hockey. "When Lafleur retired, it made me open my eyes," he said.

35 Lafleur, who quit suddenly in 1984 (temporarily, as it would turn out) at the age of thirty-three after four mediocre years, had scored sixty goals in his best season, 1977–78. "I wasn't surprised he retired," Gretzky said. "You wake up, you're no longer in the top-ten scorers, you think, 'Oh, my God,' and you begin to press. When Lafleur was in his prime, it was a much rougher league, but slower. We get hit, but not as much as in the late seventies."

36 Danny Gare, the Red Wing veteran who had played against Gretzky the night before, told me, "They don't run against him like they did on Lafleur."

37 It's not true that they don't run on him. The hit men seek him here, they seek him there, but like the Scarlet Pimpernel they can't board him anywhere: he's too elusive. Gretzky can fit through a keyhole. Watching him out there, I often felt that he was made of Plasticine. I've seen him stretch his arms a seeming two feet more because that's what was required to retrieve a puck. Conversely, putting a shift on a defenceman, cruising very low on ice, he seemed to shrink to whatever size was necessary to pass. He is incomparably dangerous behind the opposition's net and unequalled at making a puck squirt free from a crowd.

38 If, to begin with, Gretzky had a fault, it was his tendency to whine. For a while, all an opposing player had to do was to skate past Gretzky thinking negative thoughts for No. 99 to fall to the ice, seemingly mortally wounded, his eyes turned imploringly to the referee. In Edmonton, this had earned him a pejorative nickname: "The Wayner."

39 In June, Gretzky won the Hart Memorial Trophy, the league's most valuable player award, for the sixth straight time, this in a year in which he had already won his fifth consecutive Art Ross Trophy, for the NHL's leading point scorer during the regular season. One hundred and eighteen years after Confederation, the only thing out of Canada more famous than Gretzky was the cold front.

40 For a hockey player, it should be noted, this was a grand accomplishment for, as a rule in 1985, NHL Stars had to cope with a difficult paradox. Celebrated at home, they could, much to their chagrin, usually pass anonymously south of the 49th parallel. Not so Gretzky. But for all his fame, he remained something of an enigma, a young man charged with contradictions. Ostensibly modest beyond compare, he had taken to talking about himself in the third person. Speaking of the endless hours he clocked on his backyard skating rink as a child, he said: "It wasn't a sacrifice. That's what Wayne Gretzky wanted to do." Discussing possible commercial endorsements, he allowed, "The thing to look for is ... is there a future in it for Wayne Gretzky?"

41 Seemingly self-composed, he didn't fly on airplanes easily. Obviously, there was a lot of inner tension bottled up in Gretzky, and at thirty thousand feet, it began to leak. In 1981, trying to beat his fear of flying, he tried a hypnotherapist, but it worked only briefly. Come 1984 he flew with pilots in the cockpit as often as possible, which helped only some, because they had to send him back into the cabin once they began landing procedures, and Gretzky had been known to sit there, unable to look, holding his head in his hands.

42 Sifting through the Gretzky file, it appeared that just about every reply he had ever given in an interview was calculated to oblige. Again and again, his answers were not only boringly proper but also tainted by what W.H. Auden once condemned as the rehearsed response. Under all the superficial sweetness, however, I suspected there was a small residue of bitterness. This, in remembrance of a boy deprived of a normal childhood, driven to compete on ice with boys four to six years his senior from the age of six.

43 Wayne was only eleven years old when he began to set all manner of amazing records in minor-league hockey, even as he would later astound the NHL. But in 1984, even as Gretzky was arguably the best player the game had ever known, a much-needed publicity bonanza for the NHL in the United States, he was also, ironically, a menace to the game.

44 Imagine, if you will, a baseball outfielder, not yet in his prime, who hits .400 or better every season as a matter of course and you have some notion of Gretzky's hockey stature. Furthermore, since Gretzky's sophomore year in the NHL, there had been no contest for the Art Ross Trophy. Gretzky is so far superior to any other forward, regularly winning the point-scoring title by a previ-

ously unheard of fifty or sixty points, that he inadvertently makes the other star players appear sadly inadequate. And while the other players tend to tell you, tight-lipped, that "Gretz is the greatest ... he has all the moves and then some," I don't think they really liked him, any more than **Salieri** did the young Mozart. Effortlessly, he made most of them look mediocre.

45 Peter Gzowski, in one of the very few intelligent books ever written about hockey, *The Game of Their Lives*, ventured, "Often the difference between what Wayne Gretzky does with the puck and what less accomplished players would have done with it is simply a *pause*, as if, as time freezes, he is enjoying an extra handful of milliseconds." Gzowski goes on to cite experiments done with athletes by a neurologist at McMaster University in Hamilton, Ontario. Based on this and other research, he suggested that Gretzky, like other superstars (say, Ted Williams or Bjorn Borg), benefited from motor neutrons that fired faster than those of mere mortals. Or, put more simply, time slowed down for him. Gretzky also profited from an uncanny ability to react quickly to everybody's position on the ice. "What separates him from his peers in the end," Gzowski wrote, "the quality that has led him to the very point of the pyramid, may well have nothing to do with physical characteristics at all, but instead be a manner of perception, not so much of what he sees—he does not have exceptional vision—but of *how* he sees it and absorbs it."

Glossary

fraternity: Brotherhood.

***Iacocca*:** Book about the former Chrysler chairman.

***Citizen Hughes*:** Book about well-known billionaire Howard Hughes.

wag: a humorous, droll, or witty person.

abominable: Morally reprehensible; very bad or unpleasant.

anachronism: Old-fashioned or out-of-date person or thing.

Salieri: Famous Italian composer who was hostile to Mozart.

Comprehension Questions

1. What is special about the year 1984, according to Richler?
2. What were Gretzky's faults, on and off the ice, according to the essay?
3. What made Gretzky so successful in hockey, according to Peter Gzowski?
4. What did the other players say about Gretzky? Did this contradict what Richler says they were feeling? Is there convincing evidence in the essay that supports Richler's claim?

Questions about Form

1. The essay begins with two fragments. Why do you think a world-renowned writer like Richler would do this deliberately? Do you think he knows what a complete sentence is?

2. You've probably noticed there is a great deal of dialogue in this essay. This is evident even before starting to read the piece due to the extensive usage of quotation marks. What effect does this dialogue have on the reader? Do you think it advances Richler's interests or not? Why or why not?

Questions for Discussion

1. It might be argued that this essay is critical of Edmonton. Would you agree or disagree. Why or why not?

2. What does the *Playboy* interview in this essay reveal about Gretzky's character? Would you have expected this of a hockey superstar?

3. What do you think, in your own words, is the author's thesis? Which sentence in the piece comes closest to your answer?

4. What is the relationship between what Peter Gzowski wrote about Gretzky's ability and the ability to have the attitude that "life takes place only in the present"?

Writing Ideas

1. In a paragraph or an essay, select someone who is, in your mind, set apart from the rest like Gretzky is set apart from other hockey players according to Richler. Give the reasons.

2. Is there a danger in becoming great at a relatively early age in life? Discuss your answer to this question in a paragraph or essay, and make references to the above piece in support of your topic sentence/thesis statement.

✦ ✦ ✦

The Other Family

Himani Bannerji

Associate Professor of Sociology at York University in Toronto, Himani Bannerji has an active teaching connection with India, especially West Bengal, through the School of Women's Studies, Jadavpur University, Kolkata. She has taught and published extensively in the areas of Marxist theory, anti-racist feminism, and nationalism. In the following story about a little girl and her mother, Bannerji gives us a glimpse into the home of an immigrant family caught between the desire to fit into a new community and the fear of losing its identity.

1 When the little girl came home it was already getting dark. The winter twilight had transformed the sheer blue sky of the day into the colour of steel, on which were etched a few stars, the bare winter trees and the dark wedges of the housetops. A few lit windows cast a faint glow on the snow outside. The mother stood at her window and watched the little hooded figure walking toward the house. The child looked like a shadow, her blue coat blended into the shadows of the evening. This child, her own, how small and **insubstantial** she seemed, and how alone, walking home through a pavement covered with ice and snow! It felt unreal. So different was this childhood from her own, so far away from the sun, the trees and the peopled streets of her own country! What did I do, she thought, I took her away from her own people and her own language, and now here she comes walking alone, through an alien street in a country named Canada.

2 As she **contemplated** the solitary, moving figure, her own solitude rushed over her like a tide. She had drifted away from a world that she had lived in and understood, and now she stood here at the same distance from her home as from the homes which she glimpsed while walking past the sparkling clean windows of the sandblasted houses. And now the doorbell rang, and here was her daughter scraping the snow off her boots on the doormat.

3 Dinner time was a good time. A time of warmth, of putting hot, steaming food onto the table. A time to chat about the important things of the day, a time to show each other what they had acquired. Sometimes, however, her mother would be absentminded, worried perhaps about work, unsettled perhaps by letters that had arrived from home, scraping her feelings into a state of rawness. This was such an evening. She had served herself and her child, started a conversation about their two cats and fallen into a silence after a few minutes.

4 "You aren't listening to me, Mother."

5 The complaining voice got through to her, and she looked at the indignant face demanding attention from the other side of the table. She gathered herself together.

6 "So what did he do, when you gave him dried food?"

7 "Oh, I don't quite remember, I think he scratched the ground near his bowl and left."

8 The child laughed.

9 "That was smart of him! So why don't we buy tinned food for them?"

10 "Maybe we should," she said, and tried to change the topic.

11 "So what did you do in your school today?"

12 "Oh, we drew pictures like we do every day. We never study anything—not like you said you did in your school. We drew a family—our family. Want to see it?"

13 "Sure, and let's go to the living room, OK? This is messy." Scraping of chairs and the lighting of the lamps in the other room. They both made a rush for the most comfortable chair, both reached it at the same time and made a compromise.

14 "How about you sit in my lap? No? OK, sit next to me then and we will squeeze in somehow."

15 There was a remarkable resemblance between the two faces, except that the face of the child had a greater intensity, given by the wide open eyes. She was fine boned, and had black hair framing her face. Right now she was struggling with the contents of her satchel, apparently trying to feel her way to the paintings.

16 "Here it is," she said, producing a piece of paper. "Here's the family!"

17 The mother looked at the picture for a long time. She was very still. Her face had set into an expression of anger and sadness. She was trying very hard not to cry. She didn't want to frighten the child, and yet what she saw made her feel distant from her daughter, as though she was looking at her through the reverse end of a telescope. She couldn't speak at all. The little girl too sat very still, a little recoiled from the body of her mother, as though expecting a blow. Her hands were clenched into fists, but finally it was she who broke the silence.

18 "What happened?" she said. "Don't you like it?"

19 "Listen," said the mother, "this is not your family. I, you and your father are dark-skinned, dark-haired. I don't have a blond wig hidden in my closet, my eyes are black, not blue, and your father's beard is black, not red, and you, do you have a white skin, a button nose with freckles, blue eyes and blond hair tied into a ponytail? You said you drew our family. This is not it, is it?"

20 The child was now feeling distinctly cornered. At first she was startled and frightened by her mother's response, but now she was prepared to be defiant. She had the greatest authority behind her, and she now summoned it to her help.

21 "I drew it from a book," she said, "all our books have this same picture of the family. You can go and see it for yourself. And everyone else drew it too. You can ask our teacher tomorrow. She liked it, so there!"

22 The little girl was clutching at her last straw.

23 "But you? Where are you in this picture?" demanded her mother, by now thoroughly aroused. "Where are we? Is this the family you would like to have? Don't you want us anymore? You want to be a *mem-sahib*, a white girl?"

24 But even as she lashed out these questions the mother regretted them. She could see that she made no sense to the child. She could feel the unfairness of it all. She was sorry that she was putting such a heavy burden on such young shoulders.

25 "First I bring her here," she thought, "and then I try to make her feel guilty for wanting to be the same as the others." But something had taken hold of her this evening. Panic at the thought of losing her child, despair and guilt galvanized her into speech she regretted, and she looked with anger at her only child, who it seemed wanted to be white, who had rejected her dark mother. Someday this child would be ashamed of her, she thought, someday would move out into the world of those others. Someday they would be enemies. Confusing thoughts ran through her head like images on an uncontrollable television screen, in the chaos of which she heard her **ultimate** justification flung at her by her daughter—they wanted me to draw the family, didn't they? "They" wanted "her" to draw "the family." The way her daughter pronounced the words "they" or "the family"

indicated that she knew what she was talking about. The simple pronoun "they" definitely stood for authority, for that uncontrollable yet organized world immediately outside, of which the school was the ultimate expression. It surrounded their own private space. "They" had power, "they" could crush little people like her anytime "they" wanted to, and in "their" world that was the picture of the family. Whether her mother liked it or not, whether she looked like the little girl in it or not, made not one jot of difference. That was, yes, that was the right picture. As these thoughts passed through her mind, her anger ebbed away. Abandoning her fury and distance, the mother bowed her head at the image of this family and burst into sobs.

26 "What will happen to you?" she said. "What did I do to you?"

27 She cried a great deal and said many **incoherent** things. The little girl was patient, quietly absorbing her mother's change of mood. She had a thoughtful look on her face, and bit her nails from time to time. She did not protest any more, but nor did she cry. After a while her mother took her to bed and tucked her in, and sat in the kitchen with the fearful vision of her daughter always outside of the window of the blond family, never the centre of her own life, always rejecting herself, and her life transformed into a gigantic peep show. She wept very bitterly because she had caused this destruction, and because she had hated her child in her own fear of rejection, and because she had sowed guilt into her mind.

28 When her mother went to bed and closed the door, the child, who had been waiting for long, left the bed. She crossed the corridor on her tiptoes, past the row of shoes, the silent gathering of the overcoats and the mirror with the wavy surface, and went into the washroom. Behind the door was another mirror, of full length, and clear. Deliberately and slowly the child took off the top of her pajamas and surveyed herself with grave scrutiny. She saw the brownness of her skin, the wide, staring, dark eyes, the black hair now tousled from the pillows, the scar on her nose and the brownish pink of her mouth. She stood a while lost in this act of contemplation, until the sound of soft padded feet neared the door, and a whiskered face peeped in. She stooped and picked up the cat and walked back to her own room.

[. . .]

29 It was snowing again, and little elves with bright coloured coats and snow in their boots had reappeared in the classroom. When finally the coats were hung under pegs with names and boots neatly stowed away, the little girl approached her teacher. She had her painting from the day before in her hand.

30 "I have brought it back," she said.

31 "Why?" asked her teacher, "don't you like it any more?"

32 The little girl was looking around very intently.

33 "It's not finished yet," she said. "The books I looked at didn't have something. Can I finish it now?"

34 "Go ahead," said the teacher, moving on to get the colours from the cupboard.

35 The little girl was looking at the classroom. It was full of children of all colours, of all kinds of shapes of noses and of different colours of hair. She sat on the floor, placed the incomplete picture on a big piece of newspaper and started to paint. She worked long at it—and with great concentration. Finally it was finished. She went back to her teacher.

36 "It's finished now," she said, "I drew the rest."

37 The teacher reached out for the picture and spread it neatly on a desk. There they were, the blond family arranged in a semicircle with a dip in the middle, but next to them, arranged alike, stood another group—a man, a woman, and a child, but they were dark-skinned, dark-haired, the woman wore clothes from her own country, and the little girl in the middle had a scar on her nose.

38 "Do you like it?"

39 "Who are they?" asked the teacher, though she should have known. But the little girl didn't mind answering this question one bit.

40 "It's the other family," she said.

Glossary

insubstantial: Not large in size or amount; weak.

contemplated: Looked at or considered in a calm, reflective manner.

ultimate: Last, final.

incoherent: Unable to speak intelligibly.

Comprehension Questions

1. Is there mutual respect between mother and daughter? Cite the evidence.
2. What was the immediate thing that upset the little girl's mother when she saw the first picture her daughter had drawn?
3. Of what does the author say the mother was afraid? Where is the evidence in the story of this?
4. How did the little girl resolve the issue?

Questions about Form

1. Is this an essay or a story? Explain.
2. Although this piece is told in third-person narration, is the narrator more knowledgeable about a particular character? Explain.

3. Does the author make effective use of transitions in this story? Give three examples of transitions.
4. How does the extensive usage of quotations affect the story?

Questions for Discussion

1. Because this piece is fictional, the thesis of the author is far from explicit. What do you think, in your own words, is the author's thesis? What evidence would you cite from the story in support of your answer?
2. How does the fear that the mother experiences in this story relate to the idea of young people dating people of other races and religions? How do problems in this area tend to get resolved?

Writing Ideas

1. How important are pictures and words when it comes to helping people develop strong self-esteem? Write a paragraph/essay supporting your answer.
2. As this story is about the conflict between the desire to fit in and the fear of losing one's identity, write a paragraph/essay in which you discuss a personal experience that relates to this story, and explain how your own situation was resolved.

✦ ✦ ✦

SELLING ILLUSIONS

Neil Bissoondath

Novelist, short story writer, and essayist Neil Bissoondath was born in Arima, Trinidad, in 1955, and now lives in Canada. The following piece is an excerpt from his book entitled *Selling Illusions: The Cult of Multiculturalism in Canada.* As this piece indicates, Bissoondath exhibits some strong feelings about multiculturalism in Canada and how it's not what perhaps it is purported to be. In the following piece, he relates his experience as an eighteen-year-old who has just come to Canada to attend York University.

1 If the York University campus was a safe haven from which to discover the pleasures of Canada, … it was also the place where I first encountered reasons for unease.

2 York operates on a college system. New students choose, or are assigned to, one of the various colleges on the campus. Unfamiliar with the system, ignorant

of the purposes behind the individual colleges, I allowed myself to be assigned to Bethune College.

3 Familiarity with the college brought a certain dismay. Bethune College, named in honour of **Dr. Norman Bethune**, is an institution devoted to Third World studies; it had a certain reputation for left-wing radicalism. The reason for my dismay was simple: my major was to be French language and literature. The bilingual Glendon College, my logical "home," was never mentioned. I can only assume that I was enrolled at Bethune in part because I had come from a Third World country and in part because my adviser assumed that I would be most comfortable in an environment where a high percentage of students were, like me, non-white. It was an assuredly benign assumption, one made with the best of intentions, but also with no regard to my personal beliefs or intellectual interests. My adviser, then, had looked at me through the lens of her own stereotype and guided me according to the presumed comforts of "sticking with your own."

4 Although I was not at first aware of it, the concept of "sticking with your own" was just then in vogue at York. This became clear the moment you entered the main cafeteria at Central Square in the massive concrete bunker of the Ross Building. It was large and brashly lit, institutional in character, a place for feeding oneself rather than enjoying a meal. I remember it as a loud and busy place, brash with the sounds of trays and cutlery roughly handled, of a multitude of voices blended into a steady roar.

5 And yet, it seemed a benign atmosphere, friendly in an impersonal way. The controlled chaos offered an anonymity that would ease the task of inserting oneself, of fitting in. Or so it seemed at first.

6 Chaos is always subtly ordered, and it did not require a very discerning eye to decode the chaos of the Central Square cafeteria. Indeed, a map could be drawn, various sections coloured in to denote defined areas. To highlight, for instance, the table at which Chinese students congregated behind a wall of Cantonese; or the tables over in the corner protected by the raucous enthusiasm of West Indian accents; or the table more subtly framed by **yarmulkes** and Star of David pendants.

7 To approach any of these tables was to intrude on a clannish exclusivity. It was to challenge the unofficially designated territory of tables parcelled out so that each group, whether racially, culturally or religiously defined, could enjoy its little enclave, its own little "homeland," so to speak, protected by unspoken **prerogatives.**

8 The idea of "sticking with your own" was reinforced by various student organizations, many of which were financially assisted by the university. Controversy arose at one point when an application for membership in the Black Students' Federation was received from a student—a writer for the campus newspaper, as it turned out—whose skin colour seemed to disqualify him. Questions arose: Was being black a prerequisite for belonging to the Black Students' Federation? Or was a commitment to the issues raised by the association suffi-

cient justification for belonging? Just how relevant was skin colour, how relevant cultural background, how relevant political belief?

9 A hint of the complexity of the question may be discerned in a story once told to me by a friend. One afternoon, he stopped in at his favourite coffee house in Toronto's Kensington Market, a small place brightly decorated in the tropical style. It featured reggae music and the rich Blue Mountain coffee from Jamaica. As he sipped his coffee, he eavesdropped on a conversation at the table behind him, three young men, evidently musicians, discussing their next gig. My friend understood little of what was said—their thick Jamaican accents made their words **undecipherable**—but he enjoyed listening to their speech in the same way that he enjoyed the sounds of reggae. Cup empty, he rose to leave. On his way out he glanced at the men and with delight saw, as he put it, "one black guy with dreadlocks and two white guys with blond hair and blue eyes." An encounter, then, with the wickedness of history. He left the coffee house thrilled at abandoning the wreckage of a stereotype.

10 The issue at York was eventually settled by the decision to admit the white student to the Federation—not on the grounds that race was irrelevant but that, as an organization financially assisted by the university, it had to respect the university's regulations prohibiting discrimination on the grounds of race and colour. I did not belong to the Federation, but the resolution was pleasing anyway, even though there was a tincture of discomfort at the way in which it had come about: through technicality, and not through the application of principle. None of the real questions had been grappled with, none answered.

11 Questions of segregation and **exclusivity** kept raising their heads. One day a Jewish friend invited me to join him for coffee in the Jewish Students' Federation lounge. I was reluctant—the lounge seemed to me governed by even stronger proscriptions than the table in the cafeteria—but he insisted. As he fixed us each a coffee, he said in a voice clearly intended for others in the room that I should feel free to help myself from the coffee-machine at any time. And then he added in strained tones that the lounge, provided by the university, was open to all: I was to ignore anyone who tried to stop me. It was in this way that he sought to make me part of unsuspected **internecine** tensions, while publicly declaring his own position.

12 The issues made me wary: I neither joined the Black Students' Federation nor revisited the Jewish Students' Federation lounge. I learned instead to keep my distance from the tables that would have welcomed me not as an individual but as an individual of a certain skin colour, with a certain accent, with a certain assumed cultural outlook—the tables that would have welcomed me not for *who* I was and for what I could do but for *what* I was and for what they presumed I represented. I had not come here, I decided, in order to join a ghetto.

13 Alone in a new land, I faced inevitable questions. Questions about my past and my present, about the land left behind and the land newly found, about the nature of this society and my place in it. At eighteen, about to embark on a new life, I felt these to be weighty issues.

14 For many people at those cafeteria tables, though, these were questions of no great importance. They were almost aggressive in dismissing any discomfort they might have experienced by flaunting the only government policy that seemed to arouse no resentment: Canada as a multicultural land. Officially. Legally. Here, they insisted, you did not have to change. Here you could—indeed, it was your duty to—remain what you were. None of this American melting-pot nonsense, none of this remaking yourself to fit your new circumstances: you did not have to adjust to the society, the society was obligated to accommodate itself to you.

15 An attractive proposal, then, a policy that excused much and required little effort. And yet I found myself not easily seduced.

16 The problem was that I had come in search of a new life and a new way of looking at the world, "to expand my horizons" (to use a cliché) from the narrow perspectives of my youth in Trinidad. I had no desire to transport here life as I had known it: this seemed to me particularly onerous baggage with which to burden one's shoulders. Beyond this, though, the very act of emigration had already changed me. I was no longer the same person who had boarded the aircraft in Trinidad bound for Toronto: I had brought with me not the attitudes of the tourist but those of someone embarking on an adventure that would forever change his life. This alone was a kind of psychological revolution.

17 Multiculturalism, as perceived by those at whom it was most explicitly aimed, left me with a certain measure of discomfort.

18 At the end of my first university year, I returned to Trinidad to visit my parents. It wasn't long before I was impatient to get back to Toronto. This had to do in part with the realization that, even after so short a time, old friends had become new strangers, and that old places had remained simply old places. More importantly, though, the desire to return had to do with me and with the life I had begun constructing in my adopted city. I relished the freedom this life offered, the liberation of the anonymity of the big city. I had made new friends—some of them from among "my own kind," some not—and had found all the books, magazines and films denied me in Trinidad. I had, for the first time in my life, found a place other than my parents' house that I wished to call home: a place where I could be myself.

19 Sharing this with those who wished me to bolster their ethnic bastion in Toronto made me distinctly unpopular. I was seen as a kind of traitor, unwilling to play the game by indulging in a life best described as "Caribbean North." If there was any **alienation**, it came not from the society at large but from those who saw themselves as the front-line practitioners of multiculturalism. By establishing cultural and racial exclusivity, they were doing their bit to preserve the multicultural character of the country, while I, seeking to go beyond the confines of my cultural heritage, was seen as acting counter to those interests.

20 To put it succinctly, they coveted the segregated tables of the cafeteria, while I sought a place at tables that would accommodate a greater variety.

Glossary

Dr. Norman Bethune: A Canadian surgeon and international humanitarian revered in China for his heroic and selfless treatment of the wounded in that country's struggle for a republic. He died of blood poisoning in 1939.

yarmulkes: Skullcaps worn always by male Orthodox Jews, and only during prayer and religious functions by others.

prerogatives: Exclusive rights or privileges.

undecipherable: Unable to be understood.

exclusivity: The act of shutting out.

internecine: Of or relating to a struggle within a nation, an organization, or a group.

alienation: Feeling estranged from one's social environment.

Comprehension Questions

1. What does Bissoondath mean by what he refers to as the "homeland" in paragraph 7? Why does he not want to join the "homelands"?
2. Why does Bissoondath think he was assigned to Bethune College?
3. What was really happening, according to Bissoondath, when his Jewish friend served him a coffee in the Jewish Students' Federation lounge?
4. What is the story told to Bissoondath by his friend who visited Toronto's Kensington Market? What is the meaning of it? How does it support Bissoondath's overall thesis?

Questions about Form

1. What does Bissoondath include in this piece that helps you to identify with his concerns?
2. What is the setting of Bissoondath's essay? Does this help to make the piece more effective? Why or why not?
3. What is the author doing in the last paragraph of this piece? Is it effective? Why or why not?

Questions for Discussion

1. Do "homelands," as Bissoondath would define them, exist at your school? What do you think are the reasons they exist there? Do they do more harm than good as Bissoondath suggests?
2. Do you generally "stick" with people "of your own kind"? From your own experience, what are the advantages and disadvantages of this behaviour of yours?

3. Are there clubs at your school that seem exclusive to people of a certain skin colour, religion, or nationality? Would they refuse to accept a student who wanted to join if this student didn't seem to "belong"? Is this a violation of human rights law?
4. Judging only by this essay, what would you say is the author's attitude toward multiculturalism in this country? Do you agree with it? Why or why not?
5. Do you think Canadians in general are less racist than Americans? Why or why not? What in this article by Bissoondath supports your answer?

Writing Ideas

1. In a paragraph/essay, argue whether you think multiculturalism, the way it is promoted at your school, contributes to or combats racism.
2. In a paragraph/essay, argue whether or not a club should be able to offer exclusivity to people of only one skin colour, or one nationality or religion, etc.
3. Imagine you are creating your own college/university cultural club. In view of Bissoondath's concerns, what would the basic guidelines regarding membership of your new club be? Support them in a paragraph/essay.
4. Identify a club or society that seems to be exclusive to your race, religion, or nationality. Write a paragraph/essay supporting or criticizing this perception of exclusivity.

✦ ✦ ✦

THE THIRTEENTH MUFFIN

Rachel Manley

Rachel Manley is a writer who lives in both Jamaica and Toronto. She is also the daughter of Michael Manley, former prime minister of Jamaica. This piece was taken from a keynote address Rachel gave at a faculty dinner at Centennial College in Toronto in 2002. Speaking to an audience of mostly college faculty, and reflecting on the professions of both the writer and the teacher, Manley distinguishes between excellence and success saying the latter should not be the measure of the former. She speaks mainly of her grandfather to illustrate the point.

1 Norman Manley was the most influential teacher in my life. And you probably think by the drum roll with which I introduce his name, that his own life was a huge success. He is now a National Hero and is respectfully honored by his nation. But the irony of his life is that for the most part, it is remembered for

its failures. He was a champion athlete who never made it to the Olympics because of the Great War. He was probably the finest advocate the West Indies ever produced, but he died virtually a pauper. He honed a two-year Caribbean political federation that was disbanded when he made the fatal error of calling a referendum in Jamaica on the issue of regional integration and lost, defeated by the adult **suffrage** for which he'd fought. He was the major force behind Jamaica's independence and wrote the country's new constitution, but he lost the campaign that would have elected him Jamaica's first Prime Minister.

2 And yet he is remembered for his honesty and, yes, his excellence. For he gave each of those things, in turn, his full **integrity** and his whole heart. He was respectful of human endeavor and did honour to everything he touched.

3 "Success is only braata," he would say to me. "Braata" is a Jamaican word for unexpected extras ... like the 13th muffin in the baker's dozen—a notion strange to us today when heroes seem to represent stardom and wealth over the less glamourous ventures of hard work, public service and integrity, the grueling tiny footsteps of true excellence.

4 And I mention these things because I feel too often we measure this very concept of excellence only by the notion of success.

5 When I was invited to address your distinguished institution for this occasion, I noticed that it features two awards, one for achievement and the other for excellence. I began to ponder these two concepts—Achievement and Excellence—concepts that sometimes go hand in hand, and sometimes do not. And I thought of the importance of coming to terms with the fact that endeavour may be in itself worthy of the description of excellence even if it fails to reach its target of some longed-for goal, or fails to end in a predetermined point of identifiable success. Not all ambitions are realized, not all battles are won. We are not all headed for Everest; it couldn't hold us all. Not all of us are born to be in the bright lights ... to be modern heroes and stars. I think young people need to know that doing their best, is in itself proof of excellence.

6 Allow me to turn to my own field of endeavour ... writing ... with which I am familiar. Like most things we pursue, its **genesis** is buried in our childhood and nurtured by the role models and teachers who were there for us along the way. I grew up with my paternal grandparents. Most Jamaicans may remember Norman Manley as the father of Jamaican independence, but to me he was just a beloved old man I called Pardi. My grandmother Mardi was a sculptress who was always teaching and encouraging young people and artists to create Jamaican themes and not imitate colonial English ones. And if there were two themes that best express their lives, it would be reflected in two pieces of advice they gave me, which it has taken me my lifetime to understand.

7 My grandfather told me that the least interesting premise on which to base a life is oneself.

8 My grandmother startled me by saying, "The point of life is to earn one's death."

9 About my writing, they had more advice: As I'd struggle with my poems, my grandmother who was very dramatic would wave her arms inspirationally around her head and say to me "Imagine…"

10 My grandfather, on the other hand, would point at the piece of paper and advise me: "Edit."

11 These two words, "imagine" and "edit" became like a **mantra** … and I spent my youth hopping along in the Left Right march of imagine and edit as though one foot were round and the other sharp as a knife. Left, Right, Imagine and Edit.

12 I would discover beyond my writing that their advice was complementary as they themselves were to each other, and necessary to most quests in life.

13 But back to the question of how we measure achievement. I offer you what is, I hope, a humorous example of what I mean within my field.

14 A writer friend of mine tells me this story, in the first person, and as a fellow writer, I gave him the benefit of the doubt that all he says is true. He is, after all, a writer. This is what he says:

> 15 I just died, and I'm on my way to the other place. But before I get to wherever it is I'm destined for, I meet St. Peter, who will give me the grand tour—he'll be my guide. He greets me and asks me what did I do in life. "I was a writer," I tell him.
>
> 16 So we arrive at the Gates of Hell. There are several doors. He opens one a crack, and I peer in. There are thousands of people there. Men and women are hunched over writing tables, with quills and parchment and inkwells. Others are staring at blank pieces of paper tucked into ancient typewriters. There are others, agonizing at blank computer screens. Their faces are contorted in pain. Some are tearing at their hair. Others are pacing up and down, howling with frustration. Their discomfort is seeping out of them. I ask him what is this place. And St. Peter says this is the place in Hell where writers dwell. "Seen enough?" he asks. I say, "Yes. Please show me the other place."
>
> 17 We are whisked up, up and up. There's another door. And St. Peter lets me peep.
>
> 18 And there, too, are thousands of people, men and women, hunched over parchment, quills in hand, others staring blankly at a page tucked into old Olivetti's or Remington's, others staring at blank computer screens…all in the throes of some private agony; faces contorted with pain; tears streaming down their cheeks, hands tearing at their hair. It's a scene of pain and desolation. I ask St. Peter, "Who are these people?" " These are writers," he says.
>
> 19 "But St. Peter," I say, "You showed me writers in Hell, and now you're showing me writers in Heaven. But it looks the same to me. What's the difference?"
>
> 20 "Ah," says St. Peter, " In Heaven, writers get published."

21 I think we're all familiar with this feeling in any profession, in any endeavour on any subject, as teachers, as artists, as students. As I speak about this from my point of view as a writer…the difference is between writing for the drawer, and

writing to be published. It is the difference between anonymity and recognition, but it is NOT the test of our worth, and it is not the measure of excellence.

22 As writers, we want other people to hear our stories, to share our experience, to enter and live, to know and understand our world; we need that recognition to provide us with the exposure. We need the sales to earn a living. But our achievement is not in winning awards but in writing books that bring characters and places and situations to life. Awards are only recognition of the thousands of hours of exacting work, some of it creative explosion and some tedious repetitive fiddling—the "Imagine" and "Edit"—we have put in.

23 I am not going to presume to lecture here about writing...to talk about what is good writing and what is not. What I'd like to do is to share with you some of my views on the process of writing as I see it, as it reflects the process of all work, to share with you my own writer's Hell and my own writer's Heaven.

24 I think I've always written, as far back as I remember. But for a long time, I hesitated to call myself a writer. I thought it such a presumption, especially with a father who published eight books, and a grandmother who was an extraordinary artist and herself edited the writers of Jamaica's green time of national and cultural emergence! But at least I came from a family who thought writing worthwhile. As some of you may be aware, too often such a claim would receive rebuke...you were a slacker, that you should do something sensible with your life, that writing can't earn a living.

25 Here's another story which an old friend of mine never tires of telling, which may illustrate the point.

> 26 Arriving in Heathrow Airport one day, W.H. Auden put "poet" under Employment on the Immigration form. The stern no-nonsense immigration officer crossed it out and wrote instead: Unemployed.

27 That's the thing ... to claim to be a writer, you were either somehow disreputable, or blasphemous. In the Caribbean, the immigration officer would be more likely to suck his or her teeth and mutter, "Who do you think you are? Shakespeare?" To claim to be a writer was to be like **Icarus**: to fly perilously close to the realm and enterprise of God.

28 Why do we write? Why do we slave away over prose or over poetry? Why do you teach? After university, I actually taught for two years, and I believe teaching is a calling not unlike writing. In most cases, it will not make you rich, and it will not make your endeavours famous, but like a pebble that drops silently in the pond, the widening ripples of its influence may affect a lot of lives and hopefully for the better.

29 I suspect each of us here tonight would give a somewhat different answer to that question; but at root, it would be the same answer: We write or we teach because we have no choice. It is inevitable. We have to. It is our quest. It is a calling.

30 Otherwise, our lives and world would make no sense to us, and the need to share this is the inconsolable engine that drives the artist and the teacher.

31 But I have grave misgivings about the modern concepts of success...the modern tendency to make success a **prerequisite** of excellence. Where I grew up, every child who struggled with a ball of rag and twine hoping one day to make the West Indies cricket team, whether he made it or not, had achieved a feat...as was the case with every young Jamaican Donovan Bailey running along muddy pot-holed paths, training in underequipped gyms. Consider this...that the Michael Jordans and the Patrick Ewings are not to be respected as much as their dazzling performances frozen mid-air featured on ads on television, as for their gradual, strenuous climb from poverty or inexperience to where they are today, and the measure of them as men has more to do with how they got where they are, and the extraordinary people who helped and taught them along the way, and once they got there, what they did with their talent and with their success... Think of the unbelievably challenging road traveled by Daniel Igali as a refugee from Nigeria to becoming Canada's gold medallist in the Olympics.

32 I believe that this is more the test of excellence than the dazzling glamour of their stardom.

33 And that, ultimately, the reward of perpetually striving for excellence is a life wholeheartedly lived; a life without deadness, without patches of grey boredom or unmeaning, but a life in which you use yourself to the fullest, use yourself "up" and so earn the honoured right to die when your time comes. Norman Manley earned his death. That to me is both the meaning and inestimable value of my grandfather's life, and it is the reason why I told you about it.

34 And for the young who are here tonight embarking on your own journeys, I recommend such a life to you.

Glossary

suffrage: The right to vote.

integrity: High principle; completeness.

genesis: Creation or beginning.

mantra: A word or phrase chanted inwardly in meditation.

Icarus: A character in Greek mythology who was warned by his father Daedalus not to fly too close to the sun. Icarus disobeyed his father and plunged to his death.

prerequisite: A requirement that must be satisfied in advance.

Comprehension Questions

1. Which is more important, according to Manley: excellence or success? Why?
2. What does the Jamaican word "braata" mean?
3. What does "the thirteenth muffin" represent or symbolize?

Questions about Form

1. This piece was originally written for the purposes of a speech for an audience of mainly college faculty. Why, however, is this piece likely to have a much wider appeal?
2. Manley tells two stories within her speech. Do they contribute to the effectiveness of her message? Why or why not?
3. Manley seems to talk quite a bit about her grandparents. In fact, "Norman Manley" are the very first two words of the piece. Why do you think her grandparents, and not her father Michael Manley, former prime minister of Jamaica, are so prominent here?

Questions for Discussion

1. What is the lesson of the story about the writers in Heaven and Hell?
2. Manley's grandmother taught her "the point of life is to earn one's death." What does this mean? And why does she recommend this kind of life to everyone at the end of her speech?
3. In paragraph 27, Manley makes a reference to "Icarus." How does this reference illustrate the overall point she's making in her essay?

Writing Ideas

1. What is Manley's thesis? Why is this thesis an especially important one to hear in North America today? Write a paragraph/essay answering these questions.
2. Write a paragraph/essay on a personal experience (yours or one of someone close to you) that exemplifies Manley's thesis.

✦ ✦ ✦

Lessons of Love from Stories of Old

Gary Lipschutz

Ideas we have about love are often harmful. According to Gary Lipschutz, we get some of these ideas from the misinterpretations of stories—stories we've known and embraced since childhood. The stories themselves might have a great deal of wisdom to offer, but, unfortunately, these stories often are misinterpreted by a society that is generally lazy and materialistic. And the result is damage in our lives around the whole issue of love. In this essay, Lipschutz, who teaches mythology and English composition at Centennial College in Toronto, not only blames "external sources" (religious organizations, businesses, the media, etc.) for this damage, but also those among us who would listen to them. Most tragic, he says, is that these misinterpretations too often defy what is in our own hearts.

1 Why is it that the very thing so many people want so badly is the one thing they never seem to find? Why is it that people, young and old, spend so much time on chat lines, so much money on dating services and so much energy obsessing over the "perfect" love and/or marriage? Why is it that the success rate of getting these things is pretty low?

2 Well, did it ever occur to you that our ideas about love are often unrealistic? We may get some of them from movies, from TV sitcoms, and worse, I dare say, from so-called reality TV shows such as *The Bachelor* or *Joe Millionaire* (a title that, in itself, suggests less-than-virtuous values). How often do we ask why the media seem to sell the idea that fashion, sex appeal and money are the most important parts of any relationship?

3 One reason for these false and damaging ideas is **commercialism.** Large businesses spend inordinate amounts of money on research into the human psyche. They know that "sex sells." They know that in their appeal to the sexual urges of a person, especially the person within a certain age range, they are more likely to exert influence over the consumer's buying choices. But is there an adverse if **inadvertent** effect as well? Do these ads in any way cause us to go after certain things in relationships that are inaccessible, things that have absolutely nothing to do with love and therefore things that do not contribute to the staying power of a relationship?

4 Advertisements and "reality" TV shows are not the only things brainwashing us. We've all grown up with certain stories: stories from religious scripture, fairy tales such as "Sleeping Beauty" and "Cinderella" and Shakespearean plays such as *Romeo and Juliet.* Most of us are familiar with the latest cinematic rendition of *Titanic,* especially the love story in it that took place between Jack and Rose.

5 Why are such stories so predominant in our lives? They help to maintain our hopes and dreams when it comes to the very thing we want the most: love, no, the perfect love. But the problem is they probably cause more harm than good, even if the intentions of those who make them up are honourable. The problem is not

the stories themselves. The problem lies in the interpretation of these stories. Let's look at a classic example of misinterpretation of the story "Sleeping Beauty."

6 Everyone knows more or less what happens in "Sleeping Beauty," regardless of the version to which one was exposed. *A king and queen give birth to a daughter after many years of trying. Upon the girl's birth, the king is so overjoyed, he decides to hold a great feast to which he invites many people. There are 13 wise women in his kingdom, but the king only invites 12 because he had only 12 golden plates from which they could eat. To get revenge for not being invited, the thirteenth "wise" (and scornful) woman arrives at the feast and cries out, "In her fifteenth year, the princess shall prick herself with a spindle and fall down dead!"*

7 *By the time this thirteenth wise woman had cursed the princess, 11 wise women who were invited had given gifts to the princess, but the twelfth had not yet spoken. Although she could not undo the evil spell, she could, however, soften it with a wish: "The princess shall not die," she said. "Instead, she shall fall into a deep sleep for one hundred years."*

8 Of course, it's the following part, more than any other, for which the whole story is known and loved:

9 *After the princess's 100-year slumber was over, a prince approaches the sleeping beauty and kisses her lips. She awakens, smiles at him fondly, and they, of course, marry each other and live happily ever after.*

10 Before discussing the interpretation of "Sleeping Beauty," it's first necessary to note the difference between an interpretation that is literal and one that is symbolic. Understanding the difference may result in a very different way of understanding not only "Sleeping Beauty" but also most other stories regardless of their source.

11 People who take things **literally** take what is spoken or written at face value. Even when it comes to religious scripture, Joseph Campbell, world-renowned mythologist, says that most of us belong to two schools of thought: in one school, there are those who believe the stories of religious scripture are true because they're believers of the miraculous; yes, Moses parted the Red Sea with his hands, or yes, Jesus raised Lazarus from the dead simply because the (Judaeo-Christian) Bible says so. And in the second school of thought, there are those who do not believe in these types of miracles simply because they are unrealistic. In other words, the difference as to whether people "believe" in scripture or not seems to depend on what they believe has literally happened two or three thousand years ago. Whether they believe in miracles or not, most people take these stories literally.

12 What if a third situation were possible? Those who study mythology may realize that myth (including religious stories) is not meant to be interpreted literally, but symbolically. In other words, things that are spoken or written might be meant to represent ideas, usually relating to some aspect of our humanity, that are otherwise difficult to understand. In fact, originally, the word *myth* did not mean "falsehood" the way it does today. The word *myth* referred to (and still does for those who are educated in the area) a story about the divine mysteries of life, thus the letters "MY..." suggesting MYstery or **MYstical.** In this context, the body of mythology is not just about Greek gods and Celtic wizards, but also heroes such as Moses of the Old Testament and Jesus of the New and, by extension, ALL of the characters of stories in every religion of the world, bar none. All such stories shed light on the mystery of humanity. They all include characters of the divine. Symbolically speaking, it could be argued that Moses represents every person in the world who eventually gets called by a higher power to do something heroic and can succeed against insurmountable odds if the holy deed is faced with a great deal of courage and conviction. Did Moses actually part the Red Sea? Only those who are literalists care, not to mention those who are bent on insisting their religion is superior to all others. The difference between "our" truth and "their" truth is what unfortunately causes **acrimony** among the religions of the world. Many present-day wars are testimony to this unfortunate side of our human nature.

13 What if the messages of these divine stories, regardless of whether we relegate them to myth, religion or fairy tales, are the same? Undeniably, regardless of interpretation, they all seem to have certain messages in common: Arrogance and selfishness are bad. Humility and sacrifice are good. Treat your neighbour as

yourself. (And don't forget, your neighbour might be of a different skin colour or religious background or social class—a detail that too often gets lost in people's interpretations, sometimes for evil reasons.) Be fair and kind to people. Don't kill people (unless you are 100 per cent sure your killing them is in self-defence). Don't lie because, as psychiatrist and prolific author M. Scott Peck (famous for his book called *The Road Less Traveled*) says in his book *People of the Lie*, the lie is the very root of human evil. Judge a person by her or his character and not on the basis of how much money he makes or how intelligent he is or how beautiful she is on the outside. And one's character, to quote the wizard in *Harry Potter and the Chamber of Secrets*, is determined not by a person's abilities but by her or his choices. Wouldn't the world be a better place if we all recognized that all these stories are telling us not only the same things, but that the important things in life are things universal to human consciousness? Doesn't it make more sense to concentrate on our similarities rather than our differences? Is religion meant to unite or divide us? Is the answer not obvious?

14 And what about Sleeping Beauty's never-ending naptime? Bruno Bettelheim, famous child psychologist and psychological interpreter of children's literature, said that what's important among other things is what Sleeping Beauty's 100-year slumber symbolizes or represents. Why, for that matter, is the 100-year sleep important at all? Literally speaking, nobody sleeps for 100 years. Then this part of the story has no meaning, right? Wrong! It has a world of meaning if it's interpreted symbolically. A cigar, symbolically speaking, is never a cigar. The 100-year sleep, it could be argued, should be the focal point of the story. The title, after all, is "*Sleeping* Beauty."

15 A more prevalent reason for ignoring the significance of the centennial snooze is that it seems to have nothing to do with the message of this story that most people desperately want to cling to: that a woman must be rescued by a man. (The first time I shot down the "rescuing" message of "Sleeping Beauty" in a class I was teaching, a young female student stormed out of the room in angry protest and promptly proceeded to drop my course.) Too many of us think, or at least hope, the rescuing part is realistic because we're basically selfish (or chauvinistic if we're male) and lazy. Too many women want to be "rescued," and too many men think they have to do the "rescuing." And that, to too many men, means making lots of money and perhaps getting a hair transplant or wearing thousand-dollar suits because if you don't look like a prince and you don't own a white horse (in modern-day terms, an expensive car and/or a condo), Sleeping Beauty won't even look at you, much less ride off with you into the sunset.

16 If the wedding of Prince Charles and Princess Diana seemed like a "fairy tale," their lives together certainly did not. Why did Sleeping Beauty and her prince get to ride off into the sunset, while Princess Diana and her lover (a lover other than her dashing prince) died a violent death? Why did a life for the world's favourite royal start out as a fairy tale and end up in a fiery and fatal car crash? Wasn't Diana meant to be "rescued" by her charming (not to mention, rich) prince?

17 If Sleeping Beauty doesn't look at you because you don't dress fashionably or you don't have a full head of hair or you don't have a nice car and condo, she's not worth your time because these things have absolutely nothing to do with love. She may be attracted to you for your sense of style, your hair, or your money, and she may feel like she's being "saved" from poverty, or her parents, or both, but she will only stay with you until she finds a richer or better looking prince or until you lose your money or, better yet, until you leave her first when you finally realize what your "princess's values" really are.

18 The 100-year slumber, according to Bettelheim, represents a stage in a person's life (not just a female's) during which she must develop her own mind away from her parents and away from her friends. Call it mental and emotional downtime or a physical or inner journey to "find oneself," an accounting of the soul, whatever you wish. The point is, too often young people make the biggest mistakes in their lives because they don't listen to an inner voice. It's much easier to "take the path of least resistance" and do what your parents tell you in order to make them happy. It's easier to follow your friends' advice; after all, they have your best interests in mind, right? Actually they probably don't, even if they don't realize it themselves. Thomas Hobbes, a 17th-century social theorist, said that people are basically selfish. And chances are we haven't gotten less selfish in the last 400 years. If anything, with more affluence in our lives, with the Internet and other types of "instantly gratifying technology" at our fingertips, we're more selfish than ever. So when we tell our friends what they should do, we're actually telling them what WE want them to do. If we were real friends, we'd try to find out what they want and then support them unconditionally.

19 When Sleeping Beauty wakes up from her 100-year slumber, she's grown. She hasn't grown old physically, of course. If she had, Prince Charming would not be kissing her, right? But how else has she grown? Having spent the time BY herself, she's learned ABOUT herself. She's "slept," which might symbolize she's spent time understanding her **unconscious**, the voice inside, the voice we tend to hear when we turn off the cell phone, the TV and the computer—the noise and chatter we hear every day. Technology makes it even more difficult than ever before to shut out the noise. For this reason, the message of the 100-year sleep in "Sleeping Beauty" becomes more relevant today than ever. We all desperately need this downtime, this distance from the noise, if we're ever going to know what our own hearts are saying. There are two problems, as I see it. First, we don't take the time or make the effort to challenge our assumptions of the interpretations of most stories, especially ones with which we've grown up. Second, even if we did, and even if people did understand what Bettelheim was trying to say, shutting out the noise of our cell phones, the TV and our computers would still be too difficult, the usual excuse made by spiritually lazy and unawakened people.

20 "Sleeping Beauty," simply put, is not about a princess being "rescued" by a prince; it's about the importance of a **spiritual awakening**. After all, the story is called "Sleeping Beauty" (becoming beautiful from self-knowledge), not "The Poor Girl Who Turns into a Princess Because She Gets Rescued by a Rich Man." Don't forget Diana wasn't even poor to begin with. And secondly, if she were "rescued," one would think she'd live to see forty.

21 When Sleeping Beauty awoke, having learned who she was and what she really wants, she was then, and only then, able to *recognize* the right man for her. The prince doesn't rescue her; she saves her own soul by choosing the man she is meant to be with because she now knows who that man is, and she has the courage to go after him regardless of what her friends or family might say or do. To her, this right man *becomes* her prince. This prince will look handsome and rich not because he's got model-good looks and drives a Jaguar or BMW but because to her, the princess who now knows what's right for herself, the man whom she has recognized as the right one LOOKS handsome, and he SEEMS rich, but in non-material ways. That, after all, is the story of *Titanic.* Rose saved her own soul when she dumped the rich, handsome fiancé (the one her mother wanted her to marry) and made the commitment to love a penniless man whom she had just met. She *knew* he was her soulmate. Nobody else could tell her this, certainly not her mother. Those who take the time to learn about themselves and follow their own hearts once they realize what their hearts are saying ... it is they who have grown up. It is they who have lived their own authentic lives. It is they who are rich.

Glossary

commercialism: Emphasis on financial profit as a measure of worth.

inadvertent: Unintentional.

literally: Taking what is spoken or written at face value, without symbolic interpretation.

mystical: Of spiritual truth beyond human understanding.

acrimony: Bitter disagreement, hostility.

unconscious: Part of the mind of which we are unaware, but which is largely responsible for our emotions, behaviour, etc.

spiritual awakening: New awareness of the importance of soul as opposed to physical things.

Comprehension Questions

1. What ideas, according to the author, do most people have about love?
2. What causes people to have these ideas?
3. How do most people interpret "Sleeping Beauty"?
4. What is different about Bruno Bettelheim's interpretation of "Sleeping Beauty"?
5. Why did the author's student walk out of his class in anger?
6. What does the author mean by the last sentence in the essay: "It is they who are rich"?

Questions about Form

1. What does the author do to make this essay effective?
2. What are the intended audience and purpose of this essay?
3. Why do you think the author mentions the movie *Titanic*?
4. Why are paragraphs 6, 7, and 9 largely in italics?

Questions for Discussion

1. What is the more believable fairy tale in our society, "Sleeping Beauty" or "Beauty and the Beast"? Why?
2. What is your definition of the perfect love?
3. Where do you think your idea (in your answer to question 2) of this definition comes from?
4. Do you think the perfect love according to your definition exists?
5. Compare this essay to "Don Juan/Doña Juana" by Rosemary Sullivan. What do they have in common? How do they differ?
6. Woody Allen, a very controversial film director/actor on the celebrity love scene (because of his marriage to the adopted daughter of his former partner, Mia Farrow), once interviewed a seemingly happy couple on the street in one of his movies. He asked to what they attributed their happiness as a couple. The male of the couple responded that they were both superficial: they both loved talking about fashion and other materialistic interests that they had in common. Do you think Woody Allen is saying these two people are likely to stay happy as a couple? Do you agree with him? Why or why not?

Writing Ideas

1. In a paragraph/essay, explain where people get their ideas of love.
2. In a paragraph/essay, identify the story that you believe best illustrates your ideas about love, and explain why.
3. What are the most important things in a relationship? What often attracts us first to the one we want to date? Why do the answers to these questions often cause trouble later on? Based on your answers to the above questions, write a paragraph/essay in which you discuss the reasons why many relationships break down.

✦ ✦ ✦

BAD GIRLS

Shari Graydon

Shari Graydon is a writer, educator, and media analyst living in Vancouver. She's been the press secretary for former B.C. premier Ujjal Dosanjh, and she's been the president of MediaWatch, a non-profit women's group that monitors the media for sexist content. For the *Vancouver Sun*, she's been a columnist, and for WTN, she's produced a 13-part TV series about women and media. In this piece from *Homemaker's* magazine (1999), Graydon interviews one of the murderers of Reena Virk, a B.C. teen violently murdered by a group of her classmates.

1 Dressed in a baggy T-shirt, cotton pants and runners, her long, wavy hair gelled and falling around her shoulders, she looks like an ordinary teenager. The stories she tells me about being spoiled as a child, rebelling as a young teen against her mom and hanging out at the mall with her friends sound like pretty common teenage experiences. Yet she spent her "Sweet 16" birthday behind bars, locked up in one of British Columbia's closed custody units for youth. "Janice" (the Young Offenders Act prohibits publication of her real name) is in jail for her part in the brutal murder of 14-year-old Reena Virk in November, 1997, an event that stunned the nation and prompted "Bad Girl" headlines coast to coast. About life in the detention centre, she says, "It's not so bad; I already knew lots of the kids."

2 The vicious attack leading to Virk's murder by a group of teenagers in a middle-class suburb of Victoria wasn't the first such incident to make headlines. In recent years stories of teen violence—usually involving testosterone-pumped boys carried away by their own misplaced **machismo**—have disturbed us all.

3 What made Reena Virk's case so shocking was that seven out of eight of the kids who participated in butting out a cigarette on her forehead, and punching and kicking her until she was dazed and bleeding, were girls. And one of them is alleged to have returned to the scene of the initial attack with a male friend, battered Virk unconscious and thrown her in the river, where she drowned, her body discovered a week later.

4 In the wake of **burgeoning** news reports about girl-to-girl violence, the case **galvanized** growing concerns across the country about just what young women are up to these days. The answer appears to be "No good." Statistics Canada reported in July that while the overall crime rate fell for the sixth consecutive year, it escalated among teenage girls by five per cent. The big picture seems to be even more alarming: from 1987 to 1997 the number of young women charged with violent crime grew from about 900 to 4,800, a staggering five-fold increase and twice that of same-aged boys.

5 Despite these figures and sensational Bad Girl headlines, the jury's still out on how widespread the problem is. For one thing, the actual numbers are relatively small: 1997's five per cent increase brought the rate to 472 offences per 100,000 population. That compares with 1,328 per 100,000 among male offenders,

which represents a four per cent drop from the previous year. For another, two-thirds of those charges were for minor assault, involving hitting or shoving that didn't result in bodily harm. The aggravated assault charges laid against the girls who attacked Reena Virk represented less than one per cent of the violent offence charges in that year.

6 Experts also point out that the numbers have risen because more charges are being laid. Alan Markwart, director of the Youth Justice team with the B.C. Ministry for Children and Families, attributes this in part to the "zero tolerance" policies now popular in schools struggling to deal with student violence. "Cases formerly dealt with by school principals are now more likely to result in legal charges," he says. He also speculates that police may be less inclined today to dismiss physical aggression between two girls as merely a "cat fight." Instead, they've begun to apply to girls the same standards used to determine the seriousness of crimes committed by boys.

7 **Mitigating** factors notwithstanding, criminologists and youth workers say that teenage girls are much more likely these days to express their anger over trivial things—and in increasingly physical ways. Once-persistent "sugar and spice" cultural stereotypes are dying hard as researchers point to evidence showing that girls have always felt just as much anger as boys; they've just been encouraged to channel their aggression into more socially acceptable "feminine" behaviors—like gossiping, name-calling and excluding the kids they want to punish. That girls are now expressing their anger physically is largely a sign of the times, attributable to the growing acceptance of violence in the teenage subculture. Studies have shown that exposure to violence can lead to increased violent behavior on the part of girls, desensitizing them to the point where they no longer feel emotional distress.

8 But the attack on Reena Virk was so frenzied—the girl's skull was fractured, her back broken—the issue takes on confounding proportions. How can young girls be capable of such shocking cruelty? What's going on in their heads?

9 Prying answers out of Janice isn't easy. Throughout our conversation, she is distracted by the comings and goings of people on the other side of the Plexiglas wall. At one point she interrupts herself to declare with pride, "That was my boyfriend who just walked by."

10 When I ask her about the night that Reena Virk died, I can tell that she doesn't really want to think—let alone talk—about what happened. But she does tell me that the source of the conflict was her belief that Virk had spread rumors about her and messed around with her boyfriend.

11 She says that the testimony and news stories describing her and a friend as "luring" Reena Virk to the site of a planned attack were false. "Fights happen every day," she says. "It just got out of hand."

12 Judging by the experiences of Stacey and Camille (pseudonyms), two Vancouver-area girls who have been on both the delivery and receiving ends of teen violence, the circumstances leading to Reena Virk's death were chillingly common. Rumors, jealousy, competition over boyfriends, they say, are the issues

most likely to ignite a fight among teenage girls. As to why more and more of those fights seem to be escalating into physical aggression, Stacey says: "You want to look big in front of your friends, to have a 'Don't mess with me' attitude. And if someone goes after you, you can't just sit there and take it."

13 Dr. Sibylle Artz, director of the School of Child and Youth Care at the University of Victoria, has authored one of the few studies of violence among teenage girls. Her book, *Sex, Power and the Violent School Girl* (Trifolium Books, 1998), provides insights into the profile of the "typical" violent teenage girl.

14 Violent girls often emerge from home lives in which they've been physically, sexually and/or emotionally abused, experienced significant alienation from at least one parent and observed chronic drug or alcohol misuse.

15 Not surprisingly, staying focused in school and fitting in generally are often a challenge for these kids, who quickly gravitate towards other teenagers with similar backgrounds. The subculture that develops reflects the same kinds of conflict and substance abuse that they see at home. And belonging to the rebel group becomes a desperate survival issue.

16 As Camille sees it, "If you're not getting attention at home, your friends—and belonging—are really important. You basically do whatever's necessary to get talked about"—including violence—"because attention, even if it's negative, is better than nothing."

17 This sounds perverse to most adults—and indeed, to most teenagers. But for the kids involved, says Shawn McNabb, a Youth Services worker in Burnaby, B.C., "Social interaction built around a constant battle for dominance is often consistent with what they experience at home."

18 The rites of passage required for acceptance into the tough crowd still include the traditional sources of peer pressure: smoking, drinking, taking drugs. Stacey explains that these are now accompanied by the expectation that girls, like boys, will demonstrate their worth in the gang by "beating up someone who has called you down." The ethic of revenge is often accompanied by the assumption that the victims "deserve" their treatment. Camille describes the **coveted** male attention won by "defending your rep" with fists and feet: "You get talked about and you get respect."

19 Some experts have suggested that girls are becoming more violent because they want to be more like boys, leading to speculation that feminism factors into the issue. By encouraging young women to seize power and go after what they want, the theory goes, we've created a monster—transforming girls into aggressive, insensitive takers.

20 Reality tells a different story. Youth workers say that girls who use violence as a means of resolving conflict typically have much more emotional investment in the traditional female goals of getting married and having a family than pursuing independence and a career. They are also more prone to seek validation through men than compete with them. The **icons** of popular culture—from the bikini-clad "warrior babes" to the ubiquitous Spice Girls—reinforce this notion.

Although lip service is paid to female power, the images of women predominating in the media send overwhelmingly sexist and **misogynist** messages, says Dr. Artz, teaching that "females are inferior to males and, in the last analysis, sexual objects."

21 Dr. Artz believes that understanding this dynamic is crucial to resolving violence among teenage girls. "The extent to which girls from troubled homes buy into messages about women's inferiority and see status as something to be gained through male attention supports their inclination to judge each other harshly."

22 Most experts agree that solutions do not include tightening up the Young Offenders Act. "The research is pretty clear," says Alan Markwart: "Get-tough approaches won't solve youth crime." Instead, training and education are paramount. Markwart stresses the importance of identifying kids in troubled homes at a young age. Then, he says, "there are two components: strong support for and training of parents, and enhanced early education to encourage kids' success in school."

23 Violence-prevention programs in the schools are useful too, says Dr. Artz, as long as they're geared to those they're intended to help. An antiviolence initiative she and project partner Dr. Ted Riecken, acting associate dean of education at the University of Victoria, introduced into B.C.'s Sooke school district underscores the need for gender-specific training programs.

24 This particular program, whose initiatives range from installing playground equipment to "bully-proofing" courses involving role-playing, was prompted by a University of Victoria 1993 survey of 1,500 grade 8 to 10 students, which revealed that 51 per cent of boys and 21 per cent of girls had admitted to beating up another person in the previous year. A sampling of the same age group taken last spring, five years into the project, showed a decrease in physical aggression of over 20 per cent among males and of 50 per cent among females. "Girls are clearly more ready to respond to this type of program," says Dr. Artz. Adds Dr. Riecken, "Girls respond to programs that focus on social skills training and desire to build positive relationships."

25 Angst among teenage girls is often provoked by the difficulty in forming trusting relationships with peers. When this is compounded by parental neglect and feelings of worthlessness—especially in the context of society's profoundly contradictory messages about female power, the importance of male attention and acceptable sexual behavior for women—the situation is ripe for violent behavior.

26 Violence begets violence. It also creates victims, who could be our daughters. If the price Reena Virk paid with her life has any meaning at all, it has at least sounded a wake-up call to the pressing need for more research into the real lives of teenage girls today.

Glossary

machismo: Exaggerated expression of masculinity.

burgeoning: Quickly growing or multiplying.

galvanized: Stimulated.

mitigating: Making less severe or more moderate.

coveted: Desired, sought-after.

icons: Representative images or figures.

misogynist: Antiwomen.

Comprehension Questions

1. Describe the murderer being interviewed.
2. How does the crime rate for teenage girls compare to the general crime rate?
3. Why are the numbers of crimes by young women in Canada on the rise, according to the article?
4. What does "Janice" say was the reason she murdered Reena Virk?
5. What does Dr. Sibylle Artz say is the typical background profile of a young woman who becomes violent?

Questions about Form

1. What does Graydon do to lend credibility to her article?
2. What kind of effect are quotations by "Janice" likely to have on the reader?
3. Graydon's article seems to be divided into two parts: the first on effects and the second on causes. Where does the change take place? What do you think the author is trying to achieve by doing this? Does she succeed?
4. Why is Reena Virk referred to in the first and, again, in the last paragraph? Do you think the author achieves her goal?

Questions for Discussion

1. Based on what you have read in Graydon's article, do young males and young females fight for the same reasons?
2. What is your perception of teenage violence in this country? Do you agree with the article as to its causes?
3. Why do you think the crime rate among teenage girls is increasing? Does it have anything to do with feminism? Explain.

Writing Ideas

1. Write a paragraph/essay explaining why you think teens often resort to violence. Refer to Graydon's article for at least one supportive detail (but not all) in your composition. Draw from your personal experience, also.
2. Write a paragraph/essay on what you think the solutions to the problem of teenage violence are. Do not discuss the causes or the effects; these should be somewhat evident from the solutions.

✦ ✦ ✦

In My Secret Life

Leonard Cohen

Most famous for his song "Suzanne," this Montreal-born poet has put much of his internationally-acclaimed poetry to music. Singers such as Jennifer Warnes and bands such as REM and the Neville Brothers have performed Cohen's work, but most of Cohen's fans prefer to hear the poet himself perform his own music. Cohen's collections of poetry, novels, and recordings have earned him the reputation as one of the most influential artists in Canada, the U.S., and Europe. The poem/song below is taken from his latest CD, *Ten New Songs*.

1 I saw you this morning.
You were moving so fast.
Can't seem to loosen my grip
On the past.
And I miss you so much.
There's no one in sight.
And we're still making love
In My Secret Life.

2 I smile when I'm angry.
I cheat and I lie.
I do what I have to do
To get by.
But I know what is wrong,
And I know what is right.
And I'd die for the truth
In My Secret Life.

3 Hold on, hold on, my brother.
My sister, hold on tight.
I finally got my orders.

I'll be marching through the morning,
Marching through the night,
Moving cross the borders
Of My Secret Life.

4 Looked through the paper.
Makes you want to cry.
Nobody cares if the people
Live or die.
And the dealer wants you thinking
That it's either black or white.
Thank **G-d** it's not that simple
In My Secret Life.

5 I bite my lip.
I buy what I'm told:
From the latest hit,
To the wisdom of old.
But I'm always alone.
And my heart is like ice.
And it's crowded and cold
In My Secret Life.

Glossary

G-d: In Judaism, a way of referring to the deity without taking His name in vain.

Comprehension Questions

1. In stanza 4, Cohen refers to "the dealer" and how he "wants you thinking / That it's either black or white." What do you think Cohen means by this?
2. What do you think the last stanza means? In particular, focus on "It's crowded and cold / In My Secret Life."

Questions about Form

1. What writing strategy or rhetorical mode does Cohen seem to be using, in part, within his poem/song?
2. Notice how each stanza ends with either "In" or "Of My Secret Life." Is this effective? Why?
3. What are the similarities or differences between the first and last stanzas? How does your answer contribute to the theme of the poem/song?

4. Are the words Cohen uses simple or complicated? Are they short or long? Notice how short the glossary is compared to that of other readings. What does this suggest? Do the answers to these questions contribute to the effectiveness of the work?

Questions for Discussion

1. What do you think Cohen is trying to say in this poem/song?
2. What is Cohen's "secret life"?
3. With regard to the two parts in conflict, which stanza seems to most clearly make a value judgment about each part? Explain.
4. Does Cohen resolve his conflict? What evidence from the poem/song supports your answer?

Writing Ideas

1. Identify two parts of you that always seem to be in conflict with each other. Write a paragraph/essay contrasting both.
2. Write a paragraph/essay interpreting the above poem/song by Leonard Cohen.

UNIT FIVE V

Appendices

APPENDIX A

Distinguishing between Words Often Confused

Words That Sound Alike

allowed (*verb*) permitted
aloud (*adv.*) out loud

Example:
The boy was finally allowed to stay up late.
Her question was stated aloud for all to hear.

altar (*noun*) an elevated place or table for religious rites
alter (*verb*) to change or adjust

Example:
The altar was decorated for the church service.
If you alter the plans, they won't work out.

aural (*adj.*) having to do with the ear or hearing
oral (*adj.*) having to do with the mouth or speech

Example:
I have poor aural skills because I won't listen.
The history of the First Nations is kept alive through their oral traditions.

brake (*verb*) to stop
(*noun*) a device used for slowing or stopping
break (*verb*) to smash, crack, or come apart
(*noun*) a crack, severing; an interruption, change

Example:
Apply the brake when you want to stop.
You'll have to break the lock to get in.
Give me a break!

capital (*adj.*) chief; major; fatal
(*noun*) leading city; money

capitol (*noun*) a building in which a U.S. state legislature assembles

Example:
Ottawa is the capital of Canada.
The capitol building for the legislature is in Albany.

chord (*noun*) three or more musical tones sounded together; harmony
cord (*noun*) a small rope of twisted strands; any ropelike structure; a unit of cut fuel wood

Example:
Many guitar chords are easy to play.
A strong cord is needed to tie the bundle together.

close (*verb*) to shut
clothes (*noun*) garments
cloth (*noun*) fabric; a piece of material

Example:
Close the door and keep the cold out.
T-shirts are our favourite type of summer clothes.
His coat was made of cloth, not leather.

coarse (*adj.*) rough; not fine; common or of inferior quality
course (*noun*) direction or path of something moving; part of a meal; a school subject

Example:
Coarse sandpaper is used to make a rough finish.
One course I'm taking this year is English grammar.

complement (*noun*) something that completes or makes up a whole
(*verb*) to complete; to supplement, enhance
compliment (*noun*) an expression of praise
(*verb*) to give praise

Example:
A blue blazer complements grey slacks.
Good work deserves a compliment.

complementary (*adj.*) complementing, often completing a pair or group of things that go together
complimentary (*adj.*) expressing a compliment; given free as a favour

Example:
With the textbook, he assigned the complementary study guide.
I have complimentary tickets to the game.

fair (*adj.*) unbiased; light colour; free of clouds; promising; lovely
(*noun*) an exhibition; regional event; market

fare (*noun*) a charge for transportation; food
(*verb*) get along; do

Example:
A pink sunset means a fair day will follow.
The train fare is increasing yearly.

flour (*noun*) the powder produced by grinding a grain
flower (*noun*) a blossom of a plant
(*verb*) to blossom

Example:
Wheat flour is used to make bread.
Tulips flower in early spring.

for (*prep.*) directed to; in the amount of; on behalf of; to the extent of
(*conj.*) because
four (*noun, adj.*) number
forty: Notice that this number is spelled differently from *four, fourteen*, or *twenty-four*.
fore (*noun, adj.*) situated near the front

Example:
This gift is for you.
There are four people in attendance.
His ideas came to the fore at work.

forth (*adv.*) onward in time, place, or order
fourth (*noun, adj.*) number

Example:
Go forth from this place.
She is fourth in line for tickets.

forward (*verb*) to send on to another address
(*adj.*) bold; progressive
(*adv.*) moving toward the front
foreword (*noun*) introduction to a book; preface

Example:
Move forward so you can hear the speaker.
The foreword to a book is sometimes called the preface.

grate (*verb*) to shred; to annoy or irritate
(*noun*) a metal grill
grateful (*adj.*) appreciative
great (*adj.*) large; significant; excellent; powerful; skillful; first-rate

Example:
Her negative attitude grates on my nerves.
Winning the prize was a great achievement.

it's contraction of *it is*
its possessive

Example:
It's a nice day today.
The bush has all of its new buds.

knew (*verb*) past tense of *know*
new (adj.) not old

Example:
The student knew the correct answer.
His new car is this year's model.

know (*verb*) to understand
no (*adv.*) a negative response
(*adj.*) not any; not one

Example:
You would know the work if you'd study.
Having no money means that you are poor.

pain (*noun*) suffering
pane (*noun*) a panel of glass

Example:
A cut finger can cause a lot of pain.
Windows contain panes of glass.

passed (*verb*) the past tense of *to pass*—to move ahead
past (*noun*) time before the present
(*prep.*) beyond
(*adj.*) no longer current

Example:
I passed the exam and moved to the next grade.
I was past the exit before I noticed that I had missed it.

patience (*noun*) calm endurance; tolerant understanding
patients (*noun*) persons under medical treatment

Example:
Waiting for someone usually takes patience.
Patients in hospitals often are very ill.

peace (*noun*) absence of war, calm
piece (*noun*) a portion, a part

Example:
Peace came when the war was over.
His piece of cake was huge.

plain (*adj.*) simple; ordinary; unattractive; clear
(*noun*) a flat, treeless land region
plane (*noun*) an aircraft; a flat, level surface; a carpenter's tool for levelling wood; a level of development

Example:
The flat plain stretched for miles without a tree.
I used a plane to make the wood smooth.

presence (*noun*) the state of being present; a person's manner
presents (*noun*) gifts
(*verb*) (third person singular) to introduce; to give a gift

Example:
The presence of the teacher kept the students quiet.
Presents are given on birthdays.

principal (*adj.*) most important; chief; main
(*noun*) the head of a school; a sum of money
principle (*noun*) rule or standard

Example:
The principal rule is the most important guideline.
There are principles of conduct to be followed at school.

rain (*noun, verb*) water falling to earth in drops
reign (*noun, verb*) a period of rule for a king or queen
rein (*noun*) a strap attached to a bridle, used to control a horse

Example:
A good rain will soak the crops.
The monarch's reign extended for many years.
To control a horse, learn how to use the reins.

raise (*verb*) to move upward; to awaken; to increase; to collect
(*noun*) an increase in salary
rays (*noun*) thin lines or beams of radiation
raze (*verb*) to tear down or demolish

Example:
A raise in pay often rewards good work.
The sun's rays contain harmful radiation.
The old building was razed to the ground.

sight (*noun*) the ability to see; a view
site (*noun*) the plot of land where something is located; the place of an event
cite (*verb*) to quote as an authority or example

Example:
Some people with perfect sight don't see clearly.

The opera house's site is between two theatres.
I can cite my grammar text as my authority.

stair (*noun*) one of a flight of steps
stare (*noun, verb*) a fixed gaze; to look at insistently

Example:
Each stair climbed brings you farther up the steps.
A steady gaze can be considered a stare.

stake (*noun*) a post sharpened at one end to drive into the ground; a financial share
(*verb*) to attach or support; to set limits with a stake
steak (*noun*) a slice of meat, usually beef

Example:
My stake in the profits amounted to a quarter share.
I like my steak well done and thick.

stationary (*adj.*) standing still
stationery (*noun*) writing paper and envelopes

Example:
Anything that is stationary does not move.
Stationery can be written upon.

they're contraction of *they are*
their possessive
there at that place

Example:
They're a happy couple.
This antique is their prized possession.
I'll meet you over there, behind the store.

to (*prep.*) in a direction toward
to (+ *verb*) the infinitive form of a verb
too (*adv.*) also; excessively; very
two (*noun*) number

Example:
Go to school.
To see is to believe.
I, too, am going to the party.
Two is one more than one.

vain (*adj.*) conceited; unsuccessful
vane (*noun*) a plate of wood or metal, often in the shape of a rooster, that pivots to indicate the direction of the wind; the weblike part of a feather

vein (*noun*) a blood vessel; the branching framework of a leaf; an occurrence of an ore; a strip of colour; a streak; a transient attitude

Example:
A vain person spends a lot of time in front of a mirror.
The vane on the roof tells the wind direction.
Veins in your body contain blood.

waist (*noun*) the middle portion of a body, garment, or object
waste (*verb*) to use thoughtlessly or carelessly
(*noun*) objects discarded as useless

Example:
A belt around your waist holds your pants up.
Excess packaging contains much waste.

wait (*verb*) to remain inactive
weight (*noun*) the measure of the heaviness of an object

Example:
Remain here and wait for my arrival.
My weight goes up every time I eat.

ware (*noun*) an article of commerce
wear (*verb*) to have on
(*noun*) deterioration as a result of use
where (*adv.*) at or in what place

Example:
You can sell your wares at the flea market.
What clothes will you wear?
He asked where the museum could be found.

weather (*noun*) atmospheric conditions
whether (*conj.*) if it is the case that

Example:
The weather report calls for rain.
She will go whether I go or not.

whole (*adj.*) complete
hole (*noun*) an opening

Example:
A pie is whole before it is sliced and served.
Holes in the road need to be filled in.

who's contraction of *who is*
whose possessive

Example:
Who's going for pizza?
Whose garbage can is blocking the driveway?

wood (*noun*) the tough tissue from trees
would (*verb*) past tense of *will*

Example:
Most paper is made from wood fibre.
He would go, he said, if he could find a ride.

write (*verb*) to form letters and words; to compose
right (*adj.*) conforming to justice, law, or morality; correct; toward a conservative political point of view
(*noun*) that which is just, morally good, legal, or proper; a direction; a political group whose policies are conservative
(*adv.*) directly; well; completely; immediately
rite (*noun*) a traditional, solemn, and often religious ceremony

Example:
Write a letter to your aunt.
You should legally do what is right.
Last rites were said over the dying person.

yoke (*noun*) a harness fastening two or more animals together; a form of bondage
yolk (*noun*) the yellow of an egg

Example:
Animals in a team are joined by a yoke.
Some diners like their eggs cooked without the yolks broken.

you're contraction of *you are*
your possessive

Example:
You're my best friend.
Take your gift to the party.

Words That Sound or Look Almost Alike

Some words are often confused with other words that sound or look almost the same. Learning to spell these words correctly involves a careful study of pronunciations along with meanings.

	Pronunciation	**Meaning**
accept	*a* as in *pat*	*verb:* to receive; to admit; to regard as true or right
except	the first *e* as in *pet*	*prep.:* other than; but; only

Example:
I accepted the parcel from the courier.
Everyone was there except the two of us.

access	*a* as in *pat*	*noun:* a means of approaching; the right to enter or make use of
excess	the first *e* as in *pet*	*noun:* a quantity or amount beyond what is required

Example:
Access to the files will provide you with information.
Overeating is an unnecessary excess.

advice	Pronounce *-ice* like the word *ice*.	*noun:* opinion as to what should be done about a problem
advise	Pronounce *-ise* like the word *eyes*.	*verb:* to suggest; to counsel

Example:
My best advice is to accept the offer.
I advise you to do what is right.

affect	*a* as in *about*	*verb:* to influence
effect	the first *e* as the *e* in *pet* or *i* in *pit*	*noun:* result *verb:* to bring about a result

Example:
I can affect his decision with my advice.
The effect of the rain was to cancel the game.

allusion	*a* as in *about*	*noun:* an indirect reference
illusion	the first *i* as in *pit*	*noun:* a mistaken concept or belief

Example:
An allusion was made to my great intelligence.
It is an illusion to think you will get rich without working.

breath	*ea* as the *e* in *pet*	*noun:* the air that is inhaled or exhaled in breathing
breathe	the *ea* as the *e* in *be*	*verb:* to inhale and exhale air

Example:
You can see your breath on the window on a cold day.
Breathe deeply and inhale the clean country air.

clothes	*o* as the *oe* in *toe*	*noun:* garments; wearing apparel
cloths	*o* as the *aw* in *paw*	*noun:* pieces of fabric

Example:
The clothes you are wearing are fashionable.
Pieces of cloth can be torn from the fabric to make rags.

conscience	kŏn′ shəns (two syllables)	*noun:* recognition of right and wrong
conscientious	kŏn shē en′ shəs (four syllables)	*adj.:* careful; thorough
conscious	kŏn′ shəs (two syllables)	*adj.:* awake; aware of one's own existence

Example:
My conscience told me to do the right thing.
I conscientiously performed my duty to the best of my ability.
She was conscious of the fact that he was behind her.

costume	*o* as in *pot*, *u* as the *u* in you	*noun:* a special style of dress for a particular occasion
custom	*u* as in *cut*, *o* as in *gallop*	*noun:* a common tradition

Example:
The costume he wore reflected his Ukrainian heritage.
It is our custom to wash our hands before eating.

council	*ou* as in *out*	*noun:* a group that governs
counsel	*ou* as in *out*	*verb:* to give advice *noun:* a lawyer; advice
consul	*o* as in *pot*	*noun:* a governmental official in the foreign service

Example:
The town council passed a by-law.
Good counsel is advice well received.
Canada has a consul in many foreign countries.

desert	di zurt′ *i* as in *pit*	*verb:* to abandon *noun:* something deserved (often plural)
	dez′ ert the first *e* as in *pet*	*noun:* barren land
dessert	di zurt′ *i* as in pit	*noun:* last part of a meal, often a sweet

Example:
The desert is usually a hot, arid place.
Our family usually eats dessert following dinner.
He got his just deserts.

diner	*i* as the *ie* in *pie*	*noun:* a person eating dinner; a restaurant with a long counter and booths
dinner	*i* as in *pit*	*noun:* chief meal of the day

Example:
A diner is a place where meals are served.
Dinner is usually eaten in the early evening.

emigrate **emigrant**	*e* as in *pet*	*verb:* to go out of a country *noun:* someone who leaves a country to settle in another country
immigrate **immigrant**	the first *i* as in *pit*	*verb:* to come into a country *noun:* someone who enters a country to settle there

Example:
Many people decided to emigrate from Ireland during the famine.
Immigrants to our country bring valuable skills.

farther	*a* as in *father*	*adj., adv.:* greater physical or measurable distance
further	*u* as in *urge*	*adj., adv.:* greater mental distance; more distant in time or degree; additional

Example:
Montreal is farther than Toronto from Windsor.
We drew further apart in our approach to the problem.

local	lo′ kəl *a* as in *about*	*adj.:* relating or peculiar to a place
locale	lo kal′ *a* as in *pat*	*noun:* a place, scene, or setting, as of a novel

Example:
Everyone here goes to the local school on the next block.
Our town was the locale for a movie.

moral	mor′ al *a* as in *about*	*adj.:* a sense of right and wrong *noun:* the lesson of a story, fable, or event
morale	mo ral′ *a* as in *pat*	*noun:* the attitude or spirit of a person or group of people

Example:
The moral of the story taught us never to cheat.
Their morale was shown by their enthusiasm for their jobs.

personal	per′ son al	*adj.:* pertaining to a particular person
personnel	per son nel′	*noun:* the people employed by an organization; an administrative division of an organization concerned with the employees

Example:
The matter is a personal one between him and me.
Most of the plant's personnel were laid off.

precede	the first *e* as the *i* in *pit*	*verb:* to come before
proceed	the *o* as the *oe* in *toe*	*verb:* to continue

Example:
You go first and precede me down the hall.
Proceed with the story you started yesterday.

quiet	qui′ et *i* as the *ie* in *pie,* *e* as in *pet*	*adj.:* silent *noun:* silence
quit	*i* as in *pit*	*verb:* to give up; to stop
quite	*i* as the *ie* in *pie*; the *e* is silent	*adv.:* somewhat; completely; truly

Example:
It was a quiet night when no sound could be heard.
Quit what you are doing and start something else.
It is quite true that I am guilty.

receipt	the first *e* as the *i* in *pit*, *ei* as in the *e* in *be*; the *p* is silent	*noun:* a bill marked as paid; the act of receiving something *verb:* to mark as paid
recipe	the first *e* as in *pet*, the *i* like the *a* in *about*, the final *e* as in *be*	*noun:* a formula for preparing a mixture, especially in cooking

Example:
The receipt for the dinner was marked "paid."
The recipe calls for more chocolate in the cookies.

special	spĕsh′ əl	*adj.:* exceptional; distinctive
especially	Notice the extra syllable at the beginning.	*adv.:* particularly

Example:
She was a special person, one of a kind.
It is especially important to file an income tax return.

than	*a* as in *pat*	*conj.:* used to make a comparison
then	*e* as in *pet*	*adv.:* at that time; in that case

Example:
She is smarter than I am.
It was then that I made up my mind.

thorough	the first *o* as the *u* in *urge, ou* as the *oe* in *toe*	*adj.:* all that is needed; fully done
though	*ou* as the *oe* in *toe*	*conj.:* despite the fact
thought	*ou* as the *aw* in *paw*	*verb:* past tense of *to think*
through	*ou* as the *oo* in *boot*	*prep.* used to indicate entrance at one side and exit from the other; finished
threw	sounds like *through*	*verb:* past tense of *to throw*

- *Thru* is only an informal spelling for the word *through*.

Example:
The thorough investigation found a hidden clue.
It's not true, though, that I told a lie.
He thought of the answer before he spoke.
Go through that exit to get outside.
He threw the ball as far as he could.

Words That Sound or Look Almost Alike: *sit/set; rise/raise; lie/lay*

These six verbs are among the most troublesome in English because each is similar in sound, spelling, and meaning to another verb. Since they are all irregular verbs, students must be careful to learn to spell the principal parts correctly. The key to learning how to use the verbs *sit, rise*, and *lie* is to remember that these are actions the subject can do without any help; no other person or thing has to be included in the sentence. When you use the verbs *set, raise*, and *lay* in a sentence, the actions of these verbs are done to other persons or objects; these persons or things have to be included directly in the sentence. For example, when you use the verb *to sit*, all you need is a subject and a form of the verb:

I sit.

However, when you use the verb *to set*, you need a subject, a form of the verb, and an object. For example:

I set the glass on the table.

The subject *I* and the verb *set* are followed by the object *glass*, which is what the subject set on the table.

sit: to take a sitting position *never* takes an object		***set:*** to place something into position *always* takes an object
Present:	I sit.	I *set the glass* down.
Present participle:	I am sitting.	I *am setting the glass* down.
Past:	I sat.	I *set the glass* down.
Past participle:	I have sat.	I *have set the glass* down.

rise: to stand up; to move upward *never* takes an object		***raise:*** to make something move up or grow; *always* takes an object
Present:	I *rise.*	I *raise the flag.*
Present participle:	The sun *is rising.*	I *am raising* the flag.
Past:	He *rose* at eight o'clock.	I *raised the flag.*
Past participle:	I *have risen* early today.	I *have raised the flag.*

The verbs *lie* and *lay* are easily confused because two of their principal parts have the same spelling. It takes concentration to learn to use these two verbs correctly.

lie: to recline *never* takes an object		***lay:*** to put *always* takes an object
Present:	I *lie* down.	I *lay the pen* down.
Present participle:	I *am lying* down.	I *am laying the pen* down.
Past:	Yesterday I *lay* down.	I *laid the pen* down.
Past participle:	I *have lain* down.	I *have laid the pen* down.

- The verb *lie* can also be a regular verb meaning "to tell an untruth." The principal parts of this verb are *lie, lying, lied, has lied.*

Words That Sound or Look Almost Alike: *choose/chose; lose/loose; lead/led; die/dye*

These verbs are often misspelled because there is confusion about how to spell the vowel sounds of the verbs. Study the spelling of the principal parts below.

Present	Present Participle	Past	Past Participle
choose	choosing	chose	has chosen
lose	losing	lost	has lost
lead	leading	led	has led
die	dying	died	has died

- *Loose* is an adjective meaning "not tightly fitted." Remember, it rhymes with *goose.*
- *Lead* can also be a noun meaning a bluish-grey metal. Remember, it rhymes with *head.*

- *Dye* is another verb meaning "to colour." Its principal parts are *dye, dyeing, dyed,* has *dyed.*

Words That Sound or Look Almost Alike: *use/used; suppose/supposed*

To use means *to bring or put into service*; *to make use of.*

Present: I *use* my brother's bike to get to school.
Past: Yesterday I *used* my father's car.

Use to means *to have as a custom* or *regular practice* in the past. It usually occurs in its past form, *used to*:

I *used to* take the bus downtown, but now I get a ride with my neighbour.

Note, however, that in expressions with the auxiliary *did*, you use the present form:

Did you use to take the bus?

A form of *to be* + *used to* means *to be familiar with or accustomed to.*

I am *used to* walking to school.

To suppose means *to guess.*

Present: I *suppose* he is trying.
Past: I *supposed* he was trying.

A form of *to be* + *supposed to* means *ought to* or *should.*

Waiters *are supposed to* be courteous.

Many people have difficulty knowing when to choose *used* and *supposed* in their writing because in speaking, the final *d* is often not clearly heard.

Incorrect: I am *suppose to* be in school today.
Correct: I am *supposed to* be in school today.

Solving Spelling Problems

Learning to Spell Commonly Mispronounced Words

Several common English words are often mispronounced or pronounced in such a way that the result is incorrect spelling. Below are sixty common words that are often misspelled. As you study them, be careful to spell each of the underlined syllables correctly.

I. Common Omission of Vowels

1. Do not omit the underlined syllable with the *a*:

accidentally	literature
basically	miniature
boundary	separate
extraordinary	temperament
incidentally	temperature

2. Do not omit the underlined syllable with the *e*:

considerable	mathematics
difference	numerous
funeral	scenery
interesting	

However, notice the following words in which the *e* is omitted:

disaster	*becomes*	disastrous
enter	*becomes*	entrance
hinder	*becomes*	hindrance
hunger	*becomes*	hungry
launder	*becomes*	laundry
monster	*becomes*	monstrous
remember	*becomes*	remembrance

3. Do not omit the underlined syllable with the *i*:

aspirin	family	similar

4. Do not omit the underlined syllable with the *o*:

chocolate
environment
favourite
humorous
laboratory
sophomore

5. Do not omit the underlined syllable with the *u*:

luxury
accuracy

6. Do not omit the underlined syllable with the *y*:

studying

II. Common Omission of Consonants

1. *b*
probably

2. *c*
arctic

3. *d*
candidate
handkerchief
handsome
supposed to
used to

4. *g*
recognize

5. *n*
government

6. *r*
February
library
surprise

7. *t*
authentic
identical
identity
partner
promptly
quantity

III. Common Addition of a Syllable

Do not add unnecessary syllables (e.g., athelete):

athlete
athletic

IV. Common Transposition of Letters

Do not transpose the underlined letters:

perform
persuade
prefer
tragedy

PRACTICE

Identifying the Correct Spelling

Circle the correct spelling for each of the following words. Check your answers against those in the Answer Key on p. 442.

1. separate	seprate	seperate
2. probably	probaly	probly
3. ardic	arctic	artic
4. suprise	saprize	surprise
5. tragedy	tradgedy	trajedy
6. quantity	quantidy	quanity
7. litrature	literature	literture
8. hungery	hungary	hungry
9. handsome	hansome	handsom
10. favourite	faverite	favrite
11. nucular	nuclear	nuclar

Learning to Spell *ie* and *ei* Words

Use this rhyme to help you remember how to spell most *ie* and *ei* words:

i before *e*
except after *c*
or when sounded like *a*
as in *neighbour* or *weigh*.

i before *e*

The majority of all the *ie* and *ei* words use *ie*.

believe
chief
friend
shriek
yield

except after *c*

ceiling
conceit
conceive
receipt
receive

or when sounded like *a*

beige
eight
reins
sleigh
vein

Once you have learned the rhyme, concentrate on learning the following groups of words that are the exceptions to this rhyme.

caffeine
codeine
protein

neither
either

sheik
stein
their
weird

leisure
seize
seizure

counterfeit
Fahrenheit
foreign
height

ancient
conscience
efficient
sufficient

PRACTICE

Choosing *ie* or *ei*

Choose the correct combination of ie or ei for the following words. Check your answers against those in the Answer Key on p. 442.

1. sl_______gh
2. bel_______ve
3. s_______ge
4. v_______l
5. l_______sure
6. dec_______t
7. n_______ce
8. w_______ght
9. prot_______n
10. anc_______nt

Forming the Plurals of Nouns

Almost all nouns are made plural simply by adding *-s* to the singular form:

girl	*becomes*	girl*s*
dinner	*becomes*	dinner*s*

However, each of the following groups of words has its own special rule for forming the plural.

1. **Words ending in *-y:***

   In words ending in *-y* preceded by a *consonant*, change the *y* to *i* and add *es*.

la*dy*	*becomes*	lad*ies*
ceremo*ny*	*becomes*	ceremon*ies*

Words ending in *-y* preceded by a *vowel* form their plurals in the regular way, by just adding *-s*.

d*ay*	*becomes*	day*s*
monk*ey*	*becomes*	monkey*s*
vall*ey*	*becomes*	valley*s*

2. **Words ending in *-o:***

Most words ending in *-o* preceded by a consonant add *-es* to form the plural.

ec*ho*	*becomes*	echo*es*
he*ro*	*becomes*	hero*es*
pota*to*	*becomes*	potato*es*

However, musical terms or names of musical instruments (which derive from Italian) add only *-s*.

piano	*becomes*	piano*s*
solo	*becomes*	solo*s*
soprano	*becomes*	soprano*s*

Words ending in *-o* preceded by a *vowel* add *-s*.

pat*io*	*becomes*	patio*s*
rad*io*	*becomes*	radio*s*
rod*eo*	*becomes*	rodeo*s*

Some words ending in *-o* may form their plural with *-s* or *-es*.

memento	*becomes*	memento*s*	*or*	memento*es*
pinto	*becomes*	pinto*s*	*or*	pinto*es*
zero	*becomes*	zero*s*	*or*	zero*es*

If you are uncertain about the plural ending of a word ending in *-o*, it is best to use the dictionary. The dictionary gives all the endings of irregular plurals. If no plural form is given, you know the word will form its plural in the regular way, by adding only *-s*.

3. **Words ending in *-ch, -sh, -s, -x,* and *-z:***

For words ending in *-ch, -sh, -s, -x,* and *-z*, add *-es*.

witch*es*
dish*es*
dress*es*
tax*es*
buzz*es*

4. **Words ending in *-fe* or *-f:***

   Some words ending in *-fe* or *-f* change the *f* to *v* and add *-es*. You can hear the change from the *f* sound to the *v* sound in the plural.

wi*fe*	*becomes*	wi*ves*
lea*f*	*becomes*	lea*ves*

   Other words ending in *-f* or *-ef* keep the *f* and just add *-s*.

sherif*f*	*becomes*	sheriff*s*
belie*f*	*becomes*	belief*s*

   Again, you can hear that the *f* sound is kept in the plural. Some words can form their plural either way. If so, the dictionary will give the preferred way first.

5. **Foreign words:**

   Some words borrowed from other languages keep the plurals from those languages to form the plural in English.

alg*a*	*becomes*	alg*ae*
alumn*a*	*becomes*	alumn*ae*
alumn*us*	*becomes*	alumn*i*
cris*is*	*becomes*	cris*es*
phenomen*on*	*becomes*	phenomen*a*

6. **Compound nouns:**

   Compound nouns make their plurals by putting the *-s* on the end of the main word.

brother-in-law	*becomes*	brother*s*-in-law
passer-by	*becomes*	passer*s*-by

7. **Irregular plurals:**

   Some nouns in English have irregular plurals.

Singular	**Plural**
child	children
deer	deer
foot	feet
goose	geese
man, woman	men, women
moose	moose
mouse	mice
ox	oxen
sheep	sheep
tooth	teeth

PRACTICE

Forming the Plurals of Nouns

Using the rules you have learned, make the following words plural. Check your answers against those in the Answer Key on p. 442.

1. puppy ______________
2. mother-in-law ______________
3. tooth ______________
4. cameo ______________
5. phenomenon ______________
6. loaf ______________
7. match ______________
8. mix ______________
9. enemy ______________
10. bag ______________

Prefixes and Suffixes

Like everything else in this world, words had to begin somewhere. Many English words come from (had their *roots* in) other languages; others were created to describe something new. For example, modern English has many roots in Old English, ancient Greek, and Latin. For example:

Roots and Derivatives

Old English		**Latin**	
akr	a field, acre	*audio*	to hear, audience
foda	food, fodder	*dignus*	dignity, worth
haelan	to heal, health	*clarus*	clear, clarify
war	defence, war	*nomen*	name
Greek			
angelos	angel		
gramma	a letter		
kosmos	the world		
logos	word		

Prefixes and suffixes can be added to the roots of words to alter the meaning of the words or to create new words with new meanings. A *prefix* is a word or part of a word placed before the root of a word, and a *suffix* is placed after the root. As is the case with root words, the English language derives many of its prefixes and suffixes from Latin and Greek. For example:

Some Latin Prefixes

ante-	before
contra-	against
extra-	beyond
in-	in, into
non-	not
post-	after
pro-	before
super-	above

Some Greek Prefixes

ampli-	on both sides
anti-	opposite
auto-	self
hemi-	half
hyper-	over, above
mono-	alone, single
para-	beside
pro-	before

Some Latin Suffixes

-ary	belonging to
-ess	feminine of
-et, ette	denoting diminution
-ty	quality, state, condition

Some Greek Suffixes

-ic	pertaining to
-ism	act, state, condition
-ist	a doer

Some examples of English words with prefixes and suffixes added include

anti	+	biotic	= antibiotic
benefit	+	ary	= beneficiary
communist	+	ism	= communism
hemi	+	sphere	= hemisphere
host	+	ess	= hostess
in	+	dispensable	= indispensable
pro	+	claim	= proclaim

Adding prefixes and suffixes may change the spelling of the former roots. This occurs most frequently when suffixes are added to words. Consult the basic spelling rules on the following pages when prefixes and suffixes are parts of words.

Should the Final Consonant Be Doubled?

The answer to the question of whether a final consonant should be doubled involves the most complicated spelling rule. However, the rule is well worth learning because once you know it, you will suddenly be able to spell thousands of words correctly.

In order to understand the rule, remember first the difference between vowels (*a, e, i, o, u,* and sometimes *y*) and consonants (all the other letters in the alphabet). The problem in spelling occurs when you want to add an ending that begins with a vowel, such as *-ed, -er, -est,* or *-ing*. Sometimes a word will double the last letter before adding an ending:

trap + ing = trapping The fur traders spent their time tra*pp*ing animals.

Sometimes the word will *not* double the last letter before adding the ending:

turn + er = turner He dropped the pancake tur*n*er.

How do you know when to double the final consonant?

Rule for Doubling One-Syllable Words

Double the final consonant of a one-syllable word when adding an ending that begins with a vowel only if the last three letters of the word are a consonant-vowel-consonant combination.

Since *rap* in the word *trap* is a consonant-vowel-consonant combination, this one-syllable word will double the final consonant when adding an ending beginning with a vowel. Since the last three letters *urn* in the word *turn* are a vowel-consonant-consonant combination, this one-syllable word does not double the final consonant when adding an ending beginning with a vowel.

Note that in words with *qu* like *quit* or *quiz*, you should think of the *qu* as a consonant. (The *u* does have a consonant *w* sound.) *quit* + ing = qui*tt*ing.

Rule for Doubling the Consonant in Words of More Than One Syllable

For words of more than one syllable, the rule adds one more condition: if the first syllable is accented in the newly formed word, you do not double the final consonant.

pre fer′ + ed = pre ferred′

but

pre fer′ + ence = pref′ er ence
(The accent has changed to the first syllable.)

PRACTICE

Doubling the Consonant?

For each of the following one-syllable words, determine whether or not the word will double the final consonant when adding an ending beginning with a vowel. The first two are done for you. Check your answers against those in the Answer Key on p. 443.

One-Syllable Word	Consonant-Vowel-Consonant Combination?	Double?	Add *-ing* Ending
drag	yes	yes	dragging
drain	no	no	draining
slip			
crack			
broil			
win			

Try these two-syllable words:

con *trol′* + ing = ______________________

fe′ *ver* + ish = ______________________

For each of the following words of more than one syllable, determine whether or not the word will double the final consonant when adding an ending beginning with a vowel.

com *pel′* + ed = ______________________

dif′ *fer* + ence = ______________________

be *gin′* + ing = ______________________

PRACTICE

Doubling the Final Consonant When Adding Endings That Begin with Vowels?

Decide whether or not to double the final consonant when adding the endings to the following words. Check your answers against those in the Answer Key on p. 443.

Word		Ending		New Word
1. bit	+	en	=	______________________
2. oc cur′	+	ence	=	______________________
3. wa′ ver	+	ing	=	______________________
4. pre fer′	+	ed	=	______________________
5. pre′ fer	+	ence	=	______________________
6. thin	+	er	=	______________________
7. trans fer′	+	ed	=	______________________
8. sail	+	ing	=	______________________
9. pro pel′	+	ent	=	______________________
10. o mit′	+	ed	=	______________________

Words Ending in *-y*

1. When a *y* at the end of a word is preceded by a consonant, change *y* to *i* and add the ending.

car*ry*	+	er	=	carr*ier*
mer*ry*	+	ment	=	merr*iment*
fun*ny*	+	er	=	____________
pret*ty*	+	ness	=	____________
va*ry*	+	es	=	____________

Exceptions: Do not change the *y* to *i* if the ending starts with an *i*. Few English words have two *i*'s together.

stu*dy*	+	ing	=	stud*ying* (not studiing)
rea*dy*	+	ing	=	____________

Some long words drop the *y* when adding the ending. You can hear that the *y* syllable is missing when you pronounce the word correctly.

milit*ary*	+	ism	=	militar*ism*
accompany	+	ist	=	____________

2. When *y* at the end of a word is preceded by a vowel, do *not* change the *y* when adding the ending. Simply add the ending.

surve*y*	+	s	=	surve*ys*
enj*oy*	+	ment	=	____________

PRACTICE

Adding Endings to Words That End in *-y*

Add endings to the following words, being sure to change the y to i whenever necessary. Check your answers against those in the Answer Key on p. 443.

Word		Ending		New Word
1. key	+	s	=	____________
2. lonely	+	ness	=	____________
3. cry	+	ing	=	____________
4. cry	+	s	=	____________
5. pray	+	er	=	____________
6. employ	+	ment	=	____________

7. monkey + ing = ____________________
8. beauty + ful = ____________________
9. theory + es = ____________________
10. ceremony + al = ____________________

Is It One Word or Two?

There is often confusion about whether certain word combinations should be joined together to form compound words. Study the following groups of words to avoid this common confusion.

These words are always written as one word:

another	everything	playroom
bathroom	grandmother	schoolteacher
bedroom	nearby	southeast, northwest, etc.
bookkeeper	nevertheless	workplace
cannot	newspaper	yourself
downstairs		

These words are always written as two words:

a lot	high school
all right	living room
dining room	no one
good night	

These words are written as one or two words depending on their use:

all ready (*pronoun and adj.*) — completely prepared
already (*adv.*) — previously; before

all together (*pronoun and adj.*) — in a group
altogether (*adv.*) — completely

all ways (*adj. and noun*) — every road or path
always (*adverb*) — on every occasion

any one (*adj. and pronoun*) — one person or thing in a specific group
anyone (*indef. pronoun*) — any person at all

every one (*adj. and pronoun*) — every person or thing in a specific group
everyone (*indef. pronoun*) — all of the people

may be (*verb*) — might be
maybe (*adv.*) — perhaps

PRACTICE

One Word or Two?

Fill in the blank in each of the following sentences by choosing the correct word or words to complete that sentence. Check your answers against those in the Answer Key on p. 443.

1. The blue rug looks beautiful in the white ________________.
   (bed room, bedroom)
2. The room is usually occupied by our ____________________ but she is not here right now. (grandmother, grand mother)
3. She has ______________ left for a winter vacation.
   (all ready, already)
4. Last night we all called her and __________________ we sang "Happy Birthday" over the phone. (all together, altogether)
5. We ______________ remember her birthday, no matter where we are.
   (all ways, always)
6. _____________ likes to be remembered on special days, particularly a birthday.
   (Every one, Everyone)
7. Next year, ______________ all the members of the family will be able to
   (may be, maybe)
   celebrate her birthday with us.
8. If she ______________ come to us, we will drive up and surprise her.
   (cannot, can not)
9. Most families have members who do not live ______________.
   (near by, nearby)
10. ______________________, we can keep in touch by letter, phone, or visits.
    (Never the less, Nevertheless)

Spelling 200 Tough Words

Word List 1: Silent Letters

b
clim*b*
crum*b*
de*b*t
dou*b*t
su*b*tle

c
indi*c*t

d
knowle*d*ge
We*d*nesday

h
ex*h*ibit
r*h*etoric
r*h*ythm
sc*h*ool

l
co*l*onel

n
autum*n*
colum*n*
condem*n*

p
*p*neumonia
*p*sychology

s
ai*s*le
debri*s*
i*s*land

t
depo*t*
lis*t*en
mor*t*gage

w
ans*w*er

Word List 2: Double Letters

a*cc*identa*ll*y
a*cc*o*mm*odate
acro*ss*
a*dd*re*ss*
a*nn*ual
a*pp*arently
a*rr*angement
co*mmittee*
emba*rr*a*ss*
exa*gg*erate
fina*ll*y
guarant*ee*
hara*ss*
nece*ss*ary
o*cc*asiona*ll*y
omi*ss*ion
po*ss*e*ss*ion
prefe*rr*ed
questio*nn*aire
reco*mm*end
sheri*ff*
su*ccee*d
su*cc*e*ss*
su*gg*est
su*mm*arize
tomo*rr*ow
wri*tt*en *but* wri*t*ing

Word List 3: *-able* or *-ible*

-able

Usually, when you begin with a complete word, the ending is *-able*.

acceptable
agreeable

- These words keep the *e* when adding the ending:

  peaceable
  noticeable
  manageable
  knowledgeable

- These words drop the *e* when adding the ending:

  conceivable
  desirable
  dispensable
  imaginable

-ible

Usually, if you start with a root that is not a word, the ending is *-ible*.

audible
compatible
eligible
feasible
illegible
incredible
permissible
plausible
possible
sensible
susceptible
tangible

Word List 4: *de-* or *di-*

de-	di-
decide	dilemma
decision	dilute
delinquent	discipline
descend	discuss
describe	disease
despair	disguise
despicable	dispense

despise
despite
despondent
destructive
develop
device
dispute
dissent
divide
divine
division

Word List 5: The *-er* Sound

Most words ending with the *-er* sound are spelled with *-er*, as in the words *prisoner, customer*, and *hunger*. Words that are exceptions to this should be learned carefully.

-ar

beggar
burglar
calendar
collar
dollar
grammar
pillar
polar
similar
vulgar

-or

actor
author
bachelor
doctor
emperor
governor
motor
professor
sailor
scissors

-our

humour
labour
neighbour

-re

centre
litre
theatre

-ur

murmur

-yr

martyr

Word List 6: *-ance* or *-ence*

Most words with the *-ence* sound at the end are spelled *-ence*. Here are a few examples:

audience
correspondence
excellence
existence
independence
insistence
intelligence
licence (noun)
presence
reference

Learn these exceptions:

-ance
allowance
ambulance
appearance
assistance
attendance
balance
deliverance
dominance
guidance
ignorance
nuisance
observance
resistance
significance
tolerance

-ense
license (verb)

-eance
vengeance

Word List 7: Problems with *s, c, z, x,* and *k*

absence
alcohol
analyze/analyse
auxiliary
awkward
biscuit
complexion
concede
consensus
criticize
ecstasy
emphasize
especially
exceed
exercise
fascinate
magazine
medicine
muscle
prejudice
recede
sincerely
supersede
vacillate
vicious

Word List 8: Twenty-four Demons

acquire
argument
benefit
cafeteria
category
cemetery
conquer
corroborate
courageous
extremely
frightening
grateful
inoculate
lightning
ninety
ninth
occurred
occurrence
privilege
ridiculous
secretary
truly
until
village

Irregular Verbs

Principal Parts of Irregular Verbs

Simple Form	Past Form	Past Participle
1. Principal parts are the same.		
beat	beat	beat or beaten
bet	bet	bet
burst	burst	burst
cast	cast	cast
cost	cost	cost
cut	cut	cut
fit	fit	fit
hit	hit	hit
hurt	hurt	hurt
let	let	let
put	put	put
quit	quit	quit
read	*read	*read
rid	rid	rid
set	set	set
shut	shut	shut
split	split	split
spread	spread	spread
wet	wet	wet
2. The past form and past participle are the same.		
bend	bent	bent
lend	lent	lent
send	sent	sent
spend	spent	spent
build	built	built

*Pronunciation changes.

Simple Form	Past Form	Past Participle
creep	crept	crept
feel	felt	felt
keep	kept	kept
sleep	slept	slept
sweep	swept	swept
deal	dealt	dealt
mean	meant	meant
leave	left	left
bleed	bled	bled
feed	fed	fed
flee	fled	fled
lead	led	led
speed	sped	sped
cling	clung	clung
dig	dug	dug
spin	spun	spun
stick	stuck	stuck
sting	stung	stung
strike	struck	struck
swing	swung	swung
wring	wrung	wrung
win	won	won
lay (to put)	laid	laid
pay	paid	paid
say	said	said
sell	sold	sold
tell	told	told
bind	bound	bound
find	found	found
grind	ground	ground
wind	wound	wound
bring	brought	brought
buy	bought	bought
fight	fought	fought
find	found	found
think	thought	thought
seek	sought	sought
catch	caught	caught
teach	taught	taught

Simple Form	Past Form	Past Participle
have	had	had
sit	sat	sat
hear	heard	heard
hold	held	held
shoot	shot	shot
stand	stood	stood

3. All forms are different

Simple Form	Past Form	Past Participle
draw	drew	drawn
fall	fell	fallen
shake	shook	shaken
take	took	taken
bear	bore	borne
swear	swore	sworn
tear	tore	torn
wear	wore	worn
blow	blew	blown
fly	flew	flown
grow	grew	grown
know	knew	known
throw	threw	thrown
begin	began	begun
drink	drank	drunk
ring	rang	rung
shrink	shrank	shrunk
sing	sang	sung
sink	sank	sunk
spring	sprang	sprung
swim	swam	swum
bite	bit	bitten (or bit)
hide	hid	hidden (or hid)
drive	drove	driven
ride	rode	ridden
stride	strode	stridden
rise	rose	risen
write	wrote	written
dive	dove	dived
break	broke	broken
freeze	froze	frozen
speak	spoke	spoken

Simple Form	Past Form	Past Participle
steal	stole	stolen
weave	wove	woven
get	got	gotten
forget	forgot	forgotten
choose	chose	chosen
give	gave	given
forgive	forgave	forgiven
forbid	forbade	forbidden
do	did	done
eat	ate	eaten
go	went	gone
lie (to recline)	lay	lain
see	saw	seen

PRACTICE

Irregular Verbs

Supply the past form or the past participle for each verb in parentheses. Check your answers against those in the Answer Key on p. 443.

1. We ________________ four trout in the stream.
   (to catch)
2. I shouldn't have ________________ my gloves on the counter.
   (to lay)
3. The audience ________________ when the singer attempted the high notes.
   (to flee)
4. The pipe ________________ yesterday; we are waiting for a plumber.
   (to burst)
5. He has ________________ aimlessly around the city for several hours.
   (to ride)
6. The firefighters ________________ down the ladder.
   (to slide)
7. The elevator ________________ quickly to the tenth floor.
   (to rise)
8. She had ________________ her job because of her medical condition.
   (to quit)
9. It was clear he had ________________ about our agreement.
   (to forget)
10. He had washed and ________________ out all his clothes in the bathtub.
    (to wring)

APPENDIX D

Answer Key to Practices

UNIT I: GRAMMAR

Chapter 2: Recognizing Subjects and Verbs

Finding the Subject of a Sentence

PRACTICE (P. 16)

1. The plane landed.
2. Michelle Bates gathered her bags.
3. She was so excited.
4. Strange sounds filled her ears.
5. A mother and her three children shared a lunch.
6. The battered red taxi idled outside.
7. A light rain had fallen recently.

Finding Hidden Subjects

PRACTICE (P. 20)

1. (You) look ~~at a map of South America~~.
2. Where is the ancient city of Chan Chan?
3. Here ~~on the coastal desert of northern Peru~~ stand the remains ~~of this city of the kings~~.
4. Chan Chan, ~~once the fabulously wealthy centre of the Chimor~~, is situated ~~in one of the driest, bleakest regions in the world~~.
5. It was the largest pre-Columbian city ~~in South America~~.
6. ~~In the ruins of this city~~, scientists have found fragments to piece together the mystery ~~of the past~~.
7. How could this civilization have survived this hostile environment and become so advanced?

Finding Action Verbs

PRACTICE (P. 22)

1. Some people collect very strange objects. (present)
2. One man saved the fortunes ~~from fortune cookies~~. (past)
3. A group of people ~~in Alberta~~ often met to discuss their spark plug collections. (past)
4. People ~~in Brandon~~ will gather many types ~~of barbed wire~~. (future)
5. Collectors take pride ~~in the possession of unusual items~~. (present)
6. A collection, ~~like odd rocks or unique automobiles~~, will let a person express his or her individuality. (future)
7. Collections keep us entertained ~~from childhood to old age~~. (present)

Chapter Review Exercises
Finding Subjects and Verbs in Simple Sentences

PRACTICE (P. 26)

1. Mother and Dad always blame me ~~for any trouble with my sister~~.
2. My sister, ~~the most popular girl in her class~~, is two years older than I.
3. Yesterday, ~~for instance~~, she was trying on her new graduation dress.
4. Helpfully, I took out her new shoes and purse ~~for her~~.
5. Margaret instantly became furious ~~with me~~.
6. I was only sharing Margaret's excitement ~~about her new clothes~~.

Chapter 3: More Work with Verbs

Correcting Unnecessary Shifts in Verb Tense

PRACTICE 1 (P. 33)

Answers will vary. These are sample answers.

1. After I complete that writing course, I will take the required history course.
2. In the beginning of the movie, the action was slow; by the end, I was sitting on the edge of my seat.

3. The textbook gives the rules for writing a bibliography, but it doesn't explain how to do footnotes.
4. I was walking in the park when all of a sudden I saw her running toward me.
5. The encyclopedia gave several pages of information about astronomy, but it didn't give anything about black holes.
6. The invitation requested that Juan be at the ceremony and that he attend the banquet as well.
7. That Web site gives you excellent information, but it is too cluttered.

PRACTICE 2 (P. 34)

Doctor Norman Bethune grew up in Gravenhurst, Ontario. He was educated in Toronto and served as a stretcher bearer in World War I. He contracted tuberculosis and thereafter devoted himself to helping other victims of the disease when he practised surgery in Montreal. He also invented or redesigned twelve medical and surgical instruments. Bethune travelled to Russia in 1935, joined the Communist Party, and went to Spain in 1936, where he organized the first mobile blood transfusion service during the Spanish Civil War. After returning to Canada, he shortly left for overseas again, this time to China, where he helped the Chinese Communists in their fight against Japan. "Spain and China," he wrote, "are part of the same battle." While there, he contracted an infection and died. Mao's essay "In Memory of Norman Bethune," prescribed reading during China's Cultural Revolution, urges all Communists to follow Bethune's example of selfless dedication to others. Bethune is the best-known Canadian to the Chinese, and many Chinese visit his Canadian birthplace.

Using the Correct Tense

PRACTICE (P. 35)

1. have stopped
2. would have
3. will buy
4. had never been
5. liked
6. will soon be
7. is

Chapter Review Exercises
Solving Problems with Verbs

PRACTICE (P. 41)

1. He ought not to drive so fast *or* He shouldn't drive so fast.
2. It is essential that Lynn take her dog to the vet.
3. I wish I were a chef.
4. She sang for a huge crowd Saturday night.
5. I was shaken up by the accident *or* The accident shook me up.
6. The skiers climbed the hill.
7. My father asked me last night to help him build a deck.

Chapter 4: Subject-Verb Agreement

Making the Subject and Verb Agree

PRACTICE (P. 44)

1. cycles
2. amazes
3. vary
4. cheer
5. hope

Chapter Review Exercises

PRACTICE 1 (P. 47)

1. doesn't
2. were
3. doesn't
4. Were
5. doesn't

PRACTICE 2 (P. 47)

1. price, has
2. decision, requires
3. She, doesn't
4. guide or security guard, sees
5. committee, agrees
6. Potato chips and cola, are
7. One, is

Chapter 5: Coordination and Subordination

Recognizing the Comma and Coordinating Conjunction

PRACTICE (P. 51)

1. The audience was packed into the room (, for) this was a man with an international reputation.
2. He could have told about all his successes (, but) instead he spoke about his disappointments.
3. His words were electric (, so) the crowd was attentive.
4. I should have brought a tape recorder (, or) at least I should have taken notes.

Recognizing the Semicolon, Adverbial Conjunction, and Comma

PRACTICE 1 (P. 53)

1. The restaurant is always too crowded on Saturdays (; nevertheless,) it serves the best food in town.
2. The land was not for sale (; however,) the house could be rented.
3. The lawsuit cost the company several million dollars (; consequently,) the company went out of business a short time later.

4. The doctor told him to lose weight ; furthermore, she insisted he also stop smoking.

Combining Sentences Using Adverbial Conjuctions

PRACTICE 2 (P. 54)

Answers will vary. These are sample answers.

1. People once preferred to write with a pen or pencil; however, the computer has now become a favourite writing tool.
2. Computers provide a powerful way to create and store pieces of writing; furthermore, they make the editing process fast and efficient.
3. Computers have revolutionized today's offices; consequently, no modern business is without them.
4. Computers have become relatively inexpensive; accordingly, most people own a computer.
5. Many children know more about computers than many adults; moreover, many children are teaching adults how to operate computers.
6. Professional writers have become enthusiastic about the use of computers; nonetheless, there are still some writers who will use only a ballpoint pen.
7. We have many technological aids for writing; nevertheless, let us not forget that the source of all our ideas is the human brain.

Recognizing Dependent and Independent Clauses

PRACTICE 1 (P. 59)

1. DC
2. DC
3. IC
4. DC
5. IC
6. DC
7. DC

Combining Sentences Using Subordination

PRACTICE 2 (P. 59)

Answers will vary. These are sample answers.

1. While he was eating breakfast, the results of the election came over the radio.
2. Simon gave up his plan to launch a dot-com company because he felt it was too risky.
3. I will see my teacher tonight, as she is speaking at the university this evening.
4. The designer hoped for a promotion, although not one person in the department was promoted last year.
5. Since the designer hoped for a promotion, she made sure all her work was done accurately and on time.

Combining Sentences Using a Relative Pronoun

PRACTICE (P. 62)

Answers will vary. These are sample answers.

1. The chemistry lab that I attend is two hours long.
2. The student assistant who is standing by the door is very knowledgeable.
3. The equipment that was purchased last year will make possible some important new research.

Recognizing Restrictive and Nonrestrictive Clauses

PRACTICE (P. 63)

1. Canada's first census, which was taken in 1667, showed 3215 non-Native inhabitants in 668 families.
2. Most of these families were French Canadians who lived near the St. Lawrence River.
3. By the time of Confederation, the population of the country had risen to 3 463 000, which was an increase of 1077 percent over 200 years.
4. If the population, which is about 30 000 000 persons in Canada now, increases by a similar percentage, we'll have a population of 280 200 000 by the year 2167.
5. Where, do you think, will we put everyone who will live in Canada then?

Chapter Review Exercises

Combining Sentences Using Coordination and Subordination

PRACTICE (P. 65)

Answers will vary. This is a sample paragraph.

The wind is strong; the waves are choppy and growing larger. I paddle my kayak harder, but my arms are getting tired. As the energy drains from them, they grow limp and heavy. The other side of the harbour seems distant. The glow of the setting sun is behind me, spreading orange and purple fingers across the sky. The wall of rocks that lies offshore picks up the last light of the setting sun, becoming a silver beacon. I focus on that wall and paddle harder. The sea smashes against my bow, pushing me away from shore. As flecks of spray hit my face, I taste the salt on my lips. With that taste of the sea, the beauty of the sea and shore strikes me. I am distracted from my labour and absorbed by the world around me. As my kayak finally glides past the rocks to the sheltered beach beyond, I am exhilarated and exhausted.

Chapter 6: Correcting Fragments

Correcting Fragments

PRACTICE 1 (P. 71)

1. You are early again.
2. I want to get a front-row seat.
3. Is your homework done yet?
4. It is nearly finished.
5. Do you think the professor will give us a quiz today?
6. I certainly hope not.
7. It looks like rain today.
8. It had better not rain. I haven't got a bag for these new books.
9. Are you going to the game on Saturday?
10. I will probably go.

Understanding Fragments

PRACTICE 2 (P. 72)

1. a. subject
2. b. verb
3. c. both subject and verb
5. b. verb
6. a. subject
7. d. contains subject and verb, but lacks complete thought
4. b. verb

Turning Fragments into Sentences

PRACTICE 3 (P. 73)

Answers will vary. These are sample answers.

1. The otter returned to the river.
2. A bird on the oak branch sang.
3. The river flowed between the island and the mainland.
4. The hawk in a soaring motion flew into the sky.
5. The fishing boats on the lake glided over the water.
6. The loon dropped like a stone into the water.
7. The fisherman put the net away.

Identifying Phrases

PRACTICE 1 (P. 75)

1. infinitive
2. infinitive
3. prepositional
4. prepositional
5. noun
6. noun
7. prepositional

PRACTICE 2 (P. 76)

1. prepositional
2. infinitive
3. prepositional
4. noun
5. verb
6. prepositional
7. infinitive
8. verb
9. infinitive
10. prepositional

Correcting the Fragment That Contains a Participle

PRACTICE 1 (P. 77)

Answers will vary. These are sample answers.

1. a. He is climbing in the Rockies.
   b. He climbs in the Rockies.
   c. Climbing in the Rockies, he left his stereo behind.
   d. Climbing in the Rockies is the thing to do.
2. a. He is playing video games.
   b. He plays video games.
   c. Playing video games, he didn't hear the robbers.
   d. Playing video games is time-consuming.
3. a. She is going clubbing on Tuesdays.
   b. She goes clubbing on Tuesdays.
   c. Going clubbing on Tuesdays, she met her best friend.
   d. Going clubbing on Tuesdays is tiring.

Recognizing the Fragment

PRACTICE 2 (P. 78)

1. complete
2. fragment
3. fragment
4. fragment
5. complete
6. fragment
7. complete
8. fragment
9. fragment
10. fragment

Chapter 7: Correcting Run-ons

Correcting Run-ons

PRACTICE 1 (P. 84)

Answers will vary. These are sample answers.

1. Simple: Certain Web sites offer free recorded music. Artists who own rights to the music are trying to stop them.

   Compound: Certain Web sites offer free recorded music, but artists who own rights to the music are trying to stop them.

   Certain Web sites offer free recorded music; however, artists who own rights to the music are trying to stop them.

Complex: Although certain Web sites offer free recorded music, artists who own rights to the music are trying to stop them.

2. Simple: Many people are opposed to gambling in all its forms. They will not even buy a lottery ticket.

   Compound: Many people are opposed to gambling in all its forms, so they will not even buy a lottery ticket.

   Many people are opposed to gambling in all its forms; indeed, they will not even buy a lottery ticket.

   Complex: Since many people are opposed to gambling in all its forms, they will not even buy a lottery ticket.

3. Simple: Hockey may be Canada's national sport. The game can be quite brutal.

   Compound: Hockey may be Canada's national sport, but the game can be quite brutal.

   Hockey may be Canada's national sport; however, the game can be quite brutal.

   Complex: Although the game can be quite brutal, hockey may be Canada's national sport.

4. Simple: Many young people manage to travel. They find ways to do it cheaply.

   Compound: Many young people manage to travel, for they find ways to do it cheaply.

   Many young people manage to travel; they find ways to do it cheaply.

   Complex: Many young people manage to travel because they find ways to do it cheaply.

5. Simple: The need for a proper diet is important in any health program. All the junk food on the grocery shelves makes it hard to be consistent.

   Compound: The need for a proper diet is important in any health program, yet all the junk food on the grocery shelves makes it hard to be consistent.

   The need for a proper diet is important in any health program; however, all the junk food on the grocery shelves makes it hard to be consistent.

   Complex: Even though the need for a proper diet is important in any health program, all the junk food on the grocery shelves makes it hard to be consistent.

PRACTICE 2 (P. 87)

Answers will vary. These are sample answers.

1. Simple: The airline has begun its new route to the islands. Everyone is looking forward to flying there.

   Compound: The airline has begun its new route to the islands, so everyone is looking forward to flying there.

   The airline has begun its new route to the islands; consequently, everyone is looking forward to flying there.

   Complex: Ever since the airline began its new route to the islands, everyone has been looking forward to flying there.

2. Simple: The movie begins at nine o'clock. Let's have dinner before the show.

   Compound: The movie begins at nine o'clock, so let's have dinner before the show.

   The movie begins at nine o'clock; therefore, let's have dinner before the show.

   Complex: Since the movie begins at nine o'clock, let's have dinner before the show.

3. Simple: The studio audience screamed at the contestant. They wanted her to try for the big prize.

   Compound: The studio audience screamed at the contestant, for they wanted her to try for the big prize.

   The studio audience screamed at the contestant; they wanted her to try for the big prize.

   Complex: The studio audience screamed at the contestant because they wanted her to try for the big prize.

4. Simple: Maya needs new shoes. She is running in the marathon.

   Compound: Maya needs new shoes, for she is running in the marathon.

   Maya needs new shoes; she is running in the marathon.

   Complex: Since she is running in the marathon, Maya needs new shoes.

5. Simple: My actor friend grabbed my arm. She wanted to tell me about her new part in the movie.

   Compound: My actor friend grabbed my arm; she wanted to tell me about her new part in the movie.

   My actor friend grabbed my arm, for she wanted to tell me about her new part in the movie.

   Complex: My actor friend grabbed my arm because she wanted to tell me about her new part in the movie.

Chapter 8: Parallel Structure

Making Sentences Parallel

PRACTICE 1 (P. 92)

1. dirty
2. sewing her own clothes
3. willingly explain material more than once

PRACTICE 2 (P. 93)

Answers will vary. These are sample answers.

1. Winter in Edmonton is very windy and bitterly cold.
2. I would prefer fixing an old car to watching television.
3. Alex is a talented athlete, a top student, and even a generous friend.
4. The apartment is crowded and dark.
5. The dancer is slender and graceful.
6. The trees were tall and leafy.
7. My friend loves to play chess, to read science fiction, and to work out at the gym.

PRACTICE 3 (P. 94)

Answers will vary. These are sample answers.

1. The dog had to choose between jumping over the fence or digging a hole underneath it.
2. She was great at swimming, canoeing, and rock climbing.
3. As I looked down the city street, I could see the soft lights from restaurant windows, I could hear the mellow sounds of a nightclub band, and I could sense the carefree moods of people walking by.
4. The singers have been on several road tours, have recorded for two record companies, and have expressed a desire to make a movie someday.
5. They would rather order a pizza than eat home cooking.
6. I explained to the teacher that my car had broken down, my books had been stolen, and my assignment pad had been left at home.
7. That night the prisoner was sick, discouraged, and lonely.

Chapter 9: Pronouns

Chapter Review Exercises
Making Pronouns and Antecedents Agree

PRACTICE (P. 104)

Answers will vary. These are sample answers.

1. The father mailed his son's high school yearbook to him.
2. No one wants his or her income reduced.
3. When a company fails to update its equipment, it often pays a price in the long run.
4. Graduates today have many more options open to them than ever before.
5. Everybody knows his or her own strengths best.
6. All the soccer players put effort into their game.
7. If the campers want to eat quickly, they should help themselves.

Chapter 10: Modifiers: Misplaced and Dangling

Chapter Review Exercises
Revising Misplaced or Dangling Modifiers

PRACTICE (P. 109)

Answers will vary. These are sample answers.

1. Wearing his tuxedo, Victor fed the dog.
2. While we were visiting Vancouver Aquarium, the otters entertained us.
3. Wanting to make a good impression, I wore a conservative, well-cut suit.
4. A band that we had heard earlier was playing in the park.
5. After running over the hill, I noticed that the farm was visible in the valley below.
6. The truck, which was broken down on the highway, caused a traffic jam for kilometres.
7. I saw three spiders hanging from the ceiling in my bedroom.

Chapter 11: Punctuation

Insert Necessary Commas

PRACTICE 1 (P. 113)

1. Problems with the water supply of Canada, the United States, Europe, and other parts of the world are growing.
2. Water is colourless, tasteless, odourless, and free of calories.
3. You will use on an average day 90 L of water for flushing, 120 L for bathing and washing clothes, and 95 L for other uses.
4. It took 450 L of water to create the eggs you ate for breakfast, 13 250 L for the steak you might eat for dinner, and over 200 000 L to produce the steel used to make your car.

5. By 1970, the English–Wabigoon river system, which runs through Grassy Narrows, Ontario, had become polluted with mercury.

PRACTICE 2 (P. 114)

1. The most overused bodies of water are our rivers, but they continue to serve us daily.
2. Canadian cities often developed next to rivers, and industries followed soon after in the same locations.
3. The people of the industrial age can try to clean the water they use, or they can watch pollution take over.
4. The Great Lakes are showing signs of renewal, yet the struggle against pollution there must continue.
5. Most people have not been educated about the dangerous state of our water supply, nor are all our members of Parliament fully aware of the problem.

PRACTICE 3 (P. 115)

1. A total solar eclipse, when the moon's shadow blots out the sun completely, is an outstanding cosmic event.
2. Once you see your first solar eclipse, you start looking forward to the next one.
3. However, witnessing this spectacle takes planning and the ability to travel to the best viewing spots.
4. In eastern Turkey, on August 11, 1999, a crowd of astronomers and "eclipse chasers" watched the last total eclipse of the millennium.
5. At the moment of totality, people cheer, clap, and often cry.

PRACTICE 4 (P. 116)

1. Natural disasters, I believe, have not been historically significant.
2. They have, however, significantly affected the lives of many Canadians.
3. Canada's worst coal-mine disaster, at Hillcrest, Alberta, occurred on June 19, 1914.
4. In Springhill, Nova Scotia, furthermore, 424 persons were killed in the mines between 1881 and 1969.
5. Avalanches, storms, and floods, which are natural disasters, have also made their marks on the face of our country.

PRACTICE 5 (P. 116)

1. Honey, I hope you're not planning to wear that hat.
2. I wonder, Samir, if the game has been cancelled.
3. Dad, could I borrow five dollars?
4. Can you help me, doctor?
5. Ayesha, is that you?

PRACTICE 6 (P. 117)

1. "I'm innocent," he cried, "of all charges against me."
2. He mumbled, "I won't incriminate myself."
3. "I was told," the defendant explained, "to answer every question."
4. "This court," the judge announced, "will be adjourned."
5. "The jury," said Al Tarvin of *The Star,* "was handpicked."

PRACTICE 7 (P. 117)

1. Kicking, the child was carried off to bed.
2. To Maria, Florence Suzuki was the boss from hell.
3. When you can, come and visit us.
4. Whoever that is, is going to be surprised.
5. Skin cancer seldom kills, doctors say.

Using the Apostrophe

PRACTICE 1 (P. 120)

1. boys'
2. their
3. Moses's or Moses'
4. Antony and Maria's
5. nobody's
6. his
7. 1700's or 1700s
8. It's
9. Vancouver's
10. Wendy's

PRACTICE 2 (P. 121)

1. Cherry's
2. geese's
3. Carol's and Tess's
4. somebody's
5. hers
6. two's
7. can't

Insert Necessary Quotation Marks

PRACTICE 1 (P. 123)

1. "The Hot House" is one of the stories contained in Rosemary Sullivan's *More Stories by Canadian Women.*
2. Nellie McClung said, "I'll never believe I'm dead until I see it in the papers."
3. no quotation marks needed
4. To "diss" is a slang term meaning to show disrespect.
5. She read the article "Whiz Kids" in *The Review.*

Using Semicolons

PRACTICE 2 (P. 123)

1. One of the best ways to remember a vacation is to take numerous photos; one of the best ways to recall the contents of a book is to take notes.
2. The problem of street crime must be solved; otherwise, the number of vigilantes will increase.
3. The meal was composed of bruschetta, an appetizer; roast duck, the house specialty; and lemon mousse, a tart dessert.
4. The bank president was very cordial; however, he would not approve the loan.
5. New methods of production are being used in the factories of Japan; eventually they will be common in this country as well.

Using Colons

PRACTICE 3 (P. 124)

1. Two Canadian-born comedians have achieved great success in the United States: Jim Carrey and Mike Myers.
2. The official has one major flaw in his personality: greed.
3. no colons needed
4. The college offers four courses in English literature: Romantic Poetry, Shakespeare's Plays, The British Short Story, and The Modern Novel.
5. Arriving at 6:15 in the morning, Marlene brought me a sausage-and-cheese pizza, ginger ale, and a litre of ice cream.

Using Dashes or Parentheses

PRACTICE (P. 127)

1. Herbert Simon is—and I don't think this is an exaggeration—a genius.
2. George Eliot (her real name was Mary Ann Evans) wrote Silas Marner.
3. You should—in fact I insist—see a doctor.
4. Health Canada's Web site has suggestions to help smokers quit (visit www.infotobacco.com).
5. Mass media (television, radio, movies, magazines, and newspapers) are able to transmit information over a wide range and to a large number of people.

Chapter Review Exercises
Punctuation Overview

PRACTICE 1 (P. 127)

1. To measure crime, sociologists have used three different techniques: official statistics, victimization surveys, and self-report studies.
2. "David" is one of the best-loved poems of Earle Birney.
3. That show uses one thing I hate: a laugh track.
4. Farley Mowat has written numerous books for adults; however, he also writes very popular books for children.
5. Tuberculosis (also known as consumption) has been nearly eliminated by medical science.
6. The Victorian Period (1837–1901) saw a rapid expansion in industry.
7. He told me—I remember the day—that he would never give up.

PRACTICE 2 (P. 127)

1. Many young people have two feelings about science and technology: awe and fear.
2. Mr. Doyle, the realtor; Mrs. Tong, the bank officer; and Ivan Petroff, the lawyer, are the three people to help work out the real estate transaction.
3. The book was entitled *English Literature: The Victorian Age*.
4. "My computer," she said, "has been crashing all day."
5. She brought a bathing suit, towel, sunglasses, and several books to the beach. (no colon after brought)
6. The meeting to discuss a pay increase—I'll believe it when I see it—has been rescheduled for Friday.
7. The complex lab experiment has these two major problems: too many difficult calculations and too many variables.

Chapter 12: Capitalization

Capitalization

PRACTICE (P. 133)

1. Italian
2. Canadian Rockies
3. Bible
4. University of Alberta
5. Hallowe'en
6. Bell Canada, Friday, Winnipeg, Manitoba

7. Cobalt-60, Canadian, Dr. Donald Green
8. Why
9. Canadian Auto Workers
10. Women of the Klondike, North

Chapter 13: Unit I Review: Using All You Have Learned

There is more than one way to correct the fragments and run-ons in the rest of the practices in this part. The following answers are possible.

Editing Sentences for Errors

PRACTICE 1 (P. 135)

1. Roma now are living in many countries of the world.
2. The international community of scientists agrees that these Roma originally came from India thousands of years ago.
3. After the original Roma people left India, they went to Persia; there they divided into groups.
4. One branch of Roma went west to Europe, while the other group decided to go east.
5. In the Middle Ages ... Little Egypt.
6. C
7. Today, Roma families may be found from Canada to Chile, living much as their ancestors did thousands of years ago.

PRACTICE 2 (P. 136)

1. The laser beam, a miracle of modern science, already has many practical uses in today's world.
2. Laser beams are narrow, highly concentrated beams of light that burn brighter than the light of the sun.
3. Scientists have found many possible military uses for the laser, but they are hoping these can be converted into constructive uses.
4. C
5. The possibility of making a laser was first described in 1958, and two years later, in California, the first laser beam was created.
6. Since they are so precise, laser beams are used in medicine to help make a specific diagnosis and to perform operations such as repairing delicate retinas and removing cancerous tumours.
7. The future uses of the laser seem endless, and it is up to us to decide whether we want to use this invention for war or for peaceful purposes.

UNIT II: THE WRITING PROCESS

Chapter 15: The Paragraph I: Structure, Topic, and Controlling Idea

Finding the Topic Sentence of a Paragraph

PRACTICE (P. 160)

1. Love is a crazy, complicated affair, made trickier by the tangle of superstitions that go along with it.
2. The brain is one of the most remarkable organs, a part of the body that we have only begun to investigate.

Finding the Topic in the Topic Sentence

PRACTICE (P. 161)

1. Remodelling an old house
2. College work
3. A well-made suit
4. Growing up near a museum
5. My favourite room in the house
6. A student who goes to school full-time and also works part-time
7. One of the disadvantages of skiing
8. the change that had come over my friend
9. current tax laws
10. Greek restaurants

Finding the Controlling Idea

PRACTICE (P. 162)

1. T: vigorous exercise CI: reduces stress
2. T: St. John's and Corner Brook CI: differ
3. T: wonder foods CI: less than wonderful
4. T: athletic scholarships available to women CI: increasing
5. T: caffeine CI: adverse effects
6. T: Madame Benoît CI: amusing personality
7. T: computers CI: will make newspapers obsolete

Chapter 16: The Paragraph II: Supporting Details

Avoid Restating the Topic Sentence

PRACTICE (P. 171)

1. a. SD	b. R	c. SD	d. SD
2. a. SD	b. SD	c. R	d. SD

Chapter 17: The Essay

Thesis or Fact?

PRACTICE 1 (P. 178)

1. F
2. T
3. T
4. F

Recognizing the Thesis Statement

PRACTICE 2 (P. 179)

1. thesis
2. title
3. fact
4. thesis
5. title
6. fact
7. fact

Chapter 20: Writing under Pressure

Methods of Development

PRACTICE (P. 212)

1. narration
2. comparison and contrast
3. discussion
4. definition
5. summary

UNIT III: WRITING STRATEGIES

Chapter 21: Narration

Coherence: Placing Details in Order of Time Sequence

PRACTICE (P. 223)

2. 4, 5, 1, 6, 2, 3

Chapter 22: Description

Coherence: Putting Details in Spatial Order

PRACTICE (P. 238)

1. 3, 5, 2, 1, 4
2. 2, 3, 1, 4

Chapter 23: Process

Coherence: Order in Logical Sequence

PRACTICE (P. 247)

7, 5, 1, 8, 2, 6, 3, 9, 4

Chapter 24: Comparison or Contrast

Evaluating the Two-Part Topic

PRACTICE (P. 258)

Answers could vary depending on the purpose of the paragraph.

3. too broad
4. suitable
5. too broad
6. too broad

Recognizing the Two Methods

PRACTICE (P. 260)

1. block; differences
2. point-by-point; similarities

Chapter 27: Cause and Effect

Looking for the Causal Relationship

PRACTICE 1 (P. 294)

1. T
2. C
3. T
4. C
5. C
6. T
7. C

Separating the Cause from the Effect

PRACTICE 2 (P. 295)

1. a. C b. C c. E d. E e. C f. E
2. a. C b. C c. E d. E e. C f. C

UNIT V: APPENDICES

Appendix B: Solving Spelling Problems

Identifying the Correct Spelling

PRACTICE (P. 415)

1. separate
2. probably
3. arctic
4. surprise
5. tragedy
6. quantity
7. literature
8. hungry
9. handsome
10. favourite
11. nuclear

Choosing *ie* or *ei*

PRACTICE (P. 416)

1. sleigh
2. believe
3. siege
4. veil
5. leisure
6. deceit
7. niece
8. weight
9. protein
10. ancient

Forming the Plurals of Nouns

PRACTICE (P. 419)

1. puppies
2. mothers-in-law
3. teeth
4. cameos
5. phenomena
6. loaves
7. matches
8. mixes
9. enemies
10. bags

Doubling the Consonant?

PRACTICE (P. 421)

slip: yes, yes, slipping
crack: no, no, cracking
broil: no, no, broiling
win: yes, yes, winning;
control: controlling
fever: feverish
compel: compelled
differ: difference
begin: beginning

Doubling the Final Consonant When Adding Endings That Begin with Vowels?

PRACTICE (P. 422)

1. bitten
2. occurrence
3. wavering
4. preferred
5. preference
6. thinner
7. transferred
8. sailing
9. propellent
10. omitted

Adding Endings to Words That End in *-y*

PRACTICE (P. 423)

1. keys
2. loneliness
3. crying
4. cries
5. prayer
6. employment
7. monkeying
8. beautiful
9. theories
10. ceremonial

One Word or Two?

PRACTICE (P. 425)

1. bedroom
2. grandmother
3. already
4. all together
5. always
6. Everyone
7. maybe
8. cannot
9. nearby
10. Nevertheless

Appendix C: Irregular Verbs

Irregular Verbs

PRACTICE (P. 432)

1. caught
2. laid
3. fled
4. burst
5. ridden
6. slid
7. rose
8. quit
9. forgotten
10. wrung

Credits

Page 229: "Transparent Silhouette" by Akis Stylianou. Reprinted with permission of the author.

Page 242: "A Profile of Daphne" by Alexandra Savage-Ferr. Reprinted with permission of the author.

Page 253: "Inner-Peace Process" by Jenny Yuen. Reprinted with permission of the author.

Page 278: "Love Hurts" by Jenny Yuen. Reprinted with permission of the author.

Page 308: "Individuals Must Spur Change" by Leanne C. Southall. Reprinted with permission of the author.

Page 318: "Don Juan/Doña Juana" by Rosemary Sullivan. From *Labyrinth of Desire: Women, Passion and Romantic Obsession* by Rosemary Sullivan. Published by HarperCollins*Publishers*, Copyright © 2001 by Rosemary Sullivan. All rights reserved.

Page 321: "Hidden Lessons" by David Suzuki. Reprinted by permission of the author.

Page 325: "In Praise of Old Women" by Marya Fiamengo. © Copyright 1976 Mosaic Press, Oakville. Reprinted by permission.

Page 328: "Heart of Loneliness" by Jean Vanier. Excerpt from *Becoming Human* by Jean Vanier. Copyright © 1998 by Jean Vanier and the Canadian Broadcasting Corporation. Reprinted by permission of House of Anansi Press.

Page 333: "Canada, My Canada" by Tomson Highway. Copyright © 2000 by Tomson Highway. First published by *Imperial Oil Review*, Spring 2000 Volume 84, No. 436. Reprinted by permission of Tomson Highway and Susan Schulman, A Literary Agency, New York.

Page 336: "My Body is My Own Business" by Naheed Mustafa. Reprinted by permission of the author.

Page 339: "The Jade Peony" by Wayson Choy. Copyright © 1977 by Wayson Choy. First published in the *UBC Alumni Chronicle* in 1979. Reprinted by permission of the author.

Page 346: “Leaving the Cave” by John Artibello. Reprinted by permission of the author.

Page 353: “I Lost My Talk” by Rita Joe. From *Song of Eskasoni*. Reprinted by permission of Canadian Scholar’s Press Inc. and Women’s Press.

Page 355: “Rats” by W. Frank Epling. Reprinted by permission.

Page 359: “Gretzky in Eighty-Four” by Mordecai Richler. From *Belling the Cat* by Mordecai Richler. Copyright © 1998 by Mordecai Richler Productions Limited. Reprinted with permission of Alfred A. Knopf Canada.

Page 366: “The Other Family” by Himani Bannerji. Reprinted by permission of the author.

Page 371: “Selling Illusions” by Neil Bissoondath. From *Selling Illusions: The Cult of Multiculturalism in Canada*. Copyright © 1994 Neil Bissoondath. Reprinted by permission of Penguin Group (Canada), a division of Pearson Penguin Canada Inc.

Page 376: “The Thirteenth Muffin” by Rachael Manley. Reprinted with permission of the author.

Page 389: “Bad Girls” by Shari Graydon. Reprinted by permission.

Page 394: “In My Secret Life” by Leonard Cohen. Written by Leonard Cohen and Sharon Robinson from *Ten New Songs*. Published by Sony Music and Sharon Robinson Songs. © 2002. Reprinted by permission Sony Music Entertainment Inc, Toronto, 2001, and by Wixen Music Publishing, Inc.

Index